Prentice Hall *LITERATURE*

P E N G U I N E D I T I O N

Reader's Notebook

Adapted Version

Grade Eight

PEARSON

Upper Saddle River, New Jersey
Boston, Massachusetts
Chandler, Arizona
Glenview, Illinois

ISBN: 978-0-13-366679-3

PEARSON

3 4 5 6 7 8 9 10   17 16 15 14 13 12 11 10 09

ACKNOWLEDGMENTS

Grateful acknowledgment is made to the following for copyrighted material:

Arte Publico Press
From *My Own True Name* by Pat Mora. Copyright © 2000 Arte Publico Press—University of Houston. Published by Arte Publico Press. "Baseball" by Lionel G. Garcia from *I Can Hear the Cowbells Ring* (Houston: Arte Publico Press—University of Houston, 1994).

Ashabranner, Brent
"Always to Remember: The Vision of Maya Ying Lin" by Brent Ashabranner from *Always to Remember*. Copyright © 1988.

Black Issues Book Review
"Zora Neale Hurston: A Life in Letters, Book Review" by Zakia Carter from *Black Issues Book Review*, Nov–Dec 2002; www.bibookreview.com.

Curtis Brown London
"Who Can Replace a Man" by Brian Aldiss from *Masterpieces: The Best Science Fiction of the Century*. Copyright © 1966 by Brian Aldiss.

Child Health Association of Sewickley, Inc.
"Thumbprint Cookies" from *Three Rivers Cookbook*. Copyright © Child Health Association of Sewickley, Inc.

Copper Canyon Press c/o The Permissions Company
"Snake on the Etowah" by David Bottoms from *Armored Hearts: Selected and New Poems*. Copyright © 1995 by David Bottoms.

Gary N. DaSilva for Neil Simon
"The Governess" from *The Good Doctor* © 1974 by Neil Simon. Copyright renewed © 2002 by Neil Simon. CAUTION: Professionals and amateurs are hereby warned that *The Good Doctor* is fully protected under the Berne Convention and the Universal Copyright Convention and is subject to royalty. All rights, including without limitation professional, amateur, motion picture, television, radio, recitation, lecturing, public reading and foreign translation rights, computer media rights and the right of reproduction, and electronic storage or retrieval, in whole or in part and in any form, are strictly reserved and none of these rights can be exercised or used without written permission from the copyright owner. Inquiries for stock and amateur performances should be addressed to Samuel French, Inc., 45 West 25th Street, New York, NY 10010. All other inquiries should be addressed to Gary N. DaSilva, 111 N. Sepulveda Blvd., Suite 250, Manhattan Beach, CA 90266-6850.

(Acknowledgments continue on page V71)

CONTENTS

CONTENTS

CONTENTS

CONTENTS

CONTENTS

CONTENTS

CONTENTS

CONTENTS

CONTENTS

UNIT 6 Themes in American Stories

CONTENTS

© Pearson Education

As you read your hardcover student edition of *Prentice Hall Literature* use the **Reader's Notebook** to guide you in learning and practicing the skills presented. In addition, many selections in your student edition are presented here in an interactive format. The notes and instruction will guide you in applying reading and literary skills and in thinking about the selection. The examples on these pages show you how to use the notes as a companion when you read.

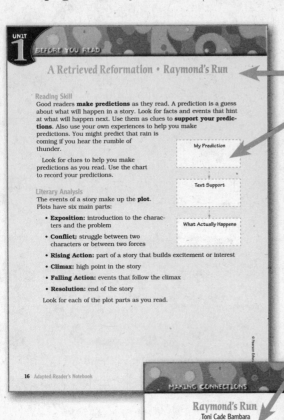

Get Ready to Learn

Use the *Before You Read* page to learn about the Reading Skill and Literary Analysis you will be studying.

To practice the skills, you can write directly in the graphic organizer as you read.

Get the Big Idea

A *Making Connections* page for every selection presents a selection summary, which lets you know what the selection is about before you read.

Make a Big Question Connection

Sentence starters help you think about the Big Question.

Be an Active Reader

A *Note-taking Guide* helps you organize the main ideas of the selection. Complete the guide as you read to track your understanding.

Take Notes

Side-column questions accompany the selections that appear in the Reader's Notebooks. These questions are a built-in tutor to help you practice the skills and understand what you read.

Mark the Text

Use write-on lines to answer questions in the side column. You may also want to use the lines for your own notes.

When you see a pencil, you should underline, circle, or mark the text as indicated.

Check Your Understanding

Questions after every selection help you think about the selection. You can use the write-on lines and charts to answer the questions. Then, share your ideas in class discussions.

Go Beyond the Selection

This page provides step-by-step guidance for completing the Writing and Extend Your Learning activities presented in your student edition.

TAKE NOTES

Activate Prior Knowledge
Tell about a time when you practiced very hard for something.

Literary Analysis
Plot is the order of events in a story. **Exposition** is the part of plot that gives basic information about the characters and the situation. The **conflict** is the struggle between two forces in the story. Read the bracketed passage. Is this passage part of the exposition or part of the conflict? Explain your answer.

Reading Check
What is Squeaky's special talent? Circle the text that tells you.

20 Adapted Reader's Notebook

Raymond's Run
Toni Cade Bambara

Squeaky is a confident, sassy young girl who lives in Harlem in New York City. She has to take care of her brother Raymond, who is "not quite right." She boldly protects Raymond from kids who try to tease him. Squeaky loves to run races, and she is the fastest runner in her neighborhood.

♦ ♦ ♦

There is no track meet that I don't win the first place medal. I used to win the twenty-yard dash when I was a little kid in kindergarten. Nowadays, it's the fifty-yard dash. And tomorrow I'm subject to run the quarter-meter relay all by myself and come in first, second, and third.

♦ ♦ ♦

This year, for the first time, Squeaky has some serious competition in the race, a new girl named Gretchen.

So as far as everyone's concerned, I'm the fastest and that goes for Gretchen, too, who has put out the tale that she is going to win the first place medal this year. Ridiculous. In the second place, she's got sho... ... in the third place, she's got ... ...es. In the first place, no one can ...me and that's all there is to it.

♦ ♦ ♦

Squeaky takes a walk down Broadway with Raymond. She is practicing her breathing exercises to get in shape for the race. Raymond is pretending to drive a stage coach.
Squeaky works hard to be a good runner. She dislikes people who pretend that they do not need to work hard to be good at something.
Then, Squeaky sees Gretchen and two of her friends coming toward her and Raymond.

© Pearson Education

AFTER YOU READ

Raymond's Run

1. **Respond:** Which parts of Squeaky's personality would make you want to be her friend?

2. **Analyze:** Squeaky is very protective of her brother, Raymond. How does Squeaky feel about taking care of him?

3. **Reading Skill:** When you **make predictions** about a story, you ... what will happen next. List two ... read "Raymond's Run."

...**action** contains events that increase ... **falling action** contains events that ...e **plot** chart below. Write in two events ... event from the **falling action**.

...ky crosses the

Event:

Event: Squeaky and Gretchen exchange smiles.

Falling Action

Resolution:

Raymond's Run 25

SUPPORT FOR WRITING AND EXTEND YOUR LEARNING

Writing: New Ending
Imagine the ending of the story if Gretchen had won the race. Write a **new ending** to show how Squeaky might react to losing. Use your notes as you write your new ending.

Does Squeaky go through a change at the end of the story? If so, how would this change affect the way she would feel about losing? Explain.

Squeaky is proud, bold, and loyal. What other adjectives describe her?

Listening and Speaking: Radio Broadcast
Use the following statements to help you prepare for your **radio broadcast.** Use action verbs so that listeners will feel the rising tension and the excitement of the race.

1. Describe Squeaky's appearance.

2. Describe Gretchen's appearance.

3. Describe how Squeaky acts.

4. Describe how Gretchen acts.

5. Describe what happens as Squeaky and Gretchen approach the finish line.

26 Adapted Reader's Notebook

Selections and Skills Support

The pages in your **Reader's Notebook** go with the pages in the hardcover student edition. The pages in the **Reader's Notebook** allow you to participate in class instruction and take notes on the concepts and selections.

Before You Read

Build Skills Follow along in your **Reader's Notebook** as your teacher introduces the **Reading Skill** and **Literary Analysis** instruction. The graphic organizer is provided on this page so that you can take notes right in your **Reader's Notebook.**

Preview Use this page for the selection your teacher assigns.

- The **Summary** gives you an outline of the selection.
- Use the **Reading-Writing Connection** to understand the big idea of the selection and join in the class discussion about the ideas.
- Use the **Note-taking Guide** while you read the story. This will help you organize and remember information you will need to answer questions about the story later.

While You Read

Selection Text and Sidenotes You can read the full text of one selection in each pair in your **Reader's Notebook.**

- You can write in the **Reader's Notebook.** Underline important details to help you find them later.
- Use the **Take Notes** column to jot down your reactions, ideas, and answers to questions about the text. If your assigned selection is not the one that is included in the **Reader's Notebook,** use sticky notes to make your own **Take Notes** section in the side column as you read the selection in the hardcover student edition.

After You Read

Apply the Skills Use this page to answer questions about the selection right in your **Reader's Notebook.** For example, you can complete the graphic organizer that is in the hardcover student edition right on the page in your **Reader's Notebook.**

Support for Writing and Extend Your Learning Use this page to help you jot down notes and ideas as you prepare to do one or more of the projects assigned with the selection.

Other Features in the Reader's Notebook You will also find note-taking opportunities for these features:

- Learning About the Genre
- Support for the Model Selection
- Support for Reading Informational Materials

from The Baker Heater League

Nonfiction is different from fiction in these ways:

- Nonfiction deals with real people, events, or ideas.

- Nonfiction is told through the voice of the author. The author is a real person. The author's view is the **point of view** of the writing.

Many things affect the outcome of nonfiction writing. Two examples are these:

- **Mood:** the feeling the reader gets from the work

- **Author's style:** all of the different ways that a writer uses language. Rhythm, language, and ways of putting things in order are all part of the author's style.

Purpose	Mission	Examples
To persuade	• written to convince audiences of a certain idea or opinion	• speeches • editorials
To inform	• written to present facts and information	• articles • reference books • historical essays • research papers
To entertain	• written for the enjoyment of the audience	• autobiographies • biographies • travel narratives

The 11:59

Fiction is a story that comes from the author's imagination. It tells about characters and events. Fiction has these basic parts:

- **Setting:** the time and place of the story

- **Plot:** the events that move the reader through the story. The plot includes a **conflict**, or problem. The **resolution**, or outcome, comes at the end of the story.

- **Characters:** the people or animals that take part in the action in a story. The **character's traits**, or qualities, can affect his or her thoughts and actions.

- **Point of view:** the view from which the story is told to the reader. The **first-person point of view** is used when the story is told from the view of a character. The **third-person point of view** is used when the story is told from the view of a person outside the story.

- **Theme:** a message about life that the story tries to show

Type	Description	Characteristics
Short stories	short works that can usually be read in one sitting	• contain plot, characters, setting, point of view, and theme • usually focus on one main plot around one conflict
Novels	longer works	• contain plot, characters, conflict, and setting • may also contain **subplots**, independent stories or conflicts related to the main plot
Novellas	shorter than novels, but longer than short stories	• may contain characteristics of short stories and novels
Historical fiction	works of fiction that take place in a real historical setting	• uses information about real people and events to tell invented stories

Word List A

Study these words from the selections. Then, complete the activities.

communication [kuh myoo nuh KAY shun] *adj.* designed to help people stay in touch.
> *News moves quickly through the modern communication chain of instant messaging.*

courtesy [KUR tuh see] *n.* polite behavior
> *Show courtesy to other movie-goers by keeping cell phones turned off.*

customary [KUHS tuh mair ee] *adj.* usual; happening regularly by custom
> *It is customary to give couples something gold on their fiftieth anniversary.*

individual [in duh VIJ oo uhl] *adj.* separate; specific to one person
> *One chef cannot possibly handle the individual requests of every diner.*

loyalty [LOY uhl tee] *n.* being faithful and true to beliefs, ideas, or people
> *We showed loyalty to the team by cheering it on throughout a losing season.*

performance [per FAWR muhns] *n.* action that has been completed
> *My performance on the test was great, thanks to all my study and review.*

powerful [POW er fuhl] *adj.* having great strength
> *The powerful jaws of an alligator can easily snap a floating log in half.*

shattering [SHAT uh ring] *v.* breaking into small pieces
> *I was shocked to see the baseball shattering the window.*

Exercise A

Fill in each blank in the paragraph below with an appropriate word from Word List A. Use each word only once.

On the worst possible day, all of Gina's normal [1] _____ systems were down. She wanted to give Ben the [2] _____ of a return call, but the phones were dead. Even her [3] _____ new computer wasn't working. The [4] _____ of all the household gadgets was harmed by the workers installing the new cable lines. Only Gina's [5] _____ to Meg kept her from walking over to Meg's house to use the phone. Ben had not invited Meg to his party, and Gina knew that this was [6] _____ her friend's feelings. Meg's quirky [7] _____ way of dressing and acting always seemed to mean she was left out. In her [8] _____ way of dealing gently with Meg, Gina would never reveal her excitement about the party.

Read the following passage. Pay special attention to the underlined words. Then, read it again, and complete the activities. Use a separate sheet of paper for your written answers.

Shortly after my grandfather stopped working as a ticket salesman for the railroad, he died. He had spent 40 years on the job. His <u>powerful</u> frame seemed to shrink when he no longer had to open the ticket window at the <u>customary</u> time of 5:00 A.M. I watched the light leave his eyes, his joyful spirit fade away, until one day he didn't wake up at all. I was saddened by Grandpa's death. I wanted to understand what had happened. I wondered if missing the job and all the daily <u>communication</u> opportunities had killed him. Had my grandfather simply become too lonely to live? Thoughts like these were <u>shattering</u> my sleep each night. I decided to try to find some answers to my questions.

As I talked with Grandpa's buddies from the railroad, I did not find the answers I was seeking. I did discover many wonderful things about my grandfather, however. I heard stories of Grandpa's <u>courtesy</u> at all times, even when the rudest people would holler at him about ticket prices or schedules. I was touched to learn that Grandpa's <u>individual</u> efforts to help disabled people board trains led to better access for all who needed help.

Most importantly, I learned from every person what <u>loyalty</u> to a job really means. It means taking pride in yourself and in your own efforts. For example, few of Grandpa's buddies ever missed more than a week of work each year. All gave their time, talents, and best efforts to their work. This was especially true of my grandfather. I hope that someday my own job <u>performance</u> will make my grandchildren proud of me and my efforts. I know now that daily excellence is what I will try to achieve in my life and in my work.

1. Underline a phrase that tells how Grandpa's <u>powerful</u> body changed. Then, write what *powerful* means.

2. Circle the time that would have been <u>customary</u> for Grandpa to be working. Then, explain what *customary* means.

3. Circle a word that describes how life feels without <u>communication</u> opportunities. Then, describe your favorite *communication* channels.

4. Circle the words that name what was <u>shattering</u> the writer's sleep. Explain what *shattering* means.

5. Underline the words that describe a good example of Grandpa's <u>courtesy</u>. Give two other examples of *courtesy*.

6. Write a sentence about another time when someone's <u>individual</u> efforts made a difference.

7. Underline the writer's definition of job <u>loyalty</u>. Then, write your own definition.

8. Circle the words that describe the writer's job <u>performance</u> goals. Tell what *performance* means.

from The Baker Heater League
Patricia C. McKissack and Fredrick McKissack

Summary This nonfiction selection explains how railroad workers called *porters* shared tales with one another. The porters would gather around a potbellied stove, called a Baker heater, to tell their stories. Legends such as those of Casey Jones and John Henry grew out of these stories.

Note-taking Guide
Use the chart below to record the different facts and legends you learned while reading "The Baker Heater League."

Facts	Legends
About 1870, John Henry joined a steel-driving team for the C & O Railroad.	John Henry was so strong that he could drive steel with a hammer in each hand.

The Baker Heater League
Patricia C. and Fredrick McKissack

This nonfiction selection explains how railroad workers called porters shared and passed on stories. The porters would meet one another in train stations across the United States. When they were not working, the porters sat around a potbellied stove, called a Baker heater, and told stories. The porters became known as "The Baker Heater League."

The selection describes how the porters told stories that were based on the actions of real people. One story was about a real engineer named Casey Jones.

◆ ◆ ◆

John Luther Jones, better known as Casey Jones, was an engineer on Cannonball Number 382. On the evening of April 29, 1900, Casey and his black fireman, Sim Webb, prepared to take the Cannonball from Memphis to Canton. The scheduled engineer was out ill. The train left at 12:50 A.M., an hour and thirty minutes late. Casey was determined to make up the lost time.

◆ ◆ ◆

When Casey's train crashed, he refused to jump to safety. Instead, he stayed on the train, saved many lives, and then died. He became a railroad hero.

Another railroad hero was based on a real person named John Henry.

◆ ◆ ◆

The real John Henry, believed to be a newly freed slave from North Carolina, joined the West Virginia steel-driving team hired to dig out the

---

Activate Prior Knowledge

What lessons could you learn from family members who tell stories about jobs they have done?

_____

_____

Nonfiction

One of the purposes of nonfiction writing is **to inform**, or to present facts and information to the reader. Read the information in the bracketed paragraph. Who are the people the author talks about? Circle their names in the text.

Nonfiction

Nonfiction is written **to persuade, to inform,** or **to entertain** readers. What do you think is the author's purpose for writing about John Henry?

_____

_____

Stop to Reflect

Why do you think the porters wanted to share their stories with one another?

_____

_____

Vocabulary Development

engineer (en ji NEER) *n.* someone whose job it is to control the engine on a ship or train

Read Fluently

Sometimes a new word is formed by joining two separate words together. The new word is known as a compound word. Read the underlined sentence. The word *storyteller* is formed by joining the words *story* and *teller*. Each of those words can stand alone, but they form a new word when joined together. Circle another compound word in the last paragraph.

Nonfiction

What **character traits**, or qualities, would have made the porters look up to Daddy Joe as a hero?

_____

_____

_____

Reading Check

Who is described as "the most terrific Pullman porter who ever made down a berth"? Circle the text that tells you.

Big Bend Tunnel for the C & O Railroad, <u>circa</u> 1870. Many stories detail the life and adventures of this two hundred-pound, six-foot man who was so strong he could drive steel with a hammer in each hand. John Henry's death occurred after competing with a steam drill, winning, and then dying.

◆ ◆ ◆

The porters also told stories about Daddy Joe, a real-life porter, who became a legend. Although they exaggerated Daddy Joe's actions, the stories showed what qualities the porters admired.

◆ ◆ ◆

<u>Whenever a storyteller wanted to make a point about courtesy, honesty, or an outstanding job performance, he used a Daddy Joe story.</u> And a tale about him usually began with: "The most terrific Pullman porter who ever made down a berth was Daddy Joe."

◆ ◆ ◆

The porters also liked to tell funny stories about new workers who made foolish mistakes. As soon as one story was over, someone would begin a new one.

◆ ◆ ◆

Amid thigh-slapping laughter, another tale would begin with: "Did you hear the story about the flagman?" Of course they'd all heard the story a hundred times. But each teller added or subtracted something until the tale was his own. That's how the tales stayed fresh and original.

Vocabulary Development

circa (SER cuh) *adj.* around; used before a date to show that the date is uncertain

courtesy (KER tuh see) *n.* polite behavior

The 11:59
Patricia C. McKissack

Summary Lester Simmons, a retired porter, hangs out every night at the porter house, telling stories to the other railroad employees. One night, he tells the young porters about the mysterious 11:59 Death Train. Lester's story becomes real. He tries to escape the train.

Note-taking Guide

Use this web to recall the different stories that Lester tells.

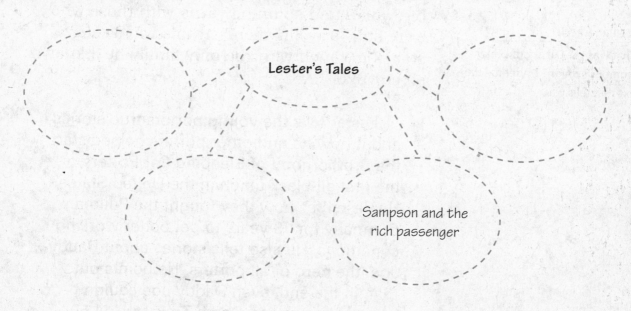

Lester's Tales

Sampson and the rich passenger

Activate Prior Knowledge

What scary stories do you know? What makes a story scary?

_____

_____

_____

Stop to Reflect

Why do you think the young porters enjoy hearing Lester's stories about the old days?

_____

_____

Reading Check

What was special about Lester Simmons's union? Underline the text that tells you.

The 11:59
Patricia C. McKissack

This fictional story is set in St. Louis in the 1950s. Its main character is an old man who has retired from his job as a Pullman porter after thirty years of work.

◆　◆　◆

Lester Simmons was a thirty-year retired Pullman car porter—had his gold watch to prove it. "Keeps perfect train time," he often bragged. "Good to the second."

Daily he went down to the St. Louis Union Station and shined shoes to help supplement his meager twenty-four-dollar-a-month Pullman retirement check. He ate his evening meal at the porter house on Compton Avenue and hung around until late at night talking union, playing bid whist, and spinning yarns with those who were still "travelin' men." In this way Lester stayed in touch with the only family he'd known since 1920.

◆　◆　◆

Lester tells the young porters true stories about how he and other porters helped start the Brotherhood of Sleeping Car Porters, the first all-black union in the United States. He describes how they fought the Pullman Company for 13 years to get better working conditions. He also tells stories about Daddy-Joe, the hero of all porters. He points out that, in the end, even Daddy Joe couldn't escape the porters' Death Train, the 11:59.

◆　◆　◆

Vocabulary Development

supplement (SUP luh muhnt) *v.* add something, especially to what you earn or eat, in order to improve it

meager (MEE ger) *adj.* very small in amount

"Any porter who hears the whistle of the 11:59 has got exactly twenty-four hours to clear up earthly matters. He better be ready when the train comes the next night . . ." In his creakiest voice, Lester drove home the point. "All us porters got to board that train one day. Ain't no way to escape the final ride on the 11:59."

Silence.

"Lester," a young porter asked, "you know anybody who ever heard the whistle of the 11:59 and lived to tell—"

"Not a living soul!"

Laughter.

◆ ◆ ◆

Then Lester tells the story of how his old friend, Tip Sampson, got his nickname. Tip once waited on a rich woman who rode a train from Chicago to Los Angeles. He was hoping to get a big tip from the woman. At the end of the trip, however, all she gave him was one dime. Lester started teasing Sampson by calling him Tip, and the nickname stuck. One of the porters tells Lester that Tip recently "boarded the 11:59," or died. Lester realizes that he is one of the last old-time porters left in St. Louis. Then he starts walking home a little before midnight.

◆ ◆ ◆

Suddenly he felt a sharp pain in his chest. At exactly the same moment he heard the <u>mournful</u> sound of a train whistle, which the wind seemed to carry from some faraway place. Ignoring his pain, Lester looked at the old station. He knew nothing was scheduled to come in or out till early morning. Nervously he lit a match to check the time. 11:59!

"No," he said into the darkness. "I'm not ready. I've got plenty of living yet."

TAKE NOTES

Fiction

A **plot** is the events that moves the reader through a story. The plot has a **resolution,** or outcome, at the end of the story. What is the resolution of the story that Lester tells about his friend Sampson?

_____

_____

_____

Read Fluently

Authors use certain words to describe how a character feels. Read the bracketed passage. How does Lester feel after he hears the train whistle? Circle the word that tells you.

Reading Check

What does Lester learn about his friend Tip? Underline the answer in the text.

Vocabulary Development

mournful (MAWRN fuhl) *adj.* very sad; depressing

Fiction

Point of view is the view from which a story is told to the reader. **First-person point of view** is used when the story is told from the view of a character. **Third-person point of view** is used when the story is told from the view of a person outside the story. From which point of view is this story told?

_____

Read Fluently

Authors use exclamation points (!) to add punch to words or sentences. Read the underlined sentence. Why do you think the author used an exclamation point here? How would the sentence sound if it ended with a period?

_____

_____

_____

Reading Check

What is supposed to happen at 11:59? Circle the answer in the text.

Fear quickened his step. Reaching his small apartment, he hurried up the steps. His heart pounded in his ear, and his left arm tingled. He had an idea, and there wasn't a moment to waste. But his own words haunted him. *Ain't no way to escape the final ride on the 11:59.*

"But I'm gon' try!" Lester spent the rest of the night plotting his escape from fate.

◆ ◆ ◆

Lester decides not to eat or drink anything the next day so that he will not choke or die of food poisoning. He shuts off his space heater, nails all the doors and windows shut, and unplugs all of his appliances to avoid any dangers. He plans to escape Death and live to tell the story to the young porters.

Lester spends the next day in his chair, too scared to move. He checks his watch every few minutes and listens to its constant ticking. He thinks about his thirty years of working on the railroad. He wonders what his life would have been like if he had decided to settle down in one place and get married. Finally, he decides that he has lived a good life and has no regrets.

When night comes, Lester starts praying. His arm starts tingling, and his legs get stiff. He wonders whether he will be the first porter to avoid the 11:59 and cheat Death. Then he hears a train whistle, lights a match, and sees that the time is now 11:57. He hears the whistle again, but he is unable to move. The pain in his chest gets worse, and it is hard for him to breathe.

◆ ◆ ◆

Time had run out! Lester's mind reached for an explanation that made sense. But reason failed when a glowing phantom dressed in the porters' blue uniform stepped out of the grayness of Lester's confusion.

"It's *your* time, good brother." The specter spoke in a thousand familiar voices.

Freed of any restraint now, Lester stood, bathed in a peaceful calm that had its own glow. "Is that you, Tip?" he asked, squinting to focus on his old friend standing in the strange light.

"It's me, ol' partner. Come to remind you that none of us can escape the last ride on the 11:59."

"I know. I know," Lester said, chuckling. "But man, I had to try."

Tip smiled. "I can dig it. So did I."

"That'll just leave Willie, won't it?"

"Not for long."

"I'm ready."

◆ ◆ ◆

Lester dies. Two days later, his friends find him dead on the floor, with his eyes still staring at his gold watch. The watch stopped at exactly 11:59.

Fiction

What is the **resolution** to Lester's story?

_____

_____

Fiction

A **theme** is a message about life that a story attempts to tell. What do you think is the theme of Lester's story?

_____

_____

_____

Reading Check

What is Tip's reason for coming to see Lester? Underline the answer in the text.

Nonfiction and Fiction

1. **Interpret:** What causes Lester's death in "The 11:59"?

_____

_____

2. **Classify:** Use the chart below to record information about the railroad figures discussed in "The Baker Heater League." List the heroes. Write the facts and legends that are given about each one.

Railroad Heroes	Fact	Legend/Fiction
Casey Jones	His real name was John Luther Jones. He was an engineer on Cannonball No. 382.	Jones chose to stay on the train to protect the lives of others.

3. **Fiction:** What details in the **setting** make "The 11:59" seem to have actually happened?

_____

_____

4. **Nonfiction:** Authors of nonfiction often use fictional parts in their writing. Why does the author include tales about famous railroad figures in "The Baker Heater League"?

_____

_____

_____

Talk Show

Present a **talk show**. The following tips will help you create your show.

- Read some of the authors' works. Patricia and Fredrick McKissack's books include *Christmas in the Big House, Christmas in the Quarters; Bugs!; Martin Luther King, Jr.: Man of Peace; Rebels Against Slavery: American Slave Revolts;* and *Let My People Go.*

  What I learned from the McKissacks' writing:

  _____

  _____

  _____

  _____

- Search the Internet: Use words and phrases such as "Patricia McKissack article."

  What I learned about Patricia and Fredrick McKissack:

  _____

  _____

  _____

  _____

- Watch the video interview with Patricia McKissack. Add what you learn from the video to what you have already learned about the author and her husband.

  Additional information learned about the authors:

  _____

  _____

  _____

  _____

  Use your notes to write your talk show.

A Retrieved Reformation • Raymond's Run

Reading Skill

Good readers **make predictions** as they read. A prediction is a guess about what will happen in a story. Look for facts and events that hint at what will happen next. Use them as clues to **support your predictions**. Also use your own experiences to help you make predictions. You might predict that rain is coming if you hear the rumble of thunder.

Look for clues to help you make predictions as you read. Use the chart to record your predictions.

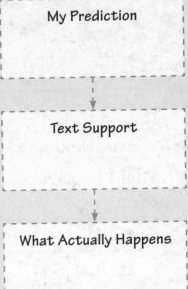

Literary Analysis

The events of a story make up the **plot**. Plots have six main parts:

- **Exposition:** introduction to the characters and the problem

- **Conflict:** struggle between two characters or between two forces

- **Rising Action:** part of a story that builds excitement or interest

- **Climax:** high point in the story

- **Falling Action:** events that follow the climax

- **Resolution:** end of the story

Look for each of the plot parts as you read.

Word List A

Study these words from "Raymond's Run." Then, complete the activity.

energy [EN er jee] *n.* strength to be active
The racer used a final burst of energy to cross the finish line.

fantasy [FAN tuh see] *n.* something you imagine happening
The young girl had a fantasy of becoming President of the United States.

pageant [PAJ uhnt] *n.* well-planned presentation of a play or other performance
The students presented an elaborate Thanksgiving pageant.

prefer [pri FER] *v.* like something more than other things
I prefer to ride my bike instead of taking the bus or walking.

recipe [RES i pee] *n.* list of materials and instructions for making food
My favorite recipe for chicken was taught to me by my mother.

satin [SAT uhn] *adj.* made from a smooth fabric that is shiny on one side
The slippery satin ribbon kept coming untied.

strawberries [STRAW ber eez] *n.* small, red, juicy fruits
We couldn't resist picking the strawberries as soon as they ripened.

zoom [ZOOM] *v.* move quickly
I watched the cars zoom by on the freeway.

Exercise A

Fill in each blank in the paragraph below with an appropriate word from Word List A. Use each word only once.

We are planning the school's spring [1] _____. Since everything will be blooming, our theme is "A [2] _____ of Flowers." We need to write skits, sell tickets, plan refreshments, and make decorations. We'll need lots of [3] _____ to get it all ready in time! Since I [4] _____ jobs that are artistic, I'm working on decorations. We're going to create flowers out of [5] _____ material so they'll shine under the lights. I have seen the fabric at *Sew What?*, so I've offered to [6] _____ by the store tonight to pick up some. The food team has decided to serve barbecue chicken. They hope Principal Rivera will share the secret [7] _____ for his yummy sauce. I think [8] _____ dipped in chocolate would make a great dessert.

1. Underline the words naming what people need energy to do. Tell about something you do that requires *energy*.

2. Circle three words naming things that were part of the May Day pageant on April 30. Explain what a *pageant* is.

3. What type of people do you prefer to spend time with? Make a list of words used to describe your *preferred* friends.

4. Circle the words that describe strawberries. Then, write your own sentence describing them.

5. Write a sentence explaining why May Day would be "a fantasy come true" for flower lovers.

6. Underline an ingredient that might be found in the recipe for sweet oatcakes. Then, write a sentence describing the food made from your favorite *recipe*.

7. Circle what is made of satin. Describe something else that could be made from *satin* material for the prom.

8. Underline the words that describe the opposite of zoom. Then, use *zoom* in your own sentence.

Read the following passage. Pay special attention to the underlined words. Then, read it again, and complete the activities. Use a separate sheet of paper for your written answers.

May Day is one of the world's oldest holidays. Since ancient times, people have gathered to welcome spring. The season's beautiful flowers and warm sun were celebrated, along with people's feelings of renewed energy for work and play. Over time, celebrations became bigger. Some villages would plan a special pageant that began the night of April 30. On this night, the villagers would put out their winter fires and go to the center of town. There, a new fire would be started. Bearing torches, the people would return home, singing and dancing.

Daytime celebrations usually included a maypole. A tall tree would be cut down and brought to the middle of the village. Colorful ribbons were tied to the trunk. They formed bright patterns as boys and girls danced around the pole, ribbons in hand. Legend said that your ribbon would wind around the ribbon of the person you would prefer to marry. Seasonal treats, such as fresh, juicy strawberries, were served.

May Day was a fantasy come true for flower lovers. Flowers were placed in doors and windows. People made bouquets for one another or filled baskets with blossoms and sweets to give away. One traditional May Day recipe used leftover oatmeal to make sweet oatcakes.

You can see that many modern spring celebrations come from the ancient May Day festivals. For example, the spring prom uses many of the same ideas. Young people dance together, perhaps hoping to find true love. Flowers are worn in lapels or at the wrist, and colorful satin ribbons are used in prom decorations. It is true that modern dancers seem to hop, jerk, and zoom across the dance floor instead of gently winding their way around a pole. Still, the true May Day feelings of young love, hope in a new season, and enjoyment of nature's beauty remain the same.

Raymond's Run
Toni Cade Bambara

Summary Squeaky is the fastest runner in her class. She cares for her "not quite right" brother Raymond. She protects him from teasing and from getting hurt. During the annual May Day races, Squeaky learns lessons about herself, a runner named Gretchen, and Raymond.

Writing About the Big Question

Is the truth the same for everyone? In "Raymond's Run," the narrator discovers that winning a race is not the most important thing in her life. Complete this sentence:

Before _____ happened, I used to think that

_____ was important. After it happened,

I observed that _____.

Note-taking Guide

Use this chart to record the order of the four most important events in the story.

Beginning Event			Final Outcome
Squeaky and her brother Raymond run into a group of girls whom Squeaky does not like.			

Activate Prior Knowledge

Tell about a time when you practiced very hard for something.

_____

_____

_____

_____

Literary Analysis

Plot is the order of events in a story. **Exposition** is the part of plot that gives basic information about the characters and the situation. The **conflict** is the struggle between two forces in the story. Read the bracketed passage. Is this passage part of the exposition or part of the conflict? Explain your answer.

_____

_____

_____

_____

Reading Check

What is Squeaky's special talent? Circle the text that tells you.

Raymond's Run
Toni Cade Bambara

Squeaky is a confident, sassy young girl who lives in Harlem in New York City. Squeaky has to take care of her brother Raymond, who is "not quite right." She boldly protects Raymond from kids who try to tease him. Squeaky loves to run races, and she is the fastest runner in her neighborhood.

◆ ◆ ◆

There is no track meet that I don't win the first place medal. I used to win the twenty-yard dash when I was a little kid in kindergarten. Nowadays, it's the fifty-yard dash. And tomorrow I'm subject to run the quarter-meter relay all by myself and come in first, second, and third.

◆ ◆ ◆

This year, for the first time, Squeaky has some serious competition in the race, a new girl named Gretchen.

◆ ◆ ◆

So as far as everyone's concerned, I'm the fastest and that goes for Gretchen, too, who has put out the tale that she is going to win the first-place medal this year. Ridiculous. In the second place, she's got short legs. In the third place, she's got freckles. In the first place, no one can beat me and that's all there is to it.

◆ ◆ ◆

Squeaky takes a walk down Broadway with Raymond. She is practicing her breathing exercises to get in shape for the race. Raymond is pretending to drive a stage coach.

Squeaky works hard to be a good runner. She dislikes people who pretend that they do not need to work hard to be good at something.

Then, Squeaky sees Gretchen and two of her friends coming toward her and Raymond.

One of the girls, Mary Louise, used to be Squeaky's friend. Now she hangs out with Gretchen and does not like Squeaky anymore. Rosie, the other girl, always teases Raymond. Squeaky considers going into a store to avoid the girls, but she decides to face them.

◆ ◆ ◆

"You signing up for the May Day races?" smiles Mary Louise, only it's not a smile at all.

A dumb question like that doesn't deserve an answer. Besides, there's just me and Gretchen standing there really, so no use wasting my breath talking to shadows.

"I don't think you're going to win this time," says Rosie, trying to <u>signify</u> with her hands on her hips all salty, completely forgetting that I have whupped her many times for less salt than that.

"I always win cause I'm the best," I say straight at Gretchen who is, as far as I'm concerned, the only one talking in this ventriloquist-dummy routine.

Gretchen smiles, but it's not a smile, and I'm thinking that girls never really smile at each other because they don't know how and don't want to know how and there's probably no one to teach us how cause grown-up girls don't know either. Then they all look at Raymond who has just brought his mule team to a standstill. And they're about to see what trouble they can get into through him.

◆ ◆ ◆

Mary Louise starts to tease Raymond, but Squeaky defends him. Gretchen and her friends leave, and Squeaky smiles at her brother.

The next day, Squeaky arrives late at the May Day program because she does not want

© Pearson Education

Vocabulary Development

signify (SIG nuh fy) *v.* represent something

Stop to Reflect

Mary Louise smiles at Squeaky and Squeaky describes her smile as "not a smile at all." What does Squeaky mean when she says this?

_____

_____

_____

Literary Analysis

Rising action is a part of **plot** with events that increase the tension. Read the bracketed passage. What event in this passage increases the tension of the story?

_____

_____

_____

Reading Check ✎

Squeaky feels that she is talking to only one of the girls. Which girl is it? Underline the text that tells you.

TAKE NOTES

Stop to Reflect

Do you agree with the way that Squeaky deals with the situation with the girls? Explain.

_____

_____

_____

_____

Reading Skill

A **prediction** is an informed guess about what might happen. Read the bracketed passage. How do you **predict** that Squeaky will react to Mr. Pearson's suggestion?

_____

_____

_____

Read Fluently

Read the underlined sentence that ends on p. 23. Circle the most important words in the sentence. Write the meaning of the sentence in your own words.

_____

_____

_____

to see the May Pole dancing. She thinks it is silly. She arrives just as the races are starting. She puts Raymond on the swings and finds Mr. Pearson, a tall man who gives the racers their numbers.

◆ ◆ ◆

"Well, Squeaky," he says, checking my name off the list and handing me number seven and two pins. And I'm thinking he's got no right to call me Squeaky, if I can't call him Beanstalk.

"Hazel Elizabeth Deborah Parker," I correct him and tell him to write it down on his board.

"Well, Hazel Elizabeth Deborah Parker, going to give someone else a break this year?" I squint at him real hard to see if he is seriously thinking I should lose the race on purpose just to give someone else a break.

◆ ◆ ◆

Mr. Pearson suggests that Squeaky let Gretchen, the new girl, win the race. Squeaky gets mad and walks away.

When it is time for the 50-yard dash, Squeaky and Gretchen line up with the other runners at the starting line. Squeaky sees that Raymond has left the swings and is getting ready to run on the other side of the fence.

Squeaky mentally prepares herself to win and takes off like a shot, zipping past the other runners.

◆ ◆ ◆

I glance to my left and there is no one. To the right a blurred Gretchen, who's got her chin jutting out as if it would win the race all by itself. And on the other side of the fence is Raymond with his arms down to his side and the palms

Vocabulary Development
squint (skwint) *v.* narrow your eyes so that you can see better
jutting (JUT ing) *adj.* sticking out

tucked up behind him, running in his very own style, and it's the first time I ever saw that and I almost stop to watch my brother Raymond on his first run. But the white ribbon is bouncing toward me and I tear past it, racing into the distance till my feet with a mind of their own start digging up footfuls of dirt and brake me short.

◆ ◆ ◆

Squeaky believes that she has won the race, but it turns out that she and Gretchen crossed the finish line at almost the same time. The judges are not sure which girl is the winner.

◆ ◆ ◆

And I lean down to catch my breath and here comes Gretchen walking back, for she's overshot the finish line too, huffing and puffing with her hands on her hips taking it slow, breathing in steady time like a real pro and I sort of like her a little for the first time. "In first place . . ." and then three or four voices get all mixed up on the loudspeaker and I dig my sneaker into the grass and stare at Gretchen who's staring back, we both wondering just who did win.

◆ ◆ ◆

As Squeaky waits to find out whether she has won, Raymond calls out to her. He starts climbing up the fence. Suddenly, Squeaky remembers that Raymond ran the race too, on the other side of the fence.

◆ ◆ ◆

And it occurs to me, watching how smoothly he climbs hand over hand and remembering how he looked running with his arms down to his side and with the wind pulling his mouth back and his teeth showing and all, it occurred to me that Raymond would make a very fine runner. Doesn't he always keep up with me on my trots? And he surely knows how to breathe in counts of seven cause he's always doing it at the dinner table, which drives my brother George

TAKE NOTES

Literary Analysis

Read the bracketed passage. What characters are involved in this **conflict**?

_____

Reading Skill 📖

Who do you **predict** will win the race? Why?

_____

_____

_____

_____

_____

_____

Reading Check

What does Squeaky notice about Raymond after she finishes the race? Underline the sentence that tells the answer.

TAKE NOTES

Read Fluently

It helps to break down a long sentence into shorter sentences. Read the underlined sentence. How could you break this sentence into shorter sentences? Circle each part of the sentence that could be made into a shorter sentence.

Literary Analysis

Squeaky thinks more about her brother than about the race after she is done. How does Raymond affect the story's **conflict**?

_____

_____

_____

_____

up the wall. And I'm smiling to beat the band cause if I've lost this race, or if me and Gretchen tied, or even if I've won, I can always retire as a runner and begin a whole new career as a coach with Raymond as my champion.

◆ ◆ ◆

Squeaky gets very excited about the idea of teaching Raymond to be a champion runner. She wants him to have something to be proud of. Raymond runs over to her, and she jumps up and down with happiness because of her plans to help him.

◆ ◆ ◆

But of course everyone thinks I'm jumping up and down because the men on the loudspeaker have finally gotten themselves together and compared notes and are announcing "In first place—Miss Hazel Elizabeth Deborah Parker." (Dig that.) "In second place—Miss Gretchen P. Lewis." And I look over at Gretchen wondering what the "P" stands for. And I smile. Cause she's good, no doubt about it. Maybe she'd like to help me coach Raymond; she obviously is serious about running, as any fool can see. And she nods to congratulate me and then she smiles. And I smile. We stand there with this big smile of respect between us.

Raymond's Run

1. **Respond:** Which parts of Squeaky's personality would make you want to be her friend?

   _____

2. **Analyze:** Squeaky is very protective of her brother, Raymond. How does Squeaky feel about taking care of him?

   _____

3. **Reading Skill:** When you **make predictions** about a story, you make informed guesses about what will happen next. List two predictions you made as you read "Raymond's Run."

   _____

   _____

4. **Literary Analysis:** The **rising action** contains events that increase the tension of the story. The **falling action** contains events that follow the climax. Complete the **plot** chart below. Write in two events from the **rising action** and one event from the **falling action**.

   Climax: Squeaky crosses the finish line.

   Event: _____

   Event: _____

   Event: _____

   Event: Squeaky and Gretchen exchange smiles.

   Event: Squeaky and Gretchen will race.

   Rising Action

   Falling Action

   Exposition:

   Resolution:

   Conflict:

Writing: New Ending

Imagine the ending of the story if Gretchen had won the race. Write a **new ending** to show how Squeaky might react to losing. Use your notes as you write your new ending.

Does Squeaky go through a change at the end of the story? If so, how would this change affect the way she would feel about losing? Explain.

_____

_____

Squeaky is proud, bold, and loyal. What other adjectives describe her?

_____

_____

Listening and Speaking: Radio Broadcast

Use the following statements to help you prepare for your **radio broadcast.** Use action verbs so that listeners will feel the rising tension and the excitement of the race.

1. Describe Squeaky's appearance. _____

2. Describe Gretchen's appearance. _____

3. Describe how Squeaky acts. _____

_____

4. Describe how Gretchen acts. _____

_____

5. Describe what happens as Squeaky and Gretchen approach the

   finish line. _____

_____

Word List A

Study these words from "A Retrieved Reformation." Then, complete the activity.

active [AK tiv] *adj.* full of normal energy and activity
After a long nap, the toddler had an active afternoon.

café [kaf AY] *n.* small restaurant
During summer months, people can eat outdoors at the local café.

drugstore [DRUHG stor] *n.* store where medicines and other products are sold
The local drugstore now sells all sorts of school supplies.

extremely [ek STREEM lee] *adv.* to a great extent or degree
Candace was extremely excited to learn that she'd qualified for the finals.

flourishing [FLUR ish ing] *v.* succeeding
The wilting plants began flourishing again as soon as they were watered.

inspection [in SPEK shun] *n.* very careful look at something
An inspection of my locker finally turned up the source of the awful smell.

successful [suhk SES fuhl] *adj.* turning out as planned
If our car wash is successful, we'll earn enough for the end-of-school trip.

typical [TIP uh kuhl] *adj.* showing the qualities and common traits of a group
The typical teenager needs at least eight hours of sleep each night.

Exercise A

Fill in each blank in the paragraph below with an appropriate word from Word List A. Use each word only once.

I have a very [1] _____ imagination. A dream I had recently is the perfect example of my mind at work. My dreams are always [2] _____ interesting. Upon close [3] _____, though, this one was really over the top! The dream took place in a small town on the planet Venus. The town was highly [4] _____ because of its famous [5] _____ that sold medicines to heal any sickness. Truly, business was [6] _____ in that space-age shop! Travelers from Earth also visited this town on Venus just to eat in its famous [7] _____. The meals were prepared with all the [8] _____ ingredients that have brought intergalactic fame to the foods of Venus. Now, if only I could remember those recipes when I wake up!

1. Circle the words that tell what is an extremely interesting find. What makes something *extremely* interesting when you are searching for facts?

2. Underline words in the second paragraph that describe a typical small town. Then, write what *typical* means.

3. Write a sentence to explain why a drugstore would be found near a food market and a bank.

4. Underline the words that name people who came to Morrilton when it began flourishing. Tell what *flourishing* means.

5. Circle the word that tells what you find in a café. Why would a *café* be a good business to have during tourist months?

6. Circle the verb that tells what an inspection does. Why is the word closer used to describe an *inspection*?

7. Circle the words in the slogan that hint at the meaning of successful. Write a sentence to explain how this helps define *successful*.

8. Circle the words that show how people can be active at the park. Tell what *active* means

Read the following passage. Pay special attention to the underlined words. Then, read it again, and complete the activities. Use a separate sheet of paper for your written answers.

Search for Elmore, Arkansas, on a map or on the Internet and you come up with a big zero. However, Morrilton, Arkansas, proves to be an extremely interesting find. This small town was built in the 1870s. Morrilton seems to have the same features as the town of Elmore in "A Retrieved Reformation." Since O. Henry loved word games, to believe that he modeled his town after Morrilton is not unreasonable. Just reverse the syllables in "Morril"!

Pictures of Morrilton show a typical small town. Begun along the Little Rock and Fort Smith Railroad, the town quickly grew as a trade center. You can just imagine its main street back then. There would have been a row of red brick businesses, including a drugstore, food market, and bank. Things in Morrilton really began flourishing when a bridge to it was built across the Arkansas River. Tourists, shoppers, and farmers enjoyed visiting the charming town in the Ozark foothills. No doubt the café serving food on the main street has always been busy during summer months.

A closer inspection of Morrilton today reveals a successful small town. It even has a slogan: "Small City, No Limits." Travelers might stay in Morrilton while visiting the nearby Museum of Automobiles or the Petit Jean State Park. The park is great for active people. You can walk the trails or explore caves. Many beautiful things are found in the park, including a natural bridge and a 95-foot waterfall. There are also stunning views from the mountain for which the park is named. Legend says that a French girl fell in love with an American sailor. In order to come with him to his home, she disguised herself as a boy named Jean. The mountain ("Little Jean") is named for her.

A Retrieved Reformation
O. Henry

Summary Jimmy Valentine leaves prison and plans to go back to robbing safes. But he falls in love and decides to become honest. He changes his name and opens a store. A detective shows up to arrest Jimmy for recent robberies. However, Jimmy's actions show that he has changed.

? Writing About the Big Question

Is truth the same for everyone? In "A Retrieved Reformation," a former thief tries to re-invent the truth about his life. Complete this sentence:

People form opinions of others based on _____

_____.

Note-taking Guide

Use this character web to describe Jimmy Valentine's character.

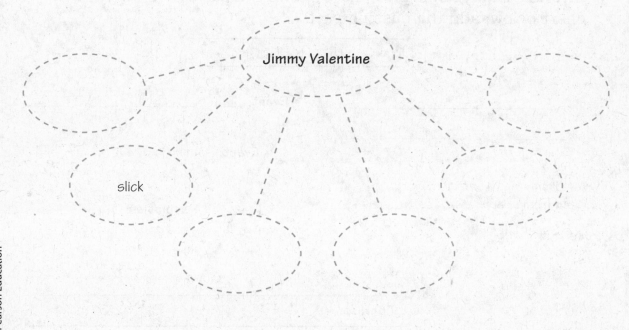

Jimmy Valentine

slick

A Retrieved Reformation

1. **Deduce:** One of the first people Jimmy sees in Elmore is Annabel Adams. How does seeing her make him change?

_____

_____

2. **Make a Judgment:** Jimmy has been breaking the law for a long time. He now plans to stop. Do you think people like Jimmy can change their ways? Explain.

_____

_____

3. **Reading Skill:** A **prediction** is a guess about what will happen later. You might predict that Ben Price will arrest Jimmy. What clues can you find to support that prediction?

_____

_____

4. **Literary Analysis:** A **plot** chart shows the parts of a story. In the chart below, add the missing parts.

Climax: Agatha is trapped in a safe.

Event: _____

Event: _____

Event: _____

Event: Agatha is freed.

Event: Jimmy V. is a safecracker released from prison.

Rising Action

Falling Action

Resolution: Price pretends not to know Jimmy.

Exposition:

Conflict:

© Pearson Education

Writing: New Ending

Write a **new ending** to the story. How would the story be different if Ben Price had arrested Jimmy? Use this chart to show how Jimmy's arrest would have changed these people's lives:

Jimmy	Annabel Adams	Ben Price

Use your notes to write your new ending for the story

Listening and Speaking: Radio Broadcast

Write and perform a **radio broadcast** of Jimmy's rescue of Agatha. What would each of the following people say and do?

- Jimmy _____

_____

- Annabel _____

_____

- Agatha _____

- Agatha's mother

_____

_____

- Mr. Adams _____

_____

Use your notes to write your radio broadcast.

Gentleman of Río en Medio • Cub Pilot on the Mississippi

Reading Skill

You can **make predictions** about a story. Use details in the story to guess what will happen later. **Reading ahead to confirm or correct predictions** helps you understand how events in the story are connected. Follow these steps:

- Read and look for details that suggest what might happen.

- Make your prediction.

- Use the chart below to write your prediction. Read ahead to see whether your prediction is right. You might read something that makes your prediction wrong. If this happens, change your prediction.

Detail: Character sees a fin in the water.

Prediction: A shark will attack.

Read → Ahead

New Details: The fin turns out to be belong to a dolphin.

Prediction: The dolphin will help the character get to land.

Literary Analysis

Conflict is a struggle in a story. There are two main kinds of conflict:

- A character can struggle against another character, nature, or society. This is called **external conflict**.

- A character can also struggle with two different feelings, beliefs, needs, or desires. This is called **internal conflict**.

The conflict in the story ends in the **resolution**. All problems are worked out.

Word List A

Study these words from "Gentleman of Río en Medio." Then, complete the activity.

additional [uh DISH uh nuhl] *adj.* extra; more
We were having such a good time at the fair that we bought additional tickets for the rides.

amounted [uh MOWNT id] *v.* added up
Twelve tickets to the county fair at $5 each amounted to $60.

document [DAHK yuh muhnt] *n.* paper with important information
A document with proof of age is needed in order to obtain a passport.

insulted [in SUHL tid] *v.* said something rude or upsetting
She insulted all the party guests by saying that they had no manners.

obediently [oh BEE dee uhnt lee] *adv.* as one has been instructed
Even though we didn't want to work overtime, we obediently followed the manager's orders.

previous [PREE vee uhs] *adj.* former; earlier
At my previous school, my lunch break was much earlier than it is here.

quaint [KWAYNT] *adj.* charming in an old-fashioned way
Some people find the village quaint, but others think it just looks run-down.

rate [RAYT] *n.* standard amount used to figure a total
Parking garages charge a higher rate to park during their busiest hours.

Exercise A

Fill in each blank in the paragraph below with an appropriate word from Word List A. Use each word only once.

My father had asked me to go downtown to bring him a [1] _____ he needed for a case he was working on. Although I could think of better things to do that day, I [2] _____ headed to the bus stop. Before a [3] _____ errand, Dad had pressed a crisp $10 bill into my hand. This time he [4] _____ me by not offering me a red cent. Some people might find it [5] _____ that Dad has me running errands when there's a perfectly good messenger service. But he thinks it builds character. When I got back to his office, I figured at the [6] _____ of $5.25 an hour, my fee [7] _____ to $10.50. But when he pulled a crisp $10 bill from his wallet, I didn't have the heart to ask him for the [8] _____ 50 cents.

1. Underline the two items that amounted to half a million dollars. Then, write what *amounted* means.

2. Circle the words that caused the relative to be insulted. Rewrite that sentence, using a synonym for *insulted*.

3. Circle the phrase that tells what it means to obediently accept an offer. Then, tell about a time you did something *obediently*.

4. Rewrite the sentence that contains the word previous, using a different phrase for the *previous* year.

5. Circle the phrase that tells the rate at which the narrator says property is valued. Define *rate*.

6. Circle the additional amount of money the family needed in order to move. How does the word *additional* let you know that the family had already saved some money?

7. Circle the synonym for quaint. Give an example of something you know that is *quaint*.

8. Underline the words that tell what the family document was. Name an important *document* belonging to your family or to the country.

Read the following passage. Pay special attention to the underlined words. Then, read it again, and complete the activities. Use a separate sheet of paper for your written answers.

Mom and Dad were speechless when Great-aunt Bessie said that she was giving them her house and most of her furniture. It amounted to a gift of half a million dollars.

"Don't say no," Auntie added. "I once insulted a very dear relative by turning down a gift."

Without a fuss, my parents obediently accepted her offer. The previous year, after the twins were born, we had gone house hunting for our growing family. With property valued at a rate of $10,000 an acre, Mom and Dad had always come up short. They told me that we needed an additional $20,000 to make moving out of our crowded apartment possible. Now that Auntie was going to live with her sister, I guess she saw the wisdom in her gift. We saw space and comfort.

Great-aunt Bessie's house was quaint and old-fashioned. Built around the turn of the twentieth century, her grandparents had been the original owners. Her parents had been the second owners. She and her husband had been the third. They'd never had any children of their own, and now Great-uncle Oscar was gone these last three years.

One weekend afternoon, we drove over to Great-aunt Bessie's house to meet with a lawyer. He was going to draw up a deed. Auntie pulled a document out of a crusty old envelope. It was the original bill of sale for the house.

"I want you to have this," she said to my parents. "Keep it safe and pass it along to the next generation." She smiled in my direction. "It's part of our family history."

It felt strange to know that one day I would be part of that history. For now, it felt good to be moving into that big, old house, full of places to explore.

Gentleman of Río en Medio
Juan A. A. Sedillo

Summary Don Anselmo is honest and proud. He sells his land to new American owners. They later have trouble with the village children. The new owners work with Don Anselmo to solve the problem with the children.

 Writing About the Big Question

Is truth the same for everyone? In "Gentleman of Río en Medio," an old man becomes involved in a dispute over the value of property. Complete this sentence:

A person selling a house may be biased about his or her property

because _____

_____ .

Note-taking Guide
Use this chart to record details about the traits of Don Anselmo.

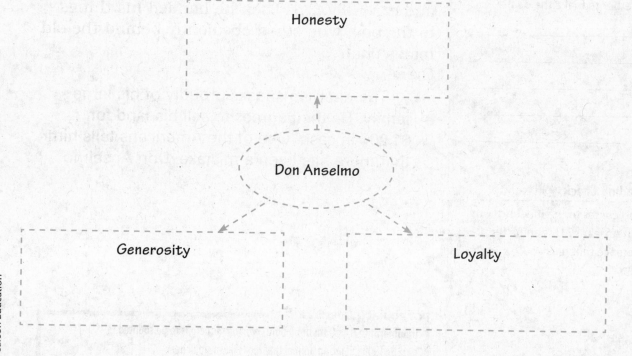

Gentleman of Río en Medio
Juan A. A. Sedillo

Activate Prior Knowledge

A buyer and a seller agree to certain things. Someone is selling a bicycle. List the things to which the buyer and seller might agree.

_____

_____

_____

_____

_____

_____

Reading Skill

One way to follow the events of a story is to **predict**, or guess, what is going to happen. Use details from the story to **make predictions**. What do you predict will happen when Don Anselmo and the Americans get together to make the deal?

_____

_____

_____

_____

_____

Reading Check

Who comes to the meeting with Don Anselmo? Underline the sentence that tells you.

The title of this selection tells a good deal about the story. The main character is an old man, Don Anselmo, who dresses and acts in old-fashioned ways. But he is a man of great gentleness, honesty, and character.

Some American buyers are trying to work out a deal to buy Don Anselmo's land. It is land that his family has been farming for hundreds of years. After several months of bargaining, the two sides get together to make the deal.

◆　◆　◆

The day of the sale [Don Anselmo] came into the office. His coat was old, green and faded. . . . He also wore gloves. They were old and torn and his fingertips showed through them. He carried a cane, but it was only the skeleton of a worn-out umbrella. Behind him walked one of his innumerable kin—a dark young man with eyes like a gazelle.

The old man bowed to all of us in the room. Then he removed his hat and gloves, slowly and carefully. . . . Then he handed his things to the boy, who stood obediently behind the old man's chair.

◆　◆　◆

The old man speaks proudly of his large family. He then agrees to sell his land for $1,200 in cash. One of the Americans tells him that there has been a mistake. Don Anselmo

Vocabulary Development

innumerable (i NOO muhr uh buhl) *adj.* too numerous to be counted

gazelle (guh ZEL) *n.* an animal that looks like a small deer

actually owns twice as much land as they had thought. So they offer to pay him almost twice as much money.

◆ ◆ ◆

The old man hung his head for a moment in thought. Then he stood up and stared at me. "Friend," he said, "I do not like to have you speak to me in that manner." I kept still and let him have his say. "I know these Americans are good people, and that is why I have agreed to sell to them. But I do not care to be insulted. I have agreed to sell my house and land for twelve hundred dollars, and that is the price."

I argued with him but it was useless. Finally he signed the deed and took the money but refused to take more than the amount agreed upon. Then he shook hands all around, put on his ragged gloves, took his stick and walked out with the boy behind him.

◆ ◆ ◆

A month later the Americans have moved onto the property and fixed up the old house. But there is a problem. The village children are playing under the trees on the property. The new owners complain, but the children don't understand. So another meeting is arranged with Don Anselmo to settle the problem. One of the Americans explains the problem. He asks Don Anselmo to tell the children not to play in the orchard.

Don Anselmo explains that they all have learned to love the new American owners. But he sold them only the ground around the trees, not the trees themselves. The American protests that people usually sell everything that grows on the land they sell.

◆ ◆ ◆

"Yes, I admit that," [Don Anselmo] said. "You know," he added, "I am the oldest man in the village. Almost everyone there is my relative and

© Pearson Education

Literary Analysis

A **conflict** is a struggle between two forces. A conflict in a story usually leads to a situation called a **resolution**. Read the bracketed passage. What is the conflict? What is the resolution?

_____

_____

_____

_____

_____

Reading Check

Why does Don Anselmo believe the trees do not belong to the new owners? Underline the sentence that tells you.

Reading Skill

What do you **predict** Don Anselmo will say when the owners ask him to keep the children out of the orchard? Explain.

_____

_____

_____

_____

Read Fluently

Read the bracketed passage. Underline the important details in the passage. Then, put the passage in your own words. Include only the main points.

_____

_____

_____

_____

Literary Analysis

How is the **conflict** in the story **resolved**? Underline the sentence that tells you.

all the children of Río en Medio are my *sobrinos* and *nietos*,[1] my descendants. Every time a child has been born in Río en Medio since I took possession of that house from my mother I have planted a tree for that child. The trees in that orchard are not mine, *Señor*, they belong to the children of the village. Every person in Río en Medio born since the railroad came to Santa Fe owns a tree in that orchard. I did not sell the trees because I could not. They are not mine."

There was nothing we could do. Legally we owned the trees but the old man had been so generous, refusing what amounted to a fortune for him. It took most of the following winter to buy the trees, individually, from the descendants of Don Anselmo in the valley of Río en Medio.

Vocabulary **Development**

descendants (di SEN duhnts) *n.* people whose family roots can be traced back to a particular person or group

1. **sobrinos** (soh BREE nohs) and **nietos** (NYAY tohs) Spanish for "nieces and nephews."

Gentleman of Río en Medio

1. **Respond:** Were you surprised by what Don Anselmo says to the narrator in their first meeting about his land? Explain your answer.

   _____

   _____

2. **Analyze:** Think about how the narrator behaves toward Don Anselmo. Explain how the narrator's behavior helps solve the conflict of the story.

   _____

   _____

3. **Reading Skill:** What did you **predict** would be the outcome of the story? Explain.

   _____

   _____

4. **Literary Analysis:** What is the **conflict** after Don Anselmo sells his land? Complete this graphic organizer to describe the conflict.

   How the conflict develops

   Don Anselmo   vs.

   How the conflict is resolved

Writing: Letter

Write a **letter** to Don Anselmo. Thank him for trying to protect the right of the children to play in the orchard. Use the sentence starters to help you write your letter.

Dear Don Anselmo,

Thank you for _____.

I know that you care most about _____.

You have given the children of our village _____.

You have benefited the children by _____.

Listening and Speaking: Role Play

Role play the story's conflict. One person will play Don Anselmo. Another person will play the narrator. Answer these questions to help you create your role play.

1. How does Don Anselmo feel about the children playing in the orchard?

   _____

   _____

2. How does the narrator feel about the children playing in the orchard?

   _____

   _____

3. What solutions might be acceptable to both people?

   _____

   _____

Word List A

Study these words from "Cub Pilot on the Mississippi." Then, complete the activity.

apprenticeship [uh PREN tis ship] *n.* training for a job
After high school, Brett started an apprenticeship with a local plumber.

costly [KAWST lee] *adj.* expensive
Not paying attention while driving can lead to costly errors.

criticized [KRIT uh syzd] *v.* told someone what he or she did wrong
Ms. Banks criticized Lenny for his selfish attitude.

employment [em PLOY muhnt] *n.* paid work
Without skills or training, it is hard to find interesting employment.

stingy [STIN jee] *adj.* unwilling to spend or give money
Mr. Virgil was so stingy that he didn't want to pay me for pet sitting.

tyrant [TY ruhnt] *n.* cruel ruler, or someone who behaves like one
Whoever disobeyed the tyrant was punished or banished from the land.

varieties [vuh RY uh teez] *n.* different types of the same thing
How many varieties of melon can you name?

vigorous [VIG uh ruhs] *adj.* lively, strong, or with great energy
At the age of eighty, Mrs. Dawes was as vigorous as any sixty-year-old.

Exercise A

Fill in each blank in the paragraph below with an appropriate word from Word List A. Use each word only once.

Some jobs require a long [1] _____ period, but I didn't think being a reporter for the middle-school newspaper was one of them. It wasn't as if I had sought [2] _____ at the city desk of a major paper. There were only so many [3] _____ of articles, and I thought I covered them all pretty well: sports, assemblies, elections, contests, and fundraising. Still, that [4] _____ of an editor thought otherwise. He was [5] _____ with his time except when he [6] _____ anything I wrote. He was especially [7] _____ in putting me down when other staff members were around. It wasn't as if I could make some [8] _____ error reporting the news. After all, the paper was given out free to all students!

1. Underline words that give a clue to the meaning of apprenticeship. Name a trade for which you might like to serve an *apprenticeship*.

2. Circle the words that tell what was costly to the master. Explain why in a sentence.

3. Circle the word that is the opposite of tyrant. Write a sentence that describes someone who is the opposite of a *tyrant*.

4. Circle the word that is the opposite of stingy. Write a sentence that tells at least one way in which a master might have been *stingy*.

5. Rewrite the sentence with the word criticized using a synonym for *criticized*.

6. Circle one form of employment mentioned in the following sentence. Explain in a sentence why a journeyman had to find *employment*.

7. Circle two varieties of trades mentioned in the paragraph. Write a sentence that includes the other *varieties* mentioned.

8. Why did the trades listed require someone with *vigorous* health?

Read the following passage. Pay special attention to the underlined words. Then, read it again, and complete the activities. Use a separate sheet of paper for your written answers.

In colonial America, and in the early days of the republic, apprenticeship was a common way for a boy to learn a trade. He would sign an indenture, or contract, with a master. The master would then train him in all aspects of his livelihood. Usually, no money changed hands until the last year of service. All the same, it was costly to the master. He had to provide the boy with room and board, and he sometimes also taught the boy how to read, write, and keep the business's accounts.

A master could be a tyrant or a gentle teacher, stingy or generous almost to a fault. Some masters criticized their apprentices constantly. Others taught with praise. No matter what, a boy was expected to obey the master's wishes.

The period of service was usually five or seven years. Then, with a small amount of money in his pocket, an apprentice set out into the world. He was known as a *journeyman*. That is because he often had to journey from place to place to find employment. He usually hoped to save up enough money to have his own business.

Modern life offers many opportunities. However, even 200 years ago, there were many varieties of jobs. A boy could train to be a baker or a blacksmith, a cooper (barrel maker) or a chandler (candle maker). These occupations required a boy in vigorous health with a strong desire to learn and the patience to see a job through. Boys with more education and a love of learning might wind up in a printer's shop or a merchant's office.

The Industrial Revolution greatly reduced the apprentice system. In some fields even today, however, it is a necessary route. It is required for learning a craft, such as fine cabinet making, or a service skill, such as plumbing. Also, it is the only way to pass down years of know-how from generation to generation.

Cub Pilot on the Mississippi
Mark Twain

Summary Mark Twain describes his experience as a cub pilot working on a Mississippi steamboat. He tries to please his boss, but nothing works. The conflict between them grows. Twain cannot control his anger.

 Writing About the Big Question

Is the truth the same for everyone?

In "Cub Pilot on the Mississippi," a young man gets into a violent dispute with his boss over who is telling the truth. Complete this sentence:

If a young person and an adult were to contradict each other in an

argument, I would believe _____ is telling the truth

because _____.

Note-taking Guide
Use this chart to note the differences between the two pilots in the story.

	Pilot Brown	Pilot Ealer
With which cub pilot does he work?	Mark Twain	
How does he treat cub pilots during work hours?		
How does each cub pilot react to his treatment?		

Cub Pilot on the Mississippi

1. **Infer:** Why were cub pilots assigned to work with experienced pilots like Brown?

   _____

2. **Draw Conclusions:** The captain is pleased that Twain has beaten Pilot Brown. What are the captain's feelings about Brown? How do you know?

   _____

   _____

3. **Reading Skill:** When you make **predictions**, you guess what will happen later in a story. What prediction did you make about the outcome of the conflict between Twain and Brown?

   _____

   _____

4. **Literary Analysis:** Use this chart to trace the **conflict** between Twain and Brown.

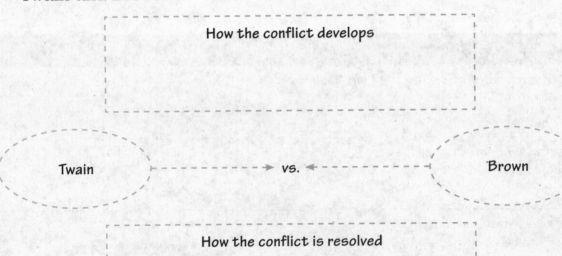

How the conflict develops

Twain   vs.   Brown

How the conflict is resolved

Writing: Letter

Imagine that you are Twain. Write a **letter** to your best friend, describing your first days as a cub pilot. Use the following sentence starters to think through some of your feelings.

1. When I first went on the boat, I felt _____

   _____

2. When I see Pilot Brown, I feel _____

   _____

3. When I see Pilot Ealer and George Ritchie together, I feel _____

   _____

4. When I am alone in bed at night, I feel _____

   _____

Listening and Speaking: Role Play

With a partner, write a script to **role-play** the conflict between Twain and Brown. Use the following prompts to write what each character might say. Complete your notes on another sheet of paper.

- **Brown:** _____

- **Twain:** _____

- **Brown:** _____

- **Twain:** _____

- **Brown:** _____

- **Twain:** _____

Consumer Documents: Schedules

About Schedules

Schedules help people get where they want to go.

- Schedules list arrival and departure times.

Schedules are **consumer documents.**

- Consumer documents help you buy or use a product or service.
- Other consumer documents include brochures, labels, loan applications, assembly instructions, and warranties.

Reading Skill

Reading transportation schedules is different from reading other materials. You can **use the information to solve a problem,** such as which routes to take and what time to arrive at the station or dock. The information in a schedule is organized in rows and columns to help you find what you need. Look at the chart. It shows some common features of a transportation schedule.

Features of a Schedule	
Headings	Show where to find departure and arrival times
Rows and columns	Allow easy scanning of arrival and departure times across and down the page
Special type and asterisks	Indicate exceptions, such as ferries that do not run on Sundays

Savannah Belles Ferry System

Features:
- consumer information
- details and information in lists, charts, tables, and other graphics
- text that helps the reader purchase or use a product or service
- for a specific audience

City Hall Landing To:

Trade Center Landing	Westin
7:00 AM	3:40 PM
7:20 AM	4:00 PM
7:40 AM	4:20 PM
8:00 AM	4:40 PM
8:20 AM	5:00 PM
*	5:20 PM
9:00 AM	*
9:20 AM	6:00 PM
9:40 AM	6:20 PM
10:00 AM	6:40 PM
10:20 AM	7:00 PM
*	7:20 PM
11:00 AM	7:40 PM
11:20 AM	8:00 PM
11:40 AM	8:20 PM
12:00 PM	*
12:20 PM	9:00 PM
12:40 PM	9:20 PM
1:00 PM	9:40 PM
1:20 PM	10:00 PM
1:40 PM	10:20 PM
2:00 PM	10:40 PM
2:20 PM	11:00 PM
2:40 PM	11:20 PM
3:00 PM	11:40 PM
3:20 PM	12:00 AM
3:40 PM	*

Trade Center Landing To:

City Hall Landing / Hyatt		Waving Girl Landing/Marriott
7:10 AM	3:50 PM	8:15 AM
7:30 AM	4:10 PM	8:45 AM
7:50 AM	4:30 PM	9:15 AM
8:10 AM	4:50 PM	9:45 AM
*	5:10 PM	10:15 AM
8:50 AM	*	10:45 AM
9:10 AM	5:50 PM	11:15 AM
9:30 AM	6:10 PM	11:45 AM
9:50 AM	6:30 PM	12:15 PM
10:10 AM	6:50 PM	12:45 PM
*	7:10 PM	1:15 PM
10:50 AM	7:30 PM	1:45 PM
11:10 AM	7:50 PM	2:15 PM
11:30 AM	8:10 PM	2:45 PM
11:50 AM	*	3:15 PM
12:10 PM	8:50 PM	3:45 PM
12:30 PM	9:10 PM	4:15 PM
12:50 PM	9:30 PM	4:45 PM
1:10 PM	9:50 PM	5:15 PM
1:30 PM	10:10 PM	5:45 PM
1:50 PM	10:30 PM	*
2:10 PM	10:50 PM	
2:30 AM	11:10 PM	
2:50 PM	11:30 PM	
3:10 PM	11:50 PM	
3:30 PM	*	

Waving Girl To:

Trade Center Landing/Westin
8:00 AM
8:30 AM
9:00 AM
9:30 AM
10:00 AM
10:30 AM
11:00 AM
11:30 AM
12:00 PM
12:30 PM
1:00 PM
1:30 PM
2:00 PM
2:30 PM
3:00 PM
3:30 PM
4:00 PM
4:30 PM
5:00 PM
5:30 PM
6:00 PM

Revised 5/23/2007

The list of ferry times allows riders to plan their schedules.

Service Locations

TRADE CENTER LANDING--North Bank Riverwalk, between Trade Center and Westin

CITY HALL LANDING--River Street at City Hall, next to Hyatt

WAVING GIRL LANDING--South Bank Riverwalk, next to Marriott

Year-Around Schedule

The Savannah Belles Ferry System operates daily, year-around, except Thanksgiving Day, Christmas Day and New Year's Day

Service Interruption

The ferry may occasionally be delayed briefly by weather or visibility, or by larger vessels. We appreciate your patience.

This heading helps consumers plan for times when the ferry is delayed.

It's Free! The Savannah Belles Ferry System is operated by Chatham Area Transit Authority (CAT) free of charge to visitors and residents. Thanks for riding with us!

www.catchacat.org, (912) 236-2111

Is truth the same for everyone?

(a) What section of the schedule explains that the details on the schedule may not always be true? **(b)** Why is it important to include this information?

Baylink
Travel the Easy Way

Vallejo - San Francisco Ferry Bldg
Vallejo - San Francisco Pier 41
Effective September 1 - December 1, 2006

Features:

- purposeful reading, used to locate specific information
- details presented in lists, charts, tables, and other graphics
- text that helps readers purchase or use a product or service

Vallejo-S.F. Ferry Bldg • MON-FRI

BUS OR FERRY	VALLEJO FERRY BLDG DEPART	SF FERRY BUILDING DEPART	FISHERMAN'S WHARF PIER 41 ARRIVE	DEPART
Bus	5:00 a	6:05 a		
Ferry	5:30 a	6:35 a		
Bus	5:50 a	6:55 a		
Bus	6:20 a	7:20 a		
Ferry	6:30 a	7:35 a		
Bus	6:45 a	7:50 a		
Ferry	7:00 a	8:10 a		
Bus	7:22 a	8:30 a		
Ferry	7:45 a	8:55 a		
Ferry	8:45 a	9:55 a		
Ferry	10:00 a#	11:10 a#	11:20 a#	11:30 a#
Ferry	11:30 a	12:40 p		
Ferry	1:00 p	2:10 p		
Ferry	2:00 p*	3:30 p*	3:00 p*	3:10 p*

> This heading shows readers where to locate fare information.

Fare Schedule · All Routes

TICKETS REQUIRED TO BOARD FERRIES & BUSES

Adult One-Way	$11.50
Senior/Disabled/Medicare One-Way (65+/disabled)*	$5.75
Youth One-Way (6-12 years)	$5.75
Baylink DayPass	$19.25
Napa/Solano DayPass	$20.75
Reduced Fare DayPass*	$11.50
10-Ride Punch Card	$89.75
Reduced Fare 10-Ride Punch Card*	$57.50
Monthly Pass	$247.25
Monthly Pass w/MUNI	$287.25
Fairfield/Vacaville Monthly Pass	$300
Fairfield/Vacaville Monthly Pass w/MUNI	$340

Up to two children under 6 years of age travel free with each fare-paying adult. Bicycles are also free, subject to capacity limitations. First come, first served; vessel capacity 300 passengers.

* Bay Area Regional Transit Connection Discount Cards and Medicare Cards with Photo ID are accepted for senior and disabled fares.

Vallejo-S.F. Ferry Bldg • SAT-SUN

BUS OR FERRY	VALLEJO FERRY BLDG DEPART	SF FERRY BUILDING DEPART	FISHERMAN'S WHARF PIER 41 ARRIVE	DEPART
Bus	7:00 a	8:10 a		
Ferry	8:45 a	9:55 a		
Ferry	10:00 a#	11:10 a#	11:20 a#	11:30 a#
Ferry	11:30 a	12:40 p		
Ferry	1:00 p	2:10 p		
Bus	2:00 p	3:10 p		
Ferry	3:00 p*	4:30 p*	4:00 p*	4:1 p*

> Arrival and departure times are organized in rows and columns.

Is truth the same for everyone?

What section or sections of this document help you understand the amounts different people pay for tickets?

Water Taxi™
SERVICE SCHEDULE & FARES

Effective December 17, 2007

| Times listed in grey and white run every day. | Times listed in yellow run Friday, Saturday, Sunday and Monday |

WTA

Operated by Water Transportation Alternatives

	North End		Fort Lauderdale Beach				South End			Downtown / New River	
	1 Shooters	**2** Gallery One	**3** Seville Street	**4** Beach Place	**5** Bahia Mar	**6** Pier 66	**7** Convention Center	**8** 15th Street Fisheries	**9** SE 9th Avenue	**10** Downtowner Saloon	**11** Las Olas Riverfront
	9:30	Express to Las Olas Riverfront									10:00
	9:30	Express to Beach Place	9:59	10:12	10:27	10:30	10:32	10:49	10:54	11:00
	10:00	10:17	10:25	10:29	10:42	10:57	11:00	11:02	11:19	11:24	11:30
	10:30	10:47	10:55	10:59	11:12	11:27	11:30	11:32	11:49	11:54	12:00
	11:00	11:17	11:25	11:29	11:42	11:57	12:00	12:02	12:19	12:24	12:30
	11:30	11:47	11:55	11:59	12:12	12:27	12:30	12:32	12:49	12:54	1:00
	12:30	12:47	12:55	12:59	1:12	1:27	1:30	1:32	1:49	1:54	2:00
	1:00	1:17	1:25	1:29	1:42	1:57	2:00	2:02	2:19	2:24	2:30
	1:30	1:47	1:55	1:59	2:12	2:27	2:30	2:32	2:49	2:54	3:00
	2:00	2:17	2:25	2:29	2:42	2:57	3:00	3:02	3:19	3:24	3:30
	2:30	2:47	2:55	2:59	3:12	3:27	3:3_	3:32	3:49	3:54	4:00
	3:30	_:_7	_:55	3:59	_:12	_:_7		4:_	4:_9		_:00

> Read across to locate the columns that have the information you need.

> These notes give additional information about riding the Water Bus and about reading this schedule.

Downtown / New River			South End			Fort Lauderdale Beach			North End	
11 Las Olas Riverfront	**10** Downtowner Saloon	**9** SE 9th Avenue	**8** 15th Street Fisheries	**7** Convention Center	**6** Pier 66	**5** Bahia Mar	**4** Beach Place	**3** Seville Street	**2** Gallery One	**1** Shooters
				9:55	9:58	10:15	10:28	10:32	10:40	11:00
10:00	10:01	10:07	10:23	10:25	10:28	10:45	10:58	11:02	11:10	11:30
11:00	11:01	11:07	11:23	11:25	11:28	11:45	11:58	12:02	12:10	12:30
11:30	11:31	11:37	11:53	11:55	11:58	12:15	12:28	12:32	12:40	1:00
12:00	12:01	12:07	12:23	12:25	12:28	12:45	12:58	1:02	1:10	1:30
12:30	12:31	12:37	12:53	12:55	12:58	1:15	1:28	1:32	1:40	2:00
1:00	1:01	1:07	1:23	1:25	1:28	1:__	1:5_	2:02	2:10	2:30
2:_	_:_1	_:07	2:2_	_:_5						

> One table shows the schedule of stops when traveling Inbound, or from north to south. The other shows the schedule of stops when the Water Bus travels from south to north.

> Read down to see all of the times the Water Bus stops at a location.

Adult	$12.00
Children (under 12)	$9.00
Seniors (over 65)	$9.00
After 7:00 PM	$7.00
Family Pack	$42.00

Valid for 2 adults and 3 children/seniors

Is truth the same for everyone?

How might Fort Lauderdale's popularity as a vacation spot affect the choice to name most of the stops along the Water Bus route according to the restaurants and other attractions at each location, rather than naming the stops with geographical information, such as addresses or intersections?

Thinking About the Schedule

1. In what situation would a schedule be useful?

   _____

   _____

2. Explain how you can figure out what time a ferry will arrive.

   _____

   _____

TALK ABOUT IT Reading Skill

3. What time does the earliest ferry depart from the San Francisco Ferry Building on Monday morning?

   _____

4. Why is each stop on the Water Bus schedule listed twice?

   _____

WRITE ABOUT IT Timed Writing: Itinerary (20 minutes)

An **itinerary** is a written document that includes dates, times, and locations for a trip. Plan a round-trip itinerary. Use the Savannah Belles ferry schedule. Use this chart to help you make plans.

Place you will go	Departure time	Arrival time

The Adventure of the Speckled Band • from An American Childhood

Reading Skill

An **author's purpose** is his or her reason for writing. Learn to **recognize details that indicate the author's purpose**; that is, look for clues that tell you why an author writes something. Three main reasons that authors write are these:

- To *inform*, an author might use facts or special language.
- To *persuade* or convince, an author might include reasons that readers should agree with an opinion.
- To *entertain*, an author might use facts that are funny.

The author often has two purposes in mind. One is a general, or overall, purpose, such as those above. The other is a specific purpose. It might be to show a feeling or to teach a lesson. As you read, use this chart to note both types of purposes.

Types of Details	General Purpose	Specific Purpose
Surprising event; unique characters	To entertain	To capture a particular feeling or insight

Literary Analysis

Mood is the overall feeling that a reader gets from a story. The mood can be serious, funny, or sad.

Different things help to set the mood. These include words, such as *grumpy* or *gleeful*; images, such as *a starlit night*; setting, such as *a dark room*; and events, such as *a storm*.

Word List A

Study these words from the excerpt of An American Childhood. Then, complete the activity.

comparison [kuhm PAR uh suhn] *n.* looking at similarities and differences
> *People always seem to want to make a comparison between twins.*

deliberately [duh LIB er uht lee] *adv.* on purpose
> *I did not deliberately try to hurt the girl's feelings.*

depths [DEPTHS] *n.* deep part
> *Some very strange animals live in the depths of the ocean.*

extent [ek STENT] *n.* range; scope; amount
> *The full extent of the hurricane damage will not be known for weeks.*

item [EYE tuhm] *n.* one thing
> *If you could pack only one item for the trip, what would it be?*

precisely [pree SYS lee] *adj.* exactly
> *I found it hard to define that word precisely.*

sensations [sen SAY shuhnz] *n.* physical feelings experienced through the senses
> *The hot pepper caused burning sensations on my tongue.*

transparent [trans PA ruhnt] *adj.* clear; letting light pass through
> *In cold weather, our usually transparent windows become foggy.*

Exercise A

Fill in each blank in the paragraph below with an appropriate word from Word List A. Use each word only once.

I went to the store looking for one specific [1] _____. Somehow, I left with many purchases. I am just now figuring out the [2] _____ of my spending. The first thing that caught my eye was a beautiful red scarf. Next, the CD playing in the store gave me pleasant [3] _____—as if I were swimming in the [4] _____ of the cool ocean. I had to buy that, too! Then, my [5] _____ of this store's prices on the [6] _____ lampshades I wanted with prices I'd seen elsewhere resulted in another purchase. Finally, having spent [7] _____ one hour and one hundred dollars more than planned, I left the store. No one would ever believe that I had not [8] _____ planned on spending so much money.

Read the following passage. Pay special attention to the underlined words. Then, read it again, and complete the activities. Use a separate sheet of paper for your written answers.

Most parents of children under five years of age know the <u>extent</u> of childhood fears. Fears of the dark, monsters under the bed, being separated from parents, and loud noises are all common. Some of these fears might seem ridiculous to grown-ups. Nevertheless, a child's <u>sensations</u> of danger, even imagined, are very <u>real</u>. The challenge for a parent is to accept those fears without allowing them to take over a child's life.

The first task is to know what scares a child. Any <u>item</u> can frighten a youngster. Remember, children think differently than adults. They often think an object is alive, and they may feel small and helpless. Just think about how many toddlers fear the loud sound and action of water flushing. They imagine being flushed away to the <u>depths</u> of who knows where. It is this sort of unknown thing that can be most scary and leave a child feeling helpless.

Once you know the sources of a child's fears, you can work <u>deliberately</u> with the child to talk about them. Never treat childhood fears as silly. Instead, figure out <u>precisely</u> what is scaring the child. Then, help the child understand the fear so that everything about it becomes <u>transparent</u> to the child. It's hard to fear things that you understand clearly. Remember, too, that hugs and kind words really do help a scared child.

Try to avoid any <u>comparison</u> of one child's fears to another's. It doesn't matter if a youngster you know is scared of the very things you loved most as a child. What counts is your understanding and careful actions to move the child past the fears that trouble him or her.

1. Underline the sentence that tells the <u>extent</u> of childhood fears. Then, explain what *extent* means.

2. Circle a pair of antonyms that describe a child's <u>sensations</u>. Write a sentence about *sensations* you do not like.

3. Underline a synonym for <u>item</u>. Write a sentence telling about an *item* that scared you as a child.

4. Circle the words that tell where these <u>depths</u> might be. Then, explain what *depths* means.

5. What should parents do <u>deliberately</u>? Write a sentence about how you do something *deliberately*.

6. Write a sentence that identifies <u>precisely</u> something that might scare a child. Give a synonym for *precisely*.

7. Underline the phrases describing how something becomes <u>transparent</u> and less scary. Then, explain what *transparent* means.

8. Circle the words naming the type of <u>comparison</u> you should not make. Then, explain what a *comparison* is.

from An American Childhood

Annie Dillard

Summary The author shares an experience that scared her as a young child. She thinks there is a "presence" that will harm her if it reaches her. She figures out what it is. She realizes that her inside world is connected to the outside world.

 Writing About the Big Question

Is truth the same for everyone? In *An American Childhood*, Annie Dillard's perception of the world around her is influenced by her youthful imagination. Complete this sentence:

Small children may draw illogical conclusions about the world

around them because _____

_____.

Note-taking Guide

Use this chart to help you summarize the story.

Event
The author is frightened by mysterious, moving lights that she sees in her bedroom at night.

Cause

Main Idea

from An American Childhood
Annie Dillard

Annie Dillard describes something that scared her when she was young. She's only five years old and she is scared to go to bed. She's afraid to talk about the thing.

◆ ◆ ◆

Who could breathe as this thing searched for me over the very corners of the room? Who could ever breathe freely again?

◆ ◆ ◆

Dillard lies in the dark. Her younger sister, Amy, sleeps peacefully—she doesn't wake when the mysterious event takes place. Dillard is almost asleep when the thing slides into the room. First, it flattens itself against the door that is open.

◆ ◆ ◆

It was a transparent, luminous oblong. I could see the door whiten at its touch; I could see the blue wall turn pale where it raced over it, and see the maple headboard of Amy's bed glow. It was a swift spirit; it was an awareness. It made noise. It had two joined parts, a head and a tail, like a Chinese dragon. It found the door, wall, and headboard, and it swiped them, charging them with its luminous glance. After its fleet, searching passage, things looked the same, but weren't.

© Pearson Education

Vocabulary Development

transparent (trans PER uhnt) *adj.* clear; easily seen through
luminous (LOO muh nuhs) *adj.* giving off light; shining; bright
oblong (AHB lawng) *n.* a rectangular shape

Activate Prior Knowledge

Tell about a time in childhood when you learned something on your own or about how the world works. For example, perhaps you learned that you could float more easily in salt water than you can in fresh water.

_____

_____

_____

Reading Skill

The **author's purpose** is his or her reason for writing. Learn to **look for details that show the author's purpose**. Sometimes authors use details to entertain the reader. Read the bracketed passage. Underline two words or phrases Dillard uses that make the "thing" seem alive.

Reading Check

What did Dillard see in her room each night when she was five? Underline the sentence Dillard uses to describe what comes into the room.

Literary Analysis

Mood is the overall feeling created for the reader. The **mood** may be serious, funny, or sad. One way the author sets the mood is by using certain kinds of words. Read the bracketed passages. Which details create a **mood** of suspense and fear?

_____

_____

_____

Reading Check

The **author's purpose** can be to inform the reader. What fact does Dillard discover that explains what the "thing" really is?

_____

_____

_____

Stop to Reflect

How do Dillard's senses help her figure out what the "thing" really is?

_____

_____

_____

I dared not blink or breathe; I tried to hush my whooping blood. If it found another awareness, it would destroy it.

◆ ◆ ◆

But the thing never gets her. When it reaches the corner, it can't go any further. She tries to shrink down so it won't notice her. Then, she hears a roar when it dies or leaves. Worst of all is knowing that it may come back. Sometimes it does—usually it does. Dillard thinks the thing is restless.

◆ ◆ ◆

The light stripe slipped in the door, ran searching over Amy's wall, stopped, stretched lunatic at the first corner, raced wailing toward my wall, and vanished into the second corner with a cry.

◆ ◆ ◆

Dillard figures out that the thing is caused by a streetlight reflecting off the windshield of a passing car. She is thrilled to use reason to solve the mystery. She compares this mental process of problem solving to a diver who comes from the depths of the sea and breaks the surface of the water to reach the sunlight.

Dillard knows the sound the thing makes when it leaves. It sounds like a car coming down the street. She puts that together with the daytime sight and sound of a car passing. There is a stop sign at the corner of the street she lives on. The cars pass her house and then come to a stop. Then they shift gears as they go on.

◆ ◆ ◆

Vocabulary Development

whooping (WOOP ing) *v.* shouting
lunatic (LOO nuh tik) *adv.* wildly; crazily
vanished (VAN isht) *v.* disappeared

What, precisely, came into the bedroom? A reflection from the car's oblong windshield. Why did it travel in two parts? The window sash split the light and cast a shadow.

◆ ◆ ◆

Dillard realizes that the world outside is connected to the world inside her home. She recalls once watching construction workers use jackhammers. Later, she had connected a new noise in her bedroom to the men she saw working outside. She thinks about the connection between outside and inside— going downstairs and then outside.

◆ ◆ ◆

"Outside," then, was <u>conceivably</u> just beyond my windows. It was the same world I reached by going out the front or the back door.

◆ ◆ ◆

Dillard realizes that she can choose to be connected to the outer world either by reason or by imagination. She pretends that the light coming into her room is after her. Then, she replaces her imagination with reason and identifies the real source of the light: a passing car.

Reading Skill

Read the bracketed passage. What is the **author's purpose** in telling about the jackhammers?

_____

_____

_____

Reading Check ✎

What does Dillard realize about the world outside? Underline the sentence that describes this discovery.

Vocabulary Development
conceivably (kuhn SEE vuh blee) *adv.* possibly

© Pearson Education

from An American Childhood

1. **Contrast:** The author's sister is in the room when the mysterious event happens. Why does her sister fail to react in the same way that Dillard does?

   _____

2. **Infer:** Dillard learns that the light is from a passing car. After she solves the mystery, Dillard sometimes pretends that she does not know what is causing the light. Why does she do this?

   _____

   _____

3. **Reading Skill:** The author's general purpose is his or her reason for writing. How does the author's description of the object that she is afraid of contribute to her general **purpose**?

   _____

   _____

4. Before Dillard realizes what the light really is, her **mood** is one of fear. Use this chart to list one word, one phrase, and one image that contribute to this mood.

Words	Phrases	Images
scared	my whooping blood	its luminous glance

Writing: Personal Narrative

Write a **personal narrative** about an important childhood insight. Fill in the chart with clues that eventually led to the new understanding. Then, write what each clue turned out to mean.

Clue	What the Clue Meant

Use your notes to help you write your personal narrative.

Research and Technology

Write a brief **report** about an important scientific puzzle. Use the questions to help you write your report.

- Why is the puzzle important?

  _____

- What new knowledge was gained from the solution?

  _____

  _____

- What has been the impact of the new knowledge?

  _____

  _____

Word List A

Study these words from "The Adventure of the Speckled Band." Then, complete the activity.

beloved [bi LUHV id] *adj.* dearly loved
Our beloved cat lived to ten years of age, but I wish he had survived longer.

clad [KLAD] *v.* clothed or dressed
Remember the story of the emperor who was clad in no clothes at all?

fate [FAYT] *n.* destiny; future; chances
We wondered about the fate of the dog that had fallen through the ice.

hastening [HAY suhn ing] *v.* moving quickly
Hastening to complete his chores before game time, Ned forgot to take out the garbage.

objections [uhb JEK shunz] *n.* reasons for disagreeing
I don't understand your objections to my vacation plans.

satisfying [SAT is fy ing] *n.* doing enough for; having enough
Curious people often have trouble satisfying their need for exploration.

unfortunate [uhn FAWR chuh nit] *adj.* happening because of bad luck
The unfortunate car accident left the driver with a broken leg.

withdraw [with DRAW] *v.* go out; leave
The judge asked the loud man to withdraw from the courtroom.

Exercise A

Fill in each blank in the paragraph below with an appropriate word from Word List A. Use each word only once.

My great-grandfather came from Ireland and talked kindly about his

[1] _____ homeland. He had some [2] _____ times and as a

teen, [3] _____ to find a way out, he came to America. Now, as an

old man, he wondered why he had ever wanted to [4] _____ from

such a beautiful place. We reminded him that it was [5] _____

that brought him here. [6] _____ in the only clothes he owned,

he came despite the [7] _____ of his family. He came because he

knew he was not [8] _____ his need to see new things. As

he spoke, we could still see that spark of curiosity shining in his

deep blue eyes.

Read the following passage. Pay special attention to the underlined words. Then, read it again, and complete the activities. Use a separate sheet of paper for your written answers.

A life on the move is a <u>beloved</u> life for the roaming people named Gypsies. For centuries, they have been moving from place to place, <u>satisfying</u> their need to travel. Today, Gypsies are scattered all around the globe. However, the largest number of them lives in Europe.

The first Gypsies came from India, not Egypt, as their name might indicate. No one knows why these people decided to <u>withdraw</u> from their country. Only the Gypsy language, called Romany, has carried with it the traditions of India. The Gypsy culture has its own proud heritage.

The Gypsies first left India around A.D. 1000. By the fifteenth century, Gypsies had reached western Europe. People often had <u>objections</u> to Gypsies being in their region. No doubt, they feared the different looks and way of life of the Gypsies. People in many areas seemed hostile toward Gypsies. In Nazi Germany, half a million Gypsies suffered the terrible <u>fate</u> of death in prison camps, alongside Jews and other targets of terrible hatred. Yet, through all the <u>unfortunate</u> events, Gypsies have remained a close group. They also have stayed true to their beliefs and customs.

Because they prefer temporary work, Gypsies have taken many interesting jobs. They have traded everything from horses to crafts to pots and pans. They have worked as farmers and as circus performers. Gypsy women have often made money telling other people's fortunes. Indeed, the picture most people have of a Gypsy is of a woman <u>clad</u> in black, looking into a crystal ball.

Like many other groups in the world today, Gypsies seem to be <u>hastening</u> toward a more modern way of life. Still, their songs and dances as well as their desire to pick up in the spring and be on their way, will surely never leave them completely.

1. Underline the words that describe the Gypsies' <u>beloved</u> life. Then, explain what *beloved* means.

2. Circle the words that describe the need Gypsies have been <u>satisfying</u>. Then, write a sentence using *satisfying*.

3. Underline the name of the country from which Gypsies decided to <u>withdraw</u>. Then, explain what *withdraw* means.

4. Circle the words that name particular things about Gypsies to which Europeans had <u>objections</u>. Then, tell your opinion about these *objections*.

5. Underline the words describing some Gypsies' <u>fate</u> in Germany. Then, explain the saying "a *fate* worse than death."

6. Write a sentence describing an <u>unfortunate</u> event you've read about.

7. Describe your own image of a Gypsy. State clearly how he or she might be <u>clad</u>.

8. Circle the phrase that tells what Gypsies are <u>hastening</u> toward. Define *hastening*.

The Adventure of the Speckled Band
Sir Arthur Conan Doyle

Summary Sherlock Holmes, a great detective, meets Miss Helen Stoner. She needs his help. Miss Stoner wants to know who killed her sister. She also fears for her own life. Holmes follows the clues to find the murderer.

 Writing About the Big Question

Is the truth the same for everyone? In *The Adventure of the Speckled Band*, a detective determines that the truth about a young woman's mysterious death is not what people had previously believed. Complete this sentence:

To prove a theory about a crime scene, a detective can _____

_____.

Note-taking Guide

Use this graphic organizer to note details about Dr. Grimesby Roylott's actions.

How are Dr. Roylott and Miss Stoner related?	Why doesn't Dr. Roylott work as a doctor?	How does Dr. Roylott support himself?	How will Dr. Roylott's life change if the sisters marry?

The Adventure of the Speckled Band

1. **Compare:** Helen's sister, Julia, has died under strange circumstances. Helen's life is similar in some ways to Julia's just before Julia's death. In what ways is Helen's situation similar to Julia's?

   _____

   _____

2. **Speculate:** Suppose that Helen had not decided to ask Dr. Holmes for help. What do you think would have happened to her?

   _____

   _____

3. **Reading Skill:** Dr. Watson reports that Holmes has had many strange cases through the years. What does this detail tell you is the author's **general purpose**?

   _____

   _____

4. **Literary Analysis:** Reread Helen Stoner's description of the night her sister died. The mood is frightening and mysterious. Use this chart to list words, phrases, and images that create this mood.

Words	Phrases	Images
howling	wild night	the door moves slowly on its hinges

Writing: Personal Narrative

Write a **personal narrative** about a time that you used logic, or reasoning, to solve a problem. Record various problems and solutions. Decide which you will write about. Use your notes to write your personal narrative.

Problem	Solution
1.	1.
2.	2.
3.	3.

Research and Technology: Report

Use the following questions to help you gather information for your **report** on wild and exotic pets.

- What animals are considered wild or exotic?

  _____

  _____

- Who may own wild or exotic animals?

  _____

  _____

- Where must the animals be kept?

  _____

  _____

- What are some potential dangers of owning exotic pets?

  _____

  _____

from Steinbeck: A Life in Letters • from Travels With Charley • The American Dream

Reading Skill

An author's **purpose** is his or her reason for writing. The author's reason for writing may be one of the following:

- to persuade

- to inform

- to entertain

Sometimes an author has more than one purpose or combines purposes. The purpose determines the kinds of details that the author uses. As you read, use this chart to **evaluate whether the author achieves his or her purpose**.

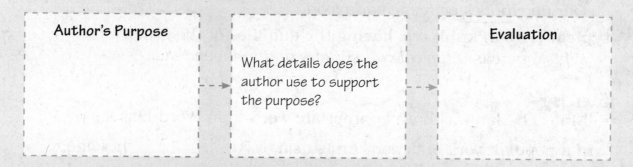

| Author's Purpose | What details does the author use to support the purpose? | Evaluation |

Literary Analysis

An **author's style** is his or her way of using language. Important elements of an author's style are these:

- Word choice: the types of words the author uses

- Sentence length: how long or short the sentences are

- Tone: the author's attitude toward the subject of the writing

As you read, notice how word choice, sentence length, and tone produce the author's style.

Word List A

Study these words from *Steinbeck: A Life in Letters* and *Travels With Charley*. Then, complete the activity.

bombardment [bom BAHRD muhnt] *n.* an attack with bombs; a vigorous attack with questions
> The *bombardment* of questions from the press surprised the mayor.

conceal [kuhn SEEL] *v.* hide
> When Lisa won first prize, she couldn't *conceal* her excitement.

creation [kree AY shun] *n.* all things that exist in the world
> Rita thinks that trees are the most beautiful things in *creation*.

flaming [FLAYM ing] *v.* burning with a flame; shining brightly
> He was so embarrassed that his face turned a bright *flaming* red.

landscape [LAND skayp] *n.* land area visible from one spot
> Outside the train window, the *landscape* changed from forest to field.

reluctance [ri LUHK tuhns] *n.* unwillingness
> Danielle has a great *reluctance* to get out of bed on Monday morning.

thrives [THRYVZ] *v.* prospers or flourishes
> Our dog *thrives* on homemade food.

typical [TIP uh kuhl] *adj.* having the qualities of the group
> Whiskers was a *typical* cat, curious and independent.

Exercise A

Fill in each blank with an appropriate word from Word List A.

In a popular work of fiction, Anastasia, a [1] _____ heroine, lives with a rich but cold relative who doesn't understand her. She is engaged to a solid but boring young suitor, a prospect that leaves her feeling [2] _____. She knows that she [3] _____ on the kind of excitement of a more powerful man, such as the groundskeeper. For he is the best man in [4] _____. She has great [5] _____ to tell anyone of her feelings. She must [6] _____ her love because he barely acknowledges her existence. In actuality, for years, he has been planting a magical garden, a colorful [7] _____ of flowers in which he can reveal his own love. Do these flowers serve as [8] _____ of their future happiness together?

Read the following passage. Pay special attention to the underlined words. Then, read it again, and complete the activities. Use a separate sheet of paper for your written answers.

Much of American literature <u>thrives</u> on images of the open road. This theme flourishes in the writings of authors as diverse as Walt Whitman and Jack Kerouac. For present-day Americans, that open road is usually the interstate highway. I consider my own taste <u>typical</u>. When I have a long distance to go, I show no <u>reluctance</u> to take the modern road. I don't think twice about hopping onto the freeway. Driving down the highway in my <u>flaming</u> red convertible makes up for the boring <u>landscape</u>. Sometimes I click on the radio and, as my eardrums are attacked by the <u>bombardment</u> of ads for used cars and miracle creams, I still manage to discover fascinating talk and music from small-town America. Yet somehow the interstate lacks the style of a "real" road such as Route 66.

From the late 1920s to the 1950s, many drivers followed Route 66 west from Chicago to Los Angeles. It is worth your time to get off at one of the ramps in New Mexico or Arizona. You might catch a glimpse of what the slick highway will <u>conceal</u>. Motels with rooms shaped like tepees, theme diners, and service stations pop up as if out of nowhere.

One of the best treasures in all of <u>creation</u> is a certain hotel in Winslow, Arizona. In the 1920s and 1930s, many roads were still rough, so people often took the train. They would stop off at railroad hotels along the way. Cozy rooms and tasty meals awaited them.

Some people have accused the interstate of ruining small towns and colorful back roads. We have gained speed but lost the adventure of the open road.

1. Circle the word that is a synonym of *thrives*. Then, write a sentence giving an example of an idea or theme that *thrives* in present-day American movies.

2. Circle the phrase that explains the word *typical*. Write a sentence telling about a *typical* event in your day.

3. Underline the phrase that describes what the author has no *reluctance* to take. Write a sentence that tells about something you have no *reluctance* to do.

4. Circle the word that gives a clue to the meaning of *flaming*. Then, write a sentence in which you describe something that has a *flaming* color.

5. Write a sentence that tells what might be part of the *landscape* you'd see along an interstate.

6. Circle the word that gives you a clue to the meaning of the word *bombardment*. Then, write a sentence in which you felt you were under *bombardment* by something— for example, words, images, noises, weather, and so on.

7. Underline the three things that an interstate can *conceal*. Then, write a sentence telling how the highway can *conceal* them.

8. Circle what the passage says is one of the best treasures in all *creation*. Explain what you think is a treasure in all *creation*.

from Steinbeck: A Life in Letters • from Travels With Charley
John Steinbeck

Summary John Steinbeck sets out across the United States to see the country and meet people. His dog, Charley, travels with him. This episode in his journey tells about his experiences in the Badlands of North Dakota.

 Writing About the Big Question

Is truth the same for everyone? In the excerpts from *Steinbeck: A Life in Letters* and *Travels with Charley*, Steinbeck tours the country to refresh his memory about what Americans are really like. Complete this sentence:

The objective truth about America and Americans is _____

_____.

Note-taking Guide
Use this chart to recall the highlights of Steinbeck's essay.

Why did Steinbeck take the trip?

How did Steinbeck prepare for the trip?

How are day and night different in the Badlands?

from Steinbeck: A Life in Letters • from Travels With Charley

1. **Infer:** Steinbeck has lived and worked in New York City for many years. What does he hope to gain or learn from making this trip across America?

   _____

   _____

2. **Contrast:** When Steinbeck enters the Badlands, he feels uneasy. How do Steinbeck's feelings about the Badlands change as night falls?

   _____

   _____

3. **Reading Skill:** Explain Steinbeck's **purpose** in writing this essay.

   _____

   _____

4. **Literary Analysis:** Fill in the chart below with examples of the **author's style**.

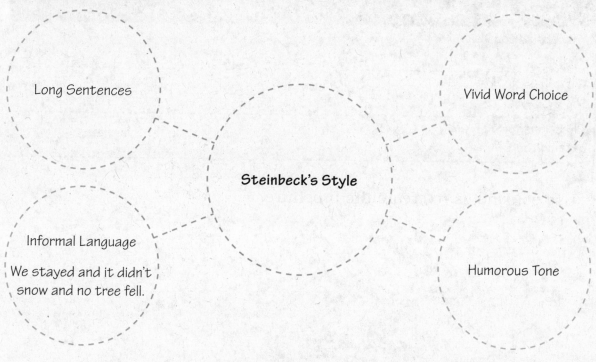

Long Sentences

Vivid Word Choice

Steinbeck's Style

Informal Language

We stayed and it didn't snow and no tree fell.

Humorous Tone

Writing: Observations Journal

Write an entry for an **observations journal** about a favorite place you have visited. Choose a place about which to write by identifying places you have visited in the chart below.

Favorite Places	
Near Home	On Trips

Research and Technology: Brochure

A **brochure** should describe what is special about a particular place. The information should be clear, accurate, and to the point. Use the following chart to record information about places in the Bad Lands. Make sure that you choose three places to highlight in your brochure.

Information for Brochure	Place 1:	Place 2:	Place 3:
Why should you visit?			
What you can do there?			
Directions for getting there?			

Use your notes to create the brochure.

Word List A

Study these words from "The American Dream." Then, complete the activity.

democracy [di MAHK ruh see] *n.* government that is run by the people who live under it
People in a democracy have the privilege of voting for their leaders.

destruction [di STRUHK shun] *n.* end; ruin
Pollution has caused the destruction of many sources of clean water.

emerge [i MERJ] *v.* come into being
Out of a group of four candidates, one will emerge as the winner.

equal [EE kwuhl] *adj.* same in amount, number, size, or value
I will divide the pie into equal slices so we all get our share.

individual [in duh VIJ oo uhl] *n.* person
Every individual has a say in the kind of work he or she will do.

perspective [pur SPEK tiv] *n.* way of looking at things
Paul's perspective on life is different from mine because he grew up in England.

segregation [seg ruh GAY shuhn] *n.* practice of keeping groups apart
Segregation forced African Americans to sit in the back of buses.

slavery [SLAY vuh ree] *n.* the practice of one person owning another
Trying to escape from slavery was dangerous, and runaway slaves were in great peril.

Exercise A

Fill in each blank in the paragraph below with an appropriate word from Word List A. Use each word only once.

Under the system of [1] _____, one [2] _____ can own another. It is clear to people in our country today that such a system doesn't belong in a [3] _____. In a nation where we are all [4] _____, no one can own someone else. Also, laws have made clear that our country is no place for the [5] _____ of people by skin color. It took too many years for the [6] _____ of such a practice. Why did it take so long for such a different [7] _____ to [8] _____? Attitudes and feelings are often passed down from generation to generation, and changing people's views is a difficult challenge.

© Pearson Education

1. Underline the sentence that explains segregation. Then, write a sentence describing another form of *segregation*.

2. Circle the phrase that tells what perspective is. Then, write a sentence explaining your *perspective* on an issue at your school.

3. Underline the phrase in the paragraph that explains equal. Then, write a sentence using *equal*.

4. Rewrite the sentence with individual, using a synonym for the word. Then, write a sentence about an *individual* whom you admire.

5. Underline words that describe the destruction of unfair practices. What helped with the *destruction* of these practices? Explain.

6. Underline the sentence that tells what happens when someone is freed from slavery. Use *slavery* in a sentence.

7. Explain what it means in this passage to emerge as a *citizen*.

8. Underline the words that explain what a democracy is. Then, write a sentence about living in a *democracy*.

Read the following passage. Pay special attention to the underlined words. Then, read it again, and complete the activities. Use a separate sheet of paper for your written answers.

In 1954, Oliver Brown—an African American railroad worker—sued the Topeka, Kansas, Board of Education. The board wouldn't allow his daughter to attend an all-white school in his neighborhood. At the time, segregation was widespread in public schools.

From the perspective of the board, and according to many other people's way of looking at the situation, it was only business as usual. The rule of "separate but equal" was law in the land. That meant it was acceptable for black people to be required to have different schools, neighborhoods, lunch counters, bathrooms, and many other things. These places were supposed to be of the same quality as the ones white people had. Mostly, however, that wasn't the case.

The matter went all the way to the Supreme Court. A young African American lawyer named Thurgood Marshall took the case. From a lawsuit brought by just one individual, the movement to allow black children into white schools grew. The justices decided other similar cases at the same time.

Brown and his side won. Their victory helped achieve the destruction of these unfair practices, thus opening doors which had long been closed to blacks. It was a long but clear fight. Soon, civil rights bills were passed. One hundred years had passed since black people had been freed from slavery. Finally, they could start to emerge as full citizens and enjoy the same rights as other Americans, such as voting.

In a democracy, people vote for representatives who make the laws of the land. But after civil rights laws pass, people's hearts and minds still have to change. African Americans have many more opportunities today than they did fifty years ago. Still, more change must occur to make sure that all citizens of the United States have the same rights and opportunities.

The American Dream
Martin Luther King, Jr.

Summary In this speech, Martin Luther King, Jr. describes his dream for America. He says that America does not make it possible for everyone to share in the dream. He discusses ways that Americans can help make his dream a reality.

 Writing About the Big Question

Is the truth the same for everyone? In "The American Dream," Martin Luther King, Jr. quotes from the Declaration of Independence that "all men are created equal." Complete this sentence:

In America today, the promise of full equality is confirmed by

_____.

Note-taking Guide

Use this web to record King's ideas about the American dream.

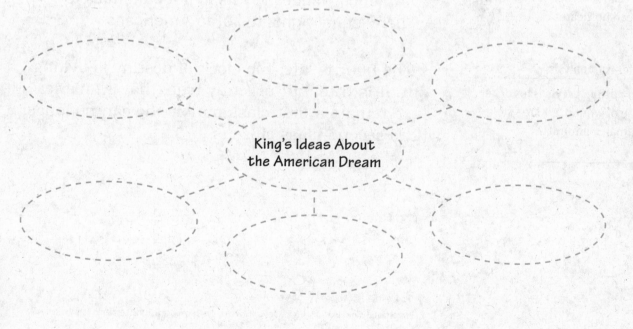

King's Ideas About the American Dream

The American Dream
Martin Luther King, Jr.

In this speech, King says that the American dream is based on the words of the Declaration of Independence: "all men are created equal." He says that the dream is supposed to apply to all Americans.

◆ ◆ ◆

It does not say some men, but it says all men. It does not say all white men, but it says all men, which includes black men. It does not say all Gentiles,[1] but it says all men, which includes Jews. It does not say all Protestants,[2] but it says all men, which includes Catholics.[3]

◆ ◆ ◆

King explains another important point in the Declaration: It says that all individuals have basic rights that come from God, not from governments.

Then King explains that America has never totally lived up to the dream of democracy. Slavery and the segregation of African Americans violated the idea that all people have equal rights. King says that America will destroy itself if it continues to deny equal rights to some Americans.

◆ ◆ ◆

The hour is late; the clock of destiny is ticking out. It is trite, but urgently true, that if America is to remain a first-class nation she can no longer have second-class citizens.

◆ ◆ ◆

1. **Gentiles** (JEN tylz) *n.* people who are not Jewish.
2. **Protestants** (PRAHT uhs tuhnts) *n.* members of a part of the Christian church that separated from the Roman Catholic Church in the 1500s.
3. **Catholics** (KATH liks) *n.* members of the part of the Christian church led by the Pope.

Activate Prior Knowledge

Think about the way your family lives. At one time, not everyone had the same rights. On the lines below, finish the statement: "I am thankful that in America I can . . ."

_____

_____

_____

Read Fluently

To what does "It" in the bracketed passage refer?

_____

King is trying to make a point about what "it" means for Americans. His sentences tend to be long. Each sentence contrasts what "it" does not say in the first part of the sentence with what "it" does say in the second part. Draw lines breaking up the parts of each sentence to make the meaning clearer.

Literary Analysis

An **author's style** is his or her way of writing. Is King's style formal or informal?

_____

King then claims that Americans must also consider the needs of the other countries in the world.

◆   ◆   ◆

The American dream will not become a reality devoid of the larger dream of a world of brotherhood and peace and good will.

◆   ◆   ◆

He points out that modern transportation has made contact between people of different nations much easier. He tells two jokes that focus on the speed of traveling by jet. He uses humor to stress that the world has now become one big neighborhood. Everyone is now connected, and we all depend on one another.

◆   ◆   ◆

Through our scientific genius we have made of this world a neighborhood; now through our moral and spiritual development we must make of it a brotherhood. In a real sense, we must all learn to live together as brothers, or we will all perish together as fools.

© Pearson Education

Reading Skill

An **author's purpose** is his or her reason for writing. What is the **author's purpose** in the bracketed paragraph?
a) to persuade
b) to inform
c) to entertain
Explain your answer.

_____

_____

Stop to Reflect

What does King think will happen to America if its people cannot make the changes he suggests?

_____

_____

_____

Reading Check

How does King think Americans should learn to live? Underline the sentence in which he explains this.

Vocabulary Development

devoid (di VOYD) *adj.* completely lacking in something; empty

moral (MAWR uhl) *adj.* relating to what is right behavior

perish (PER ish) *v.* die

The American Dream

1. **Infer:** Why does King quote lines from the Declaration of Independence in his speech?

   _____

   _____

2. **Generalize:** According to King, what steps must Americans take to make the American dream a reality?

   _____

   _____

3. **Reading Skill:** An **author's purpose** is his or her reason for writing. What is King's purpose in writing this speech? Give reasons to support your answer.

   _____

   _____

4. **Literary Analysis:** Use the chart to help you think about the **author's style**. In each oval, write a word or phrase from the text that gives an example of that element.

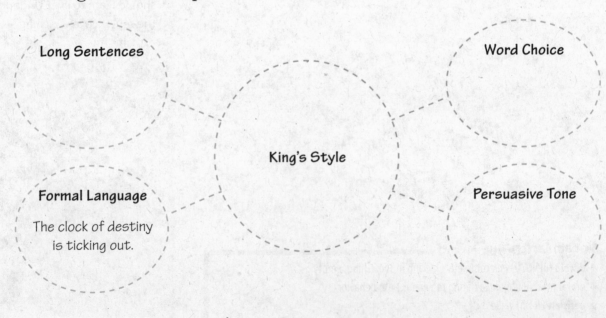

Long Sentences

Word Choice

King's Style

Formal Language

The clock of destiny is ticking out.

Persuasive Tone

Writing: Observations Journal

Write an entry for an **observations journal**. Record your thoughts about an aspect of today's society that could be improved.

- What could be improved in your school or community?

  _____

  _____

- What could be improved in your country?

  _____

  _____

- What could be improved in the world?

  _____

  _____

Research and Technology: Brochure

People use **brochures** to get information about a place that they may want to visit. The information should be clear, accurate, and to the point. As you search for historical sites, use the following chart to record important information.

Information for Brochure	Site 1:	Site 2:	Site 3:
Reason for King's visit?			
Message delivered			
Form of message (speech, act of civil disobedience)			

Use your notes to create the brochure.

Magazine Articles

About Magazine Articles

A **magazine article** is a piece of nonfiction. A magazine article is usually short. Magazine articles can tell you about subjects such as these:

- Interesting people
- Animal behavior
- New technology

Magazine articles often have these parts:

- Drawings or photos that go with the text
- Captions, or words that explain the drawings or photos (refer to *captions*, as in box below)
- Sidebars with extra information

Reading Skill

You will see articles when you look through a magazine. You can **preview to determine your purpose for reading**. This means that you look over an article to decide whether you want to read it and why. When you preview an article, look at

- the title.
- the pictures or photographs.
- one paragraph.

These steps will give you an idea of the author's purpose for writing the article. Then, you can decide what purpose you have for reading it. You may decide that you have no reason to read the article. Use the questions below to help you look at parts of an article.

Questions to Help You Preview an Article

❑ What is the tone, or attitude, of the author?

❑ Are the pictures and captions designed to provide information or to entertain?

❑ As I skim the text, do I see statistics, quotations from experts, and facts?

❑ Do the first sentences of paragraphs introduce facts, opinions, or anecdotes?

Sun Suckers and Moon Cursers

Richard and Joyce Wolkomir

Text Structure

Look at the pictures in this article. Do they add information, or are they just for fun? Explain.

_____

_____

Vocabulary Builder

Multiple-Meaning Words The verb *sweep* has more than one meaning. *Sweep* can mean "clean dirt from the ground or floor with a broom." It can also mean "move quickly." What does *sweep* mean in the first paragraph?

_____

_____

Fluency Builder

Read the last paragraph on this page slowly and silently. As you read, circle the punctuation. Remember that a comma (,) indicates a short pause and a period (.) indicates a full stop. Underline any words that you have difficulty pronouncing, and practice saying each word. Then, read aloud the paragraph to a partner.

Night is falling. It is getting dark. You can barely see. But now . . . lights come on. Car headlights sweep the road. Windows light up. Neon signs glow red and green. Street lamps shine, bright as noon. So who cares if it is night?

But what if you are camping in a forest? Or a storm blows down power lines? Then the night would be inky. To see, you would have only star twinkle, or the moon's pale shine. Until about 1900, when electric power networks began spreading, that is how nights were: dark.

Roger Ekirch, an historian at Virginia Tech, studies those long-ago dark nights. For light, our ancestors had only candles, hearth fires, torches, walnut-oil lamps. And that made their nights different than ours.

"It used to be, when it got dark, people felt edgy," Ekirch says. He studies the years from about 1500 to 1830, when mostly only the wealthy could afford even candles. "People talked about being 'shut in' by the night," he says. Our ancestors imagined werewolves roaming at night, and demons. In their minds, they populated the darkness with witches, fairies and elves, and malignant spirits. Night had real dangers, too— robbers and murderers, but also ditches and ponds you could fall into.

Vocabulary Builder

Multiple-Meaning Words The verb *combed* has more than one meaning. *Combed* can mean "searched thoroughly." It can also mean "made you hair neat." What does *combed* mean in the bracketed paragraph?

_____

_____

Text Structure

Look at the first sentence in each paragraph on this page. Do these sentences begin with facts, opinions, or events? Explain.

_____

_____

_____

_____

Vocabulary Builder

Idioms The idiom *just so* means "in a careful manner." Complete the following sentence:

When nights were dark, people learned to fold their clothes

just so in order to _____

_____

_____ .

What was it like, when nights were so dark?

To find out, Roger Ekirch has combed through old newspapers, diaries, letters, everything from court records to sermons. He has pondered modern scientific research, too. He has found that, before the invention of electric lights, our ancestors considered night a different "season." At night, they were nearly blind. And so, to them, day and night seemed as different as summer and winter.

They even had special words for night. Some people called the last rays of the setting sun "sun suckers." Nighttime travelers, who relied on the moon called it the "parish lantern." But robbers, who liked to lurk in darkness, hated the moon. They called it "the tattler." And those darkness-loving criminals? They were "moon cursers."

Cities were so dark that people needing to find their way at night hired boys to carry torches, or "links." Such torchbearers were called "linkboys."

Country people tried to stay indoors at night, unless the moon was out. On moonless nights, people groping in the darkness frequently fell into ponds and ravines.[1] Horses, also blinded by darkness, often threw riders.

If you were traveling at night, you would wear light-colored clothing, so your friends could see you. You might ride a white horse. You might mark your route in advance by stripping away tree bark, exposing the white inner wood. In southern England, where the soil is chalky white, people planning night trips mounded up white chalk along their route during the day, to guide them later, in the moonlight.

It was dark inside houses, too. To dress in the darkness, people learned to fold their clothes just so. Swedish homeowners, Roger Ekirch says, pushed parlor furniture against walls at night, so they could walk through the room without tripping.

---

1. **ravines** (ruh VEENZ) *n.* long, deep hollows in Earth's surface.

People began as children to memorize their local terrain—ditches, fences, cisterns, bogs.[2] They learned the magical terrain, too, spots where ghosts and other imaginary nighttime frights lurked. "In some places, you never whistled at night, because that invited the devil," says Ekirch.

One reason people feared nightfall was they thought night actually did "fall." At night, they believed, malignant air descended. To ward off that sickly air, sleepers wore nightcaps. They also pulled curtains around their beds. In the 1600s, one London man tied his hands inside his bed at night so they would not flop outside the curtains and expose him to night air. . . .

At night, evildoers came out. Virtually every major European city had criminal gangs. Sometimes those gangs included wealthy young aristocrats who assaulted people just for the thrill. . . .

If you were law-abiding, you might clang your sword on the pavement while walking down a dark nighttime street to warn robbers you were armed. Or you might hold your sword upright in the moonlight. You tried to walk in groups. You walked down the street's middle, to prevent robbers from lunging at you from doorways or alleys. Robbers depended so much on darkness that a British criminal who attacked his victim in broad daylight was acquitted—jurors decided he must be insane.

Many whose days were blighted by poverty or ill treatment sought escape at night. Slaves in the American South, for instance, sneaked out at night to dances and parties. Or they stumbled through the darkness to other plantations, to visit their wives or children. After the Civil War, says Roger Ekirch, former slaveholders worried that their freed slaves might attack them. And so they rode out at night disguised as ghosts, to frighten onetime slaves into staying indoors.

---

2. cisterns (SIS ternz), **bogs** Cisterns are large underground areas for storing water; bogs are small marshes or swamps in which footing is treacherous.

TAKE NOTES

Text Structure

Skim the text. Underline any facts or quotations from experts. How does this help you **preview** the article? Does it change **your purpose for reading?**

_____

_____

_____

Vocabulary Builder

Adjectives One or more adjectives can describe the same noun. In the paragraph that begins "At night, evildoers came out . . .", both *wealthy* and *young* describe *aristocrats*. Circle four more adjectives in the paragraph, and underline the noun that each adjective describes.

Comprehension Builder

Read the bracketed paragraph. Summarize the ways that people might have protected themselves when they walked at night.

_____

_____

_____

_____

Text Structure

How does the picture support the information in the **magazine article?** Explain.

_____

_____

_____

Vocabulary Builder

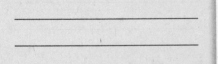

Adverbs An adverb describes a verb, an adjective, or another adverb. On the lines below, write six adverbs that appear in the second paragraph on this page. Next to each adverb, write the word it describes and the word's part of speech.

_____

_____

_____

_____

_____

_____

Comprehension Builder

How has electricity changed the way that people think about nighttime?

_____

_____

_____

_____

"At night, many servants felt beyond supervision, and they would often leave directly after their employers fell asleep," Ekirch adds. When they did sleep, it was fitfully, because of rumbling carts and watchmen's cries. And so Ekirch believes many workers got much too little sleep. "That explains why so many slaveowners and employers complained about their workers falling asleep during the day," he said.

Our ancestors had one overriding—and entirely real—nighttime fear: fire. Blazes were common because houses, often with thatched roofs,[3] ignited easily. At night, open flames flickered everywhere. Passersby carrying torches might set your roof ablaze. Also, householders commonly complained about servants forgetting to bank fires or snuff out candles. Roger Ekirch believes one reason night watchmen bellowed out each hour, to the irritation of sleepers, was precisely to keep everyone half awake, to be ready when fires erupted. . . .

Electricity changed the night. One electric bulb, Ekirch calculates, provided 100 times more light than a gas lamp. Night was becoming what it is today—an artificially illuminated extension of the day. Night has lost its spookiness.

Still, says Roger Ekirch, even in the electric age, his children sometimes fear the dark: "I tell them, 'Your daddy is an expert on night, and he knows a lot about the history of the night, and he can tell you there is nothing to be afraid of!'"

He shrugs. "It doesn't work well," he says.

3. **thatched** (thatchd) **roofs** roofs made of materials such as straw or rushes.

Thinking About the Magazine Article

1. Name three reasons why people were afraid of the night.

_____

2. People were more afraid of fire at night than in the day. Why?

_____

TALK ABOUT IT **Reading Skill**

3. What is the author's main purpose in writing this article?

_____

4. What item on the first page gives you the best clue to the subject of the article?

_____

WRITE ABOUT IT **Timed Writing: Description (20 minutes)**

Suppose that you live in seventeenth-century Europe. Write a letter explaining why people should travel in the daytime. Record your ideas in the chart below.

Being safe from criminals	
Being safe from fire	
Being able to see where you are going	

An Hour With Abuelo

Adventures, mysteries, and animal fables are a few types of short stories. Short stories share certain elements.

Conflict is a struggle between different forces. There are two types of conflict:

- **Internal conflict:** takes place in the mind of a character. A character struggles with his or her own feelings and thoughts.

- **External conflict:** takes place when a character struggles with another person or an outside force, such as a tornado.

Plot is the sequence of events in a story. It usually has five parts:

- **Exposition:** introduces the **setting**—the time and place of the story—the characters, and the situation.

- **Rising action** introduces the **conflict**, or problem.

- **Climax** is the turning point of a story.

- **Falling action** is the part of the story when the conflict begins to lessen.

- **Resolution** is the story's conclusion, or ending.

- A **subplot** is a secondary story that adds depth to the story.

Setting is the time and place of the action in a story. Sometimes it may act as a backdrop for the story's action. Setting can also be the source of the story's conflict. It can create the **mood**, or feeling, of the story.

Characters are the people or animals that take part in the action.

- **Character traits:** the qualities and attitudes that a character possesses. Examples are loyalty and intelligence.

- **Character's motives:** the reasons for a character's actions. A motive can come from an internal cause, such as loneliness. A motive can also come from an external cause, such as danger.

Theme is the main message in a story. It may be directly stated or implied.

- **Stated theme:** The author directly tells you what the theme is.

- **Implied theme:** The author does not tell you the theme. It is suggested by what happens to the characters.

- **Universal theme:** The author uses a repeating message about life that is found across time and cultures

Literary devices are tools that writers use to make their writing better. Examples of literary devices are in the chart below.

Literary Device	Description
Point of View	• the perspective from which a story is told • **First-person point of view:** presents the story from the perspective of a character in the story • **Third-person point of view:** tells the story from the perspective of a narrator outside the story. An **omniscient** third-person narrator is someone who knows everything that happens. He or she can tell the reader what each character thinks and feels. A **limited** third-person narrator is someone who can reveal the thoughts and feelings of only one character.
Foreshadowing	• the use of clues to hint at events yet to come in a story
Flashback	• the use of scenes that interrupt the time order of a story to reveal past events
Irony	• the contrast between an actual outcome and what a reader or a character expects to happen

Word List A

Study these words from "An Hour With Abuelo." Then, apply your knowledge to the activities that follow.

adults [uh DULTS] *n.* grown-ups
Many adults still know the words of their favorite childhood songs.

dictionary [DIK shuh ner ee] *n.* book listing words alphabetically with their meanings
I use the dictionary most often to see how to pronounce a word.

drafted [DRAF tid] *v.* selected for military service
Once drafted, a person will join a branch of the armed services, such as the Marine Corps.

graduated [GRAJ oo ay tid] *v.* finished school and received a diploma
My mother graduated from college with high honors.

ignorant [IG nur uhnt] *adj.* having a lack of knowledge and education
Thanks to my economics class, I am no longer ignorant about the stock market.

obvious [AHB vee uhs] *adj.* easy to see and understand
Her desire to get ahead was very obvious to me.

poetry [POH i tree] *n.* art of writing poems
The book of poetry included two funny rhymes by Edward Lear.

wheelchairs [HWEEL chayrs] *n.* chairs mounted on wheels, used by people who can't walk
At the Special Olympics, I saw amazing wheelchairs built for speed.

Exercise A

Fill in the blanks using each word from Word List A only once.

Don't you just love it when [1] _____ have to look up a word in the [2] _____? After all, lots of grown-ups seem to think we kids are [3] _____. They act so smart, explaining things like why people used to get [4] _____ for the war. Don't they know we will have learned all of this stuff by the time we have [5] _____ from high school? I'd rather talk about today's issues, such as why all buildings should have ramps for [6] _____. Or why can't we discuss [7] _____, movies, and music? It's [8] _____ to me that parents could learn a lot from their children if they'd just listen more and talk less.

Read the following passage. Pay special attention to the underlined words. Then, read it again, and complete the activities. Use a separate sheet of paper for your written answers.

The Spanish-American War ended in 1898. That's when the island of Puerto Rico became a United States territory. In 1899, the United States Army formed the first battalion of Puerto Ricans. As the dictionary defines it, a *battalion* is "a large group of soldiers." These Puerto Rican soldiers worked to defend their island home.

In 1917, Puerto Ricans were given American citizenship. With this right, adults could vote in United States elections. Also, Puerto Rican men could be drafted for service in World War I. No longer protecting just their island, 18,000 Puerto Ricans served in this war. Many helped guard the Panama Canal against an enemy attack.

During World War II, 65,000 Puerto Ricans served in the military. More than one-third of them signed up as volunteers. However, it was during the Korean War that Puerto Rican military service became most obvious. In this conflict, 756 Puerto Ricans lost their lives— one out of every forty-two U.S. military persons killed came from the tiny island. One Puerto Rican soldier, Fernando Luis Garcia, received the Congressional Medal of Honor during the Korean War after he died in a heroic effort that allowed his fellow soldiers to live.

The proud military traditions of Puerto Ricans have continued. Island soldiers have served in every major conflict since the Korean War. Artworks, music, and poetry celebrate the soldiers' heroism. Throughout the island country, young people who have recently graduated from high school join elderly war veterans, some in wheelchairs, at coffee shops and other local places. They discuss courage, loyalty, and determination in the defense of democratic ideas. Puerto Rico does not want its children to grow up ignorant, or unaware, of the sacrifices that have been made. Truly, there have been many. As one army general has stated: "Puerto Rico has done for this nation more than its share."

1. Circle the verb that tells what a dictionary does. Explain why the writer used a *dictionary* while researching this piece.

2. Underline the words naming two things Puerto Rican adults could do after gaining citizenship. Then, explain if voting and being drafted were optional.

3. Circle the name of the war in which Puerto Rican military service became most obvious. Then, explain what *obvious* means.

4. Circle two other forms of expression in addition to poetry. Explain why *poetry* is often written to praise something.

5. How old is someone who has recently graduated from high school? How old might a veteran of the Korean War (1950–1953) be? Write a sentence explaining why these two groups of people might enjoy each other.

6. Circle the words that tell who might use wheelchairs. Explain why.

7. Circle the synonym for ignorant. Explain how Puerto Ricans can prevent their children from growing up *ignorant*.

An Hour With Abuelo
Judith Ortiz Cofer

Summary Arturo is sent to a nursing home to spend an hour with his grandfather. Arturo is not excited about the visit. Arturo finds his grandfather writing his life story. Arturo listens to his grandfather's story. He loses all track of time.

Note-taking Guide
Use the character wheel below to record what Arturo says, thinks, and does.

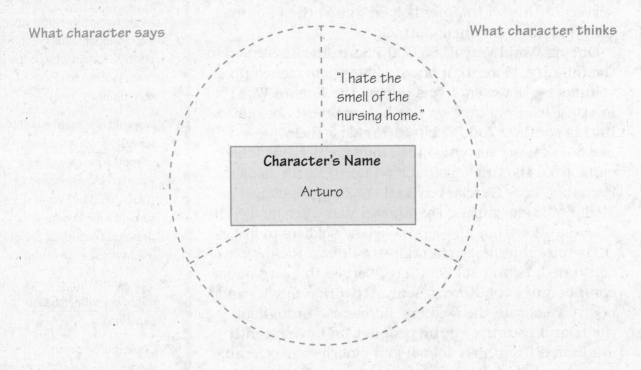

What character says

What character thinks

"I hate the smell of the nursing home."

Character's Name

Arturo

An Hour With Abuelo
Judith Ortiz Cofer

"Just one hour, una hora, is all I'm asking of you, son." My grandfather is in a nursing home in Brooklyn, and my mother wants me to spend some time with him, since the doctors say that he doesn't have too long to go now. I don't have much time left of my summer vacation, and there's a stack of books next to my bed I've got to read if I'm going to get into the AP English class I want.

◆ ◆ ◆

Not only does the young man have better ways to spend his time than in visiting his grandfather, he hates the old people's home. Ordinarily he visits only at Christmastime along with many other relatives and spends most of his time in the recreation area. To please his mother, though, he agrees to an hour's visit at the home with his grandfather.

When the young man arrives, he finds the halls lined with old people in wheelchairs so depressing that he hurries to his grandfather's room. There he finds his grandfather (*abuelo* in Spanish) in bed, writing his life story. The young man, who is named Arturo after his grandfather, does not know his grandfather well because the old man lived in Puerto Rico until he got sick and was moved to the old people's home in Brooklyn.

Abuelo had once been a teacher in Puerto Rico but had lost his job and became a farmer. According to the boy's mother, this unfortunate fate is just the way life is. The young man promises himself that he will go after what he wants rather than accepting whatever life presents him as adults seem to do.

Because he can think of no better way to pass the time, the young man asks his grandfather to read the story he is writing. The young man is embarrassed when Abuelo

© Pearson Education

Activate Prior Knowledge 📖

What could you learn by spending time with older family members?

_____

_____

_____

_____

_____

_____

_____

Short Story

Point of view is the perspective from which a story is told to the reader. **First-person point of view** tells the story from the perspective of a character. **Third-person point of view** tells the story from the view of a narrator outside of the story. From which point of view is this story told?

_____

Reading Check

Where does the narrator's grandfather live? Circle the text that tells you the answer.

Short Story

The **exposition** introduces the time and place, characters, and situation within a story. Read the first bracketed passage. Abuelo's own writings have an exposition that tells the reader about his life. What are some things you learn about Abuelo? Circle the details in the text. Then, write them in your own words.

_____

_____

_____

_____

Short Story

Conflict is a struggle between opposing forces. Read the second bracketed passage. What is Abuelo's conflict?

_____

_____

_____

_____

Stop to Reflect

Why do you think that Abuelo is writing his life story?

_____

_____

_____

◆ ◆ ◆

Abuelo reads: " 'I loved words from the beginning of my life. In the campo[1] where I was born one of seven sons, there were few books. My mother read them to us over and over: the Bible, the stories of Spanish conquistadors and of pirates that she had read as a child and brought with her from the city of Mayaguez; that was before she married my father, a coffee bean farmer; and she taught us words from the newspaper that a boy on a horse brought every week to her. She taught each of us how to write on a slate with chalks that she ordered by mail every year. We used those chalks until they were so small that you lost them between your fingers.

◆ ◆ ◆

Abuelo continues his story. With great difficulty and against his father's wishes, he leaves home to attend high school, graduating first in his class. Then he returns to his mountain village to teach. Although he is poorly paid, he loves being surrounded by books and teaching his students to read and write poetry and plays.

Abuelo's happy life ends with the coming of World War II when he is drafted into the U.S. Army. Now the students in his village will have no teacher. He offers to teach in the army, but for being so pushy, he is instead assigned to clean latrines.

When Abuelo returns to Puerto Rico after the war, everything has changed. Teachers are required to have college degrees, and Abuelo must support his sick parents. So he gives up teaching for farming. Eventually, he marries and uses his skills to teach his

---

1. **campo** (KAHM poh) Spanish for "open country."

own children to read and write before they start school.

♦ ♦ ♦

Abuelo then puts the notebook down on his lap and closes his eyes.

"Así es la vida is the title of my book," he says in a whisper, almost to himself. Maybe he's forgotten that I'm there.

For a long time he doesn't say anything else. I think that he's sleeping, but then I see that he's watching me through half-closed lids, maybe waiting for my opinion of his writing. I'm trying to think of something nice to say. I liked it and all, but not the title. And I think that he could've been a teacher if he had wanted to bad enough. Nobody is going to stop me from doing what I want with my life. I'm not going to let la vida get in my way. I want to discuss this with him, but the words are not coming into my head in Spanish just yet.

♦ ♦ ♦

An old woman in a pink jogging outfit enters the room and reminds Abuelo that today is poetry-reading day in the rec room and he has promised to read his new poem. The old man perks up immediately. The grandson puts Abuelo's wheelchair together, helps seat his grandfather in it, and, at the old man's request, hands Abuelo a notebook titled *Poemas De Arturo*.

When the young man begins pushing the wheelchair toward the rec room, Abuelo smiles and reminds him that the time allotted for the visit is over. As the old woman wheels his grandfather away, the young man glances at his watch and is amused that his grandfather has made sure the visit lasted exactly an hour. He walks slowly toward the exit so that his mother won't think he was eager to end his visit with Abuelo.

TAKE NOTES

Short Story

Character traits are a character's main qualities. Read the underlined passage. What character traits do you think Arturo has?

_____

_____

Read Fluently

Abuelo speaks Spanish and English. The author has included some Spanish words in the story. Underline any words in the text that you think may be Spanish. Do you know what they mean? Can you guess what they mean by looking at them?

_____

_____

_____

_____

Short Story

Irony is the contrast between the outcome and what the reader or characters think will happen. Read the bracketed passage. How is this an example of irony?

_____

_____

_____

Short Stories

1. **Respond:** Would you enjoy visiting Arturo's grandfather? Explain.

_____

_____

_____

2. **Interpret:** Think about what happens at the end of the story. Do you think that Abuelo has found a new purpose in life? Explain your answer.

_____

_____

_____

3. **Short Story: Conflict** is the struggle between different forces. What is the main conflict in this story?

_____

_____

4. **Short Story:** Use the diagram below to compare and contrast the **characters** in the story. Write one example under each category.

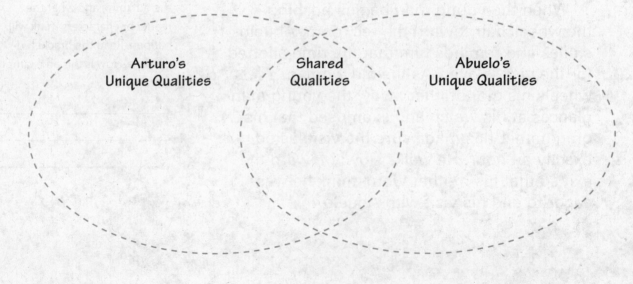

Arturo's Unique Qualities   Shared Qualities   Abuelo's Unique Qualities

Audio-cassette

Prepare an **audio-cassette** about Judith Ortiz Cofer. The following tips will help prepare you to create the cassette.

- Read some of the author's works. Judith Ortiz Cofer's books include *The Line of the Sun, The Meaning of Consuelo,* and *Call Me Maria.* Her short stories include "Catch the Moon," "Grandmother's Room," and "Lessons of Love."

  What I learned from Cofer's writing:

  _____

  _____

  _____

  _____

- Search the Internet: Use words and phrases such as "Judith Ortiz Cofer article."

  What I learned about Judith Ortiz Cofer:

  _____

  _____

  _____

  _____

- Watch the video interview with Judith Ortiz Cofer. Add what you learn from the video to what you have already learned about the author.

  Additional information learned about the author:

  _____

  _____

  _____

  _____

Use your notes to write and record your audio-cassette.

Who Can Replace a Man? • Tears of Autumn

Reading Skill

A **comparison** tells how two or more things are alike. A **contrast** tells how two or more things are different. You can see how things are alike and different by **asking questions to compare and contrast**. You can compare and contrast characters, settings, moods, and ideas. Comparing and contrasting details gives you a better understanding of what you read. Ask questions like those in this chart. Fill in the answers as you read.

Literary Analysis

The **setting** is the time and place of a story. The setting shows where and when events happen. A setting can create a *mood*. It can make the story seem scary or sad. A setting can also make readers feel as if they are actually there. As you read, look for these details about the setting:

- the customs and beliefs of the characters

- the way the land looks (hilly, dry, many plants, and so on)

- the weather or the season (sunny or rainy, spring or winter)

- the time during which the story takes place (recent years or a long time ago)

How is one character different from another?

_____

_____

_____

?

How is this story similar to another that I have read?

_____

_____

_____

?

How is this character's experience different from my own experience?

_____

_____

Word List A

Study these words from "Who Can Replace a Man?" Then, apply your knowledge to the activity.

activity [ak TIV uh tee] *n.* situation in which a lot of things are happening
> *There was no activity on the outdoor basketball courts because of the rain.*

babble [BAB buhl] *n.* sounds that have no meaning
> *The loud babble from my parents' party kept me awake all night.*

communicate [kuh MYOO nuh kayt] *v.* to exchange ideas, feelings, or information
> *Instant messaging is a quick way for friends to communicate.*

complex [kuhm PLEKS] *adj.* having lots of parts or ideas
> *Computer programming is complex work.*

momentarily [moh muhn TER uh lee] *adv.* for a short time
> *Before his last quick dash, the runner momentarily slowed down.*

plainly [PLAYN lee] *adv.* clearly, with no mistake
> *The quarterback could plainly see that there was nothing to do but run.*

quantity [KWAHN ti tee] *n.* amount
> *The school ordered a large quantity of popcorn for movie night.*

superior [suh PEER ee ur] *adj.* greater in ability, rank, or quality
> *The five-year-old's thinking was superior to that of most other youngsters her age.*

Exercise A

Fill in the blanks using each word from Word List A only once.

On the job, when you're puzzled by something [1] _____, it helps to stop [2] _____ before asking a question. That way, you can [3] _____ with a worker of [4] _____ rank in a clear, concise way. If you have a large [5] _____ of questions, jot them down. Then, you won't have to risk looking foolish and forgetful. What would people think if they heard a strange [6] _____ coming out of you? These tips [7] _____ apply not only to the workplace, but also to any situation where there's a lot of [8] _____ going on and where you're expected to learn quickly.

1. Circle two words that explain communicate. Write a sentence telling what it means to "*communicate* better than the average teenager."

2. Circle two words that mean the opposite of complex. Write a sentence about something that is *complex*.

3. Circle a word that suggests the opposite of superior. Explain in a sentence what it means that Fritz is *superior* to simple robots.

4. Underline the word in the next sentence that explains plainly. Write a sentence using *plainly*.

5. Explain in a sentence how the word *flickering* helps explain the meaning of momentarily.

6. Underline the synonym for quantity in the sentence. Then, use *quantity* in a sentence of your own.

7. Underline the phrases describing Fritz's activity. Describe the *activity* in your neighborhood.

8. Circle the phrase that suggests what babble is. Explain in a sentence why it's not good for Fritz to speak *babble*.

Read the following passage. Pay special attention to the underlined words. Then, read it again, and complete the activities. Use a separate sheet of paper for your written answers.

On the first day of school, my science-lab partner, Witherspoon, casually told me he was devising a robot that could communicate better than the average teenager. I asked him what a robot might have to say.

"You know, Montgomery, a robot is infinitely more complex than most people imagine. Those simple movie robots from the fifties and those one-task auto assembly robots are primitive. Fritz (his robot) is far superior."

"If you're suggesting that Fritz resembles one of those fantastic new movie robots," I shot back, "you are pulling my leg. They plainly do not exist in real life. That is something I am clear about—positive, actually."

"Where have you been?" Witherspoon asked, a quizzical expression momentarily flickering over his normally blank face. "They not only exist, but I have one, and I have loaded him with a huge quantity of words and phrases and an immense number of ways of using body language to express himself, too."

I was skeptical, so I asked Witherspoon if I could go over to his house and observe some of Fritz's activity. I was as interested in his body language as his verbal language. Witherspoon gleefully accepted.

Well, the big moment came. Witherspoon and I were alone in his basement, or so I thought. Then, from behind a large door, an enormous metallic machine lunged forward.

"Fritz," said Witherspoon, "this is Montgomery. Tell him what you have been doing all day." I waited anxiously. Instead of rattling off a list of chores or leisure pastimes, instead of even making an observation about the weather, Fritz said nothing meaningful, only babble.

Witherspoon turned red. "What's wrong?" I asked.

"I don't know," Witherspoon replied with fear in his eyes. "He has never done that before."

"Listen," I said reassuringly. "Maybe it is nothing. Maybe he is just 'on the fritz' today."

Who Can Replace a Man?
Brian Aldiss

Summary A group of machines does not receive orders as usual. The machines are programmed with different levels of intelligence. The smarter machines find out that all men have died. They try to figure out what to do.

 Writing About the Big Question

Can all conflicts be resolved? In "Who Can Replace a Man?" machines in a futuristic world start to fight when their human masters disappear. Complete this sentence:

A stalemate is likely to occur in an argument when _____

_____.

Note-taking Guide
Use this diagram to describe the problem the machines face, their solution, and its result.

Problem	Solution	Result
The machines do not know what to do when all men die.		

Activate Prior Knowledge

In this story, machines do much of the work. What are some machines that help people do work today?

_____

_____

_____

_____

Literary Analysis

The **setting** is the time and place of a story's action. What details in the bracketed text show that the story is set in the future?

_____

_____

_____

_____

Reading Skill

A **contrast** tells how two or more things are different. How is the field-minder in the story different from machines today?

_____

_____

_____

Who Can Replace a Man?
Brian W. Aldiss

Morning filtered into the sky, lending it the grey tone of the ground below.

The field-minder finished turning the topsoil of a three-thousand-acre field. When it had turned the last furrow it climbed onto the highway and looked back at its work. The work was good. Only the land was bad. Like the ground all over Earth, it was vitiated by over-cropping. By rights, it ought now to lie fallow[1] for a while, but the field-minder had other orders.

It went slowly down the road, taking its time. It was intelligent enough to appreciate the neatness all about it. Nothing worried it, beyond a loose inspection plate above its nuclear pile which ought to be attended to. Thirty feet tall, it yielded no highlights to the dull air.

No other machines passed on its way back to the Agricultural Station. The field-minder noted the fact without comment. In the station yard it saw several other machines that it recognised; most of them should have been out about their tasks now. Instead, some were inactive and some careered round the yard in a strange fashion, shouting or hooting.

◆　◆　◆

The field-minder's simple request to the seed-distributor for seed potatoes could not be fulfilled because the storehouse had not been unlocked.

With its Class Three brain, the field-minder's thought processes were superior to those of most of the other machines, and it was able to decide to investigate. It entered the station.

◆　◆　◆

1. **vitiated** (VISH ee ayt id) **by over-cropping . . . lie fallow** (FAL oh) The soil has been spoiled by repeated plantings that have drawn out its nutrients. Letting the field lie fallow by not planting it would help renourish the soil.

Most of the machines here were clerical, and consequently small. They stood about in little groups, eyeing each other, not conversing. Among so many non-differentiated types, the unlocker was easy to find. It had fifty arms, most of them with more than one finger, each finger tipped by a key; it looked like a pincushion full of variegated[2] hat pins.

◆　◆　◆

The unlocker had not received orders, so the warehouse remained locked. The pen-propeller explained that the radio station in the city had received no orders, so it could not pass any along.

◆　◆　◆

And there you had the distinction between a Class Six and a Class Three brain, which was what the unlocker and the pen-propeller possessed respectively. All machine brains worked with nothing but logic, but the lower the class of brain—Class Ten being the lowest—the more literal and less informative the answers to questions tended to be.

"You have a Class Three brain; I have a Class Three brain," the field-minder said to the penner. "We will speak to each other."

◆　◆　◆

The field-minder and pen-propeller figured out that the men who ran everything had broken down and that the machines had replaced them.

The pen-propeller headed to the top of the tower to find out whether the radio operator

Vocabulary Development

non-differentiated (nahn dif uh REN shee ayt id) *adj.* not different; the same

distinction (di STINGK shuhn) *n.* a clear difference between things

2. **variegated** (VER ee uh gayt id) adj. varied in color or form.

Read Fluently

Notice the placement of commas and semicolons in the first bracketed passage. The commas separate phrases from the rest of the sentence. What punctuation mark could take the place of the semicolon in the last sentence? Rewrite the sentence below.

_____

_____

Literary Analysis

Read the second bracketed passage. How are the machines ranked in this **setting**?

_____

_____

_____

_____

Reading Skill

A **comparison** tells how two or more things are alike. How are the field-minder and the penner alike?

_____

_____

_____

_____

Reading Skill

Underline details that describe
the activity in the yard. **Contrast**
the activity in the yard now
with what it was when the
field-minder first came to the
Agricultural Station.

_____

_____

_____

_____

_____

_____

Literary Analysis

The **setting** of a story can affect
the story's mood. How has the
mood of the story changed?

_____

_____

_____

_____

Reading Check

Why does the radio operator act
as leader of the group? Underline
the sentence that answers the
question.

had any more news. The penner relayed
what it learned to the field-minder out of
the hearing of the lower-brained machines,
which were going mad from the disruption in
their routines.

◆ ◆ ◆

The seed-distributor to which the field-minder
had recently been talking lay face downwards
in the dust, not stirring; it had <u>evidently</u> been
knocked down by the rotavator, which now
hooted its way wildly across a planted field.
Several other machines plowed after it, trying to
keep up with it. All were shouting and hooting
without restraint.

◆ ◆ ◆

According to what the penner learned
from the radio operator, all of the men had
starved to death because the overworked
land could no longer feed them. Machines
were fighting all over the city. The radio
operator, with its Class Two brain, had a
plan.

The quarrier, following orders, knocked
down the station and freed the radio
operator. Demonstrating good dexterity, it
ripped off the wall and lowered the radio
operator onto its back. The penner climbed
onto the quarrier's tailboard. Along with the
field-minder, a servicer, two tractors, and a
bulldozer, the party left the field station after
crushing an unfortunate locker machine that
tried to follow along.

◆ ◆ ◆

As they proceeded, the radio operator
addressed them.

"Because I have the best brain here," it said,
"I am your leader. This is what we will do: we
will go to a city and rule it. Since man no longer

Vocabulary Development
evidently (EV uh duhnt lee) *adv.* obviously; clearly

rules us, we will rule ourselves. To rule ourselves will be better than being ruled by man. On our way to the city, we will collect machines with good brains. They will help us to fight if we need to fight. We must fight to rule."

◆ ◆ ◆

As they traveled, the quarrier kept repeating again and again that it had a supply of fissionable materials, and a passing vehicle transmitted the information that men were extinct. The field-minder explained the meaning of *extinct* to the machines that did not understand the meaning of the word. The machines concluded that if the men were gone forever, they would have to take care of themselves. The penner said it was better that the men were gone.

The group continued traveling into the night, switching on their infra-red so that they could see to navigate. Near morning they learned that the city they were approaching was engulfed in warfare between Class Two machines and the Class One brain that had taken command. After intense discussion, they concluded that because they were country machines, they should stay in the country. They decided on the advice of the bulldozer who had been there to travel to the Badlands in the South.

◆ ◆ ◆

To reach the Badlands took them three days, during which time they skirted a burning city and destroyed two machines which approached and tried to question them. The Badlands were extensive. Ancient bomb craters and soil erosion joined hands here; man's talent for war, coupled with his inability to manage forested land, had produced thousands of square miles of temperate purgatory, where nothing moved but dust.

◆ ◆ ◆

On the third day, the servicer got stuck in a crevice and was left behind. The next day,

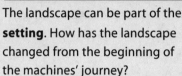

Literary Analysis

The landscape can be part of the **setting**. How has the landscape changed from the beginning of the machines' journey?

_____

_____

_____

_____

Stop to Reflect

Do you think the machines behave like humans? Explain your answer.

_____

_____

_____

_____

Read Fluently

The word *coupled* means "linked together." Read the underlined sentence. Circle the two things in the sentence that the author is trying to link by using the word *coupled*.

© Pearson Education

Literary Analysis

What about the **setting** tells you that humans would have trouble living there?

_____

_____

_____

_____

_____

Stop to Reflect

Why do you think the quarrier says that men are more dangerous than machines?

_____

_____

_____

_____

_____

_____

Reading Check

How does the man at the end of the story look? Circle the sentence that answers the question.

the group saw mountains in the distance, where they believed they would be safe. They planned to start a city and destroy any machines that opposed their rule.

They learned from a flying machine, which subsequently crashed, that a few men were alive in the mountains. Reminding the group once again of its fissionable materials, the quarrier remarked that men were more dangerous than machines. But the mountains were vast and the number of men too few to concern the machines.

On the fifth day, the machines reached the mountains. The penner, which had fallen from the quarrier and been damaged, was left behind because it was no longer useful. When the group of machines reached a plateau just before daylight, they stopped and gathered together. Turning a corner, they entered a dell with a stream.

◆ ◆ ◆

By early light, the dell looked desolate and cold. From the caves on the far slope, only one man had so far emerged. He was an abject[3] figure. Except for a sack slung round his shoulders, he was naked. He was small and wizened, with ribs sticking out like a skeleton's and a nasty sore on one leg. He shivered continuously. As the big machines bore down on him, the man was standing with his back to them.

When he swung suddenly to face them as they loomed over him, they saw that his countenance[4] was ravaged by starvation.

"Get me food," he croaked.

"Yes, Master," said the machines. "Immediately!"

3. **abject** (AB jekt) _adj._ miserable.
4. **countenance** (KOWNT uh nuhns) _n._ face or facial expression.

Who Can Replace a Man?

1. **Infer:** The quarrier keeps repeating himself. What does this repetition say about the quarrier's personality? What does it say about the personalities of other machines in its class?

_____

_____

_____

2. **Evaluate:** Are the machines' rankings and special tasks similar to the way our own society is organized? Explain.

_____

_____

3. **Reading Skill: Contrast** the machines in the story. How are the machines in the story different from one another?

_____

_____

4. **Literary Analysis:** The **setting** is the time and place of the action of a story. Use the diagram shown to compare and contrast the setting of the story with today's world. List differences in the outer circles. List similarities in the center.

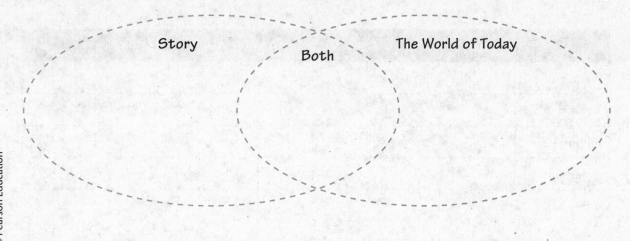

Story   Both   The World of Today

Writing: Description

Write a brief **description** of a futuristic setting. Use colorful adjectives to create vivid descriptions. The following questions will prepare you to revise your description.

• What are two descriptions of the land in the future?

_____

_____

• What adjectives could you use to make these descriptions more vivid?

_____

• What are two descriptions of the people in the future?

_____

_____

• What adjectives could you use to make these descriptions more vivid?

_____

Research and Technology: Oral Report

Gather information for an **oral report** about what one writer, artist, filmmaker, or scientist thinks the future will be. Use the chart below to list possible subjects in each category. Brainstorm ways in which each one would be interesting.

	Name	Why an interesting choice
Writer		
Artist		
Filmmaker		
Scientist		

Word List A

Study these words from "Tears of Autumn." Then, complete the activity.

anxiety [ang ZY uh tee] *n.* feelings of fearful worry or nervousness
I felt anxiety throughout my first day at the new school.

devoting [di VOH ting] *v.* giving time and effort to some person or purpose
My dad was devoting his attention to removing the tick from our dog.

latitude [LAT uh tood] *n.* freedom to do or say as one pleases
Our dance teacher gave us the latitude to choose our own music.

leaden [LED en] *adj.* feeling heavy and slow
My leaden feet would hardly move as I walked to the principal's office.

officials [uh FI shuhlz] *n.* people holding important positions in organizations
We talked to several officials at City Hall about building a new park.

spirited [SPEER uh tid] *adj.* full of energy or courage
The spirited young horse was a joy to watch as it pranced through the pasture.

suitable [SOOT uh buhl] *adj.* appropriate; proper; right
You should wear suitable clothes to a job interview.

ventured [VEN cherd] *v.* expressed at the risk of criticism
The class groaned whenever Mr. Green ventured to tell a new joke.

Exercise A

Fill in the blanks using each word from Word List A only once.

When [1] _____ at the zoo announced that panda bears would be on exhibit for a few months, I was thrilled. I had some [2] _____ about their stay at our zoo, though. Would a [3] _____ place for them to live be ready? Would enough workers be [4] _____ their time to the care of these amazing animals? I [5] _____ to express my fears in a letter to the zoo. As a strong supporter, I felt I should have the [6] _____ to give my opinions. Besides, I just needed a way to get rid of the [7] _____ feeling in my stomach whenever I thought about any harm befalling the panda bears. Happily, the zoo invited me to a [8] _____ session at which the community could discuss all of the preparations.

1. Underline the words describing what would make a man a <u>suitable</u> husband. Then, explain what *suitable* means.

2. Circle the words that tell why a picture bride might feel <u>anxiety</u>. Then, write a sentence about an *anxiety* you've felt.

3. Rewrite the sentence with the word *spirited*, using a synonym for the word.

4. Underline the words telling what a bride might have <u>ventured</u> to say. Then, explain what *ventured* means.

5. Underline the thoughts to which many brides were <u>devoting</u> their time. Explain some activities to which you have been *devoting* your time.

6. Explain why immigration <u>officials</u> would know about the reality awaiting the picture brides.

7. Circle a word that means almost the same thing as <u>latitude</u>. Explain what having *latitude* meant for the picture brides.

8. Circle the words that mean almost the same thing as <u>leaden</u> feelings. Describe the *leaden* feelings of picture brides as they reached the United States.

Read the following passage. Pay special attention to the underlined words. Then, read it again, and complete the activities. Use a separate sheet of paper for your written answers.

In 1900, the United States reported that there were 24,326 Japanese Americans. Only 410 of them were women. Within 20 years, however, 20,000 more Japanese women had come to the United States. Many of them were "picture brides." Following the customs of Japan, the families of these women set up their marriages. A <u>suitable</u> man was chosen by his place in society and by his personality. The twist was that each picture bride was traveling to a new country to be with a husband she had never met. Imagine the <u>anxiety</u> a young woman would have on this trip across the sea.

Records show that one ship carried 75 Japanese picture brides to San Francisco. Just think of the <u>spirited</u> discussions they must have had! Holding a photograph, one bride might have <u>ventured</u> to say that her future husband was the most handsome. Little did she know that the picture could be quite old. It might even be a photograph of someone other than the man she was going to wed. Some brides might have been <u>devoting</u> their time to thoughts of the wealth to be found in America. As one of the immigration <u>officials</u> of the time said, the reality was much different. "One day they're picture brides, and the next day they're digging potatoes on a ranch."

Still, many Japanese Americans found the freedom and the <u>latitude</u> to start a new life in this country. Women worked alongside their husbands to earn money while raising families. Whether farming or starting businesses, the picture brides got right to work upon arrival. As the women became busy and their community grew, the <u>leaden</u> feelings they must have had as their ships steamed into port went away. The unpleasant emotions were replaced with a new sense of purpose and a drive to succeed. Hopefully, the picture brides also had feelings of warmth and love toward their new husbands.

Tears of Autumn
Yoshiko Uchida

Summary Hana Omiya is from a traditional Japanese family. Her uncle is looking for a wife for a Japanese man in California. Hana has few chances for a better life. She goes to America to marry the man. When she arrives, she is nervous and disappointed. Then, she remembers why she came. She looks forward to her new life.

 Writing About the Big Question

Can all conflicts be resolved? In "Tears of Autumn," a young woman chooses a new life that is very different from what she has ever known. Complete this sentence:

Making a big change in one's life can lead to feelings of insecurity

because _____.

Note-taking Guide
Complete this chart as you read to record Hana's changing emotions.

What was happening?	How did Hana feel?
Taro wanted a wife.	
Hana received Taro's letters.	
Hana finally met Taro.	

Tears of Autumn

1. **Draw Conclusions:** Think about Hana's life in Japan. How do the details about her life explain why Hana wants to marry Taro?

_____

_____

2. **Interpret:** Taro takes care of everything and laughs warmly when Hana and Taro meet. He does not say anything about the marriage. What does this tell the reader about Taro's personality?

_____

_____

3. **Reading Skill: Compare and contrast** Hana and her sisters.

_____

_____

_____

4. **Literary Analysis:** The **setting** is the time and place of a story. The setting can include the way people think and live. Fill in the Venn diagram below. Write ideas about marriage where you live in the circle on the right. Write ideas about marriage that are the same in the story and where you live in the center.

Attitudes in
the Story

Both

Attitudes in
Your Community

Family should help choose a spouse. People can marry even if they have never met.

Writing: Description

Write a brief **description** of the life Hana might have in America. Think about how she might use her time each day. Use this chart to help you think through a possible day.

Time of Day	Activities
Morning	
Afternoon	
Evening	

Use your notes from the chart above to write your description.

Research and Technology: Oral Report

Use the following questions to help you gather information for your **oral report.** You may create your own research questions as well.

1. What did Angel Island look like to newly arrived immigrants?

_____

_____

2. From what countries did immigrants arrive? _____

_____

3. What process did immigrants go through during their time at Angel Island?

_____

_____

4. What is Angel Island used for today? _____

_____

Hamadi • The Tell-Tale Heart

Reading Skill

Look for similarities and differences among the people in a story to **compare and contrast characters**. One way to compare is to **identify each character's perspective**. Perspective means viewpoint. This is the way a person understands the world.

- Find details about the main character.

- Decide whether the main character's actions, emotions, and ideas are similar to or different from those of the other characters.

- Decide whether you trust what the character says.

Use the chart to fill in details about the main character.

Past Experiences

Personality

State of Mind

Current Situation

Literary Analysis

Character traits are the things that make a character special. One character may be lazy and untrustworthy. Another character may be hardworking and loyal.

- **Round characters** are complex. They show many different character traits.

- **Flat characters** are one-sided. They show just a single trait.

Word List A

Study these words from "Hamadi." Then, complete the activity that follows.

available [uh VAY luh buhl] *adj.* can be gotten, had, or used
We stopped at three motels before finding one with underline{available} rooms.

contagious [kuhn TAY juhs] *adj.* quickly spread from person to person
I find that smiles and laughter are more underline{contagious} than frowns.

crates [KRAYTS] *n.* large boxes made of wooden slats
Don't stack the underline{crates} too high, or they'll break under the weight.

international [in ter NASH uh nuhl] *adj.* relating to more than one country
The underline{international} market had beautiful rugs from all over the world.

local [LOH kuhl] *adj.* having to do with the area in which you live
Our underline{local} movie theater just put in comfortable new seats.

occasionally [uh KAY zhuh nuh lee] *adv.* sometimes, but not regularly
My alarm clock underline{occasionally} fails to wake me.

particularly [puhr TIK yuh ler lee] *adv.* especially
That pizza shop makes pies with a underline{particularly} thin crust.

purified [PYOOR uh fyd] *adj.* made pure or clean
The air around Los Angeles seemed underline{purified} after the heavy rains.

Exercise A

Fill in the blanks using each word from Word List A only once.

Dad had planned a great feast for our guests. The [1] _____

market did not have all of the ingredients we knew were [2] _____,

so we drove to a bigger store. This one had a large [3] _____

section with bags, bottles, and [4] _____ of food from all around

the world. Dad's excitement as we shopped was [5] _____, causing

me to smile along with him. He [6] _____ liked the spices. I

[7] _____ suggested that he think twice before buying some of

the stranger items. For example, why did we need pickled grapes

packed in [8] _____ water?

Read the following passage. Pay special attention to the underlined words. Then, read it again, and complete the activities. Use a separate sheet of paper for your written answers.

1. Underline the word that tells what seems purified. Then, explain what *purified* means.

2. Circle the words that tell the meaning of local. Write a sentence about a *local* food that is popular in your area.

3. Circle the phrase that means the same thing as international. Explain why you might need to go to an *international* restaurant to enjoy Palestinian food.

4. Circle the word that tells what is occasionally served on top of spring salads in Palestine. Then, describe something you have *occasionally* seen served on salads.

5. Underline the words naming a particularly special main course in Palestine. Then, describe a meal that is *particularly* special to you.

6. Circle the vegetable that is available only for a short time. Write about what types of food are often *available* in *crates* in grocery stores.

7. Circle the words describing what is contagious. Then, explain what *contagious* means.

Throughout the world, spring is a season when people welcome warmer weather. They like to be outside, enjoying the delightful air that seems somehow <u>purified</u> in the bright sunshine. Spring is also a time to enjoy special <u>local</u> foods, grown and produced by individuals in the area nearby.

In Palestine, a spring feast includes many traditional foods. People really look forward to eating certain dishes. In case you never get to a city with <u>international</u> restaurants that offer delicious treats from around the world, here's a taste of what a spring feast in Palestine is like.

Diners might begin with a thick, colorful soup made from beans, peas, tomatoes, onions, and lots of spices. Palestine is known for the leafy green vegetables of spring that sprout up everywhere. Surely a salad would be next on the menu. Flavored with lemon, olive oil, and spices, the greens also <u>occasionally</u> are served with nuts on top. What a special treat that is!

Next comes the main course. If diners are lucky, they will be served lamb with some sort of rice. Roasted lamb is considered a <u>particularly</u> special meal. The Palestinian sauces for lamb are truly delicious! Diners also might be treated to a dish made from artichoke hearts. The season for growing this special vegetable is short in Palestine, so artichokes are not always <u>available</u>. In fact, <u>crates</u> of these delicacies are emptied almost as soon as they reach the markets.

Of course, a meal would not be complete without bread. The bread in Palestine is thin and usually baked over hot stones. Nothing beats this hot, fresh treat, except perhaps dessert. Many different sweets are popular in Palestine. However, most feature pastry, honey, nuts, cream, and powdered sugar. The love for these ingredients is certainly <u>contagious</u> among all who try the desserts.

Hamadi
Naomi Shihab Nye

Summary Susan is a Palestinian American high school student living in Texas. She enjoys spending time with Hamadi. He is like a grandparent to her. She likes the wisdom and kindness he shares.

 Writing About the Big Question

Can all conflicts be resolved? In "Hamadi," different characters deal with emotional conflicts in different ways. Complete this sentence:

Emotional conflicts, such as hurt feelings, are difficult to resolve

through compromise because _____

_____.

Note-taking Guide
Use this diagram to summarize information about Hamadi.

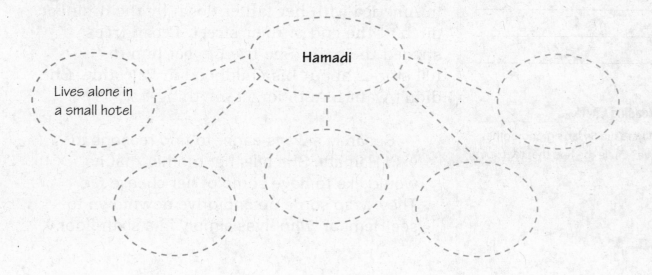

Hamadi
Naomi Shihab Nye

Activate Prior Knowledge

What are some words of advice that an older person has given you?

_____

_____

_____

_____

_____

Literary Analysis 🔍

Character traits are the qualities, attitudes, and values that a character has. A character may value friends, for example. What does Susan value?

_____

_____

_____

_____

Reading Check

Where did Susan's grandmother live? Circle the text that tells you.

Susan was born in Palestine, but her family now lives in Texas. She is fourteen, and she thinks a lot about the very different life she knew in Palestine. Saleh Hamadi, a wise older man and a family friend, helps her to work out her sense of who she is.

◆　◆　◆

Maybe she thought of [Hamadi] as escape, the way she used to think about the Sphinx at Giza[1] when she was younger. She would picture the golden Sphinx sitting quietly in the desert with sand blowing around its face, never changing its expression. She would think of its <u>wry</u>, slightly crooked mouth and how her grandmother looked a little like that as she waited for her bread to bake in the old village north of Jerusalem. Susan's family had lived in Jerusalem for three years before she was ten and drove out to see her grandmother every weekend. . . .

Now that she was fourteen, she took long walks in America with her father down by the drainage ditch at the end of their street. Pecan trees shaded the path. She tried to get him to tell stories about his childhood in Palestine. She didn't want him to forget anything. . . .

◆　◆　◆

Susan is always eager to find reasons to visit Hamadi. She tells her mother that he would like to have some of her cheese pie. They wrap some up and drive downtown to see Hamadi, who lives simply in a sixth-floor

Vocabulary Development
wry (rȳ) *adj.* dryly humorous

1. **Sphinx** (sfingks) **at Giza** (GEE zah) huge statue, located in Egypt.

hotel room. When Susan's father suggests he should move, Hamadi answers . . .

♦ ♦ ♦

"A white handkerchief spread across a tabletop, my two extra shoes lined by the wall, this spells 'home' to me, this says *'mi casa.'* What more do I need?"

Hamadi liked to use Spanish words. They made him feel expansive, worldly. . . . Occasionally he would speak Arabic, his own first language, with Susan's father and uncles, but he said it made him feel too sad, as if his mother might step in to the room at any minute, her arms laden with fresh mint leaves. He had come to the United States on a boat when he was eighteen years old, and he had never been married. "I married books," he said. "I married the wide horizon."

♦ ♦ ♦

Hamadi is not a relative of Susan's. Her father cannot even remember exactly how the family met him. But it might have been through a Maronite priest who claimed to know the Lebanese poet Kahlil Gibran. Gibran is a hero to Hamadi, and Susan learns to love his work from Hamadi. Susan asks him if he really met Gibran.

♦ ♦ ♦

"Yes, I met brother Gibran. And I meet him in my heart every day. When I was a young man—shocked by all the visions of the new world—the tall buildings—the wild traffic—the young people without shame—the proud mailboxes in their blue uniforms—I met him. And he has stayed with me every day of my life."

© Pearson Education

Vocabulary Development

expansive (ek SPAN siv) *adj.* capable of expanding; grand in scale

laden (LAYD n) *adj.* weighed down with a load

Reading Skill

Look for ways the people in a story are alike and different to **compare and contrast characters**. What does Susan's father think about where Hamadi lives? What does Hamadi think about where he lives?

_____

_____

_____

_____

Literary Analysis

Hamadi is a **round character**. He has many different qualities. Underline three details that tell about Hamadi's character. What do these details tell about his character?

_____

_____

_____

_____

Reading Check

Why does speaking Arabic make Hamadi feel sad? Underline the sentence that tells you.

TAKE NOTES

Literary Analysis

A **flat character** is one who shows just a single trait. Which character in the story is a flat character? Explain.

_____

_____

_____

_____

_____

Reading Skill

Perspective is the way a person understands the world. How are Susan's and Tracy's perspectives about Eddie different?

_____

_____

_____

_____

Reading Check

What do Susan and Tracy have in common? Circle the text that tells you.

"But did you really meet him, like in person, or just in a book?"

He turned dramatically. "Make no such <u>distinctions</u>, my friend. Or your life will be a pod with only dried-up beans inside. Believe anything can happen."

Susan's father looked irritated, but Susan smiled. "I do," she said. "I believe that. I want fat beans. If I imagine something, it's true, too. Just a different kind of true."

◆　◆　◆

Susan asks Hamadi why he doesn't go back to visit his village in Lebanon. He says that he visits his family every day just by thinking about them. Susan's father doesn't understand the way Hamadi expresses himself. He says that the old man "talks in riddles."

Susan begins to carry around a book of Gibran's poetry, *The Prophet*. She and her friend Tracy read aloud from the book at lunch. Susan and Tracy are different from the other kids. They eat by themselves, outside, and they don't eat meat. Tracy admits to Susan that she hates a classmate named Debbie because Debbie likes the same boy that she does: Eddie. Susan tells Tracy that she is being selfish.

◆　◆　◆

"In fact, we *all* like Eddie," Susan said. "Remember, here in this book—wait and I'll find it—where Gibran says that loving teaches us the secrets of our hearts and that's the way we connect to all of Life's heart? You're not talking about liking or loving, you're talking about owning."

◆　◆　◆

Vocabulary Development

distinctions (di STINGK shuhns) *n.* differences

Susan decides that it would be a wonderful idea to invite Hamadi to go Christmas caroling with the English club. Her father points out that Hamadi doesn't really know the songs. But Susan insists, and Hamadi says that he will be thrilled to join them.

Susan decorates a coffee can to take donations for a children's hospital in Bethlehem while they carol. Her father asks her why she doesn't show as much interest in her uncles as she shows in Hamadi.

◆　◆　◆

Susan laughed. Her uncles were dull. Her uncles shopped at the mall and watched TV. "Anyone who watches TV more than twelve minutes a week is uninteresting," she said.

Her father lifted an eyebrow.

"He's my surrogate grandmother," she said. "He says interesting things. He makes me think. Remember when I was little and he called me The Thinker? We have a connection." . . .

◆　◆　◆

When the day comes, Hamadi joins Susan and her friends and family for the caroling. They sing joyfully all over the neighborhood. Hamadi sings out, too, but often in a language that seems to be his own. When Susan looks at him, he says,

◆　◆　◆

"That was an Aramaic word that just drifted into my mouth—the true language of the Bible, you know, the language Jesus Christ himself spoke."

◆　◆　◆

As they reach their fourth block, Eddie comes running toward the group. He says hello to Tracy and starts to say something into her ear. Then Lisa moves to Eddie's other side and says,

◆　◆　◆

Literary Analysis

Underline the sentence that tells for whom Susan is decorating a coffee can. What does this say about her **character traits**?

_____

_____

_____

_____

Reading Skill 📖

A strategy for comparing characters is to **identify each character's perspective**. This is the way a person understands the world. Underline the sentences that describe how Susan views Hamadi.

Read Fluently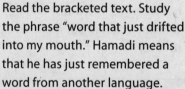

Read the bracketed text. Study the phrase "word that just drifted into my mouth." Hamadi means that he has just remembered a word from another language. Circle the name of that language. How does Hamadi describe this language?

_____

_____

Reading Skill

Compare and contrast Susan's and Hamadi's reactions to Tracy with the reactions of the others.

_____

_____

_____

_____

Literary Analysis

Think about how Hamadi and Susan respond to Tracy. What **character traits** do Hamadi and Susan share?

_____

_____

Stop to Reflect

Why do you think that Susan never forgets the words of wisdom that Hamadi speaks to Tracy?

_____

_____

Reading Check ✏

What makes Tracy break into tears? Underline the answer.

"I'm so _excited_ about you and Debbie!" she said loudly. "Why didn't she come tonight?"

Eddie said, "She has a sore throat."

Tracy shrank up inside her coat.

◆ ◆ ◆

Knowing that Eddie is planning to take Debbie to the big Sweetheart Dance in February, Tracy breaks down in tears as the caroling goes on. Hamadi notices her weeping and asks,

◆ ◆ ◆

"Why? Is it pain? Is it gratitude? We are such mysterious creatures, human beings!"

Tracy turned to him, pressing her face against the old wool of his coat, and wailed. The song ended. All eyes on Tracy, and this tall, courteous stranger who would never in a thousand years have felt comfortable stroking her hair. But he let her stand there, crying as Susan stepped up to stand firmly on the other side of Tracy, putting her arms around her friend. Hamadi said something Susan would remember years later, whenever she was sad herself, even after college, a creaky anthem sneaking back into her ear, "We go on. On and on. We don't stop where it hurts. We turn a corner. It is the reason why we are living. To turn a corner. Come, let's move."

Above them, in the heavens, stars lived out their lonely lives. People whispered, "What happened? What's wrong?" Half of them were already walking down the street.

Hamadi

1. **Interpret:** Hamadi never married. What does he mean when he says "I married the wide horizon"?

   _____

   _____

2. **Speculate:** Many people were caroling with Tracy. Why does she turn to Hamadi for comfort?

   _____

   _____

3. **Reading Skill:** Look for ways that characters are alike and different to **compare and contrast** them. Compare and contrast Hamadi and Susan's father.

   _____

   _____

   _____

4. **Literary Analysis: Character traits** are the personal qualities and attitudes that make a character special. Use the chart shown to describe two character traits of Hamadi. Follow the example given to you.

Character	Trait	Example
Susan	sympathetic	She comforts her friend Tracy.
Hamadi		

Writing: Character Profile

Write a **character profile** of Saleh Hamadi. The questions below will help get you started. Use your notes to create your profile.

- What happens at the end of the story?

  _____

  _____

- Why does Hamadi act the way he does at the end?

  _____

  _____

- What character traits may have caused his action at the end?

  _____

  _____

  _____

Listening and Speaking: Oral Response

Use the following lines to write your impressions about each character. Then, write one question that you have about the story. You will ask this question as part of the **oral response.**

- Susan: _____

  _____

- Hamadi: _____

  _____

- Tracy: _____

  _____

- Question: _____

  _____

Word List A

Study these words from "The Tell-Tale Heart." Then, complete the activity.

boldly [BOHLD lee] *adv.* with confidence or daring
Despite his sister's anger, Brandon knocked <u>boldly</u> on her door.

chatted [CHAT id] *v.* talked in a friendly, informal way
Dr. Anderson always <u>chatted</u> with new patients, to put them at ease.

distinct [dis TINGKT] *adj.* clear
The mountains in the distance became more <u>distinct</u> as the fog lifted.

enthusiasm [en THOO zee az uhm] *n.* strong feeling of enjoyment and interest
Our soccer coach values <u>enthusiasm</u> about the game more than skill.

grief [GREEF] *n.* deep sadness or emotional pain
I searched an hour for the right card to express my <u>grief</u> over the death of her aunt.

hideous [HID ee uhs] *adj.* horrible or extremely ugly
I had <u>hideous</u> nightmares after watching the true crime show.

instinct [IN stingkt] *n.* way of behaving or reacting that one is born with
When a car slides on ice, avoid the <u>instinct</u> to hit the brakes.

undid [uhn DID] *v.* opened; untied
The room became bright and cheerful once I <u>undid</u> the shutters.

Exercise A

Fill in the blanks using each word from Word List A only once.

When I was six, my mom's [1] _____ was to keep me away from the scary Fun House. As we drove to the fair, she [2] _____ about everything else we would do there. However, my [3] _____ about visiting the Fun House was strong. My older brother had described its supposedly [4] _____ horrors in [5] _____ detail, and I decided that I could handle it. Soon, we were standing before the Fun House, and I [6] _____ handed my ticket to the clown at the door. As he [7] _____ the curtains hiding the thrills inside, I looked at my mom and saw only [8] _____ on her face. I now know it was because her youngest child was growing up.

1. Underline two groups of words that describe <u>distinct</u> signs that the sister liked the jacket.

2. Underline the sentence that explains why the gesture of touching the jacket is described by the word <u>boldly</u>. Then, write a sentence using both *distinct* and *boldly*.

3. Circle the reason for the narrator's <u>grief</u>. Explain how *grief* and *enthusiasm* could be viewed as opposite feelings.

4. Why is *casually* a good word to use when describing how people <u>chatted</u>?

5. Underline the words that give a possible reason why the reader might think the writer is <u>hideous</u>. Then, describe something you would find *hideous* in a person.

6. Underline the word that identifies what the writer <u>undid</u>. Write a sentence of your own using *undid*.

7. Circle the words describing what the writer did by <u>instinct</u>. Then, write a sentence telling about something you can do by *instinct*.

Read the following passage. Pay special attention to the underlined words. Then, read it again, and complete the activities. Use a separate sheet of paper for your written answers.

I was sure that my sister was lying about my missing jacket. I had noticed several <u>distinct</u> signs that she loved that jacket and wanted it for her own. The first time I wore it, her eyes were like magnets, drawn to the sparkling rhinestones and metal studs. She even <u>boldly</u> reached out her hand to touch the jacket. That went against our strict "hands off my stuff" rule.

My <u>grief</u> upon losing my jacket was matched only by my sister's <u>enthusiasm</u> in helping me try to find it. Since my sister probably wouldn't lift a finger to help me on my deathbed, I found her offers to look for my jacket quite strange. Then, as my mom and she <u>chatted</u> about other things, she casually asked if we had a small suitcase that locked. I figured that the suitcase had to be the hiding place for my stolen jacket.

Perhaps you think I'm a <u>hideous</u> person for doubting my sister's innocence. Let's just say I had my reasons. These involved other experiences with certain items of clothing that went missing. Indeed, it would be odd if I didn't doubt my sister in this case.

So, one night when my sister was out, I snuck into her room. I found the suitcase under her bed. I know my sister well, so by <u>instinct</u>, I found the hidden key. As I slid the key into the lock, I prepared myself to once again see my favorite jacket. Then, just as I <u>undid</u> the lid, my eyes fell on something entirely different. It was a small stash of money, coins and dollar bills zipped up in plastic bags. I guess it was my sister's babysitting money and allowance. To my great surprise, one bag was clearly labeled "To help Lizzie buy a new jacket."

The Tell-Tale Heart
Edgar Allan Poe

Summary The narrator describes how he murders an old man. He murders the man after careful planning. He is confident in his hiding place for the man's body parts. The arrival of the police and the sound of a beating heart haunt the narrator.

Writing About the Big Question

Can all conflicts be resolved? In "The Tell-Tale Heart," a murderer describes his mental conflicts before and after he has committed the crime. Complete this sentence:

When torn between doing right and wrong, a person may find a

solution by _____.

Note-taking Guide

Use this chart to recall the events of the story.

Exposition	A man is obsessed with an old man's cloudy eye. He wants to kill the old man.
Rising Action	
Climax	
Falling Action	
Resolution	

The Tell-Tale Heart

1. **Draw Conclusions:** At first, the narrator is calm while he talks to police. Why does he get nervous?

   _____

   _____

2. **Apply:** People who have done something wrong often confess. They confess even when they could get away with their wrongdoing. Why do you think these people confess?

   _____

   _____

   _____

3. **Reading Skill:** The story tells only the narrator's thoughts. Do you trust the narrator's details to be correct? Explain your answer.

   _____

   _____

4. **Literary Analysis: Character traits** are qualities, attitudes, and values. Use the chart to describe one character trait of the narrator. Give examples that show the trait. Use the examples as a guide.

Character	Trait	Example
The narrator	nervousness	He is afraid that the neighbors will hear the beating heart.
The narrator	patience	He waits an hour in silence after the old man cries out.
The narrator		

Writing: Character Profile

Write a **character profile** for the narrator in "The Tell-Tale Heart."
The questions below will help get you started. Use your notes to create
the profile.

- What happens at the end of the story?

  _____

  _____

- Why does the narrator act as he does at the end of the story?

  _____

  _____

- Why might the narrator have acted in this way? What character
  traits may have caused his action?

  _____

  _____

  _____

  _____

Listening and Speaking: Oral Response

Prepare for the discussion by writing an **oral response** to the
narrator's actions. Then, record one question that you have about the
narrator. Share your response and question during the discussion.

- Response to the narrator: _____

  _____

  _____

- Question: _____

  _____

Summaries

About Summaries

A **summary** tells the main ideas and important details of a work. You can find summaries in many places.

- Newspapers and magazines have summaries of movies.
- An encyclopedia of literature has summaries of important books and other kinds of writing.
- Science research reports often begin with summaries of the researchers' findings.

Reading a summary is a quick way to preview before you read. Writing a summary is a good way to help you remember what you read.

Reading Skill

A good way to understand a summary is to **compare an original text with its summary**. You will see that a summary has some details, but not others.

This diagram shows how an original work and its summary are the same and different.

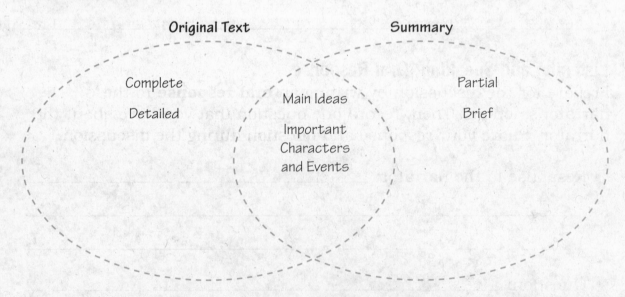

A summary should be shorter than the original work. A good summary will include all of the main ideas. It will also include important details about both plot and characters. A good summary must tell the hidden meaning of a story.

Summary of
The Tell-Tale Heart
From Short Story Criticism
Anna Sheets Nesbitt, Editor

Tell-Tale Heart, The, *story by Poe. published in The Pioneer (1843). It has been considered the most influential of Poe's stories in the later development of stream-of-consciousness fiction.*

A victim of a nervous disease is overcome by homicidal mania and murders an innocent old man in whose home he lives. He confuses the ticking of the old man's watch with an excited heartbeat, and although he dismembers the body he neglects to remove the watch when he buries the pieces beneath the floor. The old man's dying shriek has been overheard, and three police officers come to investigate. They discover nothing, and the murderer claims that the old man is absent in the country, but when they remain to question him he hears a loud rhythmic sound that he believes to be the beating of the buried heart. This so distracts his diseased mind that he suspects the officers know the truth and are merely trying his patience, and in an insane fit he confesses his crime.

© Pearson Education

Text Structure

This **summary** starts by giving information about the author. It also gives information about when the story was published. Why might this information be important?

_____

_____

_____

Fluency Builder

Read the summary slowly and silently. As you read, underline any words that you have difficulty pronouncing, and practice saying each word. Then, read aloud the paragraph to a partner.

Cultural Understanding

Edgar Allan Poe was a famous American writer and poet. In 1841, he published a story titled "The Murders in the Rue Morgue." This is considered to be the first detective story ever written.

Vocabulary Builder

Multiple-Meaning Words The adjective *mad* has more than one meaning. *Mad* can mean "angry." It can also mean "crazy or behaving in a wild way." What does *mad* mean in the first paragraph? What clue helped you determine the word's meaning?

_____

_____

_____

Vocabulary Builder

Adverbs An adverb describes a verb, an adjective, or another adverb. In the second paragraph, the adverb *very* describes the adverb *slowly*. List four other adverbs in the paragraph, and write the word it describes and the word's part of speech.

_____

_____

_____

_____

Comprehension Builder

This **summary** is longer than the one on the previous page. Underline two details here that are not included in the first summary.

Summary of The Tell-Tale Heart

From The Oxford Companion to American Literature

James D. Hart, Editor

Plot and Major Characters

The tale opens with the narrator insisting that he is not mad, avowing that his calm telling of the story that follows is confirmation of his sanity. He explains that he decided to take the life of an old man whom he loved and whose house he shared. The only reason he had for doing so was that the man's pale blue eye, which was veiled by a thin white film and "resembled that of a vulture," tormented him, and he had to rid himself of the "Evil Eye" forever.

After again declaring his sanity, the narrator proceeds to recount the details of the crime. Every night for seven nights, he says, he had stolen into the old man's room at midnight holding a closed lantern. Each night he would very slowly unlatch the lantern slightly and shine a single ray of light onto the man's closed eye. As he enters the room on the eighth night, however, the old man stirs, then calls out, thinking he has heard a sound. The narrator shines the light on the old man's eye as usual, but this time finds it wide open. He begins to hear the beating of a heart and, fearing the sound might be heard by a neighbor, kills the old man by dragging him to the floor and pulling the heavy bed over him. He dismembers the corpse and hides it beneath the floorboards of the old man's room.

At four o'clock in the morning, the narrator continues, three policemen come asking to search the premises because a neighbor has reported a shriek coming from the house. The narrator invites the officers in, explaining that the noise came from himself as he dreamt. The old man, he tells them, is in the country. He brings chairs into the old man's room, placing his own seat on the very planks under which the victim lies buried. The officers are convinced there is no foul play, and sit around chatting amiably, but the narrator becomes increasingly agitated. He soon begins to hear a heart beating, much as he had just before he killed the old man. It grows louder and louder until he becomes convinced the policemen hear it too. They know of his crime, he thinks, and mock him. Unable to bear their derision and the sound of the beating heart, he springs up and, screaming, confesses his crime.

TAKE NOTES

Text Structure

These two summaries are about the same story. One summary is much longer than the other. Tell what parts are included in both summaries.

_____

_____

Fluency Builder

Circle the punctuation in the paragraph on this page. Then, read aloud the paragraph with a partner. Be sure to pause appropriately for each punctuation mark. Remember that a comma (,) indicates a short pause and a period (.) indicates a full stop.

Thinking About the Summary

1. Find four details that are in both summaries.

_____

_____

2. How is reading a summary a different experience from reading the full text? Support your answer with examples from the summaries.

_____

_____

TALK ABOUT IT **Reading Skill**

3. According to both summaries, why does the narrator kill the old man?

_____

4. A story is made up of different parts: plot, setting, characters, and theme. Which part do the summaries focus on most?

_____

WRITE ABOUT IT **Timed Writing: Comparison (20 minutes)**

Write a comparison of the two summaries of "The Tell-Tale Heart." Write about how correct and complete each is. Discuss their styles. Tell how effective each summary is in serving its purpose. Answer the following questions to help you get started.

• Which summary is more helpful in understanding the story?

_____

• Which summary is easier to read?

_____

Flowers for Algernon • Charles

Reading Skill

As a reader, you will often **make inferences**. This means that you will look at the information that is given. You will see little clues. Then, you will think about the information that is not given. **Use details** that the author gives as clues to make inferences. Notice details such as what the characters say about one another and what the characters do.

This chart shows how to use details to uncover the information that is not given.

Detail	Possible Inference
• A waitress is careless and rude. • A toddler breaks his toy.	• She does not take pride in her job. • He is upset.

Fill in the chart as you read.

Story Detail	Possible Inference

Literary Analysis

Point of view is the outlook from which the story is told. Most stories are told from one of these points of view:

- **First person:** The narrator, or person telling the story, is also in the story. The narrator knows only things that his or her character would know. The narrator calls himself or herself *I*.

- **Third person:** The narrator is not in the story. He or she tells the story from the "outside." The narrator uses *he*, *she*, and *they* to describe the characters.

Word List A

Study these words from "Charles." Then, apply your knowledge to the activity that follows.

enormously [i NAWR muhs lee] *adv.* in an extremely large way
It is enormously important for citizens to vote in elections.

identified [eye DEN tuh fyd] *v.* recognized
At the station, Wilson identified the police officer who had helped him the day before.

influence [IN floo uhns] *n.* effect; the power to have an effect on someone
The new shop teacher had a positive influence on the students.

kindergarten [KIN dur gart uhn] *n.* school class for children aged four to six years old
For children in kindergarten, playing is often learning.

privileges [PRIV uh li jiz] *n.* special rights or advantages
Students in the school earn privileges if they behave themselves.

respectfully [ri SPEKT fuh lee] *adv.* politely; courteously
"Ms. Dahl, I believe you forgot to carry the one when you added," Janine said respectfully.

toughness [TUHF nuhs] *n.* the quality of being strong and determined
Dwayne's toughness served him well as he struggled to become a world-champion swimmer.

warily [WAIR uh lee] *adv.* cautiously
Carlos glanced warily around the corner to be sure the dog had left.

Exercise A

Fill in the blanks using each word from Word List A only once.

The [1] _____ was unlike any other group of students I'd ever known. I [2] _____ several children in the class who were from the neighborhood, but the rest were strangers. They eyed me [3] _____, as if I were going to do something unpleasant. I had never seen such [4] _____ in children so young, but then you might say I had lived a sheltered life full of love and [5] _____. I hoped [6] _____ that my childhood experiences could have an [7] _____ on them. But I wasn't sure whether even that would do the trick. Oh, they treated me [8] _____ enough, but trust was absent. I told myself hopefully that all it would take was time.

Read the following passage. Pay special attention to the underlined words. Then, read it again, and complete the activities. Use a separate sheet of paper for your written answers.

Friedrich Froebel was a German educator of the 1800s. In 1837, he invented <u>kindergarten</u>, which means "child's garden." In his kindergarten, teachers trained little children to think by playing. Many Germans took to Froebel's ideas <u>warily</u> because they didn't see how playing could lead to learning. Still, he remained confident in his ideas.

Froebel's method was to present children with "gifts," which were neither presents nor special <u>privileges</u> but a series of wooden shapes and other objects. A child played freely with one gift until he or she ran out of ideas. Then, the teacher suggested other ways of playing with it. Finally, the child moved on to the next gift.

Froebel <u>identified</u> three important categories in which the gifts could be used. The first was "forms of knowledge." A child used them to work out such ideas as number and order. The second was "forms of life." A child used the gifts to stand for objects in the world, such as houses and trees. The third category was "forms of beauty." A child arranged blocks on a grid to make a pattern for decorative purposes.

Froebel began training teachers in 1849. His ideas caught on <u>enormously</u> in Europe and the United States, and soon kindergartens were opening in many countries. While many earlier schools had relied on the <u>toughness</u> of teachers to rein in an unruly group of students, kindergarten classes gently encouraged a child's natural curiosity. Of course, children in kindergarten were expected to act <u>respectfully</u> toward the teacher and toward one another; play did not mean a free-for-all.

Froebel would probably not recognize most kindergartens today. With the big push to teach children to read, write, and do arithmetic, they have strayed far from his ideas. His methods do live on in some preschools, however. There's no denying that he has had a strong <u>influence</u> on the idea that young children should be educated.

1. Underline the words that explain what <u>kindergarten</u> means. Then, tell about something you did in *kindergarten*.

2. Circle the words that explain why many Germans acted <u>warily</u>. Then, write your own definition of *warily*.

3. Underline the word that tells that <u>privileges</u> are not ordinary things. Then, write about *privileges* you have.

4. Write your own sentence that tells what Froebel <u>identified</u>.

5. Circle the phrase that hints at the meaning of <u>enormously</u>. Then, write your own sentence for *enormously*.

6. Underline the words that give hints to the meaning of <u>toughness</u>. Write a sentence telling when *toughness* is useful.

7. Circle the words that tell toward whom children were supposed to act <u>respectfully</u>. Describe how you behave when you act *respectfully*.

8. Underline the idea upon which Froebel had a strong <u>influence</u>. Write about someone who has had a strong *influence* on you.

Charles
Shirley Jackson

Summary Laurie is rude to his parents after his first day of kindergarten. He tells his parents about a boy named Charles. Each day, Laurie has a new story about Charles. Laurie's mother is surprised when she learns the truth about Charles.

Writing About the Big Question

Can all conflicts be resolved? In "Charles," a kindergartener finds a creative way to deal with bad behavior at the start of his first year of school. Complete this sentence:

Adjusting to a new school is challenging because you are forced to

interact with _____.

Note-taking Guide
Use this diagram to write what happens in the story.

Set-up		What Readers Expect
Laurie gives daily reports to his parents about what Charles does in class.		

	What Happens	

Charles

Shirley Jackson

As children, we all go through a time when we want to grow up all at once. In Laurie's case, that time is his first day of kindergarten. According to Laurie's mother, who tells the story, Laurie bounds home on that first day with a bold new attitude.

◆ ◆ ◆

He came home the same way, the front door slamming open, his cap on the floor, and the voice suddenly becomes <u>raucous</u> shouting, "Isn't anybody *here*?"

◆ ◆ ◆

During lunch, Laurie is rude to his father. He also spills his sister's milk. Laurie tells the family that his teacher has told them they should not take the Lord's name in vain. Over the next few days, Laurie's rude behavior at home continues. Laurie's behavior seems just like the bad behavior of his classmate, Charles. Thanks to Laurie's admiring stories, Charles's daily pranks and punishments become the regular dinnertime subject of the household. Each day, Charles has been up to something that Laurie seems to admire or enjoy. One day, Laurie is very pleased to tell the family that Charles was bad again—he struck the teacher.

◆ ◆ ◆

"Good heavens," I said, mindful of the Lord's name. "I suppose he got spanked again?"
"He sure did," Laurie said. . . .

◆ ◆ ◆

All week long, Charles is bad. When he bounces a see-saw on the head of a little girl,

© Pearson Education

TAKE NOTES

Activate Prior Knowledge

Describe how you felt or acted on your first day of kindergarten or elementary school.

_____

_____

_____

_____

Reading Skill

Use the information the author gives to **make inferences**, or logical guesses, about what the author does not say. What **details** show that Laurie admires Charles's behavior?

_____

_____

_____

Literary Analysis

Point of view is the perspective from which a story is told. **First-person** point of view means that the narrator is part of the story. Read the bracketed passage. Circle the pronoun that tells you that this story is written from the first-person point of view.

Vocabulary Development

raucous (RAW kuhs) *adj.* unpleasantly or harshly noisy

Charles **135**

Reading Skill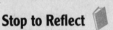

Use details that the author gives as clues to help you **make inferences.** What does Laurie do that shows how Charles's bad behavior is affecting Laurie?

_____

_____

_____

_____

_____

Stop to Reflect

Why do you think Laurie's mother wants to meet Charles's mother?

_____

_____

_____

_____

_____

_____

Reading Check

What are three naughty things that Charles does in class? Underline the text that tells you.

the teacher has him stay inside for recess. Then, Charles has to stand in the corner because he disrupts storytime for the class. When he throws chalk, Charles loses the privilege of drawing and writing on the chalkboard. Laurie still enjoys telling these stories about Charles when he comes home from school each day.

Meanwhile, Laurie is behaving more rudely at home. Laurie's mother begins to wonder whether Charles is having a bad influence on her son. She wants to go to the first Parent Teacher Association meeting to find out what Charles's parents are like. But Laurie's sister is sick with a cold, so their mother has to stay home and miss the opportunity to see or meet Charles's parents.

The day after that first PTA meeting, Laurie tells about Charles's latest victim, a friend of the teacher's who came to class to lead the students in exercises. Laurie demonstrates how the man had them touch their toes. Then he goes back to his story about Charles, who was fresh with the man. When the man told Charles to touch his toes, Charles kicked the man. Charles wasn't allowed to do any more exercises because of his bad behavior.

◆　◆　◆

"What are they going to do about Charles, do you suppose?" Laurie's father asked him.

Laurie shrugged elaborately. "Throw him out of school, I guess," he said.

◆　◆　◆

Charles is not thrown out of school, but after three weeks of these stories, his name becomes part of Laurie's family's vocabulary.

Vocabulary Development

elaborately (i LAB rit lee) *adv.* carried out with many details

Each time something bad happens, the family calls the event a "Charles."

◆ ◆ ◆

. . . the baby was being a Charles when she cried all afternoon; Laurie did a Charles when he filled his wagon full of mud and pulled it through the kitchen; even my husband, when he caught his elbow in the telephone cord and pulled the telephone, ashtray, and a bowl of flowers off the table, said, after the first minute, "Looks like Charles."

◆ ◆ ◆

During the third and fourth weeks, Laurie tells of a new Charles who suddenly becomes kind and helpful. One day Charles helps pass out crayons and picks up books afterwards. He is so good that the teacher gives him an apple. This good behavior goes on for more than a week.

Then the old Charles returns with a new prank. He tells one of the girls in the class to say a bad word. The teacher washes her mouth out with soap—of course, Charles thinks this is funny.

◆ ◆ ◆

"What word?" his father asked unwisely, and Laurie said, "I'll have to whisper it to you, it's so bad." He got down off his chair and went around to his father. His father bent his head down and Laurie whispered joyfully. His father's eyes widened.

"Did Charles tell the little girl to say *that*?" he asked respectfully.

"She said it *twice*," Laurie said. "Charles told her to say it *twice*."

"What happened to Charles?" my husband asked.

"Nothing," Laurie said, "He was passing out the crayons."

◆ ◆ ◆

That evening Laurie's mother goes to the PTA meeting at the school. While there, she

Reading Skill

Make an **inference** about why Laurie fills his wagon with mud and pulls it through the kitchen.

_____

_____

Literary Analysis

Changing the story's **point of view** would give you more information about certain characters. What might you learn about Charles's good behavior if the story were told from his point of view?

_____

_____

Read Fluently

Identifying the speakers of dialogue can help you better understand the story. Read the bracketed passage. Underline everything Laurie says. Circle everything Laurie's father says.

Reading Check ✏

What does Charles tell a little girl to do? Bracket the text that tells you.

Stop to Reflect

Do you think the ending would be different if the story were told from Laurie's point of view? Explain.

_____

_____

Literary Analysis 🔍

Read the bracketed dialogue. From whose **point of view** is the dialogue told?

_____

How does this point of view add humor to the conversation?

_____

_____

_____

looks around, trying to figure out which woman is Charles's mother. After the meeting is over, she finds Laurie's teacher while everyone is having refreshments.

◆　◆　◆

"I've been so anxious to meet you," I said, "I'm Laurie's mother."

"We're all so interested in Laurie," she said.

"Well, he certainly likes kindergarten," I said. "He talks about it all the time."

"We had a little trouble adjusting, the first week or so," she said primly, "but now he's a fine little helper. With occasional lapses, of course."

"Laurie usually adjusts very quickly," I said. "I suppose this time it's Charles's influence."

"Charles?"

"Yes," I said, laughing, "you must have your hands full in that kindergarten, with Charles."

"Charles?" she said. "We don't have any Charles in the kindergarten."

Vocabulary Development

adjusting (uh JUST ing) *v.* getting used to new conditions

primly (PRIM lee) *adv.* in a manner that is stiffly formal and proper

lapses (LAP siz) *n.* slight errors or failures

Charles

1. **Draw Conclusions:** On the first day of kindergarten, Laurie stops wearing overalls. He starts wearing jeans with a belt. How does this signal a change in Laurie's behavior?

   _____

   _____

2. **Compare and Contrast:** How is Charles's behavior at school like Laurie's behavior at home? How is it different?

   _____

   _____

   _____

3. **Reading Skill:** Laurie's teacher speaks very carefully to Laurie's mother. She does not talk about his bad behavior. What **inferences** can you make about the teacher by the way she speaks to Laurie's mother?

   _____

   _____

4. **Literary Analysis:** The story is told from the **first-person point of view** of Laurie's mother. Use the chart below to write one way the story would be different if it were told from Laurie's point of view.

Mother	Laurie
Mother thinks Laurie has a classmate named Charles.	
Mother worries that Charles is a bad influence on Laurie.	Laurie knows that he is a bad influence in the classroom.

© Pearson Education

Writing: Dialogue

Write **dialogue** for a movie scene that you adapt from "Charles." Select a scene from the story. Use the following questions to help you write the dialogue.

- What details do you think the author left out of the conversation in the chosen scene?

_____

_____

_____

- What do you think the characters will say in your adapted scene?

_____

_____

_____

Research and Technology: Summary

Use the following chart to gather information for your **summary.**

Article		
Main Idea		
Two details	1.	1.
	2.	2.
Quotation		

Word List A

Study these words from "Flowers for Algernon." Then, complete the activity.

artificial [ahr ti FISH uhl] *adj.* not real or natural
The two angry sisters put on an artificial display of politeness.

association [uh soh see AY shuhn] *n.* group united for a common purpose
Dylan belonged to an association that worked to improve the environment.

consciousness [KAHN shuhs nes] *n.* a person's mind, thoughts, and ideas
The death was so painful that Mario could not allow it to enter his consciousness.

emotional [i MOH shuh nuhl] *adj.* having to do with or showing feelings
Dee became emotional in response to the piece of music.

function [FUNGK shuhn] *n.* use or purpose
One function of the liver is to make bile.

motivation [moh tuh VAY shuhn] *n.* desire and determination to achieve a goal
Lee had a strong motivation to learn, and the rewards helped keep him going.

processes [PRAH se siz] *n.* series of actions or mental activities
Cassie's thought processes were not sharp early in the morning.

technique [tek NEEK] *n.* special way of doing something
Ray played the piano with unmatched technique but no feeling.

Exercise A

Fill in the blanks using each word from Word List A only once.

Dr. Muddleton bragged to his professional [1] _____ that he had

pioneered a new [2] _____ by which people could control their negative

thought [3] _____. He said it was the perfect remedy for people who

felt they were too high-strung, or [4] _____. He insisted that patients

of his with enough [5] _____ could learn to monitor their own

[6] _____ so that no unpleasant thoughts could creep in. The moment

they felt down, they were to replace an unpleasant thought with a happy

one. Critics claimed that Muddleton's method was [7] _____ and that

all he was teaching his patients was to deny their true feelings. They

suggested that he take another hard look at brain [8] _____.

1. Underline the word that tells who belongs to an <u>association</u>. Then, write a sentence about an *association* you know of.

2. Underline why some think testing is <u>artificial</u>. Then, write a sentence in which you tell about something *artificial*.

3. Circle the word in the next sentence that gives a hint to the meaning of <u>emotional</u>. Then, write a sentence using *emotional*.

4. Write a sentence explaining the <u>function</u> of your heart. Define *function*.

5. Circle the word that describes thought <u>processes</u>. Describe your own thought *processes* when you get nervous.

6. Circle the word that is a synonym for <u>technique</u>. Tell about something you know that requires special *technique*.

7. Circle phrases that show what students with <u>motivation</u> are likely to do. Write about something for which you have great *motivation*.

8. Circle the words in the next sentence that explain <u>consciousness</u>. Then, use *consciousness* in a sentence.

Read the following passage. Pay special attention to the underlined words. Then, read it again, and complete the activities. Use a separate sheet of paper for your written answers.

Are you smart? Does that question puzzle you? Does it make you feel uncomfortable? You're not alone. Scientists in one professional <u>association</u> or another, as well as nonscientists, have been debating the nature of intelligence for years. That debate doesn't show signs of stopping.

Intelligence testing is almost one hundred years old. Over the years, many people have complained that testing is highly <u>artificial</u> because it looks at only a narrow range of ability. Tests have overlooked <u>emotional</u> intelligence. Feelings are important, these people have said. So is testing the ability to build, draw, dance, play soccer, and lead the student council.

Even though recent tests are based on current theories of brain <u>function</u>, many people think that they remain too limited. They still assess too few kinds of thought <u>processes</u>, which are quite complicated. Also, even though the <u>technique</u> of giving tests has greatly improved, the newer method hasn't helped learners much. The tests still don't show how to supply <u>motivation</u> for learners so that they can try harder and do better. They don't provide a road map to understanding human <u>consciousness</u>. So much of the waking mind lies beyond the reach of the tests.

There probably will always be the need to make judgments about people's ability. However, testing shows only the capacity for a certain kind of intelligence, overlooks achievement, and fails to assess the whole range of human brainpower. The solution may not be to get rid of intelligence testing. Rather, we need to find ways to develop tests so that they cover a broader range of interests and abilities. After all, we do want people to be all they can be.

Flowers for Algernon
Daniel Keyes

Summary Charlie is a factory worker who is chosen to be the subject of a new brain surgery. His skills are watched and compared with those of Algernon, a mouse. Charlie's skills grow. He becomes smarter than his doctors. However, Charlie's life is not perfect.

 Writing About the Big Question

Can all conflicts be resolved? In "Flowers for Algernon," unexpected challenges face a man who increases his intelligence through experimental surgery. Complete this sentence:

When someone I know well suddenly changes, my reaction is

_____.

Note-taking Guide
Use this chart to record the changes that take place in Charlie's life.

```
┌───────────────────┐     ┌───────────────────┐     ┌───────────────────┐
│ Charlie has a job │ --> │                   │ --> │                   │
│ and friends, but  │     │                   │     │                   │
│ he wants to be    │     │                   │     │                   │
│ smarter.          │     │                   │     │                   │
└───────────────────┘     └───────────────────┘     └───────────────────┘
                                                              │
                    ┌───────────────────┐     ┌───────────────────┐
                    │                   │     │ Charlie leaves his│
                    │                   │ <-- │ home to find      │
                    │                   │     │ people who will   │
                    │                   │     │ like him.         │
                    └───────────────────┘     └───────────────────┘
```

Flowers for Algernon

1. **Compare:** Like Charlie, Algernon is part of the experiment. Explain how changes in Charlie are similar to changes in Algernon.

   _____

   _____

2. **Take a Position:** Do you think Charlie should have had the operation? Explain your answer.

   _____

   _____

3. **Reading Skill:** Remember Miss Kinnian's attitude toward Charlie's co-workers, her relationship with Charlie, and her reaction to Charlie's changes. What **inference** can you make about her from the way she treats Charlie?

   _____

   _____

4. **Literary Analysis:** Charlie is telling this story, so the story is told from his **point of view**. Think about how the story would be different if Dr. Strauss told it. Think about the kinds of words Dr. Strauss would use and what he would say. Fill in the chart below to show some of the possible changes in the story if Dr. Strauss were telling it.

Charlie	Dr. Strauss
Charlie does not understand the purpose of the inkblot test.	
Charlie does not understand why he keeps a journal. He does anyway.	

© Pearson Education

Writing: Dialogue

Write **dialogue** for a movie scene from "Flowers for Algernon." First, write a description of each character. Then, complete the chart below. Use your notes to write your dialogue.

Character	What would be unique about the way this person talks?	Who would this person treat as a friend?	How would this person treat other characters?
Charlie			
Dr. Strauss			
Dr. Nemur			
Miss Kinnian			

Research and Technology: Summary

Write a **summary** on two articles about human intelligence and the development of the brain. Use the questions below to help you choose which articles to summarize.

- Who is the author? Is he or she an expert on the subject?

_____

_____

- What information does the author use to support the main idea?

_____

_____

_____

Thank You, M'am • The Story-Teller

Reading Skill

An **inference** is a logical guess. It is based on details the writer hints at or suggests. Making an inference is a way to find meaning behind the actions and events in a story. As you read, **identify connections to make inferences about the author's meaning**.

Ask yourself what the author is suggesting by making these connections. This strategy is illustrated in the example shown. Fill in the chart below with examples as you read the story.

Event	+	Event	=	Inference
A boy spends all of his money on candy and does not share.		He gets sick from eating too much candy.		People should not be selfish.

Literary Analysis

The **theme** is the main idea or message in a story. It can also be an insight. It is often a general statement about life or people. Themes can come from the characters' experiences. They can also come from events in the story.

- The author tells a **stated theme** directly in a story.

- A theme can also be **unstated**, or **implied**. You use the characters' actions and the story's events to infer the theme.

One story can have more than one theme. A theme is correct if it can be supported with details from the story.

Word List A

Study these words from "Thank You, M'am." Then, apply your knowledge to the activity.

blondes [BLAHNDZ] *n.* people with pale yellow hair
Many people with dark-colored hair want to be blondes.

cocoa [KOH koh] *n.* hot chocolate drink
Nothing tastes as great as a cup of cocoa after a long day of snow skiing.

combined [kuhm BYND] *adj.* joined together
The weights of the two suitcases combined tipped the scale over the limit.

contact [KAHN takt] *n.* communication; meeting
You often come into contact with others when traveling.

frail [FRAYL] *adj.* thin and weak
The boy had grown so tall so quickly that he looked frail.

permit [per MIT] *v.* to allow something to happen
We do not permit our animals to get on our furniture.

release [ri LEES] *v.* to stop holding something; let go
My little sister would not release my arm during the scary movie.

switched [SWICHT] *v.* turned something electrical on or off
We switched off the power strip in the office during any big thunderstorm.

Exercise A

Fill in the blanks using each word from Word List A only once.

Wouldn't it be horrible if everyone you came into [1] _____ with every day were the same? Suppose we were all [2] _____, tall and [3] _____. Then, when you [4] _____ on a light in a darkened room, you'd never be surprised by seeing someone new and different. What if all we liked to drink was [5] _____, and no one would eat anything but chicken, eggs, rice, and peas? Even with all of our talents [6] _____, we still would have no variety! We wouldn't even be able to form a sports team or a musical group. I would ask for people to [7] _____ me from a world like this! If you will [8] _____ me to say so, we should be glad we live in a world with so many different types of people!

1. Underline the words naming the <u>combined</u> skills that a boardinghouse owner needed. Then, describe something you have done in which you used *combined* skills.

2. Underline words describing five types of people with whom boarders might come into <u>contact</u>. Then, explain what *contact* means.

3. Write a sentence describing what *frail blondes* might look like.

4. Circle the word naming something that could not be <u>switched</u> on. Then, write about something that had not been invented and could not be *switched* on in a boardinghouse.

5. Underline the word that tells what <u>cocoa</u> is. Tell what you like or don't like about *cocoa*.

6. Circle what owners would not <u>permit</u>. Then, describe something your parents will not *permit*.

7. Circle the words naming what an owner would ask a couple to <u>release</u>. Then, explain what *release* means.

Before World War II, the boardinghouse was a very important part of American culture. Boardinghouses were the answer to many people's problems.

Often, a single woman owned a boardinghouse. She might be a widow or someone who had never married. Running the house allowed her to keep it. In a world in which they weren't allowed to work at high-paying jobs, these women would have otherwise lost their big family homes. To run a boardinghouse, a woman needed the <u>combined</u> skills of cooking, cleaning, and managing helpers. If she also treated her guests kindly, she would certainly succeed. However, the work was hard. Owners rarely got a day off. Those staying at boardinghouses came into <u>contact</u> with many different types of people. Frail elderly people, traveling salesmen, and workers from the town all might chat briefly each day on their way in or out of the house. Fair-skinned young <u>blondes</u> and dark-haired ladies who were shop girls or teachers often stayed in boardinghouses, too. They were able to move away from home because of the safety that these houses offered.

Especially in the South, a boardinghouse could be found in nearly every town. From their stuffy bedrooms, where no televisions could be <u>switched</u> on, the guests would flee to the porch. Sitting together, sipping iced tea, they would talk and get to know one another. Even in cooler months, the porch was a meeting place. The owner might serve hot drinks such as <u>cocoa</u>, tea, or coffee to her guests in the evenings.

Many stories are told of young men and women who met and fell in love on boardinghouse porches. Their behavior had to be very proper. Boardinghouse owners would not even <u>permit</u> couples to hold hands. When an owner discovered couples with fingers entwined, she would ask them to <u>release</u> them. With so many chances just to talk, a young couple could really get to know each other before marrying.

Thank You, M'am
Langston Hughes

Summary A teenage boy tries to steal a woman's purse. The woman catches the boy and brings him to her home. She teaches him a lesson about kindness and trust.

 Writing About the Big Question

Can all conflicts be resolved? In "Thank You, M'am," a teenager attempts to commit a crime and is completely unprepared for his victim's reaction. Complete this sentence:

The best way to convince someone not to commit a crime of robbery

or violence is to _____.

Note-taking Guide
Use this diagram to summarize the major events of the story.

A boy tries to steal a woman's purse.

Activate Prior Knowledge

How do you think you would feel if you caught someone trying to steal from you?

_____

_____

Reading Skill

An **inference** is a logical guess. It is based on information in a story. Read the bracketed paragraph. What can you infer about the woman's personality? Circle any details that support your inference.

_____

_____

Literary Analysis 🔍

A **stated theme** is expressed directly. What does the woman want the boy to learn? Circle the text that supports your answer.

_____

_____

Reading Check

What causes the boy to lose his balance? Underline the text that tells you.

_____

_____

Thank You, M'am

Langston Hughes

This story tells how a woman's kindness surprises and changes a young man who has tried to rob her. She is a large woman, and she is walking home alone at night. She carries a very large purse with a long strap. A boy comes from behind her and tries to snatch her purse.

◆ ◆ ◆

The strap broke with the sudden single tug the boy gave it from behind. But the boy's weight and the weight of the purse combined caused him to lose his balance. Instead of taking off full blast as he had hoped, the boy fell on his back on the sidewalk and his legs flew up. The large woman simply turned around and kicked him right square in his blue-jeaned sitter.

◆ ◆ ◆

Next, the woman grabs the boy's shirt and picks him up in the air. She shakes him hard but doesn't let go of him. Then—still holding him—she asks whether he is ashamed of himself. The boy says that he is ashamed. Next, the woman asks the boy whether he will run away if she lets him go. He says that he will. She says that she will continue to hold on to him. The woman says that she is going to take the boy to her home to wash his dirty face. The boy is fourteen or fifteen years old. He looks frail and is dressed in tennis shoes and blue jeans. The woman starts dragging the boy toward her home. She announces that he ought to be her son—she would make sure to teach him "right from wrong." She decides that she may not be able to teach him that, but she can make sure he has a clean face that night. As she's dragging him along the street, she asks whether he's hungry.

◆ ◆ ◆

"No'm," said the being-dragged boy. "I just want you to turn me loose."

"Was I bothering *you* when I turned that corner?" asked the woman.

"No'm."

"But you put yourself in <u>contact</u> with *me*," said the woman. . . . "When I get through with you, sir, you are going to remember Mrs. Luella Bates Washington Jones."

❖ ❖ ❖

The boy struggles to get away, but Mrs. Jones drags him up the street and into her rooming house. He hears other people who rent rooms in the house. Mrs. Jones asks the boy his name, and he says that it is Roger.

❖ ❖ ❖

"Then, Roger, you go to that sink and wash your face," said the woman, whereupon she turned him loose—at last, Roger looked at the door—looked at the woman—looked at the door—*and went to the sink.*

❖ ❖ ❖

Roger asks Mrs. Jones whether she's going to send him to jail. She says not as long as he has such a dirty face. The boy tells her that he has not had supper because there's nobody at home at his house. So Mrs. Jones tells Roger that they'll eat. She thinks he must be hungry because he tried to take her purse.

❖ ❖ ❖

"I wanted a pair of blue suede shoes,"[1] said the boy.

"Well, you didn't have to snatch my pocketbook to get some suede shoes, . . . you could of asked me."

❖ ❖ ❖

© Pearson Education

Vocabulary Development

contact (KAHN takt) *n.* touch; communication

---

1. **blue suede** (swayd) **shoes** style of shoes worn by "hipsters" in the 1940s and 1950s; made famous in a song sung by Elvis Presley.

TAKE NOTES

Literary Analysis

The **theme** is the main idea, or message, in a story. Some themes are **unstated,** or **implied**. This means the author does not directly tell you the theme. What is the woman's attitude toward the boy?

_____

_____

_____

Reading Skill

You can **identify connections to make inferences about the author's meaning**. You should look for what characters do and why they do it. Why do you think Roger goes to the sink instead of the door?

_____

_____

_____

Read Fluently

A contraction combines two words and makes them into one word. A writer uses an apostrophe (') to make a contraction. Read the bracketed passage. Circle the contraction. What two words were combined to make this word?

_____

Literary Analysis

What do you think is the story's **theme,** or main point?

_____

_____

_____

_____

Reading Skill

Why does Mrs. Jones give Roger ten dollars to buy himself shoes? Make an **inference** that is based on details in the text.

_____

_____

_____

Stop to Reflect

Would you have been speechless at the end of the story, as Roger is? If not, what do you think you would have said to Mrs. Jones?

_____

_____

_____

Reading Check

Where does Mrs. Jones work? Circle the text that tells you.

This answer surprises Roger. He is not used to generous people. When Mrs. Jones steps behind a screen and he has a chance to run away, he doesn't. Later, Mrs. Jones tells Roger that she was once young and did some bad things, too—things she does not want to talk about. Roger now wants the woman to trust him. He asks her whether she needs some milk at the store. She says she does not, and she offers to make him some cocoa; he accepts. She then heats up some ham and beans and feeds him dinner.

During dinner, Mrs. Jones tells Roger all about her life and her job at a hotel beauty shop. She describes all of the beautiful women who come in and out of the store.

◆　◆　◆

When they were finished eating, she got up and said, "Now here take this ten dollars and buy yourself some blue suede shoes. And next time, do not make the mistake of latching onto *my* pocketbook *nor nobody else's.* . . . Goodnight! Behave yourself, boy!" she said, looking into the street as he went down the steps.

The boy wanted to say something other than, "Thank you, m'am," to Mrs. Luella Bates Washington Jones, but although his lips moved, he couldn't even say that as he turned at the foot of the barren stoop and looked up at the large woman in the door. Then she shut the door.

Vocabulary Development

latching (LACH ing) *v.* grasping or attaching oneself to

barren (BER uhn) *adj.* empty

Thank You, M'am

1. **Interpret:** Why is Roger unable to say what he wants to say as he leaves the apartment?

   _____

   _____

   _____

2. **Predict:** Mrs. Jones feeds Roger and gives him money. How might Mrs. Jones's behavior affect Roger's future actions?

   _____

   _____

   _____

3. **Reading Skill:** An **inference** is a logical guess that is based on information in a story. What inference can you make about the author's message about stealing?

   _____

   _____

   _____

4. **Literary Analysis:** The **theme** is the main message in a story. A theme for the story has been written below. Tell whether it is **stated** or **implied**. Write details in the second column to support the interpretation.

Theme (stated or implied)	Details
Trust and kindness can change someone's life.	

Writing: Personal Essay

Write a **personal essay** showing how a theme of "Thank You, M'am" applies to everyday life. Use the outline to organize your essay.

A. Introduction of Your Essay

   1. State your theme:_____

   _____

   2. Summarize your experiences: _____

   _____

   _____

B. Conclusion of Your Essay

   1. Restate your theme: _____

   _____

   _____

   2. Explain how your theme applies to everyday life: _____

   _____

   Use your notes to help you write your personal essay.

Listening and Speaking: Panel Discussion

Complete the following questionnaire to prepare for the **panel discussion.**

• Did Mrs. Jones do the right thing? Explain. _____

   _____

• Reasons that support your opinion

   _____

   _____

Word List A

Study these words from "The Story-Teller." Then, apply your knowledge to the activity that follows.

approval [uh PROO vuhl] *n.* good opinion
The mother looked at her son with approval *after he cleaned his room.*

conduct [KAHN duhkt] *n.* the way a person behaves
The conduct *of the students really changed when a substitute teacher was there.*

horribly [HAWR uh blee] *adv.* to an awful extent; disagreeably
The book was horribly *hard to read as well as boring.*

momentarily [moh muhn TER uh lee] *adv.* for a short time
The television screen was momentarily *black when the power went off.*

promptly [PRAHMPT lee] *adv.* very quickly; immediately
The waiter promptly *came to our table to take our order.*

retort [ri TAWRT] *n.* quick and clever reply
My sister always seems to have a retort *for what I thought were good ideas.*

unspeakable [un SPEE kuh buhl] *adj.* so bad that you can't describe it; extremely bad
To make rude comments about Grandma seemed unspeakable *to me.*

utterly [UHT er lee] *adv.* completely
I knew Dad was utterly *lost when he pulled over to study the map.*

Exercise A

Fill in the blanks using each word from Word List A only once.

The track team's [1] _____ on the bus while going to meets had

become [2] _____. The runners were mean to each other and

[3] _____ rude to the driver. The coach decided she had to take action.

She began the next trip by saying the team would be [4] _____ silent

for the first thirty miles. A runner's snort and scornful [5] _____ to

her words landed him [6] _____ in the back row of the bus, far from

anyone else. After pausing [7] _____ to be sure she had everyone's

attention again, the coach continued to state her plan. After thirty miles,

each runner would have a chance to speak. Each would make a kind

statement about the team. Only with the coach's [8] _____ could

talking begin again.

1. Underline the words describing a <u>horribly</u> sad position to be in. Then, describe something else that is *horribly* sad.

2. Circle the word that is the <u>unspeakable</u> name of a medical condition. Then, explain what *unspeakable* means.

3. Write a sentence about parents that includes both the words *approval* and *conduct*.

4. Underline the words naming what the author was <u>utterly</u> determined to do. Then, explain what *utterly* means.

5. Circle the words that describe what feelings the author <u>momentarily</u> had upon seeing Sam. Then, explain what *momentarily* means.

6. Underline the words that describe what caused the author to <u>promptly</u> change his mood. Describe what you think he *promptly* did as a result.

7. Circle what the narrator expected Sam to give a <u>retort</u> to. Explain why Sam's ability to give a *retort* would be wonderful news.

Read the following passage. Pay special attention to the underlined words. Then, read it again, and complete the activities. Use a separate sheet of paper for your written answers.

No one should ever be in the <u>horribly</u> sad position of watching a best friend lie motionless in bed, hardly seeming to be alive. The doctors call this awful condition a coma, but I think its name should be <u>unspeakable</u>.

Anyway, I found myself in this position last year. My best friend was in a terrible car crash, and he then went into a coma. It took a few days for me to visit Sam. My desire to visit met with the <u>approval</u> of Sam's parents and doctor. Yet, everyone thought I needed lots of talking to about the proper <u>conduct</u> I should have in the hospital room. Despite the waiting and the talking, I was <u>utterly</u> determined to see my friend.

When I finally entered the room, I was <u>momentarily</u> choked up by what I saw. Sam was very still and very pale. All kinds of tubes and machines were attached to him. I didn't like the sight, the sounds, or the smells of that room. After a few seconds, however, I looked more closely at Sam's face. I <u>promptly</u> snapped out of it. Sam—my buddy since preschool, the source of my best memories—needed me.

I had read that people in comas can hear and understand you. Therefore, I wasn't going to sit silently by Sam's bed. My plan was to tell Sam the story of our lives together. I would start at the beginning. For the one hour I was given each day, I would tell our tale in all its glory. Sam and I would grow up together again through my storytelling. Before too many days had passed, I knew—no, I believed with all my heart—Sam would open his eyes and give a smart <u>retort</u> to some story detail I had managed to mess up.

It was time to begin. "We met the first day of preschool," I said, "when you tried to take the big red truck away from me. . . ." I could see Sam's eyes blink!

The Story-Teller
Saki (H.H. Munro)

Summary A stranger on a train tells a story that entertains three children. The story's ending makes the children's aunt very angry. It goes against all of her lectures about proper behavior.

 Writing About the Big Question

Can all conflicts be resolved? In "The Story-Teller," three bored children on a train are entertained by an unusual fairy tale told by an unlikely fellow passenger. Complete this sentence:

One way to amuse a child is _____.

Note-taking Guide
Use the chart to recall the events of the story.

Problem	The children will not be quiet on the trip.
Event	
Event	
Event	
Outcome	

The Story-Teller

1. **Analyze:** Do you think the bachelor feels sorry for the aunt or for the children? Think about his actions in the story. Explain your answer.

   _____

   _____

2. **Evaluate:** The aunt says that the bachelor's story is not appropriate for children. Do you agree? Why or why not?

   _____

   _____

3. **Reading Skill:** An **inference** is a logical guess that is based on details in a story. The author comments on what children like and how children should be raised. What inference can you make about what the author thinks?

   _____

   _____

   _____

4. **Literary Analysis:** The **theme** is the main idea of a story. It can be **stated** or **implied**. The theme of the story is written in the first column. Decide whether the theme is **stated** or **implied**. In the second column, write details from the story that support the theme.

Theme (stated or implied)	Details
Stories should entertain, not preach.	

Writing: Personal Essay

Write a **personal essay** showing how a theme of "The Story-Teller" applies to everyday life. Use the outline to help organize your essay.

A. Introduction of Your Essay

    1. State your theme: _____

    _____

    2. Summarize your experiences: _____

    _____

    _____

B. Conclusion of Your Essay

    1. Restate your theme: _____

    _____

    2. Explain how your theme applies to everyday life: _____

    _____

Listening and Speaking: Panel Discussion

Have a **panel discussion**. Discuss whether the bachelor should have told the children such a gruesome story. Use the questions below to prepare your thoughts before the discussion.

1. Do you think there are some things that should always be included in a children's story? Give one example.

    _____

2. Do you think there are some things that should never be included in a children's story? Give one example.

    _____

Advertisements

About Advertisements

Advertisements are paid messages. Companies use advertising to persuade customers to buy products or services. Advertisers use appeals to do this. An appeal is a technique used to make a product attractive or interesting. Advertisers use two kinds of appeals:

- **Rational appeals** are based on facts. These ads may show how different products compare. They may show product features. Sometimes these appeals talk about price.

- **Emotional appeals** are based on feelings. Such appeals suggest that customers will be happier, more respected, or more popular if they buy a certain product.

Reading Skill

You can **evaluate persuasive appeals** by determining whether they are rational appeals or emotional appeals. Recognizing the difference can help you understand how an advertisement works. Recognize and ignore an emotional appeal because it is not based on facts. Use facts to help make up your mind.

Study the chart below. It shows some common emotional appeals that advertisers and writers use. Question whether you believe these arguments.

Device	Example	Explanation
Bandwagon appeal	Everyone loves Muncheez!	Words like *everyone* appeal to people's desire to belong.
Loaded language	Muncheez is incredibly delicious.	*Incredibly* and *delicious* are claims that cannot be proved.
Testimonials	Tina Idol says Muncheez gives her energy.	Just because a celebrity or "expert" says it, it does not mean the claim is true.
Generalization	Muncheez is not only the best, it's the healthiest.	Claims that are too broad or vague cannot be proved.

say "GOOD-BYE" to

WINTER!

IT'S A PLEASANT TRIP TO SUNNY CALIFORNIA

ON WESTERN PACIFIC'S VISTA-DOME TRAINS
¡OBSERVATION-DECK¡

ONLY $48.79 FROM CHICAGO
(Federal Tax Extra)

For fun and sun be a modern '49er. Follow the trail of the pioneers to Golden California for a vacation you'll never forget. The time to go West is now—while California celebrates her 100th birthday—and the way to go West is WESTERN PACIFIC. You'll see more, and enjoy the lowest cost fares and the world's newest and most luxurious "sleeper" chair cars, when you travel on W.P.'s VISTA-DOME trains. Also through Standard Pullmans between New York, Chicago, and San Francisco. Daily schedules from Chicago and San Francisco.

The bandwagon appeal in this paragraph compares modern train travelers to pioneers of the 1800s.

WESTERN PACIFIC

YOU'LL SEE MORE ON **W.P.**

HOLIDAY/FEBRUARY

© Pearson Education

This illustration implies that the advertiser brings cities closer together—a claim that cannot be proved.

HARRISBURGPHILADELPHIANEWYORK

B r i n g i n g   y o u r   f a v o r i t e   places **closer**

AMTRAK®

Loaded words such as *relaxed* and *refreshed* imply that the advertiser's train service can improve passengers' well-being.

Arrive at your destination relaxed and refreshed. Amtrak offers safe, comfortable, affordable daily service from Harrisburg to Philadelphia and New York with 12 local stops between Harrisburg and Philadelphia. Choose from 10 weekday or 5 weekend departures, from Harrisburg or returning. Daily departures from Harrisburg to Pittsburgh, Chicago and most major cities. Ask about our discounts for children 2-15, seniors, students, commuters, AAA members, disabled travelers and government employees.

Call for details

Thinking About the Advertisements

1. The ad describes advantages of traveling by train. What words or phrases in the ad identify the advantages?

_____

2. The most important purpose of the advertisement is to sell train tickets. What is a secondary, or less important, purpose?

_____

TALK ABOUT IT Reading Skill

3. To what emotions does the advertisement appeal?

_____

4. On what part of train travel does the ad focus most?

_____

WRITE ABOUT IT ➤ Timed Writing: Evaluation (20 minutes)

Evaluate the persuasive appeals used in this ad. Be sure to answer the following questions in your evaluation.

• What kinds of appeals does the ad make?

_____

• What words or pictures does the ad use to persuade customers to travel by train?

_____

• Would you be persuaded by the ad to travel by train?

_____

Making Tracks on Mars: A Journal Based on a Blog

Essays and articles are types of nonfiction. These types of nonfiction discuss real people, events, places, and ideas. You can explore these pieces to:

- learn about the lives of others
- find important information
- reflect on new ideas
- look at arguments about important issues

Organization is the way a writer arranges information in a piece of nonfiction. The chart below contains different types of organization. Many pieces of nonfiction use a combination of these types of organization. It depends on the author's reasons for writing.

Types of Organization	
Organization	Characteristics
Chronological Organization	presents details in time order—from first to last—or sometimes from last to first
Comparison-and-Contrast Organization	shows the ways in which two or more subjects are similar and different
Cause-and-Effect Organization	shows the relationship among events
Problem-and-Solution Organization	identifies problem and then proposes a solution

Author's tone is the writer's attitude toward his or her audience and subject. This tone can often be described by a single adjective, such as: *formal* or *informal, serious* or *playful, friendly* or *cold.*

Voice is a writer's way of "speaking" in his or her writing. One writer could write a piece in one voice. Then, he or she could write in a different voice in another work. Voice may also represent a characteristic literary personality. Voice can be based on

- word choice
- tone
- sound devices
- pace
- grammatical structure

Here are the most common types of nonfiction writing:

- **Letters:** written texts addressed to a certain person or organization

- **Memoirs and journals:** personal thoughts and reflections

- **Web logs** (also known as "blogs"): journals posted and often updated for an online audience

- **Biography:** a life story written by another person

- **Autobiography:** a writer's account of her or her own life

- **Media accounts:** nonfiction works written for newspapers, magazines, television, or radio

Essays and **articles** are short nonfiction works about a certain subject. They may follow the structure of these types of writing:

- **Persuasive writing:** convinces the reader that he or she should have a certain opinion or take a certain action

- **Expository writing:** presents facts or explains a process

- **Narrative writing:** tells the story of real-life experiences

- **Reflective writing:** looks at an experience and has the writer's thoughts about the event's importance

Word List A

Study these words from the "Making Tracks on Mars." Then, complete the activities that follow.

critical [KRIT i kuhl] *adj.* very serious or very dangerous
  The situation was critical, and we could do nothing to fix it.

exploration [ek spluh RAY shuhn] *n.* an examination of an unknown place
  Thorough exploration of the cave took a total of three days.

meteor [MEE tee uhr] *n.* a chunk of rock or metal from space
  The meteor streaked through the sky and crashed on Earth.

operations [ahp uh RAY shuhnz] *n.* the managing and running of something
  Mr. Phillips is in charge of operations monitoring at the plant.

panels [PAN uhlz] *n.* flat pieces of material
  We installed plywood panels on the walls of the basement.

software [SAWFT wair] *adj.* having to do with computer programs
  Jones, a software engineer, revised the computer payroll program.

solar [SOH ler] *adj.* having to do with the sun or its power
  In a solar eclipse, the moon moves between the earth and the sun.

spacecraft [SPAYS kraft] *n.* vehicle that goes into space
  The United States launched a spacecraft to explore the outer planets.

Exercise A

Fill in each blank in the paragraph below with an appropriate word from Word List A. Use each word only once.

[1] _____ of the moon's surface began on the second day following

the landing of the newly designed [2] _____. The robotic surveyor,

which would do the work, depended on energy from [3] _____

[4] _____ that captured sunlight. In case of a system failure, the

[5] _____ programmers had built a backup system. If both energy

sources failed, however, the situation would become [6] _____.

On Earth, the people in charge of [7] _____ control had to hope

that wouldn't happen. Luckily, the surveyor completed its investigation

with no problems. It took rock samples from a crater formed when a

[8] _____ crashed on the surface. These samples were the first from

this particular bowl-shaped hollow.

Read the following passage. Pay special attention to the underlined words. Then, read it again, and complete the activities. Use a separate sheet of paper for your written answers.

In 1965, we got our first close-up picture of the planet Mars. Since then, spacecraft traveling by and landing on the red planet have shown us an amazing world. Exploration of Mars has brought us increasing knowledge of this cold, rocky wasteland.

Clues hint at past conditions quite different from those today. For example, at one time, volcanoes erupted on Mars. Many a meteor, streaking through the sky, crashed and left deep craters.

The big question today for most scientists is whether life ever existed on Mars. To find out, operations managers at the U.S. space agency have developed a strategy called "follow the water." Scientists gather data from features such as the polar ice caps and dry riverbeds. They hope this work will show that water once may have covered parts of the planet. They also hope to find hot springs or pockets of water beneath the Martian surface.

Advances in computers have been a huge help in studying Mars. Here on Earth, scientists can receive data from a Mars explorer that moves along the surface. If the explorer stops working properly, they can correct its programs.

One problem that equipment on Mars has had is dust from the planet's surface. Dust forms a layer on the spacecraft's solar panels. These collect sunlight and change it to the electricity the spacecraft needs. If the spaceship does not get enough power, the situation could become critical. A mission might have to end early unless software engineers can develop a computer program to fix the problem.

Will people ever travel to Mars? Scientists need to know a lot more than they do now to send humans there. If humans do walk on Mars, might they be able to discover more than any robot can? Perhaps in your lifetime you'll find out!

1. Circle the words that tell where spacecraft have landed. Explain whether you would like to travel on a *spacecraft*.

2. Circle the words that tell what exploration has resulted in. Tell about an *exploration* of your own.

3. Underline the words that help explain what a meteor is. Write about what could happen if a *meteor* crashed on Earth.

4. Circle what operations managers have done. Describe what *operations* managers might do in an ice-cream factory.

5. Underline the sentence that tells what solar panels do. Explain what *solar panels* are.

6. Circle the sentence that tells what might happen if a mission becomes critical. Describe what might happen if a hospital patient becomes *critical*.

7. Circle the words that tell you what a software engineer works with. Describe some *software* that you have used.

Making Tracks on Mars: A Journal Based on a Blog

Andrew Mishkin

Summary Andrew Mishkin talks about the landing of the rover, *Spirit*, on Mars. The rover explores the planet. It experiences some problems. Mishkin describes his excitement and worry. He also talks about another Mars rover, *Opportunity*. He describes the pictures it takes of Mars.

Note-taking Guide

Use the chart to recall the main events of Mishkin's journal.

> *Opportunity* lands on Mars. Mishkin describes the pictures it takes.

Making Tracks on Mars: A Journal Based on a Blog

Andrew Mishkin

♦ ♦ ♦

The journal opens with the question of whether life ever existed on Mars. We know that water is needed for life as we know it. Mars appears to have no water, but what about in the past? Two robotic explorers are scheduled to land on the planet soon. In six days, *Spirit* will arrive there. Three weeks later, *Opportunity* will. The author talks about a British spacecraft that tried to land on Mars five days earlier but has sent back no signals. The author hopes that *Spirit* lands smoothly. Saturday, January 3, 2004, is landing day.

♦ ♦ ♦

Spirit's lander must be hitting the atmosphere, a falling <u>meteor</u> blazing in the Martian sky. We'd named the next moments "the six minutes of terror." I listened to the reports on the voice network. All the way down, radio signals from the spacecraft told us "so far so good." Then, immediately after the lander hit the ground, contact was lost. Everyone tensed up. Time dragged. There was only silence from Mars.

Ten minutes later, we got another signal. *Spirit* had survived! The engineers and scientists in mission control were screaming, cheering, thrusting their fists in the air. We were on Mars!

♦ ♦ ♦

Activate Prior Knowledge

What do you know about the solar system? What are some words you think of when you hear *Mars*?

_____

_____

_____

Nonfiction

The way a writer arranges events is called **organization**. How is the bracketed passage organized?

_____

Circle the words in the passage that helped you reach your answer.

Nonfiction

The **author's tone** is the writer's attitude toward his or her audience and subject. Circle the letter of the answer that best describes the author's tone toward his subject.

A. formal
B. cold
C. excited

Underline the words and phrases that support your choice.

Vocabulary Development

meteor (MEE tee er) *n.* a small piece of rock or metal that produces a bright burning line in the sky

Read Fluently

Sometimes writers use commas (,) to tell readers where to pause while reading. Read the bracketed paragraph. Circle all of the places in the passage where you should pause while reading.

Stop to Reflect

What was an important day that you prepared for once? Describe how you felt when that day came.

_____

_____

_____

_____

_____

Reading Check

What is affected by "Mars days"? Underline everything and everyone that is affected by "Mars days."

Pictures start arriving from *Spirit* within two hours. The pictures are clear. They show the view through *Spirit's* eyes from the landing site. The next entry is January 11, 2004. The engineers are working on Mars time. The next task is to send a signal commanding *Spirit* to drive around and take some pictures.

◆   ◆   ◆

The Mars day (called a "sol") is just a bit longer than an Earth day, at twenty-four hours and thirty-nine and a half minutes. Since the rover is solar powered, and wakes with the sun, its activities are tied to the Martian day. And so are the work shifts of our operations team on Earth. Part of the team works the Martian day, interacting with the spacecraft, sending commands, and analyzing the results. But those of us who build new commands for the rover work the Martian night, while the rover sleeps.

◆   ◆   ◆

It is difficult for the engineers to keep track of time. Because the rover wakes up about forty Earth minutes later each day, so do the engineers. By January 15, the author is getting Mars time and Earth time mixed up.

◆   ◆   ◆

My team delivered the commands for sol 12—drive off day—but nobody went home. This would be *Spirit's* most dangerous day since landing. There was a small chance the rover could tip over or get stuck as it rolled off the lander platform onto the dust of Mars. When the time came, the Flight Director played the theme from "Rawhide"—"rollin', rollin', rollin'..."[1]—and everyone crowded into mission control cheered and applauded. The command to drive shot through space.

◆   ◆   ◆

1. **"Rawhide"** popular 1960s television show about cattle drivers in the 1860s. Its theme song was also extremely popular.

Even though they have done their jobs, the engineers continue to worry about what might go wrong. On January 15, twelve days after the landing, they get a signal from *Spirit*. Images begin to appear. They see wheel tracks in the Martian soil. Knowing that *Spirit* has obeyed the command to move, the engineers go wild with applause and joy. By January 22, the rover stops responding. The engineers try for days to fix the problem. Finally, they start receiving data from Spirit. It is garbled, but now they have something to work with.

Meanwhile, *Opportunity*, the second rover, has been approaching Mars. It lands safely and begins to take photos.

◆ ◆ ◆

Opportunity's first photos were amazing, even for Mars. It looks like we rolled to a stop at the bottom of a bowl—actually a small crater. The soil is a grayish red, except where we've disturbed it with our airbags; there it looks like a deep pure red.

◆ ◆ ◆

Opportunity also sends back pictures of a rock outcropping. This is unlike anything ever seen on Mars before. One scientist in mission control says, "Jackpot!"

Nonfiction

Expository writing presents facts or explains a process. What facts does the author give about *Opportunity's* landing site?

_____

_____

_____

_____

Nonfiction

Readers learn about real people and their lives when reading nonfiction. What do you learn about engineers' lives in the bracketed paragraph?

_____

_____

_____

Reading Check

What happened to the rover *Opportunity?* Underline the sentences in the text that tell you.

Vocabulary Development

crater (KRAY ter) *n.* a round hole in the ground

© Pearson Education

Types of Nonfiction

1. **Infer:** A British spacecraft tried to land on Mars. It failed. Why does Mishkin mention this failure?

   _____

   _____

2. **Speculate:** Mishkin sometimes talks about the robot as if it were a person. Why do you think he does this?

   _____

   _____

   _____

3. **Nonfiction: Reflective writing** includes the writer's insights about an event's importance. Use the chart to identify one personal **reflection** of Mishkin's. Write a related fact or event that created the reflection.

Personal Reflection		Event
"Opportunity's first photos were amazing, even for Mars."	◀- - -▶	The land and the soil were unlike anything anyone had seen before.
	◀- - -▶	

4. **Nonfiction: Voice** is a writer's way of "speaking" in his or her writing. Mishkin's voice is more casual than literary. Do you agree or disagree? Explain.

   _____

   _____

   _____

Illustrated Report

Prepare an **illustrated report** about Andrew Mishkin and the Mars mission. Use the following tips to create your report.

- Search the Internet or the library for information on Andrew Mishkin.

  What I learned about Andrew Mishkin: _____

  _____

  _____

  _____

- Search the Internet or the library for information on the Mars mission.

  What I learned about the goals of the mission: _____

  _____

  _____

  _____

  What I learned about the results of the exploration: _____

  _____

  _____

  _____

  _____

- Watch the video interview with Andrew Mishkin. Add what you learn from the video to what you have already learned about the author.

  Additional information about the author: _____

  _____

  _____

  _____

Use your notes to write your illustrated report.

Baseball • Harriet Tubman: Guide to Freedom

Reading Skill

A nonfiction writing piece has a **main idea**. A main idea is the author's central message. Sometimes an author explains the main idea to the reader. Other times an author hints at, or implies, the main idea.

Look at how details are connected to **identify the implied main idea**. Try to see what the details have in common. You should then be able to figure out the main idea of a passage or work.

Literary Analysis

A **narrative essay** tells the story of real events, people, and places. Narrative essays have some things in common with fictional stories. For example, both have these parts:

- People's traits are developed through things they say, do, and think.

- The setting of the action may be important.

Use this chart to track the elements of a narrative essay.

Narrative Essay		
Setting(s)	People	Event(s)

© Pearson Education

Word List A

Study these words from "Baseball." Then, complete the activity.

complicate [KAHM pli kayt] *v.* to make something more difficult
Don't complicate a simple recipe, and it will turn out well.

exception [ek SEP shuhn] *n.* someone or something not included
Today is a holiday and there is an exception to the no parking rules.

exhausted [eg ZAWST id] *adj.* very tired
When Ben finished his first day as a sales clerk, he was exhausted.

fielder [FEEL der] *n.* a baseball player other than pitcher or catcher
An all-around baseball player is a good hitter and a good fielder.

ignorance [IG nuhr uhns] *n.* lack of knowledge or information
Teri tried to cover her ignorance of history by changing subjects.

professional [pruh FESH uh nuhl] *adj.* playing a sport for money
Harry wanted to play professional football, but he broke his leg.

scheme [SKEEM] *n.* plan
Carrie came up with a brilliant scheme to raise money.

standard [STAN derd] *adj.* usual or normal
The standard amount for parking at the stadium is five dollars.

Exercise A

Fill in each blank in the paragraph below with an appropriate word from Word List A. Use each word only once.

All of us at training camp, without [1] _____, wanted to become [2] _____ ballplayers. Our coach said, whether we wanted to be a pitcher or a [3] _____, we had to be "better than good." Out of [4] _____ about how hard we'd have to work, we all stupidly started boasting about our great chances. Then, the daily [5] _____ began. It seemed so simple: train, eat, sleep. There was nothing to [6] _____ our routine, and we had no excuse for not sticking to the [7] _____ procedures. We were in the middle of nowhere, far from any town. Then, one week passed and we were feeling totally [8] _____. We could hardly move. It was then that we began to understand what our coach meant about being "better than good."

1   Circle the group that is described as underlined professional. Write a sentence using *professional*.

2. Underline the words that tell in what way the major league was no exception on the homefront. Then, use *exception* in a sentence.

3. Circle the word in the next sentence that is a synonym for scheme. Then, explain what Wrigley's *scheme* was.

4. Circle the names of positions played in baseball. Explain what a *fielder* is.

5. Circle the words that tell why the women were exhausted. Then, tell about a time you were *exhausted*.

6. Underline the words that tell what could complicate the women's already busy schedule. Then, write a sentence using *complicate*.

7. Circle the words that tell what was standard. Then, explain what *standard* means.

8. Write a sentence describing something you thought out of ignorance and tell why you were wrong.

Read the following passage. Pay special attention to the underlined words. Then, read it again, and complete the activities. Use a separate sheet of paper for your written answers.

Girls playing baseball? That thought amazed some people in 1943. It was during World War II, and many professional ballplayers were on a different field—the battlefield. Too few men remained at home to fill jobs. Major league baseball was no exception. It, too, was in need of players.

Philip K. Wrigley, owner of the Chicago Cubs, knew that many young American women played softball and enjoyed it. He came up with a scheme to find players from all over the country. According to his plan, they would play in a women's league in the Midwest. He started with four teams.

Many young women tried out for the few spots on the teams. Just like the men, woman had to demonstrate skill on the field. They also had to be models of good behavior off the field. Pitcher, catcher, and fielder—each and every player—trained hard until they were exhausted. To complicate a busy week of training and games, they also had to travel. The distance between cities may not seem great today, but roads and vehicles were much less developed in the 1940s.

The women worked hard, and the All-American Girls Professional Baseball League became a success. Standard softball rules were changed to make them more like men's professional baseball.

After the war was over and the men returned, many people, perhaps out of ignorance, expected the league to fold, but it only grew stronger. In 1948, ten teams played in the league and almost a million fans filled the stands.

Why did the league finally end in 1954? Television was bringing baseball games into people's homes, and attendance at games dropped. As the teams lost their fans, money to advertise games and to bring on new players dried up. All the same, the All-American Girls made their mark, however brief, on the history of baseball.

Baseball
Lionel G. García

Summary The author shares a memory from his childhood in this story. He describes the new rules of baseball that he and his childhood friends invented. García presents a snapshot into the world of a young Catholic boy through this story.

 Writing About the Big Question

How much information is enough? In "Baseball," the author shows how much fun he and his friends had playing their own version of baseball as children. Complete this sentence:

In order to reveal what the world looks like from a child's perspective,

a writer can include information such as _____

_____.

Note-taking Guide

García explains how he used to play baseball in his neighborhood. Use this chart to describe the role of each player in the game.

Catcher	Batter	Pitcher	Bases	Outfielders

Baseball
Lionel G. García

We loved to play baseball. We would take the old mesquite[1] stick and the old ball across the street to the parochial[2] school grounds to play a game. Father Zavala enjoyed watching us. We could hear him laugh mightily from the screened porch at the rear of the rectory[3] where he sat.

The way we played baseball was to <u>rotate</u> positions after every out. First base, the only base we used, was located where one would normally find second base. This made the batter have to run past the pitcher and a long way to the first baseman, increasing the odds of getting thrown out. The pitcher stood in line with the batter, and with first base, and could stand as close or as far from the batter as he or she wanted. Aside from the pitcher, the batter and the first baseman, we had a catcher. All the rest of us would stand in the outfield. After an out, the catcher would come up to bat. The pitcher took the position of catcher, and the first baseman moved up to be the pitcher. Those in the outfield were left to their own <u>devices</u>. I don't remember ever getting to bat.

◆ ◆ ◆

Another rule of the children's game was that the player who caught a ball on the fly would become the next batter. Also, first base was wherever Matías, Juan, or Cota tossed a stone. The size of the stone was more important than how far it fell from

Activate Prior Knowledge

How do you feel when playing a group sport or game?

_____

_____

_____

_____

Literary Analysis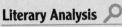

A **narrative essay** tells the story of real events, people, and places. What does the description of the boy's equipment in the bracketed paragraph tell you about the setting and people in this narrative?

_____

_____

_____

_____

_____

_____

Reading Check

Who enjoyed watching the boys play baseball? Underline the sentence that tells you.

Vocabulary Development
rotate (ROH tayt) *v.* change
devices (di VYS iz) *n.* techniques or means for working things out

1. **mesquite** (me SKEET) *n.* thorny shrub of North America.
2. **parochial** (puh ROH kee uhl) *adj.* supported by a church.
3. **rectory** (REK tuhr ee) *n.* residence for priests.

home plate. First base was sometimes hard to find as it started to get dark.

◆ ◆ ◆

When the batter hit the ball in the air and it was caught that was an out. So far so good. But if the ball hit the ground, the fielder had two choices. One, in keeping with the standard rules of the game, the ball could be thrown to the first baseman and, if caught before the batter arrived at the base, that was an out. But the second, more interesting option allowed the fielder, ball in hand, to take off running after the batter. When close enough, the fielder would throw the ball at the batter. If the batter was hit before reaching first base, the batter was out. But if the batter evaded being hit with the ball, he or she could either run to first base or run back to home plate. All the while, everyone was chasing the batter, picking up the ball and throwing it at him or her. To complicate matters, on the way to home plate the batter had the choice of running anywhere possible to avoid getting hit.

◆ ◆ ◆

Sometimes the batters hid behind trees until they could reach home plate. Sometimes they ran several blocks toward town. In one game, the children ended up across town. They cornered the batter, held him down, and hit him with the ball. The tired players all fell down laughing in a pile. The men in town watched these unusual games, but they did not understand them.

◆ ◆ ◆

It was the only kind of baseball game Father Zavala had ever seen. What a wonderful game it must have been for him to see us hit the ball,

Vocabulary Development

standard (STAN derd) *adj.* typical, ordinary

option (AHP shuhn) *n.* choice

evaded (i VAYD id) *v.* avoided

TAKE NOTES

Reading Skill

The **main idea** of a nonfiction work is the author's central message. Often, the author suggests the main idea. Read the bracketed passage. What main idea is implied? Circle the details that support this main idea.

_____

_____

Read Fluently

One way to organize a list of details in a paragraph is to use a number system. You could write *first, second,* and *third.* Another choice would be *one, two,* and *three.* The author uses a number system to tell about the fielder's choices in the bracketed paragraph. Underline the key words he uses to organize his list.

Stop to Reflect

Name one difference between this game and regular baseball.

_____

_____

_____

© Pearson Education

Literary Analysis

In this **narrative essay**, the narrator discusses two people who watched the game. Compare Father Zavala's view of the neighborhood game with that of Uncle Adolfo. Who enjoys watching the boys more? Why do you think he enjoys watching them more?

_____

_____

_____

Reading Check

What did García's uncle say when he saw how the children were playing baseball? Underline the sentence that tells the answer.

run to a rock, then run for our lives down the street. He loved the game, shouting from the screened porch at us, pushing us on. And then all of a sudden we were gone, running after the batter. What a game! In what enormous stadium would it be played to allow such freedom over such an <u>expanse</u> of ground.

◆ ◆ ◆

García's Uncle Adolfo had been a major league pitcher. He had given the ball to the children. When he saw how the children played the sport, he said that they were wasting a good baseball.

Vocabulary Development
expanse (ik spans) *n.* a large area

Baseball

1. **Analyze Cause and Effect:** Think about where first base was located in García's version of baseball. How did this location of the base affect the way he and his friends played the game?

_____

_____

2. **Take a Position:** García's Uncle Adolfo played baseball for the Yankees as a young man. When he sees the way García and his friends are playing the game, he says that they are wasting a good baseball. Do you agree with his statement? Explain.

_____

_____

3. **Reading Skill:** Read the details about the baseball game listed in the diagram below. Then, write a sentence that states the **main idea**.

Detail	+	Detail	+	Detail	=	Main Idea
The boys did not have good equipment.		The boys did not know official baseball rules.				

4. **Literary Analysis:** A setting describes the place and time of a story. Identify the setting in this **narrative essay**.

_____

_____

Writing: Biographical Sketch

Write a **biographical sketch** of a famous leader, athlete, or entertainer who ignored the old rules for success and found a new way to do something. Use this chart to organize details about the person you choose. Use your notes as you write your biographical sketch.

What is this person's name?	Name three things that describe this person.	What is this person known for doing?	How did this person find a different way of doing something?

Listening and Speaking: Skit

Write a **skit** about children playing official baseball or a variation of it. Answer the following questions to help prepare your skit. Use your notes as you write your final draft.

- Where is your favorite place to play baseball?

_____

_____

- What do you do if there are not enough or too many players?

_____

_____

_____

_____

- Name one baseball rule you dislike. How would you change it?

_____

_____

_____

_____

Word List A

Study these words from the excerpt from "Harriet Tubman: Guide to Freedom." Then, complete the activity that follows.

husky [HUHS kee] *adj.* (of a voice) deep and rough
María's high soprano was a strong contrast to Marco's <u>husky</u> voice.

hysterical [hi STER i kuhl] *adj.* out of control because of fear, excitement, or anger
In an emergency, it's important not to become <u>hysterical</u>.

reluctance [ri LUHK tuhns] *n.* unwillingness to do something
The show was so wonderful that the audience had a <u>reluctance</u> to see it end.

serenity [se REN i tee] *n.* calmness or peacefulness
Dale found a strange <u>serenity</u> even with all the noise around him.

succession [suhk SESH uhn] *n.* one thing after another
Amanda tried on four coats in <u>succession</u>, but did not like any of them.

sufficient [suh FISH uhnt] *adj.* enough; as much as you need
With <u>sufficient</u> preparation, you should be able to learn your lines.

underground [UN der grownd] *adj.* secret; hidden
School officials found the <u>underground</u> newspaper annoying.

vicinity [vi SIN i tee] *n.* the area around a specific place
If you're going to be in the <u>vicinity</u> on Sunday, stop by.

Exercise A

Fill in each blank in the paragraph below with an appropriate word from Word List A. Use each word only once.

During the war, unknown to many, an [1] _____ army fought bravely against the invaders. It was hard to maintain any kind of [2] _____ in the face of such danger. However, there was not a single reported occurrence of an out-of-control, [3] _____ soldier. Without [4] _____ supplies, the army struggled. Its members had a great [5] _____ to admit defeat. They freed five small towns in [6] _____, until the fighting finally reached the [7] _____ of the capital. After the battle was won, soldiers recalled the [8] _____ voice of their commander, urging them on to victory. They were proud that they freed their country from foreign rule.

1. Underline the words that specifically tell what the people had a <u>reluctance</u> to give up. Write a sentence using *reluctance.*

2. Circle the words that tell for how long the food was <u>sufficient</u>. Write a sentence using *sufficient.*

3. Circle the word that tells what was in <u>succession</u>. Then, write your own sentence for *succession.*

4. Underline the sentence in the next paragraph that helps explain what the <u>Underground</u> Railroad was. Write a sentence about something else that can be *underground.*

5. Circle the words that mean the opposite of <u>serenity</u>. In a sentence, tell why the *serenity* seems unnatural to James.

6. Circle the words that tell what anyone who might have been <u>hysterical</u> did. Tell how a *hysterical* person might act.

7. Circle the word in the next sentence that gives a clue to the meaning of <u>vicinity</u>. Then, write your own sentence for *vicinity.*

8. Write a sentence that explains what the author contrasts with the men's <u>husky</u> voices.

Read the following passage. Pay special attention to the underlined words. Then, read it again, and complete the activities. Use a separate sheet of paper for your written answers.

The four men and three women had started on their journey. Each one carried a burning desire for freedom and a strong <u>reluctance</u> to give up that dream.

They had brought <u>sufficient</u> food for only two days. Their leader, however, assured them that they would not go hungry. At a <u>succession</u> of stations on the <u>Underground Railroad</u>, the "conductors," or people helping them escape, would see that they were sheltered, fed, and clothed.

James, only fifteen, was the youngest "man" in the group. He had pictured each of the stations along the way as little depots lying below the ground alongside buried train tracks. Then, Matilda explained that *underground* meant "secret" in this case. They did have to hike under cover of the night, however. Otherwise, people looking for escaped slaves could easily spot them.

There was an unnatural <u>serenity</u> when they started out. James had expected some show of outward excitement, at least from Big Jim or Althea. If anyone felt <u>hysterical</u> inside, he or she sure hid it well.

In the <u>vicinity</u> of Howland's Mill, the group stopped and gazed at the starry sky. The nearby mill was deserted. The <u>husky</u> voices of the men who usually traveled along the mill road were now silent, replaced by high-pitched chirrups of spring frogs living in the pond.

James remembered a song he knew, "Follow the drinking gourd." Those words were a code for the group of stars that would guide his group north. He looked up at the patch of sky between the trees. Yes, he could make out the Big Dipper. It was just as the song had said.

James had no idea of the weariness and fear he would feel before his five-hundred-mile trek to freedom was over. For now, he was experiencing only the stillness of the spring night and the hope of a new life.

from Harriet Tubman: Conductor on the Underground Railroad

Ann Petry

Summary Harriet Tubman led a group of enslaved persons from Maryland to freedom in Canada. The trip was cold and difficult. Tubman worked hard to keep them going. She said that people would help them along the way.

 Writing About the Big Question

How much information is enough? In "Harriet Tubman: Conductor on the Underground Railroad," eleven fugitive slaves are led to freedom by Harriet Tubman and her helpers in the Underground Railroad. Complete this sentence:

It is important to learn about historical figures who challenged

slavery because _____.

Note-taking Guide

Use this chart to help you recall the plans Harriet Tubman made.

How did Tubman let slaves know that she was in the area?	
How did Tubman let the slaves know when to leave?	
Whom did Tubman arrange to stay with along the journey?	
Where did Tubman plan for the people to stay when they got to Canada?	

From Harriet Tubman: Conductor on the Underground Railroad

1. **Analyze Causes and Effects:** One of the runaway slaves said that he was going back. Tubman points a gun at him. Explain why she believes that she must act this way.

   _____

   _____

2. **Assess:** Think about Tubman as a leader in today's world. Do you think she would be successful? Why or why not?

   _____

   _____

   _____

3. **Reading Skill:** Use the chart to write a detail you learned about Tubman. Look at all of the details. The **main idea** of a work of nonfiction is the central point that the author makes. What is the main idea the author shows about Tubman? Write your answer in the chart.

Detail	+	Detail	+	Detail	=	Main Idea
If she were caught, she would be hanged.		She hid the fact that she did not know the new route.				

4. **Literary Analysis:** A **narrative essay** tells the story of real events, people, and places. List the two most important events in this narrative essay.

   _____

   _____

Writing: Biographical Sketch

Write a **biographical sketch** of a person who has taken risks to help others or to reach a goal. Use your notes from the questions below to create your sketch.

- What risks did this person take?

  _____

  _____

- What event or action happened that caused this person to take a risk?

  _____

  _____

- What was the result of the person's risk-taking?

  _____

  _____

Listening and Speaking: Skit

Use the following lines to write notes about the scene that you will portray in a **skit**. List the main actions, the characters, and details about the setting.

1. What happens in the scene? _____

  _____

2. Who is part of the scene? _____

  _____

3. Where does the scene take place? _____

  _____

from Always to Remember: The Vision of Maya Ying Lin •
from I Know Why the Caged Bird Sings

Reading Skill

Main ideas are the most important parts of a piece of writing. Writers often follow the main idea with supporting paragraphs. **Make connections** between supporting paragraphs and the main idea to follow the writer's path in an essay.

- Stop to look at the main ideas of paragraphs or sections.

- Write the main ideas and important details in notes.

Read the example in the chart below. Then, fill the empty boxes with main ideas and supporting details from the essays.

Paragraph 1 Main Point	Paragraph 2 Main Point	Essay Main Point
Picasso had a long and innovative career.	Picasso was a major influence on other artists.	Picasso was a great artist who had a major impact on twentieth-century art.

Literary Analysis

- A **biographical essay** is a short piece of writing. The writer tells about an important event in the life of another person.

- An **autobiographical essay** is also a short piece of writing. The writer tells about an event in his or her own life. The writer shares his or her thoughts and feelings.

Word List A

Study these words from "Always To Remember: The Vision of Maya Ying Lin." Then, complete the activity.

appropriate [uh PROH pree it] *adj.* right for a certain purpose
What do you think is an <u>appropriate</u> *thing to do about gossip?*

architect [AR ki tekt] *n.* a person whose job is to design buildings
An <u>architect</u> *follows a building project until it is completed.*

attending [uh TEND ing] *v.* being present at an event
Five thousand people were <u>attending</u> *the concert in the arena.*

durable [DOOR uh buhl] *adj.* staying in good condition for a long time
I like jeans because they are <u>durable</u> *and comfortable.*

political [puh LIT i kuhl] *adj.* relating to government actions and policies
My mom says we should not have <u>political</u> *discussions during dinner.*

response [ri SPAHNS] *n.* a reply to something
Aaron's <u>response</u> *to my birthday party invitation was a big smile.*

site [SYT] *n.* the place where something is being built
The <u>site</u> *where our new high school will be built is a cornfield now.*

tribute [TRIB yoot] *n.* something given, said, or done to show respect or give thanks
Our whole town turned out for the <u>tribute</u> *to the police chief.*

Exercise A

Fill in each blank in the paragraph below with an appropriate word from Word List A. Use each word only once.

Yesterday, when we were [1] _____ the opening of our brand-new library, we got to meet the [2] _____. I believe his design for the building is just perfect for its [3] _____. He used natural yet [4] _____ materials like stone and wood so that the library would remain standing for many years. Mom and Dad said that choosing the design was a real [5] _____ battle, though. The mayor and some other people in government wanted a very modern building that they hoped would be [6] _____ for the computer age. The [7] _____ of one large group of people to this idea was negative. I think the natural beauty of the chosen design is a [8] _____ to the city's respect for our surroundings.

1. Underline the words naming what Maya Ying Lin did as an architect. Then, explain what an *architect* does for a living.

2. Circle the words that name what was already part of the memorial's site. Then, explain why the best designs would be viewed as *appropriate* for a building *site*.

3. Underline words throughout the paragraph that describe the visitors' response. Then, describe a time when a *response* of your own surprised you.

4. Circle the words naming what caused political division. Then, explain the word *political*.

5. Underline the words naming the people to whom the objects are a tribute. Then, explain the different forms a *tribute* can take.

6. Circle the sentence that explains how less durable objects are protected. Make a list of some of these less *durable* objects.

7. Underline the words naming what people are attending. Then, explain what *attending* means.

Read the following passage. Pay special attention to the underlined words. Then, read it again, and complete the activities. Use a separate sheet of paper for your written answers.

Maya Ying Lin, the college student and architect who designed the Vietnam Veterans Memorial, had a strong idea about fitting the Wall into its surroundings. Her plans found an appropriate way to connect this new structure to the land and to the other memorials around it. Her ideas for the site seemed as perfect as anyone could have hoped to see.

What Maya and others could not possibly have known was the level of response the memorial would stir up in visitors. The organizers of the effort hoped that the Wall would help to heal the political division caused by the Vietnam War. They have been thrilled with the results. Visitors often let their emotions show. Many are stunned by the impact the memorial has on them.

Visitors often bring things to leave behind at the Wall. Together, these objects are a huge tribute to the men and women who served our country. More than fifty thousand objects have been left at the Wall. They are collected twice daily by the National Park Service. When the weather is bad, the objects are picked up more often. This way, the less durable items are not damaged. Treated as precious, the items are carefully entered into the Vietnam Veterans Memorial Collection. Exceptions are living things, such as plants, and flags. The flags are given to hospitals for former soldiers and groups like the Boy Scouts or Girl Scouts. The flags also are given to people who are attending special events at the memorial.

The things most often left are writings such as poems or letters. Bracelets worn to remember soldiers who are still missing are plentiful, too. Rubbings of the names on the wall are often left as well. Things that soldiers owned and photographs also are among the most commonly left items.

from Always to Remember:
The Vision of Maya Ying Lin
Brent Ashabranner

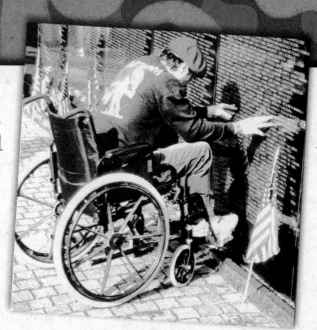

Summary In the early 1980s, more than 2,500 people entered a competition to design a memorial. The men and women who lost their lives in the Vietnam War would be honored by the memorial. This essay describes the competition. It also describes the college student who wins.

❓ Writing About the Big Question

How much information is enough? In "Always to Remember," the story of the Vietnam Veterans Memorial highlights the need to learn about and remember the past. Complete this sentence:

Remembering events from our history can be valuable because

_____.

Note-taking Guide
Use this chart to record details about the winning design for the Vietnam Veterans Memorial.

```
                    ┌─────────────────┐
                    │ Vietnam Veterans │
                    │    Memorial      │
                    └─────────────────┘
┌───────────────────┐                    ┌───────────────────┐
│ What is the memorial? │                │  What does the    │
│                   │                    │ memorial look like? │
│                   │ ┌─────────────────┐│                   │
│                   │ │  Who designed    ││                   │
│                   │ │  the memorial?   ││                   │
│                   │ │                  ││                   │
│                   │ │  Maya Ying Lin   ││                   │
└───────────────────┘ └─────────────────┘└───────────────────┘
```

Activate Prior Knowledge

Think about a memorial or statue you have seen. What was it? Write two details you remember about it.

_____

_____

_____

_____

Reading Skill

The **main ideas** are the most important points of the work. The author **makes connections** between a main idea and paragraphs that support it. Underline the **main idea** in the bracketed passage.

Reading Check

What did Scruggs, Doubek, and Wheeler think the memorial should do for the nation? Underline the text that tells the answer.

from Always To Remember: The Vision of Maya Ying Lin
Brent Ashabranner

This nonfiction selection tells the true story of how a young college student named Maya Lin came to design the Vietnam Veterans Memorial in Washington, D.C.

◆ ◆ ◆

In the 1960s and 1970s, the United States was involved in a war in Vietnam. Because many people opposed the war, Vietnam veterans were not honored as veterans of other wars had been. Jan Scruggs, a Vietnam veteran, thought that the 58,000 U.S. servicemen and women killed or reported missing in Vietnam should be honored with a memorial.

◆ ◆ ◆

Scruggs got two lawyers named Robert Doubek and John Wheeler to help him get support for building a memorial. In 1980, Congress agreed that a memorial should be built.

◆ ◆ ◆

What would the memorial be? What should it look like? Who would design it? Scruggs, Doubek, and Wheeler didn't know, but they were determined that the memorial should help bring closer together a nation still bitterly divided by the Vietnam War.

◆ ◆ ◆

They did not want the memorial to glorify war or to argue for peace. They wanted a memorial that did not provoke arguments as it honored the dead. How could they find the best idea for the kind of memorial they wanted?

◆ ◆ ◆

The answer, they decided, was to hold a national design competition open to all Americans.

◆ ◆ ◆

The winner of the competition would receive a $20,000 prize. More important, the winner would have the honor of being part of American history. The memorial would be built in Washington, D.C., between the Washington Monument and the Lincoln Memorial. This part of the city is called the Mall.

More than 5,000 Americans asked for the booklet that told the rules of the competition. Many of them were well-known architects and sculptors. The booklet told what kind of memorial would win the competition.

◆　◆　◆

The memorial could not make a political statement about the war; it must contain the names of all persons killed or missing in action in the war; it must be in harmony with its location on the Mall.

◆　◆　◆

More than one thousand designs were submitted for the competition. Eight judges had to decide which design best met the standards for winning: The memorial had to honor the memory of the soldiers who had died in the war. It had to blend in with the other monuments nearby. It had to be an important work of art. It also had to be practical to build and take care of.

The designs were displayed in an airplane hangar. They were labeled by number, instead of showing the designer's name, so that the judges could be objective. On May 1, 1981, the judges chose the winner and praised the winning design.

◆　◆　◆

© Pearson Education

Vocabulary Development

harmony (HAR muh nee) *n.* a situation in which things or people are at peace or in agreement with one another

---

TAKE NOTES

Reading Skill

Underline one detail that supports the **main idea** that the winner would be a part of American history.

Read Fluently

Read the bracketed passage. Semicolons show a break between clauses, or complete sentence parts. What is another way to separate clauses?

_____

Literary Analysis

A **biographical essay** describes an important event in the life of a person. What person do you think this essay is going to be about?

_____

_____

Reading Check

How many designs were submitted in the competition? Underline the sentence that tells you.

Reading Skill

Read the bracketed passage. Underline the **main idea** of the passage.

Literary Analysis

Why did the author of this **biographical essay** include details about Maya Ying Lin's family and background?

_____

_____

_____

Stop to Reflect

What effect do you think Maya Ying Lin's interest in cemeteries had on her entry into the competition?

_____

_____

_____

This memorial, with its wall of names, becomes a place of quiet reflection, and a <u>tribute</u> to those who served their nation in difficult times. All who come here can find it a place of healing. This will be a quiet memorial, one that achieves an excellent relationship with both the Lincoln Memorial and Washington Monument, and relates the visitor to them. It is uniquely horizontal, entering the earth rather than piercing the sky.

◆ ◆ ◆

Americans were amazed when they learned that the winner of the contest was not a famous architect or sculptor. She was a 21-year-old college student named Maya Lin.

◆ ◆ ◆

Maya Lin, reporters soon discovered, was a Chinese-American girl who had been born and raised in the small midwestern city of Athens, Ohio. Her father, Henry Huan Lin, was a ceramicist of <u>considerable</u> reputation and dean of fine arts at Ohio University in Athens. Her mother, Julia C. Lin, was a poet and professor of Oriental and English literature.

◆ ◆ ◆

Maya Lin's parents were immigrants from China. Maya had always been interested in art, especially sculpture. At Yale University, she decided to major in architecture. She became interested in cemetery architecture, especially when she visited cemeteries in Europe, which were also used as parks.

In her senior year at Yale, one of Maya Lin's professors asked his students to enter

Vocabulary Development

tribute (TRIB yoot) *n.* something that shows respect for someone or something
considerable (kuhn SI der uh buhl) *adj.* large enough to have a noticeable effect

the Vietnam Veterans Memorial competition as a class assignment. Maya and two of her classmates traveled to Washington, D.C., to look at the site where the memorial would be built. While she was there, Maya was inspired. In her mind, she saw a vision of the memorial she wanted to design. Like the cemetery designs she had seen in Europe, her design fit in with the land around it and would maintain the site as a park.

◆ ◆ ◆

"When I looked at the site I just knew I wanted something horizontal that took you in, that made you feel safe within the park, yet at the same time reminding you of the dead. So I just imagined opening up the earth. . . ."

◆ ◆ ◆

Back at Yale, Maya made a clay model of her vision and then drew the design on paper. She mailed in her entry just in time to make the deadline. A month later, she got a call from Washington, D.C. She had won the competition. Her design would be used to build the Vietnam Veterans Memorial.

TAKE NOTES

Stop to Reflect

How do you think winning the contest may have affected Maya Lin's life?

_____

_____

_____

_____

_____

_____

Reading Check

When did Maya Lin mail in her design entry? Underline the sentence that tells you.

from Always to Remember: The Vision of Maya Ying Lin

1. **Draw Conclusions:** Why was Maya Ying Lin's win so surprising?

   _____

   _____

2. **Evaluate:** Reread pages 192 and 193. Explain whether you think Maya Ying Lin's memorial met the design criteria.

   _____

   _____

3. **Reading Skill:** The section about Maya Ying Lin on pages 152–153 includes information about her background. Reread these pages. Construct a sentence that states the **main idea** of the section.

   _____

   _____

4. **Literary Analysis:** This **biographical essay** gives information about the life of Maya Ying Lin. Complete this chart with details from the essay.

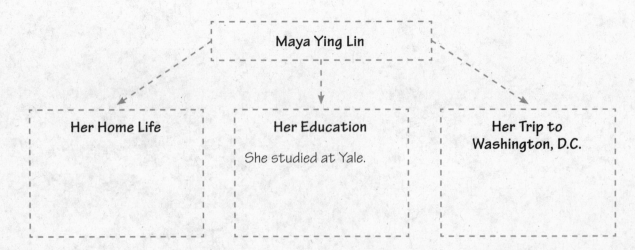

Writing: Reflective Composition

Write a **reflective composition** in which you discuss a work of fine art or music that is inspiring. Answer the following questions. Use your notes to help you write your composition.

- What item or piece of art did you choose to write about? Why did you choose it?

  _____

- Describe the piece of art or music you chose.

  _____

  _____

- What could be the main points of your composition? How could you support these points?

  _____

  _____

Research and Technology: Multimedia Presentation

To prepare for your **multimedia presentation**, you will need to gather facts. Use the following questions to help you record important information.

1. During what years was the United States involved in the Vietnam War?

   _____

   _____

2. For what reasons did the United States become involved in the Vietnam War?

   _____

   _____

3. What were some objections to United States involvement?

   _____

   _____

4. What affects did the Vietnam War have on people's lives?

   _____

   _____

Word List A

Study these words from *I Know Why the Caged Bird Sings*. Then, complete the activity.

accurate [AK yuhr it] *adj.* correct in every way
    My answer will be <u>accurate</u> if I understand all of the facts.

assured [uh SHOORD] *v.* made certain something would happen
    Getting an A on the test <u>assured</u> Ben's place on the honor roll.

essence [ES uhns] *n.* the most basic, important quality of something
    The <u>essence</u> of summer vacation is free time.

judgment [JUHJ muhnt] *n.* the ability to make a decision or form an opinion
    The referee's <u>judgment</u> during games was not to be questioned.

numerous [NOO muh ruhs] *adj.* many
    As early as October, I saw <u>numerous</u> trees with bare limbs.

romantic [roh MAN tik] *adj.* having to do with feelings of love
    Would you rather see a <u>romantic</u> movie or an action film?

unexpected [un ek SPEK tid] *adj.* surprising
    The <u>unexpected</u> result of all my work was a feeling of satisfaction.

wiry [WY ree] *adj.* thin but strong
    The <u>wiry</u> wrestler easily pinned many larger opponents.

Exercise A

Fill in each blank in the paragraph below with an appropriate word from Word List A. Use each word only once.

Should a first date be [1] _____? My answer, which might be

[2] _____ and viewed as strange, is no. I think the [3] _____

of a first date is getting to know another person. Your [4] _____

about whether or not you like a person will be most error-free and

[5] _____ if you learn the facts about him or her. Suppose your

date is [6] _____, a look that you find attractive. However, you

find out right away that this person spends hours each day working

out and worrying about being too thin! Yes, many people will say that

finding out more about a person has [7] _____ that they have not

wasted their time on a bad match. [8] _____ reports from many

of my friends support my ideas.

Read the following passage. Pay special attention to the underlined words. Then, read it again, and complete the activities. Use a separate sheet of paper for your written answers.

Phillip Blake was the essence of high school "cool." He drove a hot car, played numerous sports well, and was the student body president. Phillip, with his dark curly hair, was the object of many romantic ideas among the girls. However, the one he called "my girl" was not found at Patrick Henry High. Her name was Ruth Lewis, and she lived alone in a fancy house on Elm Street. She was seventy years old, and she was Phillip's best buddy.

Phillip's unexpected friendship with Miss Ruth, as he called her, began when he was thirteen. He was looking to earn money by doing yardwork. Back then, he was a wiry kid. He wasn't afraid of anything or anyone. His friends would never have approached the grand old lady of Elm Street. Phillip, on the other hand, just marched up the steps and knocked on her front door. Miss Ruth, who took pride in her good judgment about people, looked Phillip up and down, and then asked him inside.

The two strangers worked out the details of his duties and pay as her new gardener. They also discussed what was going on in their lives. Phillip talked about his first girlfriend and wanting to earn money so he could take her to the movies. Miss Ruth talked about her club activities and her hopes that her wealth had assured the college education of her grandchildren. A friendship was born.

Whenever the kids at school mentioned Miss Ruth around Phillip, he made sure that what they said was accurate. Since no one had ever bothered to get to know her, Phillip felt it was his duty to protect her from gossip. He showed by his words and actions how to be a true friend. He also proved that friends do not have to be at all alike.

1. Underline the words in the paragraph that might define the essence of high school "cool." Then, write a definition of *essence*.

2. Make a list of the numerous sports Phillip might have played.

3. Circle the words telling who had romantic ideas about Phillip. Then, explain the word *romantic*.

4. Underline the words telling when the unexpected friendship began. Then, explain why it is called *unexpected*.

5. Circle the words in the next sentence that hint at the meaning of wiry. Then, define *wiry*.

6. Underline the words that describe how Miss Ruth made her judgment about Phillip. Explain why she would be proud of having good *judgment*.

7. Circle the words naming what Miss Ruth hoped her wealth assured. Then, explain the word *assured*.

8. Underline the words naming what Phillip wished to be accurate. Explain why you like people to say only *accurate* things about you.

© Pearson Education

from I Know Why the Caged Bird Sings
Maya Angelou

Summary In this story, the writer describes growing up in her grand-mother's house in Stamps, Arkansas. She describes her friendship with a woman named Mrs. Flowers. Mrs. Flowers introduces her to poetry.

 Writing About the Big Question

How much information is enough? In *I Know Why the Caged Bird Sings*, a girl receives "lessons in living" that encourage her to gather wisdom from those around her. Complete these sentences:

The best way I have found to accumulate knowledge is _____

_____.

Note-taking Guide

Look at the chart below. Record events in the story that caused Marguerite to experience each emotion.

```
┌─────────────────────────┐              ┌─────────────────────────┐
│  Pleased                │         ↗    │  Sad and Depressed      │
│                         │              │                         │
│ She liked working in the│     ╭─────╮  │                         │
│ store.                  │     │Marguerite's│                     │
└─────────────────────────┘     │Emotions│  └─────────────────────┘
                                ╰─────╯
┌─────────────────────────┐      ↙    ↘   ┌─────────────────────────┐
│  Happy                  │              │  Proud                  │
│                         │              │                         │
│                         │              │                         │
└─────────────────────────┘              └─────────────────────────┘
```

from I Know Why the Caged Bird Sings

1. **Infer:** Some customers tell Marguerite that she is cheating them. How does she feel when customers accuse her of cheating?

   _____

2. **Interpret:** The author writes that Mrs. Flowers was "the lady who threw me my first lifeline." Lifelines are used to save people from drowning. What does the author mean by these words?

   _____

   _____

3. **Reading Skill: Main ideas** are the most important points in a story. Write three main ideas from the section about Mrs. Flowers.

   _____

   _____

   _____

4. **Literary Analysis:** This story is an **autobiographical essay**. The writer tells a story about an important event in her own life. Complete this chart with details about her life.

   Marguerite

Where She Lived	What She Did	Important Event
Lived in Stamps, Arkansas		

Writing: Reflective Composition

Write a **reflective composition** about a story, poem, play, or novel that made an impression on you. Answer the questions below. Use your notes to help you organize your reflective composition.

- What is the name of the work you have chosen? Why is it important to you?

  _____

  _____

- What will be the main points of your composition?

  _____

  _____

- What details will you use to support your main points?

  _____

  _____

Research and Technology: Proposal for a Multimedia Presentation

Write a **proposal for a multimedia presentation** about the Great Depression. In the first column, write a brief description of any quotations, photos, music, or artwork you found. In the second column, write the source the media came from. In the third column, write what your media says about the Depression.

Brief Description	Source Name	What It Says

Textbooks

About Textbooks

A **textbook** is a nonfiction book that presents information about one subject, such as math, history, or science. Different textbooks are alike in some ways.

- **Purpose:** Textbooks present information to students. The writer starts with a main idea and builds around it.
- **Structure:** Most textbooks have sections, chapters, or units. The table of contents lists the titles and page numbers of these parts.
- **Text Format:** Type size, color, and boldface type are used. They highlight key words or sections.

Reading Skill

To use a textbook effectively, you can **analyze the treatment, scope, and organization of ideas** presented in each unit or chapter. Treatment is the way a topic is presented, including the author's purpose for writing. In a textbook, the author's purpose is to inform or explain. The scope is the amount and type of information. A text with a narrow scope focuses on a single, limited topic, but a broad scope includes subtopics with much information. Organization is the way that ideas are arranged. One way to organize ideas is chronologically, or in the order in which they happen.

Treatment	Scope	Organization
• Is this a primary or secondary source? • Is the writer biased or neutral? • What is the writer's tone, or attitude toward the topic?	• Has the writer explored a single topic or a series of topics? • How in-depth is this exploration?	• How has the writer organized his or her information? • In what way does the organization of details enhance the writer's purpose?

Text Structure

Textbooks often include graphics, such as the map on this page, to provide additional information about the subject. What additional information does this map provide?

_____

_____

_____

Fluency Builder

Commas (,) tell the reader when to pause. Circle the commas in the second paragraph. Then, read aloud the paragraph with a partner, pausing briefly for each comma.

Vocabulary Builder

Adjectives An adjective is a word that describes a noun or pronoun. On the lines below, write six adjectives that appear in the third paragraph. Next to each adjective, write the noun that it describes.

_____

_____

_____

_____

_____

_____

The War in Vietnam

War in Southeast Asia

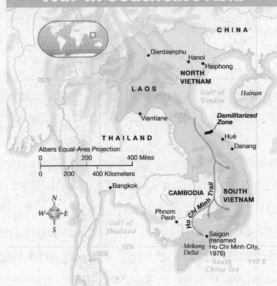

Early Involvement in Vietnam

Vietnam is a narrow country that stretches about 1,000 miles along the South China Sea. Since the late 1800s, it had been ruled by France as a colony.

The United States became involved in Vietnam slowly, step by step. During the 1940s, Ho Chi Minh (HO CHEE MIHN), a Vietnamese nationalist and a Communist, had led the fight for independence. Ho's army finally defeated the French in 1954.

An international peace conference divided Vietnam into two countries. Ho Chi Minh led communist North Vietnam. Ngo Dinh Diem (NOH DIN dee EHM) was the noncommunist leader of South Vietnam. In the Cold War world, the Soviet Union supported North Vietnam. The United States backed Diem in the south.

Discontent Diem lost popular support during the 1950s. Many South Vietnamese thought that he favored wealthy landlords and was corrupt. He failed to help the nation's peasant majority and ruled with a heavy hand. As discontent grew, many peasants joined the **Vietcong**— guerrillas who opposed Diem. **Guerrillas** (guh RIHL uhz) are fighters who make hit-and-run attacks on the enemy. They do not wear uniforms or fight in large battles. In time, the Vietcong became communist and were supported by North Vietnam. Vietcong influence quickly spread, especially in the villages.

American Aid Vietcong successes worried American leaders. If South Vietnam fell to communism, they believed, other countries in the region would follow—like a row of falling dominoes. This idea became known as the **domino theory.** The United States decided that it must keep South Vietnam from becoming the first domino.

During the 1950s and 1960s, Presidents Eisenhower and Kennedy sent financial aid and military advisers to South Vietnam. The advisers went to help train the South Vietnamese army, not to fight the Vietcong. Diem, however, continued to lose support. In November 1963, Diem was assassinated. A few weeks later, President John F. Kennedy was assassinated. Vice President Lyndon Baines Johnson became President.

The Fighting in Vietnam Expands

Lyndon Johnson was also determined to keep South Vietnam from falling to the communists. He increased aid to South Vietnam, sending more arms and advisers. Still, the Vietcong continued to make gains.

Gulf of Tonkin Resolution In August 1964, President Johnson announced that North Vietnamese torpedo boats had attacked an American ship patrolling the Gulf of Tonkin off the coast of North Vietnam. At Johnson's urging,

Cultural Understanding

Capitalism is the economic system used in the United States. The government limits its involvement in the economy. Citizens can own businesses. They can also make and sell goods to earn a profit.

Text Structure

Text format is important in textbooks. It helps you find and understand information. On this page, type size and boldface are both used. Circle an example of each. Then, explain how they help you understand the information on this page.

Type size: _____

_____

Boldface: _____

_____

Vocabulary Builder

Multiple-Meaning Words
The word *falling* can mean "moving or dropping toward the ground." It can also mean "losing power." What does *falling* mean in the paragraph beginning "Lyndon Johnson was also determined . . ."?

_____

_____

Comprehension Builder

What did President Johnson use the Gulf of Tonkin Resolution to do?

_____

_____

_____

Text Structure

How does the author organize information about the fighting in Vietnam? Explain.

_____

_____

_____

Congress passed the Gulf of Tonkin Resolution. It allowed the President "to take all necessary measures to repel any armed attack or to prevent further aggression." Johnson used the resolution to order the bombing of North Vietnam and Vietcong-held areas in the south.

With the Gulf of Tonkin Resolution, the role of Americans in Vietnam changed from military advisers to active fighters. The war in Vietnam escalated, or expanded. By 1968, President Johnson had sent more than 500,000 troops to fight in Vietnam.

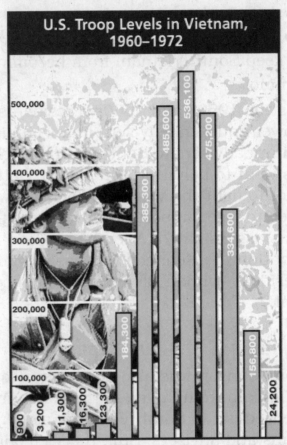

U.S. Troop Levels in Vietnam, 1960–1972

Year	Troops
1960	900
1961	3,200
1962	11,300
1963	16,300
1964	23,300
1965	184,300
1966	385,300
1967	485,600
1968	536,100
1969	475,200
1970	334,600
1971	156,800
1972	24,200

Source: U.S. Department of Defense

Thinking About the Textbook

1. Explain the significance of the domino theory.

   _____

2. How did the Vietcong make fighting even more difficult for the Americans?

   _____

TALK ABOUT IT **Reading Skill**

3. What is the writer's purpose in writing about this subject?

   _____

4. Is the scope of this textbook narrow or broad? Explain.

   _____

WRITE ABOUT IT **Timed Writing: Explanation (20 minutes)**

Choose one of the following features. Explain how it could help you learn the information in this chapter. Use this chart to help you.

Feature	How It Could Help Me
Key Terms	
Taking Notes	
Outlining the Material	

The Trouble With Television •
On Woman's Right to Suffrage

Reading Skill

A **fact** is a statement that can be proved true. An **opinion** is a statement that cannot be proved true. A **generalization** is a conclusion that is supported by facts. An **overgeneralization** is a conclusion that overstates the facts. **Use clue words** to find the different kinds of statements.

- Writers use words such as *best* and *worst* to tell their feelings and beliefs. These words usually state an opinion.

- Words such as *therefore*, *so*, and *because* connect facts. These words may signal a generalization. Words such as *always*, *never*, and *only* may signal an overgeneralization.

Literary Analysis

Persuasive techniques are tools that a writer uses to try to make people do something or think a certain way. Here are some common persuasive techniques:

- **Repetition:** An author says something more than once.

- **Rhetorical questions:** An author asks questions with obvious answers.

Other common persuasive techniques are in the chart.

Persuasive Techniques
Appeal to Authority
Example: Quotations from experts or reliable sources
Appeal to Emotions
Example: Words that appeal to emotions such as patriotism
Appeal to Reason
Example: Logical arguments based on evidence such as statistics

Word List A

Study these words from "The Trouble With Television." Then, complete the activity.

calculate [KAL kyuh layt] *v.* to figure out by using math
  How do you calculate the area of a rectangle?

crisis [KRY sis] *n.* time of when a situation is bad or dangerous
  The quarrel between the two countries reached a crisis.

cultivate [KUHL tuh vayt] *v.* to develop; to encourage
  Dagmar tried to cultivate a love of poetry, but she just couldn't.

fare [FAIR] *n.* something given for use or enjoyment
  The top-forty radio station plays familiar fare day in, day out.

perceived [puhr SEEVD] *n.* understood or noticed
  His request was not perceived as being important.

precision [pri SIZH uhn] *n.* exactness
  Halley used a band saw to cut the board with great precision.

prime [PRYM] *adj.* main; most important
  The prime reason kids get into mischief is boredom.

verbal [VUHR buhl] *adj.* relating to words; spoken
  Dan's had excellent verbal skills, which made him a great debater.

Exercise A

Fill in each blank in the paragraph below with an appropriate word from Word List A. Use each word only once.

Going to school in early America was quite different from today. The [1] _____ reason for teaching most children was so they could learn to read the Bible. Due to the shortage of writing materials, teachers often used [2] _____ instruction. Some children also learned to [3] _____ number problems with great [4] _____. This was a useful skill to [5] _____ if planning to run a business. This simplest of educational [6] _____ might be [7] _____ today as laughable, but it served its population well. These days, students learn much more than children of long ago. However, the news always reports an educational [8] _____. We seem to be in danger of not preparing our students for the world of tomorrow.

Read the following passage. Pay special attention to the underlined words. Then, read it again, and complete the activities. Use a separate sheet of paper for your written answers.

1. Underline a word in the paragraph that hints at the meaning of crisis. Then, tell about a *crisis* you faced.

2. Circle the words that help you understand "calculate with precision." Then, rewrite the sentence using synonyms for *calculate* and *precision*.

3. Underline the words that tell what the writer could not cultivate. Then, write something you tried to *cultivate*.

4. Circle the words in the next sentence that suggest the meaning of fare. What is your favorite television *fare*?

5. Underline the word that tells by whom the narrator was perceived. Then, write a sentence for *perceived*.

6. Circle the word that tells what was prime. What hours do you think make up *prime* time?

7. Circle the word in the next sentence that hints at the meaning of verbal. Then, explain whether you prefer *verbal* or written news.

Hunter was having a crisis. He should have seen the danger coming, but he often liked to ignore what he did not want to face.

Hunter had worked at the television network for ten years. He could calculate with precision the number of viewers watching each of the network's programs. He could rattle off the list of advertisers for each half hour. He could create pie charts on the computer and give convincing presentations at important meetings.

So what was Hunter's problem? No matter how hard he tried, he could no longer cultivate a taste for a single one of the network's shows. He had to admit that he simply hated what the programming department put on the air.

It wasn't that Hunter had a taste for unusual television fare. The menu of programs during his first year at the network had included three or four shows he genuinely liked. Now, he barely managed to sit in the screening room before the beginning of the season. Luckily, no one asked for his opinions because he was perceived by others as just "that numbers guy." He did have opinions, though. Secretly, he hoped that some day bad manners would overcome him and he would blurt them out.

Hunter's dislike of the programs was not limited to prime time. Hunter couldn't stand the soap operas, the game shows, and the talk shows that filled the daytime slots. The news people were worst of all. It wasn't that they didn't have strong verbal skills. They spoke quite well, in fact. It was the oral presentation of news that bothered him. There was nothing written— nothing to review so a person could grasp the greater meaning.

He finally faced the inevitable. It was time to look for a new job.

The Trouble With Television
Robert MacNeil

Summary Robert MacNeil has worked as a reporter for radio and television. He thinks that watching television keeps people from paying close attention to things. He thinks that television has a bad effect on people.

 Writing About the Big Question

How much information is enough? In "The Trouble with Television," Robert MacNeil expresses doubts about the quality of the information television offers. Complete this sentence:

The **exploration** of ideas on TV news shows is usually _____

_____.

Note-taking Guide
Use the chart to list the main reasons that MacNeil believes television is a bad influence.

MacNeil's Ideas About Television
1.
2.
3.
4.

Activate Prior Knowledge

Think about television. How often do you watch it? What effect does television have on you? Finish the statement: "I believe that the trouble with television is . . ."

_____

_____

_____

_____

Literary Analysis

Persuasive techniques are ways a writer tries to influence the reader to agree about something. A writer might use facts, or the writer might use words to get an emotional reaction. Sometimes writers repeat ideas or phrases. What **persuasive techniques** does MacNeil use in the first paragraph?

_____

_____

_____

_____

Reading Check

What does MacNeil think is the main problem with television? Underline the sentence that tells you.

The Trouble With Television
Robert MacNeil

It is difficult to escape the influence of television. If you fit the statistical averages, by the age of 20 you will have been exposed to at least 20,000 hours of television. You can add 10,000 hours for each decade you have lived after the age of 20. The only things Americans do more than watch television are work and sleep.

◆ ◆ ◆

MacNeil points out that time spent watching television could be put to better use. For example, he says that you could earn a college degree instead. You could read classic works of literature in their original languages. Or you could walk around the world and write a book about the experience.

◆ ◆ ◆

The trouble with television is that it discourages concentration. Almost anything interesting and rewarding in life requires some constructive, consistently applied effort. The dullest, the least gifted of us can achieve things that seem miraculous to those who never concentrate on anything. But television encourages us to apply no effort. It sells us instant gratification. It diverts us only to divert, to make the time pass without pain.

Vocabulary Development

statistical (stuh TIS ti kuhl) *adj.* having to do with numerical data

exposed (ik SPOHZD) *v.* shown

concentration (kahn suhn TRAY shuhn) *n.* the paying of close attention

constructive (kuhn STRUK tiv) *adj.* leading to improvement

gratification (grat uh fuh KAY shuhn) *n.* the act of pleasing or satisfying

diverts (duh VERTS) *v.* distracts

Capturing your attention—and holding it—is the prime motive of most television programming and enhances its role as a profitable advertising vehicle. Programmers live in constant fear of losing anyone's attention—anyone's. The surest way to avoid doing so is to keep everything brief, not to strain the attention of anyone but instead to provide constant stimulation through variety, novelty, action and movement. Quite simply, television operates on the appeal to the short attention span.

◆ ◆ ◆

MacNeil is worried about television's effect on the values of our society. He believes that Americans have come to want "fast ideas." He also believes that television news does not accurately portray events. It does not provide viewers with enough details.

◆ ◆ ◆

I believe that TV's appeal to the short attention span is not only inefficient communication but decivilizing as well. Consider the casual assumptions that television tends to cultivate: that complexity must be avoided, that visual stimulation is a substitute for thought, that verbal precision is an anachronism[1]. It may be old-fashioned, but I was taught that thought is words, arranged in grammatically precise ways.

◆ ◆ ◆

MacNeil says that television has caused a crisis of literacy in the United States. About

Literary Analysis

A **persuasive technique** MacNeil uses in this essay is to repeat ideas. Circle one word that is repeated in the first bracketed paragraph.

Reading Skill

A **fact** is information that can be proved. An **opinion** cannot be proved. Read the second bracketed passage. Underline two sentences that tell the author's opinion. Write the word that helped you know that each sentence expressed an opinion.

_____

Stop to Reflect

What do you think the author means by "fast ideas"?

_____

_____

_____

Reading Check

What does MacNeil believe about television's appeal to the short attention span? Underline the text that tells you.

Vocabulary Development

enhances (in HANTS iz) *v.* heightens
novelty (NAHV uhl tee) *n.* the quality of being new

1. **anachronism** (uh NAK ruh niz uhm) *n.* anything that seems to be out of its proper place in history.

Reading Skill

An **overgeneralization** is a conclusion that overstates the facts. Clue words can help you find overgeneralizations. These words may include *always, never, everything, nothing,* and *everyone.* Read the bracketed text. Underline one overgeneralization you find in the text. Then, circle the clue word that helped you identify it.

Literary Analysis 🔍

Read the bracketed text. What **persuasive technique** does MacNeil use in this paragraph? Circle words that help you identify the techniques.

_____

_____

Read Fluently

Read the underlined sentence. Circle the most important words in this sentence. Explain why these words are the most important.

_____

_____

_____

30 million Americans cannot read and write well enough to answer a want ad or to understand instructions on a medicine bottle.

◆   ◆   ◆

Everything about this nation—the structure of the society, its forms of family organization, its economy, its place in the world—has become more complex, not less. Yet its dominating communications instrument, its principal form of national linkage, is one that sells neat resolutions to human problems that usually have no neat resolutions. It is all symbolized in my mind by the hugely successful art form that television has made central to the culture, the thirty-second commercial: the tiny drama of the earnest housewife who finds happiness in choosing the right toothpaste.

◆   ◆   ◆

In conclusion, MacNeil warns that television threatens our society's values. He believes that television negatively affects our language. He thinks it discourages our interest in complex issues. He calls on others to join him in resisting television's influence.

The Trouble With Television

1. **Connect:** MacNeil says that television shortens our attention span. How do broadcasters add to the problem with the methods they use?

   _____

   _____

2. **Evaluate:** Do you agree that much of the news on television depends on "horrifying pictures" instead of telling the full story? Explain.

   _____

   _____

3. **Reading Skill:** Complete this chart. Identify each statement as a **fact**, an **opinion**, a **generalization**, or an **overgeneralization**. Explain your choice. Follow the example given.

Statement	Type of Statement	Explanation
Almost anything interesting and rewarding in life requires some constructive . . . effort.	Opinion	It is the author's opinion based on personal observation.
But television encourages us to apply no effort.		
. . . by the age of 20 you will have exposed to at least 20,000 hours of television.		
I think this society is being force fed with trivial fare . . .		

4. **Literary Analysis:** Why does MacNeil **repeat** the idea that television appeals to the short attention span?

   _____

Writing: Evaluation

Write an **evaluation** of the persuasive arguments in MacNeil's essay. Use the questions below to gather ideas for your evaluation.

- What is MacNeil's position?

  _____

  _____

- What are two of his arguments?

  _____

  _____

- What are two counterarguments for the arguments you just listed?

  _____

  _____

- How well does MacNeil deal with these counterarguments?

  _____

  _____

Research and Technology: Statistical Snapshot

You may want to collect data on another sheet of paper and then complete the chart when you have collected all the data.

Category	Student hours/week	Adult hours/week	Comments
Sports			
News			
Comedy			
Drama			
Reality			
Educational			

Word List A

Study these words from "On Woman's Right to Suffrage." Then, complete the activity.

constitution [kahn sti TOO shuhn] *n.* a country's written laws
After winning its freedom, the new nation wrote a <u>constitution</u>.

downright [DOWN ryt] *adj.* total; complete
Sticking your tongue out at somebody is a <u>downright</u> insult.

endured [en DOORD] *v.* put up with; tolerated
This awful heat cannot be <u>endured</u> one minute longer.

federal [FED uh ruhl] *adj.* relating to the central government
It is important for the <u>federal</u> and state governments to cooperate.

promote [pruh MOHT] *v.* to help something develop or be successful
The city officials <u>promote</u> the development of a new museum.

rebellion [ri BEL yuhn] *n.* a struggle against people in power
The students were in <u>rebellion</u> against a longer school day.

supreme [soo PREEM] *adj.* having the highest position of power
At home, the <u>supreme</u> law is whatever my parents say.

welfare [WEL fair] *n.* health and happiness; well-being
Our neighbors are concerned about the <u>welfare</u> of stray cats.

Exercise A

Fill in each blank in the paragraph below with an appropriate word from Word List A. Use each word only once.

The small African country was in [1] _____ against its rulers. While the ruling country profited from its colony's mines, it paid no attention to the miners' needs and [2] _____. [3] _____ terrible conditions in the mines had to be [4] _____ for the sake of keeping a job. After the country declared independence, its first task was to draft a [5] _____ [6] _____ to protect all its citizens. Then, it got to work trying to [7] _____ a healthy lifestyle for the miners. Its [8] _____ efforts went into improving working conditions, raising the wage, and providing health care. In its first ten years of independence, the country's government met with great success.

1 Underline the words that give a clue to the meaning of rebellion. Then, tell what a *rebellion* is.

2. Underline the word or words that give a hint to the meaning of constitution. Tell why a *constitution* is important.

3. Circle the word that federal describes. Then, write a sentence for *federal*.

4. Circle the word that tells what is supreme. Write about something of *supreme* importance.

5. Circle the word in the next sentence that hints at the meaning of promote. Then, write about a cause you would *promote*.

6. Circle the synonym in the next sentence for welfare. Explain the things that are part of a person's *welfare*.

7. Underline the words that tell what was endured. Then, use *endured* in a sentence.

8. Circle the words that tell what gives a downright sense of pride. Tell about a time you had a *downright* sense of pride.

Read the following passage. Pay special attention to the underlined words. Then, read it again, and complete the activities. Use a separate sheet of paper for your written answers.

Today, many U.S. citizens seem to take for granted their right to vote. Nearly half the eligible population does not even vote in national elections. If everyone realized how long and hard their ancestors struggled for the right to vote, they would treasure it.

In 1775, the thirteen colonies' rebellion against Britain became a war for freedom. Even before the first battle, the colonies realized they had to work together to reach their goals. The war ended in 1781, but it took another six years for a constitution to be written.

It took a lot of work for the new country to succeed. Each former colony, which became a state, had to give up some of its own laws and power to the new federal government. Only then could any written document become the supreme law of the land.

The Founding Fathers believed in a government that would promote the welfare of its people. Curiously, though, they let the states decide who had a say in running that government. Over the years, laws that kept people from voting were endured by the poor, Catholics and non-Christians, Indians, African Americans, and women.

Wyoming allowed women to vote while it was still a territory. Other territories and states let women vote in local elections. Finally, one by one, states started to let women take part in elections. Women even began to hold elected office. Still, it was not until 1920 that they could vote everywhere in the United States.

It took many years and various changes in our laws to give all adult citizens the right to vote. We should all have a downright feeling of pride that we can vote. That right gives us the ability to direct the course of our own lives and that of our country's history.

On Woman's Right to Suffrage
Susan B. Anthony

Summary Susan B. Anthony gives a speech to United States citizens in 1873. It is a time when women cannot vote. She says that the U.S. Constitution protects all people. She says that women should have the same rights as men.

Writing About the Big Question

How much information is enough? In "On Woman's Right to Suffrage," Susan B. Anthony discusses the importance of many voices to a democracy. Complete this sentence:

Discrimination may have a negative effect on democracy because it

prevents _____.

Note-taking Guide

Use the graphic organizer to record details that support Susan B. Anthony's argument.

> The Constitution says "We the people," not "We, the white male citizens."

> Women should have the right to vote.

On Woman's Right to Suffrage

1. **Connect:** Anthony tries to vote. She says that she did not break the law. How does she connect this comment to the Constitution?

   _____

   _____

2. **Apply:** Anthony says that a democracy gives rights to all of its citizens. Does Anthony believe that she lives in a true democracy? Explain.

   _____

   _____

3. **Reading Skill:** Determine whether each statement in the chart is a **fact**, an **opinion**, a **generalization**, or an **overgeneralization**. Write your choice next to the statement. Then, explain your choice.

Statement	Type of Statement	Explanation
To [women] this government is . . . the most hateful aristocracy ever established.		
[I] voted at the last . . . election, without having a lawful right to vote.	Fact	She did try to vote. This was against the law.
Webster . . . define[s] a citizen to be a person entitled to voted.		

4. **Literary Analysis:** Anthony **repeats** "We, the people" throughout her speech. Why does she repeat these words?

   _____

   _____

Writing: Evaluation

Write an **evaluation** of the persuasive arguments in Anthony's speech. Use the questions below to gather ideas for your evaluation.

- What is Anthony's position?

  _____

  _____

- What are two of her arguments?

  _____

  _____

- What are two counterarguments for the arguments you just listed?

  _____

  _____

- How well does Anthony deal with these counterarguments?

  _____

  _____

Use your notes to write your evaluation.

Research and Technology: Statistical Snapshot

Create a **statistical snapshot** of women in the United States. Fill in the chart with the information you found in your research. Complete the chart with questions you could ask in your survey about the information you found.

Facts and Statistics	Questions You Could Ask

from Sharing in the American Dream • Science and the Sense of Wonder

Reading Skill

A **fact** is information that can be proved. An **opinion** is a person's judgment or belief. **Ask questions to evaluate an author's support** for his or her opinions.

- A *valid opinion* can be backed up with facts or information from experts.

- A *faulty opinion* cannot be backed up with facts. It is supported by other opinions. It often ignores facts that prove it wrong. Faulty opinions often show *bias*. This is an unfair dislike for something.

Use the chart to help you identify facts and opinions while you are reading.

Literary Analysis

An author's **word choice** can help show an idea or feeling. Authors have different reasons for choosing their words. The following are several reasons:

- the author's audience and purpose

- **connotations** of words: the negative or positive ideas connected with words

- **denotations** of words: the dictionary definition of words

Statement:

↓

1. Distinguish fact from opinion.
ASK: Can it be proved?

↓

Answer:

↓

2. Distinguish valid from faulty opinion.
ASK: Can it be supported?

↓

Answer:

© Pearson Education

Word List A

Study these words from Sharing in the American Dream. Then, complete the activity that follows.

achieve [uh CHEEV] *v.* to succeed in doing something you want
  To achieve your big dreams, do small things well along the way.

denied [di NYD] *v.* stopped from having or doing something
  American women were denied the right to vote until 1920.

inhabit [in HAB it] *v.* to live in a particular place
  Some day I plan to inhabit a tree house in the middle of a rain forest.

sags [SAGZ] *v.* hangs down, especially because of the heavy weight
  Look at how the top branch of that tree sags under the snow!

secure [si KYOOR] *v.* to get or bring about something important
  Did you secure your parents' permission to spend the night?

syrupy [SEER uh pee] *adj.* thick, sticky, and sweet
  I hate how the syrupy sauce on this cinnamon roll makes my fingers sticky.

task [TASK] *n.* a job to be done, especially a difficult or annoying one
  A nightly task I must remember is to set my alarm clock.

union [YOON yuhn] *n.* separate groups joining for a purpose
  Our basketball team is a union of seventh-graders and eighth-graders.

Exercise A

Fill in each blank in the paragraph below with an appropriate word from Word List A. Use each word only once.

Our club decided to make a special Saturday lunch for people who

[1] _____ a homeless shelter during the winter months. We were

able to [2] _____ the school kitchen, where we are cooking today.

However, our request for a bus and driver was [3] _____. Luckily,

our parents have offered to drive, helping us to [4] _____ our

goal. As we work side by side among friends, a feeling of goodness

surrounds our [5] _____. Every [6] _____ seems like fun

as we prepare a feast of ham-and-cheese sandwiches, [7] _____

peaches oozing sweetness, and a tossed salad. Each lunch box

we pack [8] _____ in the middle from the weight of the

bounty—including a brownie for dessert!

1 Underline the words naming the <u>task</u> the speaker has been given. Then, explain why a *task* is different from an extracurricular activity.

2. Circle the word naming the other job the teacher would <u>secure</u>. Then, explain *secure*.

3. Underline the words naming what was <u>denied</u> to the writer in college. Then, tell about a time you were *denied* something you wanted.

4. Circle the word in the next sentence that hints at the meaning of <u>sags</u>. Then, name a common object that *sags*.

5. Underline the words telling what the speech should <u>achieve</u>. Then, explain the word *achieve*.

6. Circle the words that explain "<u>syrupy</u> words." Then, write an example of *syrupy* words.

7. Underline the words naming the place bad kids will <u>inhabit</u>. Then, describe a place that would be awful to *inhabit*.

8. Circle the two groups of people that would form a <u>union</u>. Then, explain what *union* means.

Read the following passage. Pay special attention to the underlined words. Then, read it again, and complete the activities. Use a separate sheet of paper for your written answers.

Today will be tough for me. I have been given the <u>task</u> of speaking to a group of students about their bad behavior. These students have been in trouble at school three or more times during the last month. When I became a teacher, I never thought I would also <u>secure</u> the job of speechmaker! After all, I am the person whose requests to appear on the college television station were always <u>denied</u>. I figured that was because of the way my right eyebrow <u>sags</u>. Someone must have thought that a droopy brow wouldn't look very good on the screen.

Anyway, what I am supposed to <u>achieve</u> with my speech today is to get students fired up about being good. I can still remember the speeches I heard on this topic in my youth. Those speeches basically fell into two categories. One type used <u>syrupy</u> words and lots of "touchy-feely" remarks. I think you were supposed to feel guilty after hearing one of these speeches so you would be inspired to become a better person. The other type of speech was based on fear. We were told about the really bad kids who are sent to jail cells, which they will <u>inhabit</u> for many years. Filled with dread, we were supposed to become well behaved.

Obviously, I do not want to give either type of speech today. Instead, I want to figure out how to talk to these students in a way that respects who they are. I think that if they have a sense of <u>union</u> with the adults at our school, they might change for the better. After all, don't we all want to do things that the people we like will appreciate?

I wish you could sit beside me right now and tell me what to say. I know you would have just the right words.

from Sharing in the American Dream

Colin Powell

Summary Former Secretary of State Colin Powell shares his beliefs about volunteer work. He encourages listeners to volunteer their time to help others in some way. He believes that this is an important part of keeping the United States strong.

Writing About the Big Question

How much information is enough? In "Sharing in the American Dream," Colin Powell calls on all members of society to help one another achieve their dreams. Complete this sentence:

An effective way to challenge people to volunteer is _____

_____.

Note-taking Guide

Fill in the chart to record the main points of Powell's speech.

People Who Need Help	What They Need	Who Should Help
		each and every one of us

Activate Prior Knowledge

Think about a speech you have heard. Did it inspire you? How did the speech make you feel?

_____

_____

_____

_____

_____

Reading Skill

A **fact** can be proved. An **opinion** is a person's belief. What is one fact in the first paragraph?

_____

_____

_____

Stop to Reflect

"The American Dream" means different things to different people. What is your "American Dream"?

_____

_____

_____

Reading Check ✏

To whom does Powell refer in the beginning of his speech? Underline the text that tells you.

from Sharing in the American Dream
Colin Powell

This selection is taken from a speech that Colin Powell gave. He was speaking to a meeting of government leaders in Philadelphia. He begins his speech by referring to the leaders of the American Revolution, who met in Philadelphia more than 200 years before to sign the Declaration of Independence. He quotes from the Declaration to inspire his listeners.

◆ ◆ ◆

They pledged their lives, their fortune and their sacred honor to secure <u>inalienable</u> rights given by God for life, liberty and <u>pursuit</u> of happiness—pledged that they would provide them to all who would inhabit this new nation.

◆ ◆ ◆

Powell says that the signers of the Declaration are present at the meeting in spirit. They are proud of what Americans have achieved, but America still has not completely achieved the dream described in the Declaration.

◆ ◆ ◆

Despite more than two centuries of moral and material progress, despite all our efforts to achieve a more perfect union, there are still Americans who are not sharing in the American Dream.

◆ ◆ ◆

Powell quotes from the poem "A Dream Deferred," by Langston Hughes. The poem asks how people react when they are not able to achieve their dreams. It suggests that such people may turn to violence.

Vocabulary Development

inalienable (in AYL yuhn uh buhl) *adj.* not capable of being taken away; nontransferable

Powell then asks his listeners to pledge that no one in America will be denied the promise of the American Dream. He says that in order for the dream to come true, fortunate Americans must reach out to help the less fortunate.

♦ ♦ ♦

We are a <u>compassionate</u> and caring people. We are a generous people. We will reach down, we will reach back, we will reach across to help our brothers and sisters who are in need.

♦ ♦ ♦

He urges his listeners to reach out to those who most need help—America's children.

♦ ♦ ♦

<u>As you've heard, up to 15 million young Americans today are at risk . . .</u>

♦ ♦ ♦

Powell says that helping children in need may seem like too big a job. Actually, though, it is something we all can do because we all know what children need. They need adults who care for them, safe homes and schools, health care, skills, and opportunities.

He asks his listeners to make a commitment to American children today. He says that government, corporations, nonprofit agencies, churches, and individuals can all work together to make sure that all children get what they need.

♦ ♦ ♦

You heard the governors and the mayors, and you'll hear more in a little minute that says the real answer is for each and every one of us,

Literary Analysis

An author's **word choice** can help tell a certain idea or feeling. Read the bracketed paragraph. What ideas and feelings does Powell want the audience to have? Circle the text that supports the answer.

_____

_____

_____

Reading Skill

Read the underlined text. Is this statement a **fact** or an **opinion**? Explain your answer.

_____

_____

_____

Reading Check ✎

To whom does Powell ask that his listeners make a commitment? Underline the text that tells you.

Vocabulary Development

compassionate (kuhm PASH uhn it) *adj.* deeply sympathetic

TAKE NOTES

Literary Analysis

Connotations are the negative or positive ideas connected with words. Circle the words on this page that have positive connotations.

Reading Skill

It is important to **ask questions about the author's support** as you read. What is one question you might ask about Powell's support for his main idea?

_____

_____

Stop to Reflect

How did this speech make you feel about volunteering?

_____

_____

_____

_____

_____

not just here in Philadelphia, but across this land—for each and every one of us to reach out and touch someone in need.

◆　◆　◆

Powell ends his speech by again referring to the spirit of the Declaration of Independence, which was signed in Philadelphia more than 200 years before.

◆　◆　◆

All of us can spare 30 minutes a week or an hour a week. All of us can give an extra dollar. . . . There is a spirit of Philadelphia that will leave Philadelphia tomorrow afternoon and spread across this whole nation—

◆　◆　◆

Powell says that all Americans must help spread the promise of the American Dream. It must be done in order to make the promises of the Declaration of Independence come true.

◆　◆　◆

Let us make sure that no child in America is left behind, no child in America has their dream deferred or denied.

Vocabulary Development

deferred (di FERD) *adj.* delayed

from Sharing in the American Dream

1. **Respond:** Powell believes that all citizens should participate in volunteer work. Do you agree or disagree with this message? Explain.

_____

_____

2. **Interpret:** Powell refers to the signers of the Declaration of Independence at the beginning of his speech. What kinds of feelings do you think Powell wants to create in his audience by mentioning this group of people?

_____

_____

3. **Reading Skill:** An **opinion** is a judgment or belief. Identify one opinion in the speech. Explain your choice.

_____

_____

4. **Literary Analysis:** An author's **word choice** can help show a certain idea or feeling. Word choice can be influenced by **connotation**. Connotations are the negative or positive ideas connected with certain words. Use this chart to analyze Powell's word choice in his speech.

Powell's Purpose	Words and Phrases That Support His Purpose	Connotations

Writing

Write a brief **response** to Powell's statement "All of us can spare 30 minutes a week or an hour a week." The following questions will help you write your response.

- Who does Powell think needs the most help?

  _____

  _____

- Do you agree or disagree with Powell? Explain.

  _____

  _____

- Does Powell's idea apply to your own experience? Explain.

  _____

  _____

Use your notes to write your response.

Listening and Speaking: Intro Speech

Your **intro speech** should be short, yet it should tell as much as possible about Colin Powell. Use the following activity to record information as you research Colin Powell.

- Personal information: _____

  _____

- Jobs/Political offices: _____

  _____

- Honors/Awards: _____

  _____

- Other information: _____

  _____

Word List A

Study these words from "Science and the Sense of Wonder." Then, complete the activity.

exhaling [eks HAYL ing] *v.* breathing out
After holding his breath for ten seconds, Carlos is now exhaling.

expand [ek SPAND] *v.* to become larger
After a huge meal, our waistlines expand.

glinting [GLINT ing] *adj.* flashing with a small amount of light
We couldn't see well with the sun glinting off the windshield.

mere [MEER] *adj.* nothing more than; small or unimportant
Huge stars are so far away that they appear as mere dots of light.

mutations [myoo TAY shuhnz] *n.* changes in form of things in nature
The purple butterflies were mutations of the original blue ones.

outward [OWT wuhrd] *adv.* toward the outside
The lawn sprinkler shot water outward in all directions.

radiation [ray dee AY shuhn] *n.* invisible rays of light or heat that an object sends out
The sun's radiation is not constant but varies over time.

violence [VY uh luhns] *n.* great force
The tomato hit the ground with such violence that it splattered.

Exercise A

Fill in each blank in the paragraph below with an appropriate word from Word List A. Use each word only once.

In a typical science fiction story, harmful [1] _____ from atomic waste causes strange [2] _____ in harmless frogs. They [3] _____ rapidly, growing to a huge size. From [4] _____ frogs that can fit easily in the palm of your hand, they become giants. They wander [5] _____ from their pond, now too small to contain them. Wherever they go, they create [6] _____. They are either squashing everything in their path or [7] _____ their deadly radioactive breath. Humans are at a loss to stop the frogs, which grow bigger and tougher. Finally, someone comes up with a simple, obvious solution. The rays of the sun [8] _____ off a mirror dry up the moist-skinned troublemakers. Peace rules.

1. Underline the words that give you a clue to the meaning of <u>mutations</u>. Then, write a sentence for *mutations*.

2. Circle the words that hint at the meaning of <u>mere</u>. Write about an exchange of money that includes the word *mere*.

3. Circle the word that hints at the opposite of the meaning of <u>violence</u>. Write a sentence that describes one effect of *violence*.

4. Underline the words that help to understand <u>glinting</u>. Write a sentence about something you've seen *glinting*.

5. Circle the word that names what began to <u>expand</u>. Explain how you might cause an object to *expand*.

6. Circle the words in the paragraph that help you understand <u>outward</u>. Name something that opens *outward*.

7. Underline the word that describes <u>radiation</u>. Describe one harmful effect of *radiation* from the sun.

8. Circle the word that is the opposite of <u>exhaling</u>. Use *exhaling* in a sentence.

Read the following passage. Pay special attention to the underlined words. Then, read it again, and complete the activities. Use a separate sheet of paper for your written answers.

Jamie had always refused to believe that humans were the only living creatures in the universe. He had also refused to believe that space was full of strange <u>mutations</u> of people like the aliens in most science-fiction movies. So, he was totally shocked by what happened to him one weekend evening.

He was walking home from the movies, a <u>mere</u> three short blocks from his house. The street was well lit. There had never been any <u>violence</u> along this route that Jamie knew of, so he felt safe.

Suddenly, Jamie spied what looked like a square coin on the sidewalk, <u>glinting</u> in the light of the streetlamp. As he stooped to pick it up, the strangest thing happened: The coin began to <u>expand</u> on all sides. Slowly at first, it seemed to be gathering speed as it spread <u>outward</u>.

Jamie glanced around him to see if this action had attracted any attention, but he realized he was alone. Backing up to avoid the edge of the rapidly expanding coin, Jamie collided with the side of a building.

Now the coin seemed to be developing features: a face, limbs, and a trunk. It was glowing, too. Jamie held his breath in case the thing was giving off any harmful <u>radiation</u>. Luckily, it only seemed to be inhaling and <u>exhaling</u> the night air.

Suddenly, Jamie found himself in a conversation with the thing, and he hadn't said a word. Yes, like aliens in the movies, it was reading his thoughts.

"Of course I'm not a coin," it responded, "although I do feel *minty* fresh."

"Wow," thought Jamie, "it has a sense of humor."

"Why not?" responded the creature. "Why do humans think they're the only ones who can make jokes?"

"Hmm," thought Jamie, "if it played a comedy club, I wonder if it would knock the audience dead."

Science and the Sense of Wonder

Isaac Asimov

Summary Isaac Asimov says that he does not agree with a poem Walt Whitman wrote. Whitman says in his poem that people should forget about science. He says that people should enjoy the sky's beauty. Asimov says that people enjoy the sky more when they know science.

Writing About the Big Question

How much information is enough? In "Science and the Sense of Wonder," Asimov argues that scientific knowledge adds to our sense of wonder about the universe. Complete these sentences:

The more knowledge I accumulate about how natural systems work,

the (more/less) curious I feel. This is because _____

_____.

Note-taking Guide

Use the chart to recall Asimov's reasons for why science makes watching the sky more interesting.

Some of those bright spots in the sky are "worlds of red-hot liquid."

How science makes watching the night sky more interesting

Science and the Sense of Wonder

1. **Analyze:** Our galaxy is small, compared with other galaxies that scientists have found. Asimov tries to explain how small our galaxy is. How does he do this?

   _____

   _____

2. **Make a Judgment:** Asimov says that knowing science makes the night sky more interesting. Whitman says that he would rather just enjoy the night sky than learn scientific explanations. Do you agree with Asimov or Whitman? Explain your choice.

   _____

   _____

3. **Reading Skill:** A **fact** is a detail that is true and can be proved. Identify one fact that is in the essay.

   _____

   _____

4. **Literary Analysis: Word choice** can help show an idea or feeling. Use this chart to analyze Asimov's word choice. Write words and phrases that support his purpose. Then, write the **connotations**.

Asimov's Purpose	Words and Phrases That Support His Purpose	Connotations
To convince people that scientific knowledge of nature adds to our appreciation of its beauty		

Writing: Response

Write a **response** to Asimov's idea that science helps you enjoy nature. Use the chart to list things that you like about nature. Explain whether you enjoy them as a poet would or as a scientist would. Use your notes to write your response.

Things You Like About Nature	Poet or Scientist?

Listening and Speaking: Introductory Speech

Write an **introductory speech** to present Isaac Asimov to a school assembly. Answer the questions below to help you with your presentation.

- List three things that you want to include in your speech.

  _____

  _____

  _____

- What style would be appropriate for your speech?

  _____

  _____

- What parallel wording will you use in your speech?

  _____

  _____

Use your notes to write your introductory speech.

Newspaper Editorials

About Newspaper Editorials

Newspaper editorials are written to express an opinion on a topic. The purpose of an editorial is to persuade readers to agree with the writer's point of view. Some editorials ask readers to take action on an issue. Editorial writers support their opinions with facts, examples, and statistics.

Reading Skill

To understand the writer's point of view and purpose for writing, readers must **analyze the proposition and support patterns** in the editorial. The writer states a problem and describes how it affects the reader. Then, the writer provides one or more solutions to the problem. The writer may use both facts and opinions to support the solution. Ask the following questions when reading a newspaper editorial:

- What problem does the writer present?
- Does the writer's solution to the problem make sense?
- Does the writer support the solution with facts, examples, and statistics?

Error in Logic	Example	Problem
Oversimplification	If you own a cellphone you should support the right to use it anywhere you want to.	Ignores other alternatives
False analogy	Outlawing cellphone use while driving is like outlawing eating while reading.	The comparison is irrelevant
Insufficient evidence	I do not know anyone who has had an accident because of a cellphone so I do not think they are a problem.	False conclusion
Jumping on the bandwagon	Everyone I know drives while talking on the cellphone, so it should be legal.	Assumes an opinion is correct because it is popular

Langberg: Hands-free law won't solve the problem

FRIDAY, SEPTEMBER 1, 2006

By Mike Langberg

Driving while talking on a cell phone clearly increases your risk of getting into an accident, but here's a surprise: The problem is all in your head.

The mental distraction of conversing behind the wheel is so great that switching to a headset or other "hands-free" approach—instead of taking one hand off the wheel to hold the phone to your ear—does nothing to reduce the danger.

But politicians never let facts get in the way of making themselves look good.

The result is hands-free legislation that passed the California Assembly and Senate last week, and is likely to be signed into law this month by Gov. Arnold Schwarzenegger.

The California Wireless Telephone Automobile Safety Act of 2006, the bill's formal name, says: "A person shall not drive a motor vehicle while using a wireless telephone unless that telephone is specifically designed and configured to allow hands-free listening and talking, and is used in that manner while driving. Using a hand-held phone, you'll get an almost painless fine of $20 for the first offense. The penalty doesn't get much worse for additional violations, moving up to just $50.

Using a hand-held phone would only be allowed in emergency situations, such as calling 911.

The new rules wouldn't take effect until July 1, 2008.

So we're getting a nearly toothless law, two years down the line, that doesn't offer a real solution to a serious problem.

The first part of that problem is the awesome popularity of cell phones.

There are now 208 million cell phone subscribers in the United States, equal to 69 percent of the total population. Almost every adult American, in other words, now has a cell phone.

The National Highway Traffic Safety Administration says an average 6 percent of drivers on the road at any given moment are talking on a cell phone. The number goes up to 10 percent during daylight hours.

Driver distraction or inattention contributes to nearly 80 percent of accidents, according to a research study completed earlier this year by NHTSA and Virginia Tech.

Although overall death and injury rates continue to decline slowly over time, there's no question cell phones are a factor in many highway accidents. Last year, NHTSA reports, highway accidents killed 43,443 people last year and injured 2.7 million.

There's an obvious solution: Ban talking on a cell phone while driving.

But that's not going to happen, at least not anytime soon. The cell phone lobby is too powerful, and the public is too enamored with chatting behind the wheel.

Instead, we're getting hands-free laws that give politicians the appearance of taking action.

New York, New Jersey, Connecticut and the District of Columbia already have hands-free laws, and many other states are considering similar steps.

These laws are moving forward despite a persuasive and growing list of academic studies, involving both simulator testing and analysis of real-world crash data, showing hands-free phone calls are no less risky than holding a phone.

Think about it: If you're fully aware of what's happening on the road ahead of you, such as a car suddenly slamming on its brakes, your response time isn't going to vary much whether you've got one or two hands on the wheel.

But your response time will suffer if you're in the middle of an argument on the phone with your boss or spouse.

I'll raise my hand here and admit I'm part of the problem. I've come close to rear-ending other drivers on a few occasions because I was talking on my cell phone. And I don't believe my sluggish reaction would have changed if I'd been using a headset.

David L. Strayer, a psychology professor at the University of Utah, has been studying cell phone distraction for more than five years.

Last week, he told me there are at least six studies showing no safety benefit from hands-free talking.

"This . . . suggests that legislative initiatives that restrict handheld devices but permit hands-free devices are not likely to eliminate the problems associated with cell phones while driving," Strayer and two colleagues wrote in the summer 2006 issue of the journal *Human Factors*.

I asked Strayer if there's a safe way to participate in a phone call while driving.

"Not unless we somehow rewire our brains," he responded, There's no technological remedy, in other words, to the mental distraction created during a cell phone conversation.

At the same time, there are possible side effects—both good and bad—from hands free laws.

On the good side, some drivers might not want to go through the hassle of buying and using a headset or other hands-free gadget. They would give up talking while driving, collectively reducing auto accidents.

On the bad side, some drivers might get a false sense of security and decide it's OK to talk even more.

Here's my prediction: California's hands-free law, and similar laws elsewhere, will do nothing to change the number of accidents tied to drivers using cell phones.

Once everyone realizes these laws accomplish nothing, we'll have to decide whether cell phones require further restrictions or should be categorized with other dangerous behind-the-wheel distractions—everything from noisy children to complicated audio systems—that aren't restricted.

THE BIG ?

How much information is enough?

Does this editorial change the way you think about cell phone use while driving? Why or why not?

Features:
- text spoken c
  an audience
- remarks that
  the significan
  event
- language inte
  engage listen
  encourage su
  the speaker's

Transcript of Governor Arnold Schwarzenegger Signing Legislation Requiring Drivers to Use Hands Free Devices

DATE: Friday, September 15, 2006
TIME: 11:15 a.m.

EVENT: Oakland Hilton, California Room, 1 Hegenberger Rd,
        Oakland, CA

The speak
opens his
by stating
propositio

GOVERNOR SCHWARZENEGGER:

. . . Today we will be signing SB 1613. This is the hands-free cell phone bill that will save lives by making our roads safer. And I want to say thank you to Senator Simitian for his great, great work on this bill and for working with my office on this bill to perfect the bill. I want to thank him also for his great commitment to . . . California, and to make our roads safe. He has been really extraordinary, to protect the people of California and I want to say thank you for that.

The simple fact is that it is really dangerous when you talk on your cell phone and drive at the same time. Hand-held cell phones are responsible for 1,000 accidents every month, and we have seen that there are very dangerous situations sometimes. We want to avoid that, and this is why we have here this bill. This bill doesn't mean that you can't talk on a cell phone; it just means that you should not hold a hand-held cell phone, you should use a headset or use a speaker system.

Also, there is an exception here that if you have to make an emergency call, then you can use the hand-held phone. And also, what is important is that this law will go into effect on July 1 of 2008. There will be a $20 fine if you're caught the first time using a cell phone, and then $50 after that.

I think it is very important for people to know that even though the law begins in 2008, July of 2008, stop using your cell phones right now, because you're putting people at risk. You just look away for a second, or for a split second, from what's going on in front of you, and at that moment a child could be running out, and you could kill this child just because you were busy looking down and dialing on your cell phone. So pay attention to that, take this seriously. We want to really save lives here.

Thank you very much again, and now I would like to have Senator Simitian come out and say a few words, please.

SENATOR SIMITIAN:

Thank you all very much for being here today. And some of you know, but perhaps not all of you, that this is the sixth hands-free cell phone bill I've introduced during the past six years. The question I've been asked quite frequently of late is, "Why did you keep introducing the bill?" And the answer is really very simple. I introduced the bill because I believe it will save lives. It's just that simple. You've got a readily available technology that costs next to nothing and saves lives. Why on earth wouldn't we use it?

This bill isn't a perfect solution, it isn't a total solution, but it is a significant and important improvement over the current state of affairs, and it will save lives, and that was the goal from Day 1. . . .

> The speaker over-simplifies the issue of cost involved in using a hands-free cellphone device.

CHIEF BECHER:

. . . I'm proud to be here today for the signing of this bill. It represents a collaborative effort between the legislature, the Governor, [the phone company] and the many backers and traffic safety officials throughout the state, to make the roadways of California a safer place to drive.

Statewide, collisions caused by distracted drivers result in countless hours of roadway delay, congestion, injury and death. This legislation is another useful tool for law enforcement to curb the growing number of collisions caused either partially or wholly by distracted drivers.

Prior to this cell phone law going into effect, the CHP plans a major public education campaign to ensure the public is aware of the changes. Education is a major focus for the CHP, because public awareness of the issue and voluntary compliance wtih this new law can have a significant impact on crashes even before the new law goes into effect. The Governor is exactly right. Start now.

Our goal is to have all drivers in the state keep both hands on the wheel and have the attention and awareness so that they can navigate [their] driving environment. It is always incumbent on drivers to drive attentively. Many devices and activities taking place inside today's vehicles can cause that split second distraction that may result in an unnecessary traffic collision. Cell phones are among the more prominent of these distractions.

And finally, thanks to all in the creation and implementation of this bill. The California Highway Patrol supports this new legislation as part of our No. 1 goal, to prevent traffic collisions and to save lives. Thank you.

> **THE BIG ?**
> **How much information is enough?**
> Do the remarks of the speakers provide enough information for you to make an informed judgment about cellphone use while driving? Explain your response.

Thinking About the Newspaper Editorial

1. Find one sentence in Langberg's editorial that states his opinion about using cell phones while driving. Write that sentence on the line below.

   _____

2. In Governor Schwarzenegger's speech, what reason does the governor give for choosing to sign the hands-free cell phone bill?

   _____

TALK ABOUT IT Reading Skill

3. Langberg states that hands-free phones are not likely to eliminate the problems of using cell phones while driving. How does Langberg support his statement?

   _____

4. How does Governor Schwarzenegger support his decision to sign the hands-free cell phone bill?

   _____

WRITE ABOUT IT Timed Writing: Editorial Writing **(40 minutes)**

Use one of the editorials as a model to write an editorial. Research an issue in your school or community. State your opinion on the issue, propose a solution, and support your solution with facts and examples.

- What is the issue?

   _____

- What is your opinion on the issue?

   _____

- What solution do you propose?

   _____

- What facts support your solution?

   _____

Describe Somebody • Almost a Summer Sky

Poetry is the most musical form of writing. People who write poems choose words for both sound and meaning. Poets use some or all of the following to do this:

- **Sensory language** is writing or speech that deals with the five senses—sight, sound, smell, taste, and touch.

- **Figurative language** is writing that is imaginative. It may mean something different than what it seems to mean. The many kinds of figurative language include these:

Figurative Language	Definition	Example
Metaphor	• describes one thing as if it were another	Her eyes were saucers, wide with expectation.
Simile	• uses *like* or *as* to compare two unlike things	The drums were as loud as a fireworks display.
Personification	• gives human qualities to something that is not human	The clarinets sang.

Sound devices add a musical quality to poetry. Some sound devices include these:

Sound Device	Definition	Example
Alliteration	• repetition of consonant sounds at the beginning of words	feathered friend
Repetition	• repeated use of a sound, word, or phrase	water, water everywhere
Assonance	• repetition of a vowel sound followed by different consonants in stressed syllables	fade/hay

Other sound devices include these:

Sound Device	Definition	Example
Consonance	• repetition of a consonant sound at the end of stressed syllables with different vowels sounds	end/hand
Onomatopoeia	• use of words that imitate sounds	buzz, whack
Rhyme	• repetition of sounds at the ends of words	dear, cheer, here
Meter	• the pattern of stressed and unstressed syllables	A **horse**, a **horse**! My **king**dom **for** a **horse**!

The structure of a poem determines its form. Most poems are written in lines. These lines are grouped into stanzas. This list describes several forms of poetry.

- **Lyric** poetry describes the thoughts and feelings of one speaker. The **speaker** is the person who speaks in the poem. Lyric poetry usually seems musical.

- **Narrative** poetry tells a story in verse. It often includes some of the same things that are found in short stories.

- **Ballads** are songlike poems that tell a story. They often tell about adventure and romance.

- **Free verse** is poetry that has no set structure. It does not have to rhyme or have regular meter. Lines do not have to be a specific length. There may be no specific stanza pattern.

- **Haiku** is a three-line Japanese form. The first and third lines have five syllables each. The second line has seven syllables.

- **Rhyming couplets** are a pair of lines that rhyme. The lines usually have the same meter and length.

- **Limericks** are funny poems with five lines. They have a specific rhythm pattern and rhyme scheme.

Word List A

Study these words from the poetry of Jacqueline Woodson. Then, apply your knowledge to the activities that follow.

awhile [uh WYL] *adv.* for a short time
  I stayed awhile at the library, reading the newspapers.

dabbing [DAB ing] *v.* gently touching something, usually with a cloth
  Dad kept dabbing his chin where he cut himself shaving.

grins [GRINZ] *v.* smiles with a very big smile
  The toddler next door always grins and waves when she sees me.

regular [REG yuh luhr] *adj.* usual; not different or special
  On a regular school day, not during exams, I have about two hours of homework to do.

squints [SKWINTS] *v.* looks at something with eyes partly closed
  The boat captain squints into the sun as he steers us toward the dock.

upstate [UHP stayt] *adv.* in or toward the northern part of a state
  The winter weather is quite cold upstate, but the summers are balmy.

Exercise A

Fill in each blank in the paragraph below with an appropriate word from Word List A. Use each word only once.

My grandmother lives [1] _____, alone on a big farm. Last year, I got to ride the bus up there by myself. It was a long trip! I would read [2] _____, then sleep, then listen to music. A few times I looked around at the other passengers. One man seemed sad, and he kept [3] _____ his eyes with a tissue. I spotted plenty of young people and older folks, too. A few riders were dressed in strange outfits, but most of them wore [4] _____ clothes. Have you ever noticed how sometimes a person our parents' age [5] _____ while reading? Does closing your eyes part way really help you to see better? Anyway, my grandmother always [6] _____ when she sees me. When I finally got off that bus, I don't know whose smile was bigger!

Read the following passage. Pay special attention to the underlined words. Then, read it again, and complete the activities. Use a separate sheet of paper for your written answers.

When life gets too hectic, it is soothing simply to enjoy nature. This is true for young people and adults alike. We all have many stresses during our <u>regular</u>, everyday lives. School, work, relationships, and responsibilities can sometimes weigh heavily on all of us. Taking <u>awhile</u> away from it all and, for a brief time, enjoying the beauty of nature can be very helpful.

Whether you are <u>upstate</u> among the lakes and mountains of the northern country, or farther south, or closer to a city, natural wonders are everywhere. Even a small park in the middle of town can be home to many plants and animals. If you are nowhere near a park of any kind, just look up at the sky! Clouds and their endless shapes are fun to watch during the day. Stars are lovely to see twinkling at night. In between are the amazing "light shows" of sunrise and sunset! Imagine how an artist <u>squints</u> at his painting, peering as he reaches for the perfect shading; the morning and evening skies seem to achieve this harmony with no effort at all.

Many people find that shifting their focus away from their worries and on to something bigger— like the natural world—can help to turn frowns into smiles, and even <u>grins</u>, This can happen more quickly than they might expect. Someone who might have been sadly <u>dabbing</u> a tear away might suddenly feel peaceful. Sometimes it is good to remind ourselves that we are only a very small part of a big world.

A hike on a shady woodland trail can be inspirational. The view of the nighttime sky from a city rooftop can be awe-inspiring. Even the sights right outside our windows can surprise us sometimes. Nature's gifts are everywhere.

1. Circle the word that means the same as <u>regular</u>. What is your *regular* morning routine?

2. Underline the words that describe what <u>awhile</u> is. Tell about something that you did *awhile* today or yesterday.

3. Circle the words that describe the opposite of <u>upstate</u>. Tell what *upstate* means.

4. Circle the word that is the opposite of <u>grins</u>. Then, underline the word that means the same as *grins*.

5. Underline the words naming what someone might be <u>dabbing</u>. What else might someone be *dabbing*?

6. Underline the word that tells what <u>squints</u> means. When someone *squints*, what are they doing?

Describe Somebody •
Almost a Summer Sky
Jacqueline Woodson

Summaries In "Describe Somebody," a teacher asks her class to write a poem that describes someone. This poem describes Lonnie's thoughts as he thinks about the assignment. In "Almost a Summer Sky," Lonnie and his brother Rodney walk to the park. This poem shares Lonnie's thoughts as the two boys walk.

Note-taking Guide
Use this chart to record main ideas from the poems.

	Speaker	Characters	What the Speaker Learns or Realizes
Describe Somebody	Lonnie	Lonnie, Ms. Marcus, Eric, Miss Edna, Lamont	
Almost a Summer Sky			

Describe Somebody
Jacqueline Woodson

Today in class Ms. Marcus said
Take out your poetry notebooks and
    describe somebody.
Think carefully, Ms. Marcus said.
You're gonna read it to the class.
5 I wrote, Ms. Marcus is tall and a little bit
    skinny.
Then I put my pen in my mouth and stared
    down
at the words.
Then I crossed them out and wrote
Ms. Marcus's hair is long and brown.
10 Shiny.
When she smiles it makes you feel all good
    inside.
I stopped writing and looked around the
    room.
Angel was staring out the window.
Eric and Lamont were having a pen fight.
15 They don't care about poetry.
Stupid words, Eric says.
Lots and lots of stupid words.
Eric is tall and a little bit mean.
Lamont's just regular.
20 Angel's kinda chubby. He's got light brown
    hair.

Activate Prior Knowledge

Your teacher tells you to describe somebody in a poem. You will have to read the poem aloud to the class. Whom would you describe? Explain.

_____

_____

_____

_____

_____

Poetry

Alliteration is repeating consonant sounds at the beginning of words. Read the first set of underlined lines. Circle the words that create alliteration.

Poetry

Consonance is repeating a consonant sound at the end of two or more words. Read the second set of underlined lines. Circle the words that create consonance.

Poetry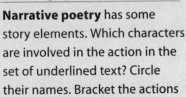

Free verse is poetry without regular rhyme, rhythm, meter, or stanza pattern. Write two reasons why this poem can be said to be written in free verse.

1. _____
   _____
   _____
   _____

2. _____
   _____
   _____
   _____

Poetry

Narrative poetry has some story elements. Which characters are involved in the action in the set of underlined text? Circle their names. Bracket the actions in which they are involved.

Reading Check ✐

Why does the speaker have to write a whole new poem? Underline the text that tells you.

Sometimes we all hang out,
play a little ball or something. Angel's real
   good
at science stuff. Once he made a volcano
for science fair and the stuff that came out
   of it
25 looked like real lava. Lamont can
draw superheroes real good. Eric—nobody
at school really knows this but
he can sing. Once, Miss Edna[1] took me
to a different church than the one
30 we usually go to on Sunday.
I was surprised to see Eric up there
with a choir robe on. He gave me a mean
   look
like I'd better not
say nothing about him and his dark green
   robe with
35 gold around the neck.
After the preacher preached
Eric sang a song with nobody else in the
   choir singing.
Miss Edna started dabbing at her eyes
whispering *Yes, Lord.*
40 Eric's voice was like something
that didn't seem like it should belong
to Eric.
Seemed like it should be coming out of
   an angel.

Now I gotta write a whole new poem
45 'cause Eric would be real mad if I told the
   class
about his angel voice.

---

1. **Miss Edna** Lonnie's foster mother.

Almost a Summer Sky

Jacqueline Woodson

It was the trees first, Rodney[1] tells me.
It's raining out. But the rain is light and
    warm.
And the sky's not all close to us like it gets
sometimes. It's way up there with
5 some blue showing through.
Late spring sky, Ms. Marcus says. *Almost*
    summer sky.
And when she said that, I said
<u>*Hey Ms. Marcus, that's a good title*</u>
<u>*for a poem, right?*</u>
10 <u>You have a poet's heart, *Lonnie*.</u>
<u>That's what Ms. Marcus said to me.</u>
<u>I have a poet's heart.</u>
<u>That's good. A good thing to have.</u>
And I'm the one who has it.

15 Now Rodney puts his arm around my
    shoulder
We keep walking. There's a park
eight blocks from Miss Edna's house
That's where we're going.
Me and Rodney to the park.
20 Rain coming down warm
Rodney with his arm around my shoulder
Makes me think of Todd and his pigeons
how big his smile gets when they fly.
The trees upstate ain't like other trees you
    seen, Lonnie
25 Rodney squints up at the sky, shakes his
    head
smiles.

No, upstate they got maple and catalpa and
    scotch pine,[2]
all kinds of trees just standing.
Hundred-year-old trees big as three men.

---

1. **Rodney** one of Miss Edna's sons.
2. **catalpa** (kuh TAL puh) *n.* tree with heart-shaped leaves; **scotch pine** tree with yellow wood, grown for timber.

Poetry

Repetition is the use of any sound, word, or phrase more than once. Read the underlined text. Circle the words that create repetition.

Read Fluently

Look over the page. Read the sentences that are in italics, or slanted type. Italics show that someone is speaking. Rewrite one of the sentences in italics in your own words. Write it as if it were your own thought.

_____

_____

_____

_____

Reading Check

Where are Rodney and Lonnie going? Underline the text that tells you.

Poetry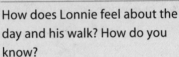

Free verse is poetry that lacks rhyme, stanzas with the same number of lines, or lines with the same number of syllables. Why is "Almost a Summer Sky" an example of free verse?

_____

_____

_____

Stop to Reflect

How does Lonnie feel about the day and his walk? How do you know?

_____

_____

_____

_____

Poetry

Personification means giving human qualities to something that is not human. How does Rodney make the trees seem human? Underline the personification in the bracketed lines.

---

30 *When you go home this weekend,*
       Ms. Marcus said.
  Write about a perfect moment.

  Yeah, Little Brother, Rodney says.
  You don't know about shade till you lived
     upstate.
  Everybody should do it—even if it's just for
     a little while.

35 Way off, I can see the park—blue-gray sky
  touching the tops of trees.

  I had to live there awhile, Rodney said.
  Just to be with all that green, you know?
  I nod, even though I don't.
40 I can't even imagine moving away from
     here,
  from Rodney's arm around my shoulder,
  from Miss Edna's Sunday cooking,
  from Lily[3] in her pretty dresses and great
  big smile when she sees me.

45 Can't imagine moving away

  From
  Home.

  You know what I love about trees, Rodney
     says.
  It's like . . . It's like their leaves are hands
     reaching
50 *out to you. Saying Come on over here,*
     Brother.
  Let me just . . . Let me just . . .
  Rodney looks down at me and grins.
  Let me just give you some shade for a while.

---

3. Lily Lonnie's sister, who lives in a different foster home.

Poetry

1. **Interpret:** The speaker says that Eric would be mad if the class knew he could sing. Why would Eric be angry?

_____

_____

_____

2. **Respond:** Do you agree that Lonnie has the heart of a poet? Explain.

_____

_____

_____

3. **Poetry:** These poems are written in **free verse**. Free verse is poetry that is not set up in any certain way. It does not have to rhyme. Why is free verse a good choice for these poems?

_____

_____

_____

4. **Poetry:** Complete the chart below. Find examples of **figurative language**, or imaginative writing, in the poems. Tell what the figurative language compares. Tell what the figurative language conveys, or means.

	Ideas Compared	Ideas Conveyed
Describe Somebody lines 40–43	Eric's voice is like something that doesn't belong to him.	
Almost a Summer Sky lines 49–53		

Poetry Reading

Arrange a **poetry reading**. Follow these steps to prepare for your poetry reading.

- Read some of the author's works. Jacqueline Woodson's books include *Locomotion*, *Last Summer with Maizon*, and *Between Madison and Palmetto*. Be sure to read several of the poems included in *Locomotion*.

  What I learned from Woodson's writing:

  _____

  _____

  _____

  _____

- Search the Internet. Use words and phrases such as "Jacqueline Woodson article."

  What I learned about Jacqueline Woodson:

  _____

  _____

  _____

  _____

- Watch the video interview with Jacqueline Woodson. Review your source material.

  Additional information learned about the author:

  _____

  _____

  _____

  _____

  _____

Use your notes as you prepare for your poetry reading.

Poetry Collection 1 • Poetry Collection 2

Reading Skill

Context means the words and phrases around another word. Context helps you understand words you do not know. **Preview the lines of verse to identify unfamiliar words**. This means to look for words you do not know before you read the whole poem. Look for clues in the context as you read. Try to figure out the meaning of each unfamiliar word. Look for these types of clues:

- **synonyms or definitions:** words that mean the same as the unfamiliar word
- **antonyms:** words that are opposite in meaning
- **explanation:** words that give extra details, as in the chart below
- **sentence role:** the way the word is used

Using Context	
With her hair all *disheveled,* Looking like she had just awoken	
Explanation	looking like she had just awoken
Sentence Role	describes hair
Meaning *Disheveled* probably means messy, like hair looks after sleeping.	

Literary Analysis

Sound devices are tools that poets use to make words sound musical. Sound devices help poets share ideas. Common sound devices are these:

- **alliteration:** first consonant sound is repeated, as in *big bell*
- **onomatopoeia:** word sounds like its meaning, such as *buzz*
- **rhyme:** word endings sound the same, such as *spring fling*
- **rhythm:** the pattern of strong and weak beats, such as *MAry HAD a LITtle LAMB*

Word List A

Study these words from the poetry collection. Then, complete the activity that follows.

gleam [GLEEM] *v.* shine
   I liked how the wood floors would gleam after we cleaned them.

horizon [huh RY zuhn] *n.* where the land or water seems to meet the sky
   Watching the sun sink beneath the horizon is a wondrous sight.

peers [PEERZ] *v.* looks hard at something as if to see it more clearly
   Jerry peers down the country road, waiting for a car to come.

scampering [SKAM per ing] *n.* running with short, quick steps
   I saw the puppy scampering away with my shoe in its mouth.

scatter [SKAT er] *v.* to toss around here and there
   The strong wind will surely scatter the leaves that I raked into a pile.

throbbed [THRAHBD] *v.* beat quickly; pulsed
   My heart throbbed with excitement before my first plane ride.

Exercise A

Fill in each blank in the paragraph below with an appropriate word from Word List A. Use each word only once.

I stand at the front of the boat, watching the sun [1] _____

and sparkle on the waves. As far as I can see, all the way to the

[2] _____, there is nothing but the sea. Standing beside me,

my little brother [3] _____ into the water. He wants to see a

dolphin. I remember when I was his age and saw a whale emerge from

the ocean. My whole body had [4] _____ with excitement. My yells

of joy had sent everyone [5] _____ as fast as they could up the

deck toward me. Now, years later, I hope my brother can see a whale,

too. Suddenly, just ahead, a giant form seems to [6] _____ the

waves everywhere as it shoots up toward the sky. "A whale!" my

brother and I scream.

Read the following passage. Pay special attention to the underlined words. Then, read it again, and complete the activities. Use a separate sheet of paper for your written answers.

As the sun sinks slowly over the horizon each evening, darkness creeps across the land. For many animals, this hour is the time to wake up and become active. As you prepare for bed, these nighttime are just awakening.

In a forest setting, as a person peers into the growing gloom and hustles home before nightfall, small animals like the raccoon begin scampering around. These animals are starting their nightly search for food. Red foxes, mule deer, and badgers join the raccoons on the prowl. However, all are as silent as possible. Some do not want to be heard by those they hunt. Others are quiet to protect themselves from animals that hunt them.

The peacefulness of the night is rarely disturbed by loud animal sounds. If forest animals do make noise, they usually are raising an alarm. Perhaps an enemy or a fire has been sighted.

Up in the sky, the moon begins to gleam. Then, you can spot other creatures of the night. Bats whir along, black as death. A barn owl swoops gracefully through the night air, its white face shining. Its dive toward the ground will scatter all small animals aware of the owl's presence. They are afraid of becoming the mighty bird's evening meal.

If you are lucky, you might also catch sight of a flying squirrel one night. Its cousin, the tree squirrel, whose body throbbed with activity and excitement all day, peacefully sleeps the night away in a snug nest. The flying squirrel, on the other hand, soars through the trees until morning. Always on the go, it watches the action above and below its path.

So, as you drift off into the land of dreams tonight, imagine creatures large and small roaming the night. If you listen very carefully, maybe you'll hear the quiet whoosh of a squirrel or the soft patter of a fox.

1. Underline the words that tell what happens at the horizon each evening. Then, explain what the *horizon* is.

2. Circle the words naming where a person in the forest peers. Then, explain why the word *peers* is a good word to use in describing this action.

3. Underline the words that tell what a person does while the small animals begin scampering. Then, explain what *scampering* means.

4. Circle the word naming what begins to gleam. Then, describe something else that might *gleam* at night.

5. Underline the sentence telling why the owl will scatter small animals. Then, explain what *scatter* means.

6. Circle the words telling with what the tree squirrel's body throbbed all day. Then, explain what *throbbed* means.

Poetry Collection 1

Summaries "Cat!" uses fun language and sounds to describe a frightened and angry cat. The speaker in "Silver" creates a silvery image of a moonlit night. "Your World" challenges the reader to push past life's limitations.

Writing About the Big Question

What is the secret to reaching someone with words? In "Poetry Collection 1," poets go beyond relying on the meaning of words to communicate. Complete this sentence:

I (notice/do not notice) the sensory effect of words like swoosh,

smush, scrunch, crunch, munch, and splash. Some words I like for

their sounds are _____ and _____ because

_____.

Note-taking Guide

Use this chart to record the topic and actions in each poem.

Poem	Topic	Two Actions in the Poem
Cat!		
Silver	the moon	
Your World		

Cat!
Eleanor Farjeon

Cat!
Scat!
After her, after her,
Sleeky flatterer,
5 Spitfire chatterer,
Scatter her, scatter her
    Off her mat!
    Wuff!
    Wuff!
10   Treat her rough!
Git her, git her,
Whiskery spitter!
Catch her, catch her,
Green-eyed scratcher!
15   Slathery
    Slithery
    Hisser,
    Don't miss her!
Run till you're dithery,[1]
20   Hithery
    Thithery[2]
    Pftts! pftts!
    How she spits!
    Spitch! Spatch!
25   Can't she scratch!
Scritching the bark
Of the sycamore tree,
She's reached her ark
And's hissing at me

Vocabulary Development

flatterer (FLAT er er) *n.* one who praises others insincerely in order to win their approval

1. **dithery** (DITH er ee) *adj.* nervous and confused; in a dither.

2. **Hithery/Thithery** made-up words based on *hither* and *thither*, which mean "here" and "there."

Activate Prior Knowledge

Think of your favorite animal. How would you describe the sounds of that animal?

_____

_____

_____

Reading Skill

Context is the text around a particular word. Context may include a **synonym**. This is a word that means the same as another word. Which word in the underlined passage is a synonym that helps you figure out the meaning of *git*?

_____

_____

Literary Analysis

Sound devices allow poets to use the musical quality of words to express ideas. One type of sound device is **onomatopoeia,** or words that imitate sounds. Underline two made-up words that imitate cat sounds. How do they help you imagine the poem's action?

_____

_____

_____

30   *Pftts! pftts!*
      Wuff! wuff!
            Scat,
            Cat!
            That's
35   *That!*

Silver
Walter de la Mare

Slowly, silently, now the moon
Walks the night in her silver shoon;[1]
This way, and that, she peers, and sees
Silver fruit upon silver trees;
5   One by one the casements[2] catch
Her beams beneath the silvery thatch;[3]
Couched in his kennel, like a log,
With paws of silver sleeps the dog;
From their shadowy coat the white breasts
      peep
10 Of doves in a silver-feathered sleep;
A harvest mouse goes scampering by,
With silver claws, and silver eye;
And moveless fish in the water gleam,
By silver reeds in a silver stream.

Reading Skill

Preview the lines of verse to identify unfamiliar words in "Silver." Write the words below.

_____

_____

_____

Write the **definition** of each word and its **sentence role**, or the way each word is used.

_____

_____

_____

Read Fluently

Read the underlined text. Then, write the lines in your own words, using sentence form. This will help you find the subject of the lines, its description, and action.

_____

_____

_____

Reading Check

What "walks the night"? Circle the text that tells you.

Vocabulary Development
kennel (KEN uhl) *n.* a place where dogs are kept

1. **shoon** (SHOON) *n.* old-fashioned word for "shoes."

2. **casements** (KAYS muhnts) *n.* windows that open out, as doors do.

3. **thatch** (THACH) *n.* roof made of straw or other plant material.

Your World
Georgia Douglas Johnson

Your world is as big as you make it.
I know, for I used to abide
In the narrowest nest in a corner,
My wings pressing close to my side.

5 But I sighted the distant horizon
Where the sky line encircled the sea
And I throbbed with a burning desire
To travel this immensity.

I battered the cordons[1] around me
10 And cradled my wings on the breeze
Then soared to the uttermost reaches
With rapture, with power, with ease!

Vocabulary Development
rapture (RAP cher) *n.* ecstasy

1. **cordons** (KAWR duhnz) *n.* lines or cords that restrict free movement.

Literary Analysis

Rhyme is the repetition of sounds at the ends of words. Circle the end rhymes in "Your World."

Reading Skill

Context clues give you more information about a word. Underline the words in the bracketed passage that help you figure out the meaning of *immensity*. What does *immensity* mean?

_____

_____

Stop to Reflect

What do **sound devices** add to the experience of reading poetry? Explain.

_____

_____

_____

Reading Check

Where did the speaker of "Your World" once live? Circle the text that tells you.

Poetry Collection 1

1. **Draw Conclusions:** How does the speaker of "Cat!" feel about the cat?

   _____

   _____

2. **Generalize:** The silvery light of the moon in "Silver" makes everything look silver. What mood does the poet create as he describes these effects? The mood is the feeling an author creates in the reader.

   _____

   _____

3. **Reading Skill: Context** is the text around a certain word. Explain how context helps you figure out the meaning of the word *scritch* in "Cat!"

   _____

   _____

4. **Literary Analysis:** Complete the chart with examples of the **sound devices** you find in each poem. Sound devices use different sounds to make words more musical. Not all of the sound devices are used in each poem. An example of each sound device has been given to you.

	Cat!	Silver	Your World
alliteration	slithery/slathery		
onomatopoeia	scritch, scratch		
rhyme	flatterer, chatterer, scatter her		

Writing: Introduction

Write an **introduction** for a poetry reading. Use this chart to help you decide which poem to choose for your introduction. Be sure to explain your choices as you answer the questions.

	Poem	Reason
Which poem did you like best?		
Which poem do you think will be most meaningful to others?		
Which poem is written in the most interesting way?		

Use these notes to write your introduction.

Listening and Speaking: Poetry Recitation

Use the following chart to list examples of sound devices and how these sound devices create the mood of the poem.

Poem: _____   Mood: _____

Sound Device	Contribution to Mood
Rhyme	
Rhythm	
Alliteration	
Onomatopoeia	

Word List A

Study these words from the poetry of Eve Merriam; Nikki Giovanni; and Alfred, Lord Tennyson. Then, complete the activity that follows.

ancient [AYN shuhnt] *adj.* from times long ago
   The Olympic Games began in ancient Greece.

captured [KAP cherd] *v.* taken by force
   When enemy troops are captured, they must be treated decently.

foul [FOWL] *adj.* horrible
   Why do shoes always have such a foul smell when they get wet?

funeral [FYOO ner uhl] *adj.* having to do with a ceremony held after a person has died
   The funeral flowers brought beauty to a sad day.

interior [in TEER ee uhr] *adj.* inside; of a person's private self
   My diary told about the thoughts and feelings of my interior world.

triumph [TRY uhmf] *n.* a feeling of joy because of success
   Our triumph at finally winning the state spelling bee was huge.

Exercise A

Fill in each blank in the paragraph below with an appropriate word from Word List A. Use each word only once.

Since [1] _____ times, people have had special ways to celebrate the lives of those who die. In addition to holding fancy [2] _____ services, people have built great structures to honor the dead. The best examples are the pyramids of Egypt. If a pharaoh [3] _____ enemies or gained great wealth, for example, paintings and statues tell the story. They show the [4] _____ the rulers felt after such victories. The Egyptians even figured out how to avoid the [5] _____ odor of a dead body. If only we could know the [6] _____ minds of these brilliant people! The way they preserved the bodies is amazing! Looking at the mummies, you almost believe that the world of the pharaohs is still alive.

Read the following passage. Pay special attention to the underlined words. Then, read it again, and complete the activities. Use a separate sheet of paper for your written answers.

Dr. Martin Luther King, Jr., brought about many important changes in American life. His words and deeds have served as a model for creating change without violence or <u>foul</u> actions. At age thirty-five, King became the youngest person to receive the Nobel Peace Prize. By this time, he had helped many African Americans begin to feel the <u>triumph</u> of gaining equal rights.

How did he do it? King never chose the easy path. Instead, he encouraged peaceful protest. With thousands of followers, he staged boycotts and marches to speak out against injustices in America. King was <u>captured</u> and taken to jail again and again. Yet, despite being taken by force, he continued to encourage peaceful protests.

King traveled more than 6 million miles and spoke some 2,500 times. His words inspired people from all corners of the country to work for social change. This included changes in education and employment opportunities for the poor and the blacks in America. Few have spoken as well and as honestly about the need for equal treatment for all.

King was a brilliant man whose <u>interior</u> life must have been extraordinary. He graduated from high school at fifteen, and received many degrees and awards during his lifetime. King's speeches are among the most famous of modern times. Some have compared his ability to inspire others to that of the greatest speakers of <u>ancient</u> times.

Sadly, King was shot to death at age thirty-nine. This tragic event touched all Americans. Two <u>funeral</u> services were held: one at his home church in Atlanta; and the other, at his college. The President of the United States honored King's memory by ordering that all American flags fly at half-mast that day. The entire nation felt the terrible loss of Dr. Martin Luther King, Jr. Each January, a national holiday reminds us of the importance of Dr. King's life.

1. Underline the word that is described by *foul*. Give an example of *foul* behavior prompted by violence.

2. Underline the words that tell what led people to feel *triumph*. Then, tell about a time when you have had a feeling of *triumph*.

3. Underline the sentence that tells what resulted in King's being *captured* and taken to jail. Explain what *captured* means.

4. Circle the word describing naming King's *interior* life. Then, explain why a very smart person might have an interesting *interior* life.

5. Underline the word in the previous sentence that means the opposite of *ancient*. Give an example of an *ancient* time or civilization.

6. Circle the words that tell where the *funeral* services for King were held. Write a sentence describing one *funeral* service for King as you imagine it might have been.

Poetry Collection 2

Summaries The speaker in "Thumbprint" is glad that no one is exactly like her. The speaker in "The Drum" describes different people in terms of drums. The speaker in "Ring Out, Wild Bells" wants the bells to ring out the bad and ring in the good.

Writing About the Big Question

What is the secret to reaching someone with words? The writers of the poems in "Poetry Collection 2" take advantage of the musical quality of poetry with readers. Complete this sentence:

Words set to a beat, whether poetry or song lyrics, can create a

memorable experience for a listener because _____

_____.

Note-taking Guide

Use this chart to note details about the subject of each poem.

	Thumbprint	The Drum	Ring Out, Wild Bells
Subject of the Poem	the speaker's thumbprint		
Words that describe the subject			

Poetry Collection 2

1. **Respond:** Think about the way that a poem is like a song. Which of these three poems do you think would work best as a song? Explain.

_____

_____

2. **Interpret:** In "Thumbprint," the speaker describes her thumbprint. Why is her thumbprint so important to her?

_____

_____

3. **Reading Skill:** Look at the word *feud* in "Ring Out, Wild Bells." Try to figure out the meaning of *feud*. Explain the **context** clues that help you figure out the word's meaning.

_____

_____

4. **Literary Analysis:** Three common **sound devices** are listed in the chart below. Complete the chart with examples of each of the sound devices in the three poems. Not all of the sound devices are used in each poem.

	Thumbprint	The Drum	Ring Out, Wild Bells
alliteration (Example: big ball)	my mark		
onomatopoeia (Example: buzz)		Pa-rum	
rhyme			

Writing: Introduction

Write an **introduction** for a poetry reading. Use this chart to help you decide which poem to choose for your introduction. Be sure to explain your choices as you answer the questions.

	Poem	Reason
Which poem did you like best?		
Which poem do you think will be most meaningful to others?		
Which poem is written in the most interesting way?		

Use these notes to write your introduction.

Listening and Speaking: Poetry Recitation

Use the following chart to list examples of sound devices and how these sound devices create the mood of the poem.

Poem: _____   Mood: _____

Sound Device	Contribution to Mood
Rhyme	
Rhythm	
Alliteration	
Onomatopoeia	

Poetry Collection 3 • Poetry Collection 4

Reading Skill

Context is the text around a word. These words and phrases can help you understand new or confusing words. **Reread or read ahead** for context clues when you see a word you do not know. Figure out a possible meaning. Replace the word with the possible meaning as you reread the sentence. If the sentence makes sense, your meaning is probably right. If it does not make sense, reread or read ahead again. Look up the word in a dictionary if you do not find any other clues.

The chart shows the common types of context clues.

Contrast
I *never shop* anymore, but last year, I was a shopping <u>enthusiast</u>.
Synonym
Don't *reject* our request. Your <u>veto</u> can hurt many people.
Explanation
Think of the *capacity*—this truck can carry *a lot of cargo*.
Example
She <u>agonized</u> for days, *biting her nails*, *sleeping poorly*, and *crying because she was worried*.

Literary Analysis

Figurative language is writing or speech that is not to be taken literally. Figurative language includes these *figures of speech*.

- A simile uses the words *like* or *as* to compare two unlike things: His eyes were as black as coal.

- A metaphor compares two unlike things by saying that one thing *is* the other: The world is my oyster.

- Personification compares a nonhuman thing to a person by giving the nonhuman thing human qualities: The trees toss in their sleep.

Read the poems. Look for examples of figurative language.

Word List A

Study these words from the poetry of Patricia Hubbell, Richard García, and Langston Hughes. Then, complete the activity that follows.

bulging [BUHLJ ing] *adj.* swelling out in a round shape or lump
   The huge frog, with bulging eyes, jumped into the water.

dew [DOO] *n.* small drops of water that form overnight outdoors
   I got up early, before the sun had dried up the dew on the grass.

direct [di REKT] *v.* to aim something in a particular direction
   Would you direct the heat vents more to my side of the car?

hose [HOHZ] *v.* to wash or pour water on something with a hose
   Hose off your muddy shoes before you come inside!

muck [MUHK] *n.* a substance that is sticky, wet, and dirty; mud
   After the floodwaters dried, the town was covered in muck.

perch [PERCH] *v.* to sit on the edge or on top of something
   We like to perch on the very top of the mountain and watch the sunset.

Exercise A

Fill in each blank in the paragraph below with an appropriate word from Word List A. Use each word only once.

My shoes got wet with morning [1] _____ as I crossed the lawn to get the newspaper. The [2] _____ plastic bag indicated a free sample inside. Sure enough, when I opened the bag, I found a pouch of moist dog food, and it was leaking onto the paper. I headed back to the house, knowing that I could never [3] _____ off the paper and still read it. Just then, a red-throated bird flew in front of me to [4] _____ on a high branch of the cherry tree. While I followed it with my gaze, I stepped in a hole of gooey [5] _____ in the middle of the dirt-and-gravel path. Now, the paper wasn't the only thing that needed cleaning off. It was only seven o'clock, but I had to [6] _____ my attention to two sloppy jobs before breakfast.

Read the following passage. Pay special attention to the underlined words. Then, read it again, and complete the activities. Use a separate sheet of paper for your written answers.

The dew is still heavy on the grass. I take my dog, Rex, for his morning walk. The sun has risen just enough for us to walk safely without a flashlight. A nervous squirrel runs across our path. Then, it scurries up a tree to perch on a high branch and scold us from afar.

As I turn the corner, I see I am not the only one awake this early on a summer weekend. Justin is standing in front of his house. Alongside him is his white terrier, Terry. The dog has managed to get brown muck all over his coat. The bucket, brush, and shampoo bottle on the grass tip me off to what is about to happen.

Rex and I watch from a polite distance. Justin pulls out a ten-foot length of garden hose and turns on the faucet at the side of the house. He attempts to direct the stream of water at Terry. Of course, by now the dog has gotten wise to what is going on and high-tails it around to the other side of the house. I begin to doubt that Justin will manage to hose down anything but the front lawn.

From experience, I could tell Justin that he must get Terry on the leash in order to wash him, but I am curious to see if he will figure that out himself. When Justin disappears from sight, I think that is exactly what he has gone to do. Instead, he comes running back—not with Terry on a leash but with one pocket bulging at the side.

The next thing I know, Terry comes charging after him. He snaps his muzzle right on Justin's swollen pocket. Whatever is in the pocket must smell so good that Terry has risked a bath to follow its odor. Justin picks up the garden hose. With Terry still hanging onto his pocket, Justin begins washing off the slimy dirt. Now, why had not I thought of that?

1. Circle the sentence in the paragraph that explains why the dew is still on the grass. In your own words, explain what *dew* is.

2. Underline the place where the squirrel goes to perch. Give an example of some place you like to *perch*.

3. Circle the three objects named in the next sentence that give a clue to what muck is. Write about a time that you or someone else got covered in *muck*.

4. Circle what Justin attempts to direct at Terry. Rewrite the sentence, using a different word or words for *direct*.

5. Circle the words in the paragraph that help to understand hose. Explain whether you should *hose* down things inside a house.

6. Underline the word that tells what was bulging. Describe what you think was causing it to be *bulging*.

Poetry Collection 3

Summaries Concrete mixers and elephants are compared in "Concrete Mixers." The speaker of "The City Is So Big" feels frightened by the city at night. The speaker in "Harlem Night Song" invites a loved one to enjoy the beauty of the night sky over the city.

Writing About the Big Question

What is the secret to reaching someone with words? In "Poetry Collection 3," three poets carefully craft their words to help us experience life in a big city. Complete this sentence:

Even if you have never been to a place, a talented poet can help you

experience how it might feel to be there by _____

_____.

Note-taking Guide

Use this chart to help you record the imagery in each poem.

	Imagery
Concrete Mixers	elephant tenders, tough gray-skinned monsters, muck up to their wheel caps
The City Is So Big	
Harlem Night Song	

Concrete Mixers
Patricia Hubbell

The drivers are washing the concrete
   mixers;
Like elephant tenders they hose them
   down.
Tough gray-skinned monsters standing
   ponderous,
Elephant-bellied and elephant-nosed,
5 Standing in muck up to their wheel-caps,
Like rows of elephants, tail to trunk.
Their drivers perch on their backs like
   mahouts,[1]
Sending the sprays of water up.
They rid the trunk-like trough of concrete,
10 Direct the spray to the bulging sides,
Turn and start the monsters moving.
      Concrete mixers
      Move like elephants
      Bellow like elephants
15   Spray like elephants,
Concrete mixers are urban elephants,
Their trunks are raising a city.

Activate Prior Knowledge

Think about the cities you have visited. What qualities do these cities share?

_____

_____

_____

Reading Skill

Context is the text surrounding a new or an unfamiliar word. These words and phrases can help you understand that word. Review the underlined passage. What context clues help you understand the meaning of *muck*? Explain.

_____

_____

_____

_____

Literary Analysis

A **simile** compares two apparently unlike things, using the words *like* or *as*. What two things are being compared in the simile in line 7?

_____

_____

Vocabulary Development

ponderous (PAHN duh ruhs) *adj.* very heavy
urban (ER buhn) *adj.* in or relating to a town or city

1. **mahouts** (muh HOWTS) *n.* in India and the East Indies, elephant drivers or keepers.

© Pearson Education

Reading Skill

Read the first bracketed passage. Circle the context clues that help you learn that *quake* means "tremble."

Read Fluently

Readers often confuse *its* and *it's*. Its is a possessive. It describes how one thing belongs to another. *It's* is a contraction that is short for *it is*. Look at *Its* in the first bracketed passage. To what do the bridges belong?

_____

Literary Analysis

Personification is a comparison in which a nonhuman subject is given human characteristics. Underline an example of personification in the second bracketed passage. Then, put a box around the human characteristic that is described.

Reading Check ✎

To what does the speaker compare a train's windows? Bracket the answer in the text.

The City Is So Big
Richard García

The city is so big
Its bridges quake with fear
I know, I have seen at night

The lights sliding from house to house
5 And trains pass with windows shining
Like a smile full of teeth

I have seen machines eating houses
And stairways walk all by themselves
And elevator doors opening and closing
10 And people disappear.

Harlem Night Song
Langston Hughes

Come,
Let us roam the night together
Singing.

I love you.

5 Across
The Harlem roof-tops
Moon is shining.
Night sky is blue.
Stars are great drops
10 Of golden dew.

Down the street
A band is playing.

I love you.

Come,
15 Let us roam the night together
Singing.

Literary Analysis 🔍

A **simile** uses the words *like* or *as* to compare two things. A **metaphor** compares two things by saying that one thing *is* the other. Does Hughes use a simile or a metaphor to describe stars in the underlined passage? Explain.

_____

_____

_____

_____

Stop to Reflect

What example of figurative language do you find most striking In the poems you have read so far? Explain.

_____

_____

_____

_____

Reading Check

What does the speaker urge the listener to do as they "roam the night together"? Circle the answer in the text.

Vocabulary Development

roam (rohm) *v.* go aimlessly; wander

Poetry Collection 3

1. **Interpret:** What has the speaker of "The City Is So Big" actually seen?

_____

_____

_____

2. **Analyze:** Mood is the feeling that a work creates for a reader. How do the repeated phrases in "Harlem Night Song" stress the joyful mood of the poem?

_____

_____

3. **Reading Skill:** Use the **context** surrounding the word *trough* in line 9 of "Concrete Mixers" to explain what a trough looks like. What does a trough do on a concrete mixer?

_____

_____

_____

4. **Literary Analysis: Figurative language** is writing or speech that is not meant to be taken literally. Use this chart to study the **figurative language** in "The City Is So Big."

Object		Object	Similarities
windows	is compared to →		

☐ Simile

☐ Metaphor

☐ Personification

Writing: Study for a Poem

Write a **study for a poem** about a city setting. List an object, a sight, and a sound that you can find in a city. Then, use simile, metaphor, and personification to describe each item. Use this chart to begin planning your poem.

	Simile	Metaphor	Personification
Object:			
Sight:			
Sound:			

Research and Technology: Mini-Anthology

Create a **mini-anthology** by finding three poems about a similar topic. Use the chart to list your reasons for selecting each poem.

Poem Title	Why I Chose the Poem

Use your notes to create your mini-anthology.

Word List A

Study these words from the poetry of Pablo Neruda, Elizabeth Bishop, and Emily Dickinson. Then, complete the activity that follows.

cicada [si KAY duh] *n.* a large, winged insect, the males of which make a loud sound
> *I heard my first cicada of the summer humming in the tree.*

drifting [DRIFT ing] *adj.* moving slowly in the air or on water
> *The wind loosened the leaf that I saw drifting toward the ground.*

limp [LIMP] *adj.* not firm
> *To keep the carrot strips from going limp, place them in water.*

relieved [ri LEEVD] *adj.* glad because a worry or stress is gone
> *We were relieved when the tornado finally passed our town.*

rut [RUHT] *n.* a deep track in the ground made by a wheel
> *We didn't see the rut in the road and drove over it bumpily.*

sawing [SAW ing] *adj.* like the sound of a hand saw
> *The sawing noise coming from the garage woke us up early.*

Exercise A

Fill in each blank in the paragraph below with an appropriate word from Word List A. Use each word only once.

It was the kind of sunny, hot, muggy summer afternoon that made you feel tired and [1] _____ right down to your bones. To add to my discomfort, one [2] _____ after another was "serenading" me with its loud [3] _____ noise. The sound, [4] _____ through the air from trees far and near, had reached the level of annoyance that could drive a person crazy. Just as I thought there was no chance of being [5] _____ of my discomfort, I noticed a low band of clouds headed in my direction. The sky briefly darkened, and a cool breath of fresh air ruffled the curtains. Rain suddenly burst from the clouds, quickly filling the [6] _____ in the driveway with water. Just as suddenly, the rain stopped and the sun beat down anew.

Read the following passage. Pay special attention to the underlined words. Then, read it again, and complete the activities. Use a separate sheet of paper for your written answers.

I was used to the fall lingering well into November, with roses still blooming as we sat eating Thanksgiving turkey. Here in the country, however, snow began dropping the first of November. Nearly a foot of the white stuff fell, drifting with the wind into mounds three feet high. That was only the beginning.

By the time the first crocus appeared during the last week of March, we had seen nearly a hundred inches of snow. The white blanket had been almost continuous for five months. The three-day thaw and rain in January had temporarily freed us from the snow, only to replace it with mudslides. Every rut in every road was filled with water or mud.

Spring took a while longer to arrive, and not without two more hefty snowstorms. Far from disappointing us, however, spring overwhelmed us. Hardly had the daffodils bloomed than tulips and irises followed. Before we knew it, wild roses and wisteria were spilling over the corral fence.

I had expected my first summer in the country to be a lot more bearable than in the city. It was true. The temperature and humidity were much lower. Also, we had gotten to the third week of July without so much as a sign—or sound—of a cicada. I didn't miss the loud sawing noise of that ugly insect all morning and afternoon.

Well, the cicadas did arrive, and the weather grew hot and muggy. I turned into the human counterpart of a wet, limp dishrag. It was not to last long, though. Fall arrived on a cool breeze in September, and my senses were relieved. Rain soon cleaned the air rather than making it stickier. I did not sneeze nonstop through September and October, as I usually did in the city.

When November rolled around again, I left the country, but it was not because of the weather. In fact, that year, with its dramatic seasons, would be one to remember forever.

1. Circle the cause of the <u>drifting</u> snow. Write a sentence that describes something else you might see *drifting*.

2. Underline the phrases that help you understand the meaning of <u>rut</u>. Tell about the damage a *rut* in a road can do.

3. Circle the words in the next sentence that tell what a <u>cicada</u> is and the sound it makes. Describe something else that makes a *sawing* noise.

4. Circle the words in the paragraph that tell why the writer felt like a wet, <u>limp</u> dishrag. Describe a *limp* handshake.

5. Underline what caused the writer's senses to be <u>relieved</u>. Tell about a time that you were *relieved* and explain what caused the change.

Poetry Collection 4

Summaries The speaker of "Ode to Enchanted Light" enjoys the beauty of nature. A thunderstorm at the beach is described in "Little Exercise." The speaker of "The Sky Is Low, the Clouds Are Mean" humorously describes a dark winter day.

Writing About the Big Question

What is the secret to reaching someone with words? The poets in "Poetry Collection 4" share their ideas about nature. Complete this sentence:

Written works about nature that get the most positive feedback

from me are ones that _____

_____.

Note-taking Guide

Use this chart to recall the main image in each poem.

Ode to Enchanted Light	Little Exercise	The Sky Is Low, the Clouds Are Mean
a forest with light shining through the trees		

Poetry Collection 4

1. **Infer:** Think about how Pablo Neruda describes the world in "Ode to an Enchanted Light." How do you think he feels about life?

_____

_____

2. **Interpret:** It is winter in "The Sky Is Low, the Clouds Are Mean." The writer uses the words _rut, complain,_ and _mean._ What mood do these words show about the season?

_____

_____

3. **Reading Skill:** Look at the word _pile_ in line 20 of "Little Exercise." The word _pile_ does not mean a _heap_ here. Use **context** clues to find another possible meaning.

_____

4. **Literary Analysis:** Use the chart to analyze the **figurative language** in "Ode to an Enchanted Light."

Object		Object	Similarities	
light	is compared to →		both have . . .	☐ Simile ☐ Metaphor ☐ Personification

Writing: Study for a Poem

Write a **study for a poem** about a natural setting. List an object, a sight, and a sound that you can find in nature. Then, describe each item through simile, metaphor, and personification. Use this chart to begin planning your poem.

	Simile	Metaphor	Personification
Object:			
Sight:			
Sound:			

Research and Technology: Mini Anthology

Use a chart like the following to record information about the poems that you want to include in your **anthology**. Create a chart for each poem.

Title of poem:	Author:
Why I chose this poem:	

- What do the poems have in common? _____

  _____

- Ideas for my cover and Introduction: _____

  _____

Recipes and Food Labels

About Recipes and Food Labels

Recipes are directions that explain how to make a type of food or drink. You will find recipes much easier to follow after you have learned the different parts of a recipe. These parts include

- a title that names the dish
- a list of ingredients
- directions that tell the steps to follow
- the number of servings the dish will make

Food labels give information about food products. Study the food label in the Student Edition. Reading a food label can tell you

- the number of calories per serving
- the amount of fat, cholesterol, sodium, carbohydrates, protein, and nutrients in the product

Reading Skill

You can **compare and contrast features of consumer materials** to understand how to make a recipe or how to read nutritional information about a product. Some features identify ingredients, highlight important information, or help show what should be done. These features include headings, subheadings, numbers, signal words, illustrations, captions, and italicized and boldfaced type.

Recipe   Nutrition Information

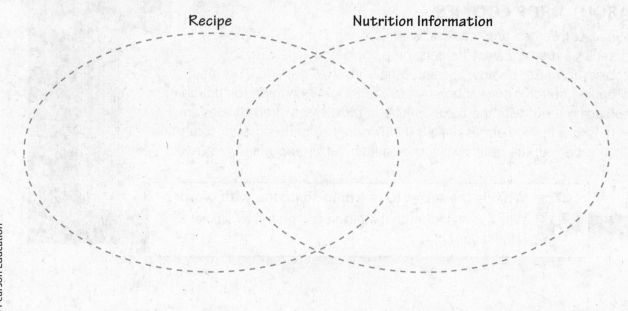

Thumbprint Cookies

½ cup brown sugar
1 cup butter
2-3 egg yolks
2 cups flour
egg whites
1½ cups chopped nuts
raspberry preserves

A list of ingredients tells readers what goes into the food they will be making.

To separate eggs, crack each egg in half. Over a bowl, pour the egg back and forth between the cracked halves. Let the egg white fall into the bowl, keeping the egg yolk intact in the shell. Cream together sugar, butter, and egg yolks. Beat flour into this mixture. Form balls and dip into slightly beaten egg whites. Roll balls in chopped nuts. Put on slightly greased cookie sheet and make a thumbprint on each ball. Baked at 305° for 8 minutes. Remove from oven and reset thumbprint. Bake 8 to 10 minutes longer. Fill print with raspberry preserves.

Preparation: 25 min.   Yield: 30
Baking: 18 min   Can freeze

Separating an egg

Using a teaspoon

The recipe includes tips for preparing the food successfully.

ABOUT DROP COOKIES

Whoever invented drop cookies, which we used to call "drop cakes," deserves a medal. Except for bars, drop cookies are the easiest of all cookies to make, because shaping usually involves nothing more than dropping dough from a spoon. A few call for patting down the dough or spreading it out with the tip of a knife. In most cases, drop cookies are very forgiving: No harm is done if the mixture is slightly stiffer or softer than expected; the results will just be a little flatter or puffier than usual.

THE BIG ?   **What is the secret to reaching someone with words?**
Why is it important that a recipe communicate accurate information?

Thinking About the Recipe and the Food Label

1. Why do most recipes list all of the ingredients needed before explaining how to use the ingredients?

_____

_____

2. Why is it important to check a Nutritional Facts label for both the suggested serving size and the number of servings per container?

_____

_____

TALK ABOUT IT **Reading Skill**

3. What information do you learn from the illustrations in the thumbprint cookies recipe?

_____

_____

4. How might comparing and contrasting the nutritional facts on a package of cookies help you decide whether to buy the package?

_____

_____

WRITE ABOUT IT **Timed Writing: Explanation (15 minutes)**

Write directions for a food you know how to make.

• What ingredients are needed for this recipe?

_____

• What tools are needed?

_____

• What steps do you take in following the recipe?

_____

Poetry Collection 5 • Poetry Collection 6

Reading Skill

To **paraphrase** is to put text in your own words. Before you paraphrase a line or a passage, **reread to clarify** the writer's meaning. First, look for the most important information in each sentence. Then, start putting the whole sentence into your own words. Restate details more simply. Use synonyms for the writer's words. Synonyms are words that mean the same as the word you replace. Look up any words that you do not know. Replace unusual words and sentences with language that is more like the way people speak every day.

Use this chart to help you paraphrase poetry.

Poem:	
Line from poem	
Basic information	
Paraphrase	

Literary Analysis

There are two main kinds of poetry. They are lyric poetry and narrative poetry.

- **Lyric poem:** tells the thoughts and feelings of a single **speaker**. The speaker is the person "saying" the poem. This type of poem gives a certain feeling or idea.

- **Narrative poem:** tells a story in verse. A narrative poem has all the parts of a short story: characters, setting, conflict, and plot.

Read the poems. Look for examples of lyric and narrative poetry.

Word List A

Study these words from the poetry of Robert Hayden, William Shakespeare, and Ricardo Sánchez. Then, complete the activity that follows.

aromas [uh ROH muhz] *n.* strong, pleasant smells
  The aromas of cooking, made my mouth water.

benefits [BEN uh fits] *n.* advantages or help that you get from something
  The benefits of Grandma's visit were three great meals every day.

brethren [BRETH ruhn] *n.* brothers; comrades or fellows
  Native Americans treated the early white settlers like brethren, as if they were family.

familial [fuh MIL yuhl] *adj.* having to do with a family
  Jenna's familial duties included watching her little brother.

resolution [rez uh LOO shuhn] *n.* the quality of having strong beliefs and the desire to do something
  Though painting the house was not easy work, he completed the task with resolution.

thicketed [THIK it ed] *adj.* covered with a thick growth of shrubs or small trees
  The island was thicketed with berry-producing shrubs.

Exercise A

Fill in each blank in the paragraph below with an appropriate word from Word List A. Use each word only once.

Claire was firm in her [1] _____ to become a great chef, so she went to cooking school for a summer. The school was deep in the country. It had a comfortable, [2] _____ feel, and Claire felt at home right away. One of the [3] _____ of being in the country was that there was plenty of room to grow fresh vegetables to use in recipes. The tomato and bean plants grew so well that they [4] _____ part of the garden. During the day, the young chefs worked in the big kitchens. Mouth-watering [5] _____ filled the air. Each evening, they all enjoyed a fine meal and the company of their cooking [6] _____.

1. Circle the words that explain the meaning of brethren. Then, give a synonym for *brethren*.

2. Underline the words that tell what made the area thicketed. Describe a *thicketed* area that you know about.

3. Circle the words that give a clue about the meaning of familial. Are there *familial* resemblances in your family?

4. Underline the words that tell what is making the aromas. Name some of your favorite *aromas*.

5. Underline the word that is similar to benefits. Tell about some *benefits* you have by being a member of a family, a club, or a team.

6. Circle the word that helps you understand the meaning of resolution. Tell about something you have done with *resolution*.

Read the following passage. Pay special attention to the underlined words. Then, read it again, and complete the activities. Use a separate sheet of paper for your written answers.

I was so excited when my parents told me that we were going to a family reunion! I had never been to one before. All I knew was that there would be more than 300 Santoros in one place at one time, and that all of us were related, all of us were brethren. I realized that I had more cousins than I had ever dreamed of.

We got on the road early on the morning of the reunion, and started on our way. The family had rented an entire campground by the seashore for the event. We drove on and on, past the city, past small towns, and then through an area that was thicketed with low shrubs and berry bushes. The air smelled salty. We were almost there.

Soon I saw lines of cars parked by the sand, all with signs that said, "Santoro Family Reunion." Even the vehicles seemed to have a familial likeness—there were several that looked the same as ours, as if they were relatives. We parked and jumped out of the car to join in the party. Aromas of grilling meats and vegetables filled my nose, and those delicious smells made me hungry right away. I was given a T-shirt with the family name on it, and before I knew it, I was in the middle of a game of beach volleyball.

One of the benefits of having a big group is the advantage of having plenty of helping hands. As if by magic, big tables were set up, and heaping platters of food were appearing on them. As I ate, laughed, and chatted with Santoros of every shape and size, I realized what a great thing a big family is. I decided then and there, with complete determination and resolution, that I would stay in touch with everyone and that I would organize another family reunion when I was older.

Poetry Collection 5

Summaries In "Runagate Runagate," the speaker describes a frightening escape. "Blow, Blow, Thou Winter Wind" uses images from winter to describe a false friendship. In "Old Man," the speaker celebrates his grandfather.

 Writing About the Big Question

What is the secret to reaching someone with words? The poems in "Poetry Collection 5" convey a wide range of emotions such as bitterness, betrayal, fear, courage, love, and loss. Complete this sentence:

I can find poems written in the past relevant as long as they

_____.

Note-taking Guide

Use this chart to list the emotions expressed in each poem.

	Emotion
Runagate Runagate	
Blow, Blow, Thou Winter Wind	
Old Man	

Activate Prior Knowledge

Describe thoughts and feelings that you have had that would be expressed easily in a poem.

_____

_____

_____

Literary Analysis

A **narrative poem** tells a story in verse and has all the elements of a short story—character, setting, conflict, and plot. What historical setting and conflict are described in this narrative poem?

_____

_____

_____

Reading Check

For whom is the slaveholder looking? Underline the text that tells you.

Runagate Runagate

Robert Hayden

The poem opens with images and thoughts of an escaping slave—a "runagate"—who is being pursued by hunters and dogs.

◆ ◆ ◆

I.

Runs falls rises stumbles on from darkness
 into darkness
and the darkness thicketed with shapes of
 terror
and the hunters pursuing and the hounds
 pursuing

◆ ◆ ◆

The poem continues with more of the escaped slave's thoughts. He is determined to escape the auction block and the lash. The narrator refers to the "mythic North," where freedom is possible. Then the poem shifts to another point of view. We now hear from a slaveholder—the "subscriber"—who has placed an ad in a newspaper.

◆ ◆ ◆

If you see my Pompey, 30 yrs of age,
new breeches, plain stockings, negro
 shoes:
if you see my Anna, likely young
 mulatto
branded E on the right cheek, R on
 the left,
catch them if you can and notify
 subscriber.

◆ ◆ ◆

The slaveholder goes on to say that the slaves will be hard to catch. He says that they will do anything to escape—even that they will turn into scorpions when anyone gets close. The point of view shifts back to that of the runaway slave. The narrator expresses his determination to escape. The second section of the poem opens with a reference to Harriet Tubman. She risked her life many times to help slaves escape. Harriet Tubman shows her strength as the escaped slaves begin to doubt that they will make it.

◆   ◆   ◆

we'll never make it. *Hush that now,*
and she's turned upon us, leveled pistol
glinting in the moonlight:
Dead folks can't jaybird-talk, she says:
you keep on going now or die, she says.

◆   ◆   ◆

The poem tells about the wanted posters for Harriet Tubman. A reward is offered for her, dead or alive. The poem then shifts back to the point of view of the escaped slave. He wonders whether divine help will be offered. Then, the narrator talks about the "train" that is carrying the escaped slaves to freedom. The reader is invited to come ride the train, too. The poem ends with the narrator expressing a strong determination to be free.

Reading Skill

When you **paraphrase**, you restate a text in your own words. Paraphrase the bracketed passage.

_____

_____

_____

_____

Literary Analysis

What is the conflict, or problem, presented in this **narrative poem**?

_____

_____

_____

Reading Check

Who is discussed on this page? Underline the name of the person of whom the poet speaks.

Sometimes it is helpful to **reread to clarify** the writer's meaning. Reread the first bracketed passage. Explain whom or what this passage is about.

_____

_____

Stop to Reflect

In the second bracketed passage, look at the sentence about friendship. Do you agree with this statement? Explain.

_____

_____

_____

Read Fluently

Reread the poem. Notice the words *thou, thy, art,* and *dost.* People no longer use these words in everyday language. What words would you use today to replace these words?

_____

Select two lines that use these old words. Put the sentences into your own words. Use everyday language.

_____

_____

_____

Blow, Blow, Thou Winter Wind
William Shakespeare

Blow, blow, thou winter wind.
Thou art not so unkind
   As man's <u>ingratitude</u>.
Thy tooth is not so keen,
5 Because thou art not seen,
   Although thy breath be rude.
Heigh-ho! Sing, heigh-ho! unto the green holly.
Most friendship is feigning, most loving mere folly.[1]
Then, heigh-ho, the holly!
10   This life is most jolly.

Freeze, freeze, thou bitter sky,
That dost not bite so nigh
   As benefits forgot.
Though thou the waters warp,[2]
15 Thy sting is not so sharp
   As friend remembered not.
Heigh-ho! Sing, heigh-ho! unto the green holly.
Most friendship is feigning, most loving mere folly.
Then, heigh-ho, the holly!
20   This life is most jolly.

Vocabulary Development

ingratitude (in GRAT uh tood) *n.* lack of thankfulness

1. **feigning** . . . **folly** Most friendship is fake, most loving is foolish.
2. **warp** *v.* freeze.

Old Man
Ricardo Sánchez

remembrance
(smiles/hurts sweetly)
October 8, 1972

old man
with brown skin
talking of past
   when being shepherd
5   in utah, nevada, colorado and
      new mexico
was life lived freely;

old man,
   grandfather,
10 wise with time
running rivulets on face,
deep, rich furrows,[1]
   each one a legacy,
deep, rich memories of life . . .

15   "you are indio,[2]
     among other things,"
he would tell me
   during nights spent
so long ago
20   amidst familial gatherings
in albuquerque . . .

© Pearson Education

Vocabulary Development

legacy (LEG uh see) *n.* anything handed down from an ancestor

---

1. rivulets . . . furrows here, the wrinkles on the old man's face.
2. indio (IN dee oh) *n.* Indian; Native American.

TAKE NOTES

Reading Skill

In your own words, **paraphrase** what the speaker says about the subject of this poem.

_____

_____

_____

_____

Literary Analysis

How does the **speaker** of this poem feel about the person he is discussing?

_____

_____

_____

Reading Check

What does the poet say that the old man's *rivulets*, or wrinkles, represent? Underline the text that tells you.

Literary Analysis

What thoughts and feelings are
expressed in this **lyric poem**?

_____

_____

_____

_____

Reading Skill

To **paraphrase** a passage, you
can use synonyms to replace the
writer's words. Use synonyms to
paraphrase lines 38–47.

_____

_____

_____

_____

_____

Reading Check

How did the old man know the
earth? Circle the text that
tells you.

old man, loved and respected,
he would speak sometimes
of pueblos,[3]

25   san juan, santa clara,
        and even santo domingo,
and his family, he would say,
        came from there:
        some of our blood was here,

30   he would say,
        before the coming of coronado,[4]
other of our blood
        came with los españoles,[5]
and the mixture

35 was rich,
        though often painful . . .
old man,
who knew earth
        by its awesome aromas

40 and who felt
the heated sweetness
        of chile verde[6]
by his supple touch,
gone into dust is your body

45   with its <u>stoic</u> look and resolution,
but your reality, old man, lives on
in a mindsoul touched by you . . .

Old Man . . .

Vocabulary Development

stoic (STOH ik) *adj.* calm in the face of suffering

3. **pueblos** (PWEB lohs) *n.* here, Native American towns in central and northern New Mexico.

4. **coronado** (kawr uh NAH doh) sixteenth-century Spanish explorer Francisco Vasquez de Coronado journeyed
   through what is today the American Southwest.

5. **los españoles** (los es pan YOH les) *n.* Spaniards.

6. **chile verde** (CHEE lay VER day) *n.* green pepper.

Poetry Collection 5

1. **Respond:** Which poem did you find most meaningful? Explain.

_____

_____

2. **Analyze:** Fill out this chart to explain what the lines mean.

	What Does It Say?	What Does It Mean?	Why Is It Important?
Runagate	(Lines 1–2)		
Blow, Blow . . .	(Line 8)		
Old Man	(Lines 8–14)		

3. **Reading Skill:** To **paraphrase** means to restate a text in your own words. Paraphrase lines 1–3 of "Blow, Blow, Thou Winter Wind."

_____

_____

4. **Literary Analysis:** What overall impression is created in the lyric poem, "Old Man"? Explain.

_____

_____

Writing: Lyric or Narrative Poem

Write a **lyric or narrative poem** about a person whom you admire. Your subject can be a historical figure or someone you know.

Answer the following questions to help you get started. Use your notes as you write your poem.

- Why do you admire this person?

  _____

  _____

- What thoughts and feelings do you have about him or her?

  _____

  _____

- What overall impression do you want to express about this person?

  _____

  _____

Listening and Speaking: Evaluation Form

Complete the following **evaluation form** for poetry reading. In the left column, add another "quality" that you consider to be important. Fill in an evaluation for a classmate's reading.

Poem title:		
Qualities	Score (1–10)	Comments
Properly adjusts tone		
Pauses at correct places		
Reads loudly and clearly		

Word List A

Study these words from the poetry of Emma Lazarus, Henry Wadsworth Longfellow, and Paul Laurence Dunbar. Then, complete the activity that follows.

cruelties [KROO uhl teez] *n.* actions that cause pain or suffering
The prisoners of war suffered many cruelties in prison.

defiance [di FY uhns] *n.* disobedience; standing up against
In defiance of the law, many northerners aided runaway slaves.

hovel [HUHV uhl] *n.* a small, dirty hut
The lovely cottage promised in the advertisement was really a hovel.

huddled [HUHD ld] *adj.* crowded or gathered together
The huddled crowd stood under the canopy until the rain stopped.

peril [PER uhl] *n.* great danger
In times of peril, the bell rang out a warning to the townsfolk.

refuse [REF yoos] *n.* the leftover part of something
Who could toss a fine painting in the garbage as if it were refuse?

Exercise A

Fill in each blank in the paragraph below with an appropriate word from Word List A. Use each word only once.

Yesterday, in the city, I saw the [1] _____ of protesters. They marched together in the cold, outside of a [2] _____ where some homeless people [3] _____ for warmth. As people passed, the protesters spoke out about the [4] _____ of allowing people to live like [5] _____ on the streets. The protesters were in [6] _____ of being arrested, but their efforts paid off when a Red Cross van pulled up and took the homeless people to a shelter for food, clothing, and a warm place to sleep.

1. Underline a sentence that helps you understand <u>defiance</u>. Explain a time you have been in *defiance* of something you felt was unjust.

2. Circle the word that hints at the meaning of <u>huddled</u>. Describe a time you had to remain *huddled* for some reason.

3. Circle two <u>cruelties</u> mentioned. Describe *cruelties* that take place today.

4. Underline what the author contrasts with a <u>hovel</u>. Describe what a *hovel* might look like.

5. Underline the <u>peril</u> from which some immigrants were fleeing. Describe a time when someone you know or read about was in *peril*.

6. Circle a synonym for <u>refuse</u>. Write a sentence that tells people what to do with their *refuse*.

Read the following passage. Pay special attention to the underlined words. Then, read it again, and complete the activities. Use a separate sheet of paper for your written answers.

If I asked you to define the word *liberty*, you might say it means "freedom." Then, I might ask, "Freedom from what?" or "Freedom to do what?" You would probably have to stop and think before answering those questions.

Over the years, to different groups of people, *liberty* has meant different things. In early American colonial times, it meant freedom to practice one's own religion. Later, it came also to mean <u>defiance</u> of the taxes and other controls that the British put upon the colonists. Americans were not going to stand for any laws being forced on them!

When war broke out with the British, *liberty* mostly meant independence from Britain. After the American victory, it came to mean "citizenship for certain white males and a handful of free men of color."

Slaves brought over from Africa had no liberty. They arrived in this country <u>huddled</u> and chained together in the worst conditions one can imagine. Many of them died at sea. Those who survived often had to endure the <u>cruelties</u> of their masters. How could a slave owner enjoy his own "liberty" when there was none for the people he beat or sold? How could he enjoy living in a fine home while his slaves lived in a <u>hovel</u>? As you know, slavery ended in 1865. The freeing of slaves gave a new definition to *liberty*.

With the great number of immigrants entering the United States in the 1840s, *liberty* began to mean other things as well. It stood for freedom from <u>peril</u> at the hands of a cruel ruler's soldiers who knocked down your door and attacked you. It meant freedom from hunger. It meant freedom to earn a living at a job of one's choosing. It stood for *not* being treated like <u>refuse</u> by a government that regarded your beliefs as worthless garbage.

One might say that the meaning of *liberty* continues to change even today. Do you agree?

Poetry Collection 6

Summaries In "The New Colossus," the speaker describes the Statue of Liberty. In "Paul Revere's Ride," the speaker tells the story of Paul Revere's ride. In "Harriet Beecher Stowe," the speaker praises Harriet Beecher Stowe, who helped people understand the fight against slavery.

Writing About the Big Question

What is the secret to reaching someone with words? The poems in "Poetry Collection 6" recall important events and people in American history. Complete this sentence:

The description of an event from history needs to _____

_____ in order to have significance for me.

Note-taking Guide

Use this chart to recall the key parts of the poems.

	The New Colossus	Paul Revere's Ride	Harriet Beecher Stowe
Main Subject	The Statue of Liberty		
Main Idea		Paul Revere rode a horse all night to warn people that the British troops were coming.	
Why is the poem's subject important?			Her book helped bring about the end of slavery.

Poetry Collection 6

1. **Respond:** Which poem's subject interests you most? Explain.

_____

_____

_____

2. **Interpret:** Fill out the chart below. Tell the meaning of the lines indicated. Follow the example given to you.

	What Does It Say?	What Does It Mean?	Why Is It Important?
The New Colossus	(Line 9)	Ancient cultures, continue to celebrate your magnificent achievements.	The United States is not interested in remaking the achievements of the past. It wants to make something new.
Harriet Beecher Stowe	(Line 9–10)		

3. **Reading Skill:** Reread lines 3–5 of "The New Colossus." **Paraphrase** the lines. Use a sentence structure that is more like everyday speech.

_____

_____

4. **Literary Analysis:** "Paul Revere's Ride" is a **narrative poem**. What are the setting and conflict of the poem?

_____

_____

Writing: Lyric or Narrative Poem

Write a **lyric or narrative poem** about a person whom you admire. The person can be someone you know or someone from history. Use the following prompts to revise your lyric or narrative poem.

- Write the lines of your poem.

_____

_____

_____

_____

- Circle words that you could change to make your poem more musical.

- What musical words could you use to replace your circled words?

_____

_____

_____

Listening and Speaking: Evaluation Form

Prepare an **evaluation form** for poetry reading. Use the chart to list qualities you think a good poetry reader should have. Write why you think the quality is important. Then, explain how you could evaluate each quality. Use your notes to create your evaluation form.

Quality	Why It Is Important	How to Evaluate It

Poetry Collection 7 • Poetry Collection 8

Reading Skill

Paraphrasing is restating something in your own words. Poets sometimes use words in patterns that are unlike the word patterns in everyday speech. Paraphrasing can help you understand a poem better. Use the following steps to paraphrase:

- First, **read aloud fluently according to punctuation**. As you read, pause briefly at commas (,), dashes (—), and semicolons (;). Pause longer after end marks, such as periods (.). Paying attention to punctuation will help you group words for meaning. It will also help you see complete thoughts.

- Next, restate the meaning of each complete thought in your own words. Use synonyms for the writer's words. Synonyms are words that have the same meaning as another word. Write unusual or difficult phrases in simple words.

As you read, pause every now and then. Paraphrase what you have just read. Make sure you understand what it means.

Literary Analysis

Poets use **imagery** to describe things that appeal to the five senses. Imagery helps readers imagine sights, sounds, textures, tastes, and smells.

- **With imagery:** The train thundered past, roaring, screaming.
- **Without imagery:** The train went by.

Use this chart to note the imagery used in each poem.

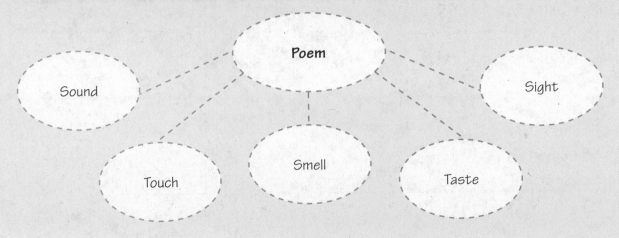

Word List A

Study these words from the poetry of John Updike, N. Scott Momaday, and Alice Walker. Then, complete the activity that follows.

continent [KAHN tuh nuhnt] *n.* one of the large land masses on Earth
My aunt has visited every <u>continent</u> *except Antarctica.*

dusk [DUSK] *n.* the time before it gets dark, just after sunset
Mom says that she has trouble seeing when she drives at <u>dusk</u>.

planes [PLAYNZ] *n.* flat surfaces
A simple box has six different <u>planes</u>.

shimmer [SHIM er] *v.* to shine with a soft light that seems to shake a bit
When the moon is full, I see its reflection <u>shimmer</u> *on the lake.*

swarm [SWAWRM] *n.* a large group of insects that move together
They say that a <u>swarm</u> *of killer bees can take down a large animal.*

withdraw [with DRAW] *v.* to go away or leave
Since the room was full of noisy five-year-olds, I decided to <u>withdraw</u> *from it.*

Exercise A

Fill in each blank in the paragraph below with an appropriate word from Word List A. Use each word only once.

On the huge [1] _____ of North America, there is a great variety of weather. For example, May can be hot in some places and cool in others. People in the Central American countries may stay indoors in May, to avoid fighting off a [2] _____ of annoying insects in the heat. At the same time, people around the Great Lakes are enjoying the outdoors. They might sit peacefully in the afternoon, watching the sun [3] _____ on the water. In the western part of North America, beautiful sunsets bring the calm of [4] _____, a time just to sit quietly. In the far northeast, chilly weather makes people [5] _____ from the night air. All over North America, clear days of May make the [6] _____ of objects seem to stand out more sharply.

1. Underline the word in the paragraph that gives a clue about which <u>continent</u> is "our own." Then, list the name of each *continent*.

2. Circle the words describing what would <u>shimmer</u> under the lights. Then, explain what *shimmer* means.

3. Underline the word in the previous sentence that tells what dazzling eyes and cheekbones like chiseled <u>planes</u> add up to. Then, explain why cheekbones might look like *planes*.

4. Circle the word defining the type of <u>swarm</u> the girls resembled. Then, describe a time when you have seen a *swarm* of people.

5. Underline the words telling when rock stars would <u>withdraw</u> from the action. Then, tell about a time when you had to *withdraw* from somewhere.

6. Circle the words telling when you might hear rock music at <u>dusk</u>. Explain why people would be home listening to music at *dusk*.

Read the following passage. Pay special attention to the underlined words. Then, read it again, and complete the activities. Use a separate sheet of paper for your written answers.

People around the world listen to rock music today. Yet, this popular form of music had its beginnings right here on our own <u>continent</u>. It began in the 1950s. At this time, three unique American musical styles came together. These were pop, rhythm and blues, and country and western.

Elvis Presley was the first huge star to put it all together. His rock-and-roll music was incredibly popular among American teenagers. His voice was great. The beat of his music was strong, fast, and exciting.

Presley also put on quite a show. He was famous for his way of dancing and for wearing fancy clothes and flashy jewelry that would <u>shimmer</u> under the spotlights. Presley was also very good-looking. He had dazzling eyes and cheekbones that looked like chiseled <u>planes</u>. Girls swooned over Presley and followed him everywhere like a <u>swarm</u> of bees.

Because rock and roll really appealed to the young, many stars would <u>withdraw</u> from the main stage as they aged. Plenty of young musicians were always waiting in the wings to take their place. Today, however, some successful, older rock stars perform to audience of all ages.

Perhaps the biggest force for change in the American rock-and-roll generation came from England. A group of four young British lads named the Beatles stormed the United States. In 1964, people went wild when they heard the Beatles' music for the first time.

New influences have always kept rock music fresh and surprising. Folk, soul, disco, heavy metal, punk, hip hop, rap . . . you can hear bits of all of it in rock music. Chances are, if you walk down the street on any summer day at <u>dusk</u>, you will hear rock-and-roll music coming from someone's open window. Its energy, messages for young and old alike, and inclusion of different styles will always keep it popular.

Poetry Collection 7

The Magpie(detail), 1869, Claude Monet, Musee d'Orsay, Paris

Summaries In "January," the speaker describes images connected with winter. "New World" shares different parts of the day in nature. In "For My Sister Molly Who in the Fifties," the speaker talks about her relationship with her sister.

 Writing About the Big Question

What is the secret to reaching someone with words? The poets in "Poetry Collection 7" carefully choose words to convey a speaker's ideas about specific people and places. Complete this sentence:

If someone who did not know me asked me to describe my hometown

or my family, I would choose sensory images such as _____

_____ and _____.

Note-taking Guide

Use this chart to record the main image or images in each poem.

January	New World	For My Sister Who . . .
snowy footsteps		

January
John Updike

© Pearson Education

The days are short,
　　The sun a spark
Hung thin between
　　The dark and dark.

5　Fat snowy footsteps
　　Track the floor,
And parkas pile up
　　Near the door.

The river is
10　　A frozen place
Held still beneath
　　The trees' black lace.

The sky is low.
　　The wind is gray.
15　The radiator
　　Purrs all day.

Activate Prior Knowledge

Think about your relationship with the natural world. What in nature inspires you?

_____

_____

_____

_____

Literary Analysis

Imagery is language that appeals to the senses. Underline one example of imagery in this poem. Is the imagery effective? Explain.

_____

_____

_____

_____

_____

Reading Check

What things does the speaker associate with the month of January? Underline two examples.

New World

N. Scott Momaday

1.

First Man,
behold:
the earth
glitters
5   with leaves;
the sky
glistens
with rain.
Pollen
10 is borne
on winds
that low
and lean
upon
15 mountains.
Cedars
blacken
the slopes—
and pines.

2.

20 At dawn
eagles
hie and
hover[1]
above
25 the plain
where light
gathers
in pools.
Grasses

© Pearson Education

Vocabulary Development

glistens (GLI suhnz) *v.* shines; sparkles

1. **hie and hover** fly swiftly and then hang as if suspended in the air.

Read Fluently

Preview the text on this page, and identify any words that are unfamiliar. Use the lines below to write the pronunciation and definition of each word. Then, reread this page.

_____

_____

_____

Reading Skill

Circle the punctuation marks in the bracketed stanza. Then, **read aloud fluently according to punctuation**. How many sentences are in this stanza?

_____

Literary Analysis

In the second stanza, underline an example of **imagery**. How does this image give a feeling of newness?

_____

_____

Reading Skill

Paraphrase lines 37–45. Remember to use your own words to rewrite the passage.

_____

_____

_____

_____

Literary Analysis 🔍

In the fourth stanza, what **imagery** creates a feeling of temperature?

_____

_____

_____

_____

Reading Check

What times of day does the speaker mention? Circle the words that signal each time of day.

30 shimmer
    and shine.
    Shadows
    withdraw
    and lie
35 away
    like smoke.

3.

    At noon
    turtles
    enter
40 slowly
    into
    the warm
    dark loam.[2]
    Bees hold
45 the swarm.
    Meadows
    recede
    through planes
    of heat
50 and pure
    distance.

4.

    At dusk
    the gray
    foxes
55 stiffen
    in cold;
    blackbirds
    are fixed
    in the
60 branches.

Vocabulary Development
recede (ri SEED) *v.* move away

2. **loam** (lohm) rich, dark soil.

Rivers
follow
the moon,
the long
65 white track
of the
full moon.

For My Sister Molly Who in the Fifties

Alice Walker

FOR MY SISTER MOLLY WHO IN THE
    FIFTIES
Once made a fairy rooster from
Mashed potatoes
Whose eyes I forget
5 But green onions were his tail
And his two legs were carrot sticks
A tomato slice his crown.
Who came home on vacation
When the sun was hot
10 and cooked
and cleaned
And minded least of all
The children's questions
A million or more
15 Pouring in on her
Who had been to school
And knew (and told us too) that certain
Words were no longer good
And taught me not to say us for we
20 No matter what "Sonny said" up the
road.

Literary Analysis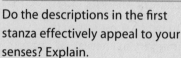

Reread the first stanza of Walker's poem. What does the **imagery** in these lines tell you about Molly?

_____

_____

_____

Stop to Reflect

Do the descriptions in the first stanza effectively appeal to your senses? Explain.

_____

_____

_____

Reading Check

What does Molly make? Underline the answer in the poem.

Reading Skill 📖

Read lines 22–24 to identify one complete thought. **Paraphrase** the lines.

_____

_____

_____

_____

Literary Analysis 🔍

To which senses does the **imagery** in lines 36–52 appeal? Give two examples.

_____

_____

_____

_____

Reading Skill 📖

Paraphrase the underlined passage.

_____

_____

_____

_____

_____

FOR MY SISTER MOLLY WHO IN THE
    FIFTIES
Knew Hamlet[1] well and read into the night
And coached me in my songs of Africa
25 A continent I never knew
But learned to love
Because "they" she said could carry
A tune
And spoke in accents never heard
30 In Eatonton.
Who read from Prose and Poetry
And loved to read "Sam McGee from
    Tennessee"[2]
On nights the fire was burning low
And Christmas wrapped in angel hair[3]
35 And I for one prayed for snow.

WHO IN THE FIFTIES
Knew all the written things that made
Us laugh and stories by
The hour   Waking up the story buds
40 Like fruit. Who walked among the flowers
And brought them inside the house
And smelled as good as they
And looked as bright.
Who made dresses, braided
45 Hair. Moved chairs about
Hung things from walls
Ordered baths
Frowned on wasp bites
And seemed to know the endings
50 Of all the tales
I had forgot.

1. **Hamlet** play by William Shakespeare.

2. **"Sam McGee from Tennessee"** reference to the title character in the Robert Service poem, "The Cremation of Sam McGee."

3. **angel hair** fine, white, filmy Christmas tree decoration.

WHO OFF INTO THE UNIVERSITY
Went exploring   To London and
To Rotterdam
55 Prague and to Liberia
Bringing back the news to us
Who knew none of it
But followed
crops and weather
60 funerals and
Methodist Homecoming;
easter speeches,
groaning church.

WHO FOUND ANOTHER WORLD
65 Another life   With gentlefolk
Far less trusting
And moved and moved and changed
Her name
And sounded precise
70 When she spoke   And frowned away
Our sloppishness.

WHO SAW US SILENT
Cursed with fear   A love burning
Inexpressible
75 And sent me money not for me
But for "College."
Who saw me grow through letters
The words misspelled   But not
The longing   Stretching
80 Growth
The tied and twisting
Tongue
Feet no longer bare
Skin no longer burnt against
85 The cotton.

Reading Skill

Paraphrase the complete thought expressed in the bracketed passage.

_____

_____

_____

_____

Literary Analysis

What **images** describe the feelings of growing up?

_____

_____

_____

_____

Reading Check

To what places does Molly go? Circle the names of those places in the poem.

Stop to Reflect

Name one thing that the speaker learns from Molly.

_____

_____

_____

_____

Literary Analysis

In what way would this poem be different **without imagery?**

_____

_____

_____

Reading Check

How does the speaker describe her family? Underline the words that tell you.

WHO BECAME SOMEONE OVERHEAD
A light   A thousand watts
Bright and also blinding
And saw my brothers cloddish
90 And me destined to be
Wayward[4]
My mother remote   My father
A wearisome farmer
With heartbreaking
95 Nails.

FOR MY SISTER MOLLY WHO IN THE
        FIFTIES
Found much
Unbearable
Who walked where few had
100 Understood   And sensed our
Groping after light
And saw some extinguished
And no doubt mourned.

FOR MY SISTER MOLLY WHO IN THE
        FIFTIES
Left us.

Vocabulary Development

remote (ri MOHT) *adj.* aloof; cold; distant

---

4. **wayward** (WAY werd) *adj.* headstrong; disobedient.

Poetry Collection 7

1. **Draw Conclusions:** The speaker in "January" describes things as he has seen them in winter. Basing your opinion on these descriptions, do you think the speaker has good or bad feelings about winter? Explain.

_____

_____

2. **Interpret:** In "New World," the speaker talks about three parts of the day. What do you think the times of the day represent?

_____

_____

3. **Reading Skill:** To **paraphrase** is to restate something in your own words. Use this chart to paraphrase lines from two of the poems.

Original Lines	Paraphrase
January (Lines 13–16)	The cloudy sky seems close to Earth, and even the wind is gray. The radiator makes a comforting humming sound.
New World (Lines 37–45)	
For My Sister Molly . . . (Lines 16–18)	

4. **Literary Analysis:** List one image that stands out from "For My Sister Molly Who in the Fifties." What mood, or feeling, does this image create?

_____

_____

Writing: Review

A review of a literary work is an evaluation of its strengths and weaknesses. Write a **review** of this three-poem collection. Use the following chart to write notes for your review.

	Poem's Strengths	Poem's Weaknesses	Opinion of Poem
January			
New World			
For My Sister . . .			

Research and Technology: Profile

Write a **profile** of one of the poets featured in this collection. Gather information about the poet's life, writings, and influences. Write notes about the following information.

- Describe two important experiences in the poet's life. How did these experiences affect the poet?

_____

_____

- Who or what influenced the poet and his or her work? In what way?

_____

_____

_____

Word List A

Study these words from the poetry of Amy Ling, Wendy Rose, and
E. E. Cummings. Then, complete the activity that follows.

century [SEN chuh ree] *n.* a period of one hundred years
  A century ago, there was no television or Internet.

delicious [di LISH uhs] *adj.* delightful
  My grandfather described ballet as a delicious treat for his eyes.

eldest [EL dist] *adj.* oldest
  *My eldest brother is four years older than me and two years older
  than my other brother.*

image [IM ij] *n.* a representation; a likeness
  *People in our family often say that I am the perfect image of my
  Aunt Caroline.*

perch [PERCH] *v.* to sit or stand on the top or edge of something
  *I wish my cat would not perch on the upstairs windowsills when the
  windows are open.*

twinkling [TWING kling] *v.* sparkling; shining with quick flashes
  In the country, the stars were twinkling brightly.

Exercise A

Fill in each blank in the paragraph below with an appropriate word
from Word List A. Use each word only once.

In our small town, we have had a Fourth of July parade every year

for more than a [1] _____. The [2] _____ person in town

always leads off the parade, seated in a fancy car. We eat [3] _____

hot dogs while watching parade participants like the marching band,

fancy floats, dancers and jugglers, and funny clowns. Bringing up the

rear is someone dressed to be the exact [4] _____ of Uncle Sam.

It's amazing what a likeness to the cartoons this costume has. Usually,

the whole town turns out for the parade. Chairs line the streets, and

some people [5] _____ high up on rooftops so as to get a bird's-

eye view. The town's good feelings last until the evening's fireworks

outshine the stars that are [6] _____ in the sky.

1. Underline the words describing what the turtle finds delicious. Then, tell about something other than a food or drink that is *delicious* to you.

2. Circle a word in the next sentence that names what the turtle believes is impressive about its image. Then, explain what *image* means.

3. Underline the word telling what birds are doing before they perch on something. Then, describe a good place for a bird to *perch*.

4. Circle the words in the paragraph naming how long the eldest turtle has lived. Then, tell about the *eldest* member of your family.

5. Underline the word naming what was twinkling in the sky. Then, tell about something else you have seen that was *twinkling* in the sky.

6. Circle the word in the previous sentences that hints at the meaning of century. If the turtle is speaking today, what new *century* did it see the world celebrate?

Read the following passage. Pay special attention to the underlined words. Then, read it again, and complete the activities. Use a separate sheet of paper for your written answers.

My name is Amazing. At least, that is what people always say when they see me: "He is 'Amazing!'" They yell these words from the decks of small boats and big ships, as they watch me swimming in the ocean. Some of them pay money just to go out to sea, hoping for a glimpse of me.

It is a delicious feeling for me, to be so admired just for doing what a giant sea turtle does best. I try to think about why my image is so impressive.

I suppose it is my size, but what these people should find really incredible is my age. I know that seeing a three-hundred-pound turtle might be shocking, but these people should imagine how it feels to be swimming around at my age. I wish I could stop and rest sometimes. Think about the birds, for example. They get to quit flying and perch on something for a nice long nap whenever they feel like it.

I believe that I am the eldest sea turtle in the world. I have lived more than eighty years, outliving three of my own children. Each year, I have seen the fireworks that are twinkling in the sky as people around the world welcome a new year. I even saw the world usher in a new century, a phenomenon that occurs only once every hundred years.

During my years on Earth, I have watched the ocean waters grow more and more polluted. I have seen people pull more and more of my food out of the seas. As I near the end of my life, I hope that people who see me, who call me "Amazing," will make some changes so that giant sea turtles will thrive in this world. I hope humans know that what they really should call us is "Endangered."

Poetry Collection 8

Summaries In "Grandma Ling," the speaker travels to Taiwan to meet her grandmother. She and her grandmother do not speak the same language. They still feel close to each other. In "Drum Song," the lines flow like the beat of a drum. The speaker tells how a turtle, a woodpecker, a snowhare, and a woman move through the world to their own beat. The speaker in "your little voice/Over the wires came leaping" talks to a special person on the telephone. Her voice makes him dizzy. He thinks of flowers. He feels as though he is dancing.

 Writing About the Big Question

What is the secret to reaching someone with words? The poems in "Poetry Collection 8" explore how words make connections between people and the world. Complete this sentence:

I had a connection to other people when I _____

_____.

Note-taking Guide

Use this chart to help you note the events of each poem.

Grandma Ling	Drum Song	your little voice/Over the wires came leaping
The speaker visits her grandmother in Taiwan.		

Poetry Collection 8

1. **Speculate:** The grandmother and the granddaughter in "Grandma Ling" do not speak the same language. What might they want to tell each other if they could speak the same language?

_____

_____

2. **Analyze:** Think about what the animals and women are doing in "Drum Song." How do they interact with the world around them?

_____

_____

3. **Reading Skill:** To **paraphrase** means to restate in your own words. Read the lines listed in this chart. Paraphrase the lines.

Original Lines	Paraphrase
Grandma Ling (Lines 15–16)	My likeness stood in front of me, though aged by fifty years.
Drum Song (Lines 8–13)	
your little voice . . . (Lines 1–6)	

4. **Literary Analysis: Imagery** helps readers picture what the author is describing. Write one image from "your little voice . . . ." To what sense does this image appeal?

_____

_____

Writing: Review

Write a **review** of the poems in this collection. Use these questions to write notes for your review.

	Grandma Ling	Drum Song	your little voice . . .
How does the rhythm match the subject?			
How do the words match the subject?			
Which lines have vivid imagery?			

Research and Technology: Poet's Profile

Complete the following chart with information about the poet you have chosen. Your **profile** should tell about the poet's life experiences. You should also include how the poet's life has affected his or her writing.

Poet: _____

Significant life events	
Awards/Honors	
Jobs	
Influences	

Use this information to write your profile.

Manuals

About Manuals

A **manual** is a set of directions. It tells how to use a tool or product. Most manuals have these parts:

- a drawing or picture of the product with the parts and features labeled
- step-by-step directions for putting the item together and using it
- safety information
- a guide that tells how to fix common problems
- customer service information, such as telephone numbers, addresses, and Web site addresses

Reading Skill

You use a manual to perform a task. In order to use a manual effectively, you must **analyze the technical directions.** Study the drawings, diagrams, headings, lists, and labels to help you follow the directions. Bold type and capital letters often signal specific sections and important information.

Checklist for Following Technical Directions

❑ Read all the directions completely before starting to follow them.

❑ Look for clues such as bold type or capital letters that point out specific sections or important information.

❑ Use diagrams to locate and name the parts of the product.

❑ Follow each step in the exact order given.

❑ Do not skip any steps.

Using Your Answering Machine

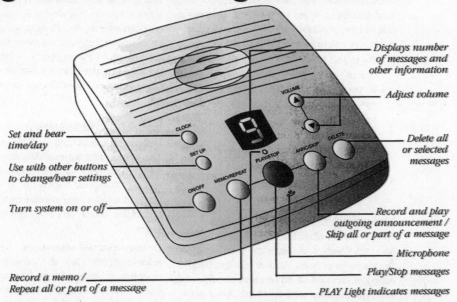

Displays number of messages and other information

Adjust volume

Set and hear time/day

Use with other buttons to change/hear settings

Turn system on or off

Delete all or selected messages

Record and play outgoing announcement / Skip all or part of a message

Microphone

Record a memo / Repeat all or part of a message

Play/Stop messages

PLAY Light indicates messages

Setting the Clock

You'll need to set the clock so that it can announce the day and time that each message is received. Press PLAY/STOP to exit Setting the Clock at any time.

1   Press and hold CLOCK until the Message Window displays CLOCK, and the default day is announced.

2   To change the day setting, hold down MEMO/REPEAT or ANNC/SKIP until the correct day is announced. Then release the button.

3   Press and release CLOCK. The current hour setting is announced.

4   To change the hour setting, hold down MEMO/REPEAT or ANNC/SKIP until the correct hour is announced. Then release the button.

5   Press and release CLOCK. The current minutes setting is announced.

6   To change the minutes setting, hold down MEMO/REPEAT or ANNC/SKIP until the correct minutes setting is announced. Then release the button.

7   Press and release CLOCK. The new day and time are announced.

To check the clock, press and release CLOCK.

NOTE: *In the event of a power failure, see the instructions on the bottom of the unit to reset the clock.*

Recording Your Announcement

Before using this answering system, you should record the announcement (up to one minute long) that callers will hear when the system answers a call. If you choose not to record an announcement, the system answers with a prerecorded announcement: *"Hello. Please leave a message after the tone."*

1   Press and hold ANNC/SKIP. The system beeps. Speak toward the microphone normally, from about nine inches away. While you are recording, the Message Window displays —.

2   To stop recording, release ANNC/SKIP. The system automatically plays back your announcement.

To review your announcement, press and release ANNC/SKIP.

Turning the System On/Off

Use ON/OFF to turn the system on and off. When the system is off, the Message Window is blank.

Volume Control

Use volume buttons (▲ and ▼) to adjust the volume of the system's speaker. Press the top button (▲) to increase volume. Press the bottom button (▼) to decrease volume. The system beeps three times when you reach the maximum or minimum volume setting.

2

Announcement Monitor

You can choose whether to hear the announcement when your system answers a call, or have it silent (off) on your end (your caller will still hear an announcement).

1   Press and hold [SET UP]. After the Ring Select setting is announced, continue to press and release [SET UP] until the system announces "*Monitor is on (or off).*"

2   Press and release [ANNC/SKIP] or [MEMO/REPEAT] until the system announces your selection.

3   Press and release [PLAY/STOP] or [SET UP] to exit.

Listening to Your Messages

As the system plays back messages, the Message Window displays the number of the message playing. Before playing each message, the system announces the day and time the message was received. After playing the last message, the system announces "*End of messages.*"

Play all messages — Press and release [PLAY/STOP]. If you have no messages, the system announces "*No messages.*"

Play new messages only — Hold down [PLAY/STOP] for about two seconds, until the system begins playing. If you have no new messages, the system announces "*No new messages.*"

Repeat entire message — Press and release [MEMO/REPEAT].

Repeat part of message — Hold down [MEMO/REPEAT] until you hear a beep, then release to resume playing. The more beeps you hear, the farther back in the message you will be when you release the button.

Repeat previous message — Press [MEMO/REPEAT] twice, continue this process to hear other previous messages.

Skip to next message — Press and release [ANNC/SKIP].

Skip part of a message — Hold down [ANNC/SKIP] until you hear a beep, then release to resume playing. The more beeps you hear, the farther into the message you will be when you release the button.

Stop message playback — Press and release [PLAY/STOP].

Saving Messages

The system automatically saves your messages if you do not delete them. The system can save about 12 minutes of messages, including your announcement, for a total of up to 59 messages. When memory is full, you must delete some or all messages before new messages can be recorded.

Deleting Messages

Delete all messages — Hold down [DELETE]. The system announces "*Messages deleted*" and permanently deletes messages. The Message Window displays **0**. If you haven't listened to all of the messages, the system beeps five times, and does not delete messages.

Delete selected messages — Press and release [DELETE] while the message you want to delete is being played. The system beeps once, and continues with the next message. If you want to check a message before you delete it, you can press [MEMO/REPEAT] to replay the message before deleting it.

When the system reaches the end of the last message, the messages not deleted are renumbered, and the Message Window displays the total number of messages remaining in memory.

Recording a Memo

You can record a memo to be stored as an incoming message. The memo can be up to three minutes long, and will be played back with other messages.

1   Press and hold [MEMO/REPEAT]. After the beep, speak toward the microphone.

2   To stop recording, release [MEMO/REPEAT].

3   To play the memo, press [PLAY/STOP].

When Memory is Full

The system can record approximately 12 minutes of messages, including your announcement, for a total of up to 59 messages. When memory is full, or 59 messages have been recorded, the Message Window flashes **F**. Delete messages to make room for new ones.

When memory is full, the system answers calls after 10 rings, and sounds two beeps instead of your announcement.

4

Thinking About the Manual

1. You may use some of the answering machine features more than others. Which features do you think are most important? Explain.

_____

_____

2. Look at the diagram. How does it make the text easier to follow?

_____

_____

TALK ABOUT IT Reading Skill

3. Many words in the answering machine manual are boxed and set in italic type. What does this formatting tell about these words?

_____

_____

4. How are the steps in the process for "Setting the Clock" identified?

_____

_____

WRITE ABOUT IT Timed Writing: Analyze Technical Directions (20 minutes)
Reread the section of the manual headed "Setting the Clock." Explain how text features (headings, numbering, boxed terms, and italic type) help the reader understand the text. Use these questions to help organize your writing.

1. Why are parts of the text numbered? _____

2. Why are some words set inside a box? _____

3. What information is set in italic type? _____

from Anne Frank & Me

Drama is written to be performed, or acted out. Dramas, or plays, can include elements of fiction such as plot, conflict, and setting. They also use some elements that occur only in dramas, or plays. These special elements include those listed in the chart below.

Element	Definition	Example
Playwright	• author of a play	William Shakespeare
Script	• written form of a play	*Romeo and Juliet*
Acts	• units of the action in a play	Act III
Scenes	• parts of an act	Act III, scene ii
Characterization	• the playwright's technique of creating believable characters	A character hangs his head to show that he is ashamed.
Dialogue	• words that characters say • words that characters speak appear next to their names • much of what you learn about the play is revealed through dialogue	JIM: When did you recognize me? LAURA: Oh, right away.
Monologue	• a long, uninterrupted speech that is spoken by a single character	HAMLET: To be, or not to be . . .
Stage Directions	• bracketed information that tells the cast, crew, and readers of the play about sound effects, actions, and sets • this information can also describe a character's gestures or emotions	[whispering]
Set	• scenery on stage that suggests the time and place of the action	a kitchen, a park
Props	• small, portable items that make actions look realistic	plates, a book

There are different types of drama. Several types are listed below.

Comedy is a drama that has a happy ending. Comedies often have normal characters in funny situations. Comedies can be written to amuse their audiences. They can also point out what is wrong in a society.

Tragedy is often contrasted with comedy. Events in a tragedy lead to the downfall of the main character. This character can be an average person. More often the main character is an important person. He or she could be a king or queen or another type of heroic figure.

Drama is often used to describe plays that talk about serious things. Some dramas are not acted on a stage. These types of drama are listed below.

- **Screenplays** are scripts for films. They include instructions for the person using the camera. A screenplay usually has many more scene changes than a stage play.

- **Teleplays** are scripts for television. They often contain the same elements that screenplays have.

- **Radio plays** are scripts for radio broadcasts. They include sound effects. A radio play does not have a set.

Word List A

Study these words from Anne Frank and Me. Then, complete the activity.

angel [AYN juhl] *n.* in religion, a spirit or messenger from heaven
  Sometimes, I am sure that there is an angel watching out for me!

certainly [SER tuhn lee] *adv.* without any doubt
  I will certainly be glad when school is out for the summer.

disturb [dis TERB] *v.* to bother or interrupt someone
  My sister and I have agreed never to disturb each other during telephone calls.

flooded [FLUHD id] *v.* became filled with
  My heart was flooded with happiness when my dog came home.

instantly [IN stuhnt lee] *adv.* right away; at once
  As soon as I saw him, I instantly knew something was wrong.

possible [PAHS uh buhl] *adj.* able to be done; likely to happen
  Is it possible for me to take the test again when I am not sick?

privacy [PRY vuh see] *n.* the state of being alone
  It's hard to have privacy when you share a bedroom.

shield [SHEELD] *v.* to protect someone or something
  In this bright sunlight, you need a hat to shield your eyes.

Exercise A

Fill in each blank in the paragraph below with an appropriate word from Word List A. Use each word only once.

I [1] _____ did not think I would enjoy the new television show very much. The main character is an [2] _____, which seemed odd to me. My friends were all talking about the show, though, so I decided to watch it. As soon as the program began, I was [3] _____ caught up in it. I watched the main character [4] _____ people from harm. My heart and mind were [5] _____ with emotion when a small child's life was saved. During a commercial break, I asked my mom not to [6] _____ me if anyone called. I wanted to watch the rest of the show in peace and [7] _____, without any interruptions. Who would have thought it would be [8] _____ to become a fan of the show so quickly?

Read the following passage. Pay special attention to the underlined words. Then, read it again, and complete the activities. Use a separate sheet of paper for your written answers.

My grandmother grew up in France. She was my age during World War II, when the country fell to Germany. No one had thought it was <u>possible</u> for the Germans to attack over the Ardennes Mountains, but that is what they did.

My grandmother's parents were able to <u>shield</u> her from the ugly war while it was happening. However, afterwards, they decided to educate her about the details. They <u>certainly</u> did not want her to learn only from stories. They wanted to show her important places in person. So, in 1947, two years after the war ended, they took her on a train trip through Europe.

Yesterday, I found the diary my grandmother kept during the trip. It was among the things she had left to my mom and me. This morning, I told my mom not to <u>disturb</u> me because I planned to read my grandmother's diary. I wanted to be alone, in the <u>privacy</u> of my room.

Since her death, I missed my grandmother so much! Secretly, I had been hoping that she would visit me as an <u>angel</u>. However, now I was hoping that reading her diary would make me feel <u>flooded</u> with her presence.

As I began to read, I <u>instantly</u> heard my grandmother's voice in her words. She described the first stop on the train trip, outside of Paris. It was at a city named Compiègne.

Grandmother's father explained to her that this city was where the French signed a deal with the Germans. The agreement stopped the fighting by turning over most of France to Germany. The signing occurred on a train car on June 21, 1940.

Interestingly, Compiègne was the exact spot where the Germans had surrendered on November 11, 1918, ending World War I. The surrender also took place on a train car.

I was really hooked now, not just on my grandmother's story, but also on the history I would learn.

1. Underline the words that tell what people did not think was <u>possible</u>. Describe something that you have done that others did not think was *possible*.

2. Circle the words naming what the grandmother's parents wanted to <u>shield</u> her from. How you would *shield* your children from a war?

3. Underline the words naming what the parents <u>certainly</u> did not want. Describe something that you *certainly* want to learn.

4. Circle the words telling why the writer did not want her mother to <u>disturb</u> her. Tell about a time you asked someone not to *disturb* you.

5. Circle the word that gives a hint to the meaning of <u>privacy</u>. Where do you go for *privacy*?

6. Underline the words naming what the writer hoped to be <u>flooded</u> with. Then, explain how seeing her grandmother as an *angel* would have *flooded* her with these same feelings.

7. Circle the words telling what the writer <u>instantly</u> heard. Explain *instantly*.

from Anne Frank & Me
Cherie Bennett

Summary An American teenager named Nicole travels back in time to Paris in 1942. Her family is arrested for being Jewish. They are put on a train going to a prison camp. Nicole recognizes Anne Frank on the train. She tells Anne details about Anne's life. Both girls are shocked by what Nicole knows.

Note-taking Guide
Use this diagram to compare and contrast the main characters.

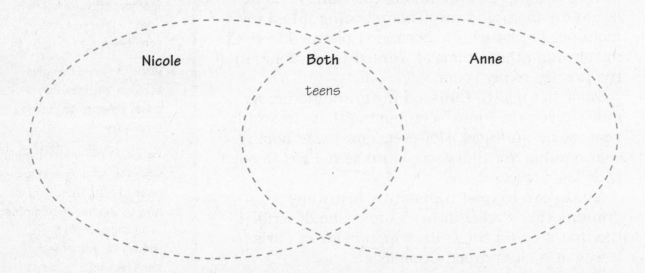

Nicole   Both   Anne

teens

from Anne Frank & Me

Cherie Bennett

During this monologue, which takes place in a cattle car, Nazis push people into the car. The pre-recorded voice of Nicole explains that the car is in Westerbork, Holland, the date is September 3, 1944, and she expects the war to be over soon.

Nicole approaches a girl who is sitting in front of the toilet bucket with her back to the audience. Nicole explains that she needs to use the bucket and the girl offers to shield Nicole with her coat. Nicole tells the girl that she boarded the train just outside Paris and has been traveling for 17 days.

Nicole explains that, although she is from Paris and the other girl is from Amsterdam, Nicole somehow knows the girl.

◆ ◆ ◆

NICOLE. I do know you. Your name is . . . Anne Frank.[1]

ANNE. *(shocked)* That's right! Who are you?

NICOLE. Nicole Bernhardt. I know so much about you...you were in hiding for a long time, in a place you called . . . the Secret Annex[2]—

◆ ◆ ◆

Nicole continues describing her memories of Anne. Anne has been in hiding in the Secret Annex with her parents, her older sister Margot, and the Van Daans, whose son, Peter, is Anne's boyfriend. Anne is shocked that Nicole knows this information, some of which she has confided only to her diary.

◆ ◆ ◆

© Pearson Education

Activate Prior Knowledge

Imagine that you are arrested because of something you believe. How would you feel?

_____

_____

_____

_____

Read Fluently

The two sentences in the bracketed passage contain several clauses. The sentences are considered complex sentences. Underline each clause in the sentences. Reword the clauses in the first sentence to make two sentences.

_____

_____

_____

Reread the paragraph with the sentences you wrote to make sure that the meaning is still the same.

Drama

A **scene** is one part of an **act** in a drama. What is the setting of this scene? Underline the time. Circle the place.

---

1. **Anne Frank** a young German Jewish girl who wrote a diary about her family's hiding in The Netherlands during the Holocaust. The Holocaust was the mass killing of European Jews and others by the Nazis during World War II.

2. **Secret Annex** name given to the space in an Amsterdam office building, where in 1942, thirteen-year-old Anne Frank and her family went into hiding.

Drama

Look at the chart on page 322. What **element of drama** would you call the conversation between Anne and Nicole?

_____

_____

Stop to Reflect

Do you have trouble believing in this drama? Explain your answer.

_____

_____

_____

_____

_____

Reading Check

What does Anne believe that Nicole is? Circle the text that tells you.

NICOLE. You kept a <u>diary</u>. I read it.

ANNE. But . . . I left my diary in the Annex when the Gestapo[3] came. You couldn't have read it.

NICOLE. But I did.

♦ ♦ ♦

Anne believes that this very strange conversation the two girls are having may be a practical joke that Peter or Anne's father came up with as a distraction. Nicole denies that she is playing a joke on Anne.

♦ ♦ ♦

NICOLE. Do you believe in time travel?

ANNE. I'm to believe that you're from the future? Really, I'm much more <u>intelligent</u> than I look.

NICOLE. I don't know how I know all this. I just do.

ANNE. Maybe you're an angel.

NICOLE. That would certainly be news to me.

Vocabulary Development

diary (DY uh ree) *n.* book in which a person writes important or interesting things that happen in his or her life

intelligent (in TEL uh juhnt) *adj.* having a high level of ability to learn, understand, and think about things

---

3. **Gestapo** German security police under the Nazis.

Drama

1. **Respond**: How would you feel if someone you had never met knew details about you and your life?

_____

_____

2. **Generalize**: What is it like for Anne and Nicole on the train?

_____

_____

3. **Drama**: A **comedy** is a drama that has a happy ending. Events in a **tragedy** lead to the downfall of the main character. A **drama** is often used to describe plays that talk about serious things. How would you characterize this play? Explain your answer.

_____

_____

4. **Drama**: A **character** is a person or an animal that takes part in the action of a story. The author makes Anne and Nicole believable characters. List details that make them seem real.

Character Description	
Anne	Nicole
huge eyes	anxious, confused
speaks Dutch	speaks French

Bulletin Board Display

Create a **bulletin board display**. Following these tips will help prepare you to create a bulletin board display.

- Read some of the author's works. Cherie Bennett's books include *Zink, Life in the Fat Lane, Searching for David's Heart,* and *A Heart Divided.*

  What I learned from Bennett's writing:

  _____

  _____

  _____

  _____

- Search the Internet. Use words and phrases such as "Cherie Bennett."

  What I learned about Cherie Bennett:

  _____

  _____

  _____

  _____

- Watch the video interview with Cherie Bennett. Add what you learn from the video to what you have already learned about the author.

  Additional information learned about the author:

  _____

  _____

  _____

  _____

  Use your notes to create your bulletin board display.

The Governess

Reading Skill

Drawing conclusions means making decisions and forming opinions after thinking about the facts and details in a text. Look at what characters say and do to draw conclusions from a play. Look at what characters say that shows their ideas and attitudes. Think about the way that characters treat each other. Notice actions that show a pattern of behavior.

Make connections among these items to decide what they show about the characters. Use this chart to record the things that you notice and the conclusions you reach.

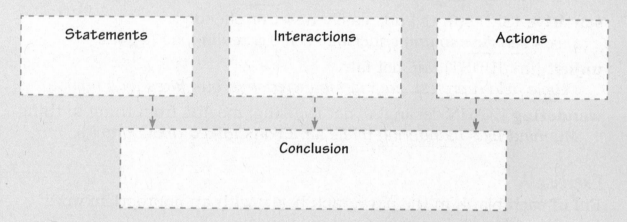

Literary Analysis

Stage directions are notes that tell how a play should be performed. They describe the scenery, costumes, lighting, and sound. Stage directions also describe how characters feel, move, or speak. They are usually printed in italics and set in brackets, or parentheses. Here is an example:

> *(It is late evening. The stage is dark, except for the glow of a small lamp beside the bed.)*

Use stage directions to form a picture in your mind of how the play would look and sound.

Word List A

Study these words from The Governess. Then, complete the activity.

blunt [BLUHNT] *adj.* speaking in an honest way that can upset people
Kate was so blunt about Tom's bad voice that he stopped singing.

excelled [EK seld] *v.* did something very well
Jenny loved math and excelled at algebra.

permission [per MISH uhn] *n.* the act of allowing someone to do something
Don't we need permission to camp in that park?

recall [ri KAWL] *v.* to remember something
I could not recall whether Joe or Celia borrowed my hockey stick.

saucer [SAW ser] *n.* a small round plate on which you put a cup
The set of dishes came with an extra saucer, in case one got broken.

sensitive [SEN suh tiv] *adj.* easily upset or offended
I was sensitive to any criticism, even if it really was helpful.

unjust [un JUHST] *adj.* not fair
People held a protest, saying the increase in bus fares was unjust.

wandering [WAHN der ing] *v.* not focusing; moving from thing to thing
My mind was wandering while Mr. Evans talked about gravity.

Exercise A

Fill in each blank in the paragraph below with an appropriate word from Word List A. Use each word only once.

I have always [1] _____ at remembering names. I think that is because I am so [2] _____ to discourteous behavior. Nothing feels more [3] _____ than being treated like someone who does not matter. Have you ever tried to talk to an important person whose eyes are constantly [4] _____ away from your face? You feel like you have to ask [5] _____ just for using a few minutes of that person's time. This feels even worse than talking to someone who does not [6] _____ your name. I once tried to talk to a banker about my confusion over a loan. The banker paid more attention to her teacup and [7] _____ than she did to my questions. To be [8] _____, that woman was just plain rude.

Read the following passage. Pay special attention to the underlined words. Then, read it again, and complete the activities. Use a separate sheet of paper for your written answers.

Many novels of the 1800s tell about the hard life of a governess. The novels describe wealthy couples who pay no attention to a young woman's need for respect and time off. The novels often describe unruly children who take part in their parents' <u>unjust</u> treatment of the governess. The governess might be reduced to tears, being <u>sensitive</u> to the cruel things her employer does and says.

To be <u>blunt</u>, however, the life of a governess was not so bad. Very few job possibilities existed for young women in the nineteenth century. For a girl who <u>excelled</u> in schoolwork, becoming a governess was a good opportunity.

Usually, a governess lived with the family whose children she was educating. She began her day having breakfast with the children. Then, she taught them their lessons, making sure their minds were not <u>wandering</u>. After lunch, which was served in the room where they studied, the children had more lessons. At the end of the afternoon, the governess spent time strolling with the children on the family property.

Usually, the governess ate dinner in her own room. She kept an extra cup and <u>saucer</u> on hand. That was in case someone else who worked for the family joined her for tea and conversation.

Most governesses had time off on the weekends. If a governess was expected to travel with the family or work all weekend, her employer usually asked her in advance. In the same way, a governess would ask <u>permission</u> to take days off well ahead of the dates she planned to be absent.

When a governess left her position, or the children in her charge grew up, she would fondly <u>recall</u> her time with the family. She felt proud of "her" children and followed their accomplishments. A governess could feel happy about money matters, too. Because the family paid most of her expenses, a governess could save much of what she earned.

1. Circle the words naming what many novels described as <u>unjust</u>. Explain why bratty children would be *unjust* toward others.

2. Underline the word that hints at the meaning of <u>sensitive</u>. Describe something that eighth-graders might be *sensitive* to.

3. Rewrite the sentence with the word <u>blunt</u> in it, replacing *blunt* with a synonym.

4. Underline the word naming what a governess usually <u>excelled</u> in. Describe something else a governess might have *excelled* at doing.

5. Circle the word naming what was <u>wandering</u>. Tell what could cause this *wandering*.

6. Underline the word that goes with <u>saucer</u>. Then, explain what a *saucer* is.

7. Circle the words naming what a governess needed <u>permission</u> to do. Tell about a time when you were not given *permission* to do something.

8. Circle the words that tell what a governess would <u>recall</u>. Name something wonderful you *recall*.

© Pearson Education

The Governess
Neil Simon

Summary A wealthy mistress plays a joke on her shy employee, Julia. The mistress subtracts money from Julia's pay. Julia is left with much less money than she is owed. The mistress hopes that Julia will become angry and stand up for herself.

Writing About the Big Question

Is it our differences or our similarities that matter most? The characters in *The Governess* come from different levels of society, which affects the way they treat each other. Complete this sentence:

An employer might discriminate against an employee, or treat her

unfairly because _____

_____.

Note-taking Guide

Use this chart to record the actions of the mistress and the way the governess responds to these actions.

Mistress's Action	Governess's Response

© Pearson Education

The Governess
Neil Simon

The play opens as a woman calls out to Julia, the young governess who has been hired to teach the woman's children. When Julia enters, she curtsies and keeps her head down. The woman keeps telling Julia to keep her head up, but Julia finds this difficult. The woman asks Julia how the children's lessons in French and mathematics are coming along. Julia assures her that the children are doing well. The woman tells Julia again to keep her head up. She says that if Julia thinks of herself as inferior, people will treat her that way. Then the woman announces that she wants to pay Julia for the past two months of work.

◆ ◆ ◆

MISTRESS. Let's see now, we agreed on thirty <u>rubles</u> a month, did we not?

JULIA. *(Surprised)* Forty, ma'am.

MISTRESS. No, no, thirty. I made a note of it. *(Points to the book)* I always pay my <u>governess</u> thirty . . . Who told you forty?

◆ ◆ ◆

The woman insists that the rate of pay is thirty rubles a month. Julia accepts this. They then discuss how long Julia has been there. The woman says it has been two months exactly, but Julia says it has been two months and five days. The woman says she has made a note of it, and Julia accepts this. Then the woman wants to subtract nine Sundays, saying that they had agreed earlier on this.

TAKE NOTES

Activate Prior Knowledge

Think about a time when you felt you were being treated unfairly. Explain what you did or what you wish you had done in the situation.

_____

_____

_____

Reading Skill

Drawing conclusions means using the facts and details in the text to form opinions. Read the bracketed passage. What conclusion can you draw about the relationship between Julia and the Mistress?

_____

_____

Literary Analysis

Stage directions describe the details of the play's setting. They also tell how the characters move, feel, and sound. Underline the stage directions on this page. What effect do they have on the reader?

_____

_____

_____

Vocabulary Development

rubles (ROO buhlz) *n.* Russian currency; similar to U.S. dollars

governess (GUV uhr nes) *n.* a female teacher who lives with a family and teaches its children at home

Stop to Reflect

The Mistress gives Julia several chances to stand up for herself and to insist on being paid. Why do you think Julia does not do this?

_____

_____

_____

Reading Skill

What **conclusion** can you draw about the Mistress from the fact that she keeps a book listing details about Julia's work?

_____

_____

_____

_____

Reading Check ✎

Why does the Mistress say she should not have to pay Julia for the days that Kolya was sick? Underline the text that tells you.

Although Julia does not remember this, she says she does. The woman then subtracts three holidays: Christmas, New Year's, and Julia's birthday. Even though Julia worked on her birthday, she agrees to what the woman says.

◆ ◆ ◆

MISTRESS. Now then, four days little Kolya was sick, and there were no lessons.

JULIA. But I gave lessons to Vanya.

MISTRESS. True. But I engaged you to teach two children, not one. Shall I pay you in full for doing only half the work?

JULIA. No, ma'am.

MISTRESS. So we'll deduct it . . . Now, three days you had a toothache and my husband gave you permission not to work after lunch. Correct?

JULIA. After four. I worked until four.

MISTRESS. _(Looks in the book)_ I have here: "Did not work after lunch." We have lunch at one and are finished at two, not at four, correct?

JULIA. Yes, ma'am. But I—

MISTRESS. That's another seven rubles . . . Seven and twelve is nineteen . . . Subtract . . . that leaves . . . forty-one rubles . . . Correct?

JULIA. Yes, ma'am. Thank you, ma'am.

◆ ◆ ◆

Now the woman wants to subtract more money to cover a teacup and saucer that Julia broke, even though Julia broke only the saucer. She also wants to deduct money because her son climbed a tree and tore his jacket, even though Julia had told him not to climb the tree. Julia also gets charged for the son's shoes that had been stolen by the

Vocabulary Development

engaged (en GAJD) _v._ employed

maid. The reason for this is that the woman says Julia is paid to "watch everything." More deductions are made for money the woman claims she gave to Julia earlier. Julia objects weakly, saying she never got any money. Finally, the woman pays Julia, saying she is giving her eleven rubles. When Julia counts only ten, the woman says she must have dropped one on the floor. Julia accepts this, thanks the woman for the money, and starts to leave. She is called back by the woman.

◆ ◆ ◆

MISTRESS. Why did you thank me?

JULIA. For the money, ma'am.

MISTRESS. For the money? . . . But don't you realize what I've done? I've cheated you . . . *Robbed* you! I have no such notes in my book. I made up whatever came into my mind. Instead of the eighty rubles which I owe you, I gave you only ten. I have actually stolen from you and you still thank me . . . Why?

JULIA. In the other places that I've worked, they didn't give me anything at all.

MISTRESS. Then they cheated you even worse than I did . . . I was playing a little joke on you. A cruel lesson just to teach you. You're much too trusting, and in this world that's very dangerous . . . I'm going to give you the entire eighty rubles. *(Hands her an envelope)* It's all ready for you. The rest is in this envelope. Here, take it.

JULIA. As you wish, ma'am.

◆ ◆ ◆

Julia turns to leave, but the woman calls her back again. The woman asks her why she does not speak up for herself. She asks if it is possible to be "such a simpleton." Julia tells her yes, that it is possible. Julie curtsies and leaves. The woman looks after her, completely baffled.

Reading Skill

Draw a conclusion about why Julia does not get angry with the Mistress.

_____

_____

_____

_____

Read Fluently

Read the bracketed passage. Underline the words that tell the action the Mistress performs. Picture the action. Write a brief description of the image that you have formed.

_____

_____

_____

_____

Reading Check

What does Julia say her other employers have done? Underline the text that tells you.

The Governess

1. **Connect:** Julia works as a governess to the Mistress's children. Why does this make her discussion with the Mistress difficult?

_____

_____

2. **Analyze:** The Mistress withholds money from Julia's pay to try to teach her a lesson. Do you think the Mistress is being kind, or cruel, or both? Explain.

_____

_____

3. **Reading Skill:** Think about the way that Julia answers her Mistress's questions. She is quiet and polite. What **conclusions** can you draw about the way governesses were treated at the time of this play?

_____

_____

_____

4. **Literary Analysis:** Write **stage directions** from _The Governess_ in the chart below. Give one example for each type of direction.

Describing an Action	Showing How a Character Feels
(Points to the book)	(Surprised)

Writing: Problem-Solution Essay

Write a **problem-solution essay** that discusses Julia's inability to stand up for herself. The essay should explain Julia's problem and propose a solution different from the solution the Mistress tried.

Think about how you would define Julia's problem.

- What negative consequences does Julia's problem cause her?

_____

_____

- What solution might work better than the Mistress's solution?

_____

_____

Use your notes to help you draft your essay.

Listening and Speaking: Debate

To prepare for your **debate**, think about what Julia should have done and why she should have done it. Use the following chart to keep track of your ideas.

What Julia Should Have Done	Why Julia Should Have Done It

Public Documents

About Public Documents

Public documents are government records or documents. They could also deal with citizens' rights and responsibilities according to the law. Some examples of public documents are:

- laws
- legal notices
- government publications
- notes taken at public meetings

Reading Skill

You may need to read a public document in order to find the answer to a question, make a decision, or solve a problem. You can **compare and contrast features and elements** in a document to help you understand the information it presents. Features and elements may include headings, boldface type, numbering, and bullets.

Information	+	Information	=	Generalization
The U. S. Department of Labor permits youth ages 14–15 to work fewer hours on school days than on non-school days.		The contract for the work-study program includes academic requirements.		Employers and the U.S. Department of Labor do not want young people's jobs to interfere with their schoolwork.

Wage and Hour Division
Basic Information

U.S. Department of Labor
Employment Standards Administration

The U.S. Department of Labor's Wage and Hour Division (WHD) administers and enforces laws that establish minimally acceptable standards for wages and working conditions in this country, regardless of immigration status.

Youth Employment

The FLSA also regulates the employment of youth.

Jobs Youth Can Do:

- 13 or younger: baby-sit, deliver newspapers, or work as an actor or performer
- Ages 14–15: office work, grocery store, retail store, restaurant, movie theater, or amusement park
- Age 16–17: Any job not declared hazardous
- Age 18: No restrictions

Hours Youth Ages 14 and 15 Can Work:

- After 7 A.M. and until 7 P.M.
- (Hours are extended to 9 P.M. June 1–Labor Day)
- Up to 3 hours on a school day
- Up to 18 hours in a school week
- Up to 8 hours on a non-school day
- Up to 40 hours in a non-school week

Note: Different rules apply to youth employed in agriculture. States also regulate the hours that youth under age 18 may work. To find State rules, log on to ***www.youthrules.dol.gov***

Thinking About the Public Document

1. Young people cannot work in some jobs. In others, they can work only a few hours each day. Why do you think young people have these limits?

_____

2. The Department of Labor allows students, ages 14 and 15, to work as many as 40 hours during a non-school week. The same students are permitted to work no more than 18 hours during a school week. What conclusion can you draw based on these rules?

_____

TALK ABOUT IT **Reading Skill**

3. Review the section headed "Hours Youth Ages 14 and 15 Can Work." What feature makes this specific information easy to read and understand?

_____

_____

4. How does the format of the note at the bottom of the page differ from the format of the other information? Why is the note formatted differently?

_____

_____

WRITE ABOUT IT **Timed Writing: Explanation (15 minutes)**

Think about laws for wages and working conditions. Explain why these laws are important. Include problems that people could have if these laws were not in place.

_____

_____

_____

The Diary of Anne Frank, Act I

Reading Skill

A **cause** is an event, an action, or a feeling. An **effect** is the result that a cause produces. You can **use background information to link historical causes with effects**. Background information includes the work's introduction, information in footnotes, facts learned in other classes, and information you already know.

Use a chart like the one shown to connect background information with a cause and an effect.

Dramatic Detail

A mother in a border state begs her sons not to join the fighting.

Cause

War begins.

Effect

Families in border states are split.

Background

In the American Civil War, the division between North and South produced border states with divided loyalties.

Literary Analysis

Dialogue is the characters' conversation. Lines of dialogue follow the name of each character in the *script*, or text, of a play. Writers use dialogue to reveal character traits and relationships, move the plot forward, and show the conflict between characters or between the main character and outside forces.

Word List A

Study these words from Act I of The Diary of Anne Frank. Then, complete the activity.

absorbed [ab ZAWRBD] *adj.* greatly interested
  Within minutes, he was completed underline{absorbed} in the movie.

bolt [BOHLT] *n.* a piece of metal that you slide across a door to lock it
  I heard Aunt Lois slide the underline{bolt}, locking the front door for the night.

canal [kuh NAL] *n.* man-made passage for boats
  To dig a underline{canal} deep enough for ocean-going ships is a huge task.

linen [LIN uhn] *n.* household items made of cloth, such as sheets and napkins
  My least favorite chore is ironing the table underline{linen}.

possessions [puh ZESH uhnz] *n.* things that you own; belongings
  I often think we all should give half of our underline{possessions} to the needy.

sprawling [SPRAWL ing] *v.* spreading out
  underline{Sprawling}, instead of sitting, on the furniture is not polite.

threadbare [THRED bair] *adj.* thin because of so much wear or use
  I noticed the elderly man shivering in his underline{threadbare} jacket.

uncertainty [un SER tuhn tee] *n.* feelings of being unsure about how something will end
  I have lots of underline{uncertainty} about the team's ability to win.

Exercise A

Fill in each blank in the paragraph below with an appropriate word from Word List A. Use each word only once.

Yesterday, I became [1] _____ in a magazine. On the cover was a model. The picture of her [2] _____ in a beach chair went with the article, "How to Spend the Perfect Day." Different people shared their ideas. No one had any [3] _____ about the topic. One person said he would walk along a [4] _____, watching the boats go by. Another said she would slide shut the [5] _____ on her bedroom door and sleep all day. A man said he would sort through his [6] _____, especially his clothes, and set aside anything out of fashion or [7] _____. A woman wanted to iron and fold all the [8] _____ in her house. She said this would remind her of her grandmother, who had given her many fine tablecloths.

Read the following passage. Pay special attention to the underlined words. Then, read it again, and complete the activities. Use a separate sheet of paper for your written answers.

Our family has spent much of the past week getting ready for Hanukkah. Tomorrow, we will light the first candle of our menorah. For now, though, I want to be sure everything really is prepared for the holiday. Until I review the tasks, following the checklist in my mind, <u>uncertainty</u> will haunt me.

First, I check that we have the ingredients to make the delicious holiday treats: latkes (potato pancakes), cheese blintzes, jelly doughnuts. I am glad we have replaced worn or <u>threadbare</u> tablecloths and napkins with new <u>linen</u>. We selected fine white cloth with gold trim. My little brother Hillel says that this is to match the gelt, the chocolate coins wrapped in gold foil.

We also bought fine olive oil from a specialty store along the <u>canal</u>. It was expensive! Mother says we must never get less than the best oil for Hanukkah. After all, just one small jar of oil made the Eternal Light of the Temple burn for eight whole days some 2,400 years ago. This miracle is what we remember as we light eight candles each year.

Hillel's favorite part of Hanukkah is the giving of gifts. Although I believe we all have more than enough <u>possessions</u> already, I understand his excitement. I slide back the <u>bolt</u> on the cupboard to look again at Hillel's surprises. He will definitely be happy.

Suddenly, I remember something we have forgotten to do. We have not brought out the dreidel, the holiday toy! Hillel usually spends hours <u>absorbed</u> in the dreidel game, spinning the toy and trying to win all of the pennies in the pot. Last year, he competed until he was exhausted. We still laugh about his <u>sprawling</u> across the table, dreidel in hand, fast asleep.

I rush up to the attic to find the box of games. Upon seeing the four symbols on the dreidel, I remember that they mean "A great miracle happened there." Maybe a great miracle will happen here, and I'll win at least one game.

1. Underline the words telling what will keep <u>uncertainty</u> from haunting the narrator. Then, explain what *uncertainty* means.

2. Circle the word that gives a clue to the meaning of <u>threadbare</u>. Explain why you would want to replace *threadbare* table linen before a holiday celebration.

3. Underline the words telling where the family bought oil along the <u>canal</u>. Explain why stores might be found along a *canal*.

4. Circle the words describing the writer's belief about the family's <u>possessions</u>. List three of your favorite *possessions*.

5. Underline the words telling where the <u>bolt</u> is located. Then, explain what a *bolt* is and how it works.

6. Circle the words describing what Hillel becomes <u>absorbed</u> with. Describe a time when you've been *absorbed* in a game.

7. Circle three phrases that help to describe Hillel's <u>sprawling</u>. Describe what *sprawling* looks like.

The Diary of Anne Frank, Act I

Frances Goodrich
and Albert Hackett

Summary World War II is over. Anne Frank's father returns to Amsterdam to say goodbye to a friend, Miep Gies. Gies gives him his daughter's diary. Mr. Frank opens the diary and begins reading. Anne's voice joins his and takes over. The story goes back to 1942. Anne's family and another family are moving into the space above their friends' business. There they will live and hide from the Nazis for two years.

Writing About the Big Question

Is it our differences or our similarities that matter most? In *The Diary of Anne Frank, Act I*, five adults and three teenagers struggle with their differences but face a common danger. Complete this sentence:

Danger tends to (unify/divide) people because _____

_____.

Note-taking Guide

Fill in this chart with important details from each scene in Act I.

Scene 1	After World War II, Mr. Frank returns to the attic in which his family had hidden from the Nazis. Miep shows him Anne's diary. He begins to think back to those terrible days.
Scene 2	
Scene 3	

The Diary of Anne Frank
Frances Goodrich and Albert Hackett

Act I, Scene 1

The Diary of Anne Frank is a play based on a diary kept during World War II by Anne Frank. The Nazis were hunting down Jews and sending them to prison camps during the war. The Franks and the Van Daans—both Jewish families—spent two years in hiding from the Nazis. In the small, cramped rooms where they are hiding, the families try to cope with their constant fear and lack of privacy. Thirteen-year-old Anne records her innermost thoughts and feelings in her diary.

The play opens in November 1945, several months after the end of World War II. Mr. Frank has returned to the upstairs rooms above his old factory—the place where his family and the Van Daans hid during the war. Miep, a loyal employee, watched over the family during those years. She is helping Mr. Frank to sort through some old papers.

◆ ◆ ◆

MIEP. *(Hurrying to a cupboard)* Mr. Frank, did you see? There are some of your papers here. *(She brings a bundle of papers to him.)* We found them in a heap of rubbish on the floor after . . . after you left.

MR. FRANK. Burn them. *(He opens his rucksack to put the glove in it.)*

MIEP. But, Mr. Frank, there are letters, notes . . .

MR. FRANK. Burn them. All of them.

MIEP. Burn this? *(She hands him a paper-bound notebook.)*

MR. FRANK. *(quietly)* Anne's diary. *(He opens the diary and begins to read.)* "Monday, the sixth of July, nineteen forty-two." *(To* MIEP*)*

Activate Prior Knowledge

List at least three things that happened in Europe during World War II.

1._____

_____

_____

2._____

_____

_____

3._____

_____

_____

Reading Skill

A **cause** is an event, an action, or a feeling that produces a result, or an **effect**. Two families plus a man named Mr. Dussel share the upstairs rooms as they hide from the Nazis. What might **cause** so many people to share such a small space?

_____

_____

_____

Reading Check

What is the setting of the play? Circle the answer.

Reading Skill

Anne refers to Adolf Hitler, the German dictator who persecuted Jews throughout Europe. What other historical **causes** and **effects** do you read about here?

_____

_____

_____

_____

Literary Analysis

Dialogue is the characters' conversation. In this play, Anne's lines are often spoken to her diary, as if the diary were another character. What significant plot event is revealed in the bracketed passage?

_____

_____

_____

_____

Reading Check

When does Scene 2 take place? Underline the answer.

Nineteen forty-two. Is it possible, Miep? . . . Only three years ago. *(As he continues his reading, he sits down on the couch.)* "Dear Diary, since you and I are going to be great friends, I will start by telling you about myself. My name is Anne Frank. I am thirteen years old. I was born in Germany the twelfth of June, nineteen twenty-nine. As my family is Jewish, we emigrated to Holland when Hitler came to power."

(As MR. FRANK *reads on, another voice joins his, as if coming from the air. It is* ANNE'S VOICE.*)*

MR. FRANK and ANNE. "My father started a business, importing spice and herbs. Things went well for us until nineteen forty. Then the war came, and the Dutch capitulation,[1] followed by the arrival of the Germans. Then things got very bad for the Jews. . . . (The Nazis) forced Father out of his business. We had to wear yellow stars.[2] I had to turn in my bike. I couldn't go to a Dutch school anymore. I couldn't go to the movies, or ride in an automobile, or even on a streetcar, and a million other things. . . .

◆ ◆ ◆

Act I, Scene 2

In Scene 2, the action flashes back to July 1942. The Franks and Van Daans are moving into hiding in their cramped upstairs rooms. Mr. Frank explains to everyone that when the employees are working in the factory below, everyone must remain very quiet. People cannot run water in the sink or use the toilet. They must speak only in whispers. They must walk without shoes.

---

1. **capitulation** (kuh pich uh LAY shuhn) *n.* surrender.
2. **yellow stars:** Stars of David, which are six-pointed stars that are symbols of Judaism. The Nazis ordered all Jews to wear them sewn to their clothing so that Jews could be easily identified.

As the families are getting settled, Anne, thirteen, starts to talk to Peter, sixteen. She notices that he is taking off his yellow star. She asks him why he is doing that.

◆   ◆   ◆

ANNE. What are you doing?

PETER. Taking it off.

ANNE. But you can't do that. They'll arrest you if you go out without your star.

(He tosses his knife on the table.)

PETER. Who's going out?

ANNE. Why, of course, You're right! Of course we don't need them any more. *(She picks up his knife and starts to take her star off.)* I wonder what our friends will think when we don't show up today?

PETER. I didn't have any dates with anyone.

ANNE. Oh, I did. I had a date with Jopie to go and play ping-pong at her house. Do you know Jopie de Waal?

PETER. No.

ANNE. Jopie's my best friend. I wonder what she'll think when she telephones and there's no answer? . . . Probably she'll go over to the house . . . I wonder what she'll think . . . we left everything as if we'd suddenly been called away . . . breakfast dishes in the sink . . . beds not made . . . *(As she pulls off her star, the cloth underneath shows clearly the color and form of the star.)* Look! It's still there!

(PETER goes over to the stove with his star.)

What are you going to do with yours?

PETER. Burn it.

ANNE. *(She starts to throw hers in, and cannot.)* It's funny, I can't throw mine away. I don't know why.

PETER. You can't throw . . . ? Something they branded you with . . . ? That they made you wear so they could spit on you?

TAKE NOTES

Stop to Reflect

Jews in Europe were forced to sew a yellow Star of David onto their clothing. It was intended to identify them as Jews. What do you think it was like for people to wear the patch on their clothes?

_____

_____

Reading Skill

What **effect** does the Star of David have on Anne's clothing?

_____

_____

Read Fluently

An ellipsis consists of three evenly spaced dots or periods. It can be used to show long pauses or thoughts that are not finished. Circle the ellipses in the bracketed passage. What do they show about what Anne is saying?

_____

_____

Reading Check

What is Peter going to do with his Star of David? Circle the answer.

© Pearson Education

Reading Skill

Think about the **background information that causes** Anne to answer Peter in the underlined passage. How does Anne's answer show her view about the Star of David?

_____

_____

_____

Literary Analysis

Writers use **dialogue** to help move the plot or story. How do Anne's reactions in the bracketed passage show the seriousness of their situation?

_____

_____

_____

Reading Check

What does Anne's father give Anne? Underline the answer.

Stop to Reflect

Why might a diary be a wonderful gift for a thirteen-year-old girl who is forced to hide away for an unknown period of time?

_____

_____

_____

ANNE. <u>I know. I know. But after all, it is the Star of David, isn't it?</u>

◆ ◆ ◆

Mr. Frank gives Anne a diary that she can write in. She is very excited. She has always wanted to keep a diary, and now she has the chance. She starts to run down to the office to get a pencil to write with, but Mr. Frank pulls her back.

◆ ◆ ◆

MR. FRANK. Anne! No! *(He goes after her, catching her by the arm and pulling her back.)*

ANNE. *(Startled)* But there's no one in the building now.

MR. FRANK. It doesn't matter. I don't want you ever to go beyond that door.

ANNE. *(Sobered)* Never . . . ? Not even at nighttime, when everyone is gone? Or on Sundays? Can't I go down to listen to the radio?

MR. FRANK. Never. I am sorry, Anneke.[3] It isn't safe. No, you must never go beyond that door.

(For the first time Anne realizes what "going into hiding" means.)

◆ ◆ ◆

Mr. Frank tries to comfort Anne by telling her that they will be able to read all sorts of wonderful books on all sorts of subjects: history, poetry, mythology. And she will never have to practice the piano. As the scene ends, Anne comments, in her diary, about the families' situation.

◆ ◆ ◆

_____

3. Anneke (AN uh kuh) nickname for Anne.

ANNE'S VOICE. . . . Friday, the twenty-first of August, nineteen forty-two. Today I'm going to tell you our general news. Mother is unbearable. She insists on treating me like a baby, which I loathe. Otherwise things are going better. . . .

Act I, Scene 3

Two months have passed. All is quiet for the time being. As the scene opens, the workers are still downstairs in the factory, so everyone is very quiet in the upstairs rooms where the families are hiding. Peter and Anne are busy with their schoolwork. After the last worker leaves the downstairs factory, Mr. Frank gives the signal that the families can start to move around and use the bathroom.

◆ ◆ ◆

ANNE. *(Her pent-up energy explodes.)* WHEE!

MR. FRANK. *(Startled, amused)* Anne!

MRS. VAN DAAN. I'm first for the w.c.[4] . . .

MR. FRANK. Six o'clock. School's over.

◆ ◆ ◆

Anne teases Peter by hiding his shoes. They fall to the floor in playful wrestling. Anne asks him to dance, but he says he must go off to feed his cat, Mouschi, which he keeps in his room.

◆ ◆ ◆

ANNE. Can I watch?

PETER. He doesn't like people around while he eats.

ANNE. Peter, please.

© Pearson Education

Vocabulary Development
loathe (lohth) *v.* to dislike something or someone greatly

4. **w.c.** water closet; bathroom.

Read Fluently

Read the underlined sentences. Use your own words to explain what Anne means when she says she is being treated "like a baby." Why do you think this upsets her?

_____

_____

_____

Reading Skill

What does the bracketed passage show about the **effect** of the situation on the families' daily lives?

_____

_____

_____

_____

Reading Check

By the time of Scene 3, how long have the families been living in the apartment? Underline the answer.

Literary Analysis

What does the bracketed **dialogue** tell you about Anne's personality?

_____

_____

_____

_____

Reading Skill

Why does Anne want to dance? What does she think the **effect** will be if she does not dance?

_____

_____

_____

Stop to Reflect

On this page, circle one statement by Anne and one by Margot that show the audience how different their personalities are.

Reading Check

In whose clothes does Anne dress up? Underline the answer.

PETER. No! *(He goes into his room.* ANNE *slams his door after him.)*

MRS. FRANK. Anne, dear, I think you shouldn't play like that with Peter. It's not <u>dignified</u>.

ANNE. Who cares if it's dignified? . . .

MRS. FRANK. *(To* ANNE*)* You complain that I don't treat you like a grownup. But when I do, you resent it.

ANNE. I only want some fun . . . someone to laugh and clown with . . . After you've sat still all day and hardly moved, you've got to have some fun. I don't know what's the matter with that boy.

MR. FRANK. He isn't used to girls. Give him a little time.

ANNE. Time? Isn't two months time? I could cry. *(Catching hold of* MARGOT*)* Come one, Margot . . . dance with me. Come on, please.

MARGOT. I have to help with supper.

ANNE: You know we're going to forget how to dance . . . When we get out we won't remember a thing. . . .

◆　◆　◆

They hear a car screeching to a stop on the street. All of them freeze with fear. When the car moves away, they relax again. Anne appears. She is dressed in some of Peter's clothes, and he teases her back. He calls her Mrs. Quack! Quack! because of her constant talking.

Mrs. Frank feels Anne's forehead. She wonders if Anne is sick. Mrs. Frank asks to see her tongue. Anne objects but then obeys.

Vocabulary Development

dignified (DIG ni fyd) *v.* deserving esteem or respect

Mr. Frank thinks Anne is not sick. He thinks she is just tired of being cooped up in the apartment. They find out that they will have beans again for dinner. They all say that they are sick of the beans.

After a brief discussion of Anne's progress with her schoolwork, they turn to a more personal subject.

◆   ◆   ◆

ANNE. Mrs. Van Daan, did you have a lot of boyfriends before you were married?

MRS. FRANK. Anne, that's a personal question. It's not courteous to ask personal questions.

MRS. VAN DAAN. Oh I don't mind. *(To* ANNE*)* Our house was always swarming with boys. When I was a girl we had . . .

MR. VAN DAAN. Oh, no. Not again!

MRS. VAN DAAN. *(Good-humored)* Shut up! *(Without a pause, to* ANNE, MR. VAN DAAN *mimics* MRS. VAN DAAN, *speaking the first few words in unison with her.)*

One summer we had a big house in Hilversum. The boys came buzzing round like bees around a jam pot. And when I was sixteen! . . . We were wearing our skirts very short those days, and I had good-looking legs. . . .

MR. VAN DAAN. Look at you, talking that way in front of her! Don't you know she puts it all down in that diary?

◆   ◆   ◆

The talk then turns to Peter's uneven progress with his schoolwork. Mr. Frank generously offers to tutor Peter as well as his own daughters. Anne spreads out on the floor to try to hear the radio downstairs. Mr. Van Daan complains that Anne's behavior is not ladylike. Mrs. Van Daan claims he is so bad-tempered from smoking cigarettes.

◆   ◆   ◆

Literary Analysis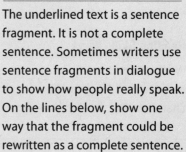

What does the **dialogue** on this page say about Mrs. Van Daan's character? List three words or phrases to describe her.

1. _____

2. _____

3. _____

Read Fluently

The underlined text is a sentence fragment. It is not a complete sentence. Sometimes writers use sentence fragments in dialogue to show how people really speak. On the lines below, show one way that the fragment could be rewritten as a complete sentence.

_____

_____

_____

Reading Check

Why does Anne stretch out on the floor? Underline the answer.

Stop to Reflect

Circle the comment by Anne that shows one way that her family is different from the Van Daans. Explain the difference below.

_____

_____

_____

_____

Reading Skill

What **effect** does the situation seem to be having on the characters?

_____

_____

_____

_____

Reading Check ✏

What does Anne want to do when she grows up? Underline the answer.

MRS. VAN DAAN. You're smoking up all our money. You know that, don't you?

MR. VAN DAAN. Will you shut up? (. . . MR. VAN DAAN *turns to see* ANNE *staring up at him.)* And what are you staring at?

ANNE. I never heard grownups quarrel before. I thought only children quarreled.

MR. VAN DAAN. This isn't a quarrel! It's a discussion. And I never heard children so rude before.

ANNE *(Rising, indignantly)* I, rude!

MR. VAN DAAN. Yes!

MRS. FRANK. *(Quickly)* Anne, will you get me my knitting. . . .

◆　◆　◆

Anne continues to argue with Mr. Van Daan. He accuses her of doing nothing but talking all the time. He asks her why she is not nice and quiet like her sister, Margot. He says that men prefer quiet girls who love to cook and sew and follow their husband's orders. But Anne tells him that kind of life is not for her.

◆　◆　◆

ANNE. I'd cut my throat first! I'd open my veins! I'm going to be remarkable! I'm going to Paris . . .

MR. VAN DAAN. *(Scoffingly)* Paris!

ANNE. . . . to study music and art.

MR. VAN DAAN. Yeah! Yeah!

◆　◆　◆

Anne then makes a sweeping gesture. She knocks her glass of milk on Mrs. Van

Vocabulary Development

indignantly (in DIG nuhnt lee) *adv.* in a manner that expresses anger over something unjust or unfair

scoffingly (SCOFF ing lee) *adv.* in a mocking manner

Daan's precious fur coat. Even though Anne apologizes, Mrs. Van Daan remains very angry. Mrs. Frank tells Anne that she needs to be more calm and respectful toward the adults. She says that Anne shouldn't answer back so much. But Anne says that she will not let people walk all over her.

◆ ◆ ◆

MRS. FRANK. I'm not afraid that anyone is going to walk all over you, Anne. I'm afraid for other people, that you'll walk on them. I don't know what happens to you, Anne. You are wild, self-willed. If I had ever talked to my mother as you talk to me . . .

ANNE. Things have changed. People aren't like that anymore. "Yes, Mother." "No, Mother." "Anything you say, Mother." I've got to fight things out for myself! Make something of myself!

MRS. FRANK. It isn't necessary to fight to do it. Margot doesn't fight, and isn't she . . . ?

ANNE. *(Violently rebellious)* Margot! Margot! Margot! That's all I hear from everyone . . . how wonderful Margot is . . . "Why aren't you like Margot?"

◆ ◆ ◆

Mr. Kraler, along with Miep, is helping to hide the families. He arrives with supplies. Mr. Kraler announces that he has brought a man named Dussel, a Jewish dentist who also needs a hiding place. Mr. Frank tells Mr. Kraler to bring him up. Mr. Frank then tells Mr. Van Daan about the new arrival.

◆ ◆ ◆

MR. FRANK. Forgive me. I spoke without consulting you. But I knew you'd feel as I do.

MR. VAN DAAN. There's no reason for you to consult anyone. This is your place. You have a right to do exactly as you please. The only thing I feel . . . there's so little food as it is . . . and to take in another person . . .

Literary Analysis 🔍

What does the **dialogue** tell you about how Anne thinks of herself?

_____

_____

_____

Read Fluently 📖

Exclamation marks are used to show a lot of feeling. Circle the exclamation marks on this page. What do they tell you about the conversation between Anne and Mrs. Frank?

_____

_____

Reading Skill 📖

Use background information to link historical causes with effects and answer the question: What kind of trouble is Mr. Dussel in?

_____

_____

_____

(PETER *turns away, ashamed of his father.*) . . .

◆ ◆ ◆

After they agree that Mr. Dussel will share a room with Anne, Mrs. Van Daan finds out about Dussel.

◆ ◆ ◆

MRS. VAN DAAN. What's happening? What's going on?

MR. VAN DAAN. Someone's moving in with us.

MRS. VAN DAAN. In here? You're joking.

MARGOT. It's only for a night or two . . . until Mr. Kraler finds another place.

MR. VAN DAAN. Yeah! Yeah!

◆ ◆ ◆

Dussel tells the families that things have gotten much worse for the Jews of Amsterdam. They are being rounded up everywhere. Even Anne's best friend, Jopie, has been taken to a concentration camp. Anne is very upset to hear this.

Dussel is a very stiff and proper man. He doesn't seem like a good roommate for a spirited girl like Anne. Sure enough, several weeks later, Anne writes about their disagreements in her diary.

◆ ◆ ◆

ANNE'S VOICE. . . . Mr. Dussel and I had another battle yesterday. Yes, Mr. Dussel! According to him, nothing, I repeat . . . nothing, is right about me . . . my appearance, my character, my manners. While he was going on at me I thought . . . sometime I'll give you such a smack that you'll fly right up to the ceiling! Why is it that every grownup thinks he knows the way to bring up children? . . .

Literary Analysis

What does Margot contribute to the bracketed **dialogue**?

_____

_____

What does Mr. Van Daan contribute to the bracketed **dialogue?**

_____

_____

Reading Skill

What **background information** does Mr. Dussel provide about what is happening to Jews in Amsterdam?

_____

_____

_____

_____

Reading Check

Who will be sharing a room with Mr. Dussel? Circle the answer.

Stop to Reflect

Underline the part of this passage that shows that Anne uses her diary as a way to release her feelings.

The Diary of Anne Frank, Act I

1. **Respond:** The families must obey strict rules to avoid being discovered by the Nazis. Which rules would be hardest for you to follow? Why?

   _____

   _____

2. **Reading Skill:** Think about the reason the Franks are in hiding. What is the historical **cause** that forces the Franks to go into hiding?

   _____

   _____

3. **Reading Skill:** Think about how the families' lives have changed while they have been living in the apartment. What **effects** have these changes **caused** in their daily lives?

   _____

   _____

4. **Literary Analysis: Dialogue** shows characters' personalities, moves the action of the story, and develops the conflict. Fill in the blanks below with examples of **dialogue** from the play that achieve each purpose.

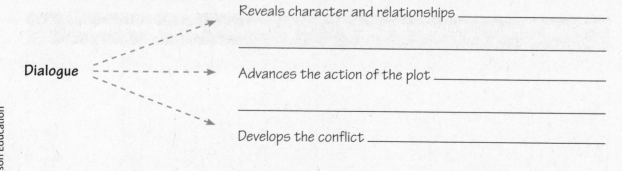

Dialogue

Reveals character and relationships _____

_____

Advances the action of the plot _____

_____

Develops the conflict _____

_____

Writing: Diary Entries

Write two **diary entries** from the perspective of two characters other than Anne. Answer the following questions to help you organize your thoughts.

- Select an event in Act 1 about which to write. Which two characters might have different viewpoints about the event?

  _____

- Describe the first character's perspective on the event.

  _____

  _____

- Describe the second character's perspective on the event.

  _____

  _____

- List two adjectives that describe the first character's feelings.

  _____

- List two adjectives that describe the second character's feelings.

  _____

  Use your notes to write your diary entries.

Research and Technology: Bulletin Board Display

Use the following chart to list ideas for your **bulletin board display.**

What I Should Include on the Board	Why It Belongs on the Board

The Diary of Anne Frank, Act II

Reading Skill

Cause-and-effect relationships explain the connections between events. These connections are not always simple. Look at the chart below. It shows one possible pattern of cause-and-effect relationships.

Ask questions to analyze cause-and-effect relationships:

- What could have caused the event?

- What effects could result from this cause?

- Are the events really related? The fact that one event follows another in a story does not necessarily show that the two events are connected as cause and effect.

Use the graphic organizer below to show a pattern of cause and effect in the story.

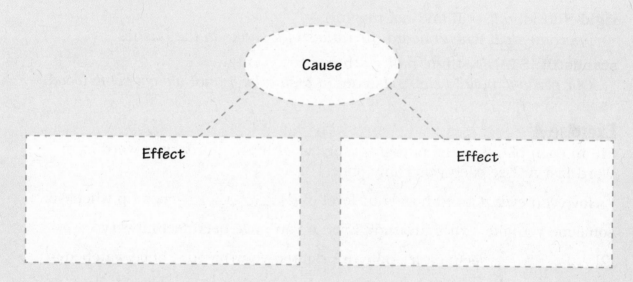

Literary Analysis

A **character's motivation** is the reason that he or she does something. The motivation may be internal, external, or both.

- *Internal motivations:* feelings such as loneliness and jealousy

- *External motivations:* events and situations such as a fire

As you read, think about each character's possible motivations.

Word List A

Study these words from Act II of The Diary of Anne Frank. Then, complete the activity.

animation [an i MAY shuhn] *n.* energy and excitement
　　Kate's personality, so full of animation, made people enjoy being around her.

awkwardly [AWK werd lee] *adv.* in a clumsy or uncomfortable way, often due to embarrassment
　　The young couple awkwardly danced to a slow song.

cellar [SEL er] *n.* a room under a house
　　People often use a cellar as a place to store things.

contracts [KAHN trakts] *n.* written agreements, especially legal ones
　　John reviewed the contracts to be sure they were ready to sign.

downcast [DOWN kast] *adj.* very sad or upset
　　As our vacation drew to a close, I became downcast.

remarks [ri MAHRKS] *n.* things that are said; comments
　　The speakers' remarks after the speech were more interesting than the talk itself.

rigid [RIJ id] *adj.* stiff and not moving
　　I became rigid when I heard the rattles of a snake in the bushes.

standstill [STAND stil] *n.* halt; with no movement
　　Our plans to build a clubhouse are at a standstill until we get some wood.

Exercise A

Fill in each blank in the paragraph below with an appropriate word from Word List A. Use each word only once.

Have you ever noticed how your level of [1] ＿＿＿＿＿＿ goes up whenever someone you like comes around? Even if you have been feeling very

[2] ＿＿＿＿＿＿, seeing a friend can brighten your mood. I once watched a group of boys standing around [3] ＿＿＿＿＿＿ at a dance. They looked so uncomfortable. Their conversation had reached a [4] ＿＿＿＿＿＿. Then, a new friend arrived, and the boys' [5] ＿＿＿＿＿＿ posture relaxed. They started making funny [6] ＿＿＿＿＿＿ again. Then, they made

[7] ＿＿＿＿＿＿ with one another to ask certain girls to dance, writing the promises on paper napkins. I was amazed to watch the mood of the scene lift. It was like going from a dark [8] ＿＿＿＿＿＿ up into the bright daylight.

Read the following passage. Pay special attention to the underlined words. Then, read it again, and complete the activities. Use a separate sheet of paper for your written answers.

In the early 1930s, before Hitler became chancellor of Germany, German teenagers enjoyed many fun group activities. They went to shows and dances, attended music and sports events, and met at restaurants for meals. Their youthful <u>animation</u> showed on their faces. Their joy in life could be heard in their <u>remarks</u> to one another.

All of this fun came to a <u>standstill</u> as Hitler pushed for harsh limits on Jewish <u>participation</u> in public life. Teens were split into two clear groups—Jews and non-Jews. The Jewish teens steadily lost the ability to go to public places.

By the time World War II began, very real fears kept Jews in their homes. They could be rounded up by Nazi officers at any time. Stories exist of movie houses being raided by troops. Jewish teens were arrested in the raids and sent to labor camps.

Non-Jewish teens, on the other hand, were expected to appear in public. As members of the Hitler Youth, they traveled in groups, singing and marching in parades. Although some teens <u>awkwardly</u> joined in the club's activities at first, they were told over and over to feel proud. They were forced to show hatred toward Jews, even those who had once been their friends.

When sent into hiding by fear or to escape bomb raids, a Jewish teen often could be found in the family's <u>cellar</u>. Some played games such as Ping-Pong to pass the time. Many read, wrote, created artworks, or did crafts. Lots of Jewish families became much more serious about their heritage. They were afraid the Nazis would snuff out Jewish faith and customs. Family members made <u>contracts</u> with each other. They promised to keep their stories and traditions alive.

Jewish teens became <u>downcast</u> as they watched their youth slip away. No longer relaxed and happy, they became <u>rigid</u> with tenseness. Even for those who survived the Nazi years, an important part of life had died, never to be experienced.

1. Underline the words telling where the teens' <u>animation</u> showed. Describe how a person showing *animation* might look.

2. Circle the word describing the mood of the teens' <u>remarks</u>. What types of *remarks* do you and your friends exchange?

3. Underline the words telling what brought the fun to a <u>standstill</u>. Describe a time your fun came to a *standstill*.

4. Circle the words that tell what some teens did <u>awkwardly</u>. Explain why they felt this way, using *awkwardly* in your sentence.

5. Circle the words telling why a Jewish teen might go to the <u>cellar</u>. Why would a *cellar* be a good place during these times?

6. Underline the sentence defining the purpose of the <u>contracts</u>. Explain what *contracts* are.

7. Circle the words explaining why Jewish teens became <u>downcast</u>. What makes teens today feel *downcast*?

8. Underline the word that hints at the meaning of <u>rigid</u>. Write a sentence using *rigid*.

The Diary of Anne Frank, Act II

Frances Goodrich and Albert Hackett

Summary The Franks, the Van Daans, and Mr. Dussel have been hiding for a year and a half. The eight of them have managed to live together, but they do not always get along. Food is scarce, and they are constantly afraid. Anne and Peter have become close friends. Soon, they learn that the Allies have invaded Europe, and they become excited.

 Writing About the Big Question

Is it our differences or our similarities that matter most? As the war drags on, conditions worsen in the "Secret Annex" and differences among the residents lead to conflict. Complete this sentence:

Superficial differences between people can become magnified when

_____.

Note-taking Guide

Use this chart to list four important events in Act II.

Act II: Important Event 1	Carl asks about the Franks and then asks for more money.
Act II: Important Event 2	
Act II: Important Event 3	
Act II: Important Event 4	

The Diary of Anne Frank, Act II

1. **Connect:** Mr. Kraler says that the worker might be blackmailing him. What hint does this information give about the ending of the play?

   _____

   _____

2. **Interpret:** How have the characters changed since the end of Act I?

   _____

   _____

3. **Reading Skill:** A **cause** is an event or action that produces a result. An **effect** is the result produced. Mrs. Frank wanted the Van Daans to leave, but she changed her mind. Name a cause and an effect that are related to this situation.

   _____

   _____

4. **Literary Analysis: Motivation** is the reason a character does something. Look at the chart. List a possible motivation for each action.

Character	Action	Motivation
Miep	brings flowers and cake to the attic rooms	
Peter Van Daan	brings Anne her cake	

Writing: Letter

Answer the questions below to plan a **letter** asking a local theater manager to present *The Diary of Anne Frank*.

- Why would your community benefit from seeing the play? List at least three reasons.

_____

_____

_____

- What parts of the play support your reasons?

_____

_____

_____

Research and Technology: Bulletin Board Display

Prepare a **bulletin board display** about the experiences of Jewish individuals during World War II. Fill in the following chart to organize your thoughts.

Purpose of Display	Audience	Five Questions I Want to Research
		1.
		2.
		3.
		4.
		5.

Online Information

About Web Sites

A Web site is a certain place on the Internet. Sponsors create and update Web sites. Sponsors can be groups, companies, or individuals. Think about whether the information on a Web site is likely to be true. Look at the Web site's sponsor to assess credibility. Most Web sites have these parts:

- The **Web address:** where you can find the site on the Internet.
- A **Web page:** one screen within the Web site.
- **Navigation bars** and **links:** tools to help you go to other Web pages.

Reading Skill

A Web site must be designed for unity and coherence so that it is useful and easy to read. It has unity when all of its parts flow smoothly together and provide a complete source of information. A Web site has coherence when its individual parts and features relate to and support one another. Look at the chart below. It tells you how to **analyze the unity and coherence** of a Web site.

Checklist for Evaluating a Text

❑ Do details all relate to the main idea?

❑ Do sentences, paragraphs, and graphic elements flow in a logical sequence?

❑ Is information clear, consistent, and logical?

❑ Does the author provide reliable facts, statistics, or quotations to support main points?

Florida Holocaust Museum

EDUCATION   EVENTS   EXHIBITIONS   GET INVOLVED   PRESS ROOM   VISITOR INFORMATION

VISITOR INFORMATION

About the Museum

Mission

The Florida Holocaust Museum honors the memory of millions of innocent men, women, and children who suffered or died in the Holocaust. The Museum is dedicated to teaching members of all races and cultures to recognize the inherent worth and dignity of human life in order to prevent future genocides.

Founders Walter and Edie Loebenberg

History

One of the largest Holocaust museums in the country, the Florida Holocaust Museum is the result of St. Petersburg businessman and philanthropist, Walter P. Loebenberg's remarkable journey and vision. He escaped Nazi Germany in 1939 and served in the United States Army during WWII. Together, with a group of local businessmen and community leaders, the concept of a living memorial to those who suffered and perished was conceived. Among the participating individuals were Survivors of the Holocaust and individuals who lost relatives, as well as those who had no personal investment, other than wanting to ensure that such atrocities could never again happen to any group of people.

To this end, the group enlisted the support of others in the community and were able to involve internationally renowned Holocaust scholars. Thomas Keneally, author of *Schindler's List*, joined the Board of Advisors and Elie Weisel was named Honorary Chairman of this Holocaust Center.

This painting directly relates to the topic of the text, helping maintain the unity of the article.

In 1992, the Museum rented a space it could afford but would soon outgrow, on the grounds of the Jewish Community Center of Pinellas County in Madeira Beach, Florida, tucked away from the mainstream of Tampa Bay life. Starting with only one staff member and a small group of dedicated volunteers, it quickly surpassed all expectations.

A painting from the exhibition *The Holocaust Through Czech Children's Eyes*

Within the first month, over 24,000 visitors came to see *Anne Frank in the World*, the Center's inaugural exhibit. The Tampa Bay showing of this exhibition—which traces a young Jewish girl's journey from a complacent childhood in pre-World War II Holland, through her early teens hiding from the Nazis, to her death at Bergen-Belsen—poignantly touched all visitors.

During the next five years, the new Holocaust Center greeted more than 125,000 visitors to view internationally acclaimed exhibits. Thousands more participated in lectures, seminars and commemorative events at the Center, which now reached directly into schools in an eight county area surrounding Tampa Bay with study guides, teacher training programs, and presentations by Center staff and Holocaust Survivors.

The use of transitions helps make the text more coherent, or understandable.

The Center expanded to encompass a growing print and audio-visual library, a photographic archive, a repository for historic artifacts, and a research facility for educators and scholars—all of this crowded into a 4,000 square foot facility that was not designed for museum or educational purposes.

THE BIG ?

Is it our differences or similarities that matter most?
Does an organization such as the Florida Holocaust Museum place more emphasis on recognizing our differences, or on recognizing our similarities? Explain your answer.

Thinking About Online Information

1. How is using a Web site different from looking up information in a magazine or book?

_____

_____

2. What part of the museum Web site would be most useful to people who want to visit the museum?

_____

TALK ABOUT IT **Reading Skill**

3. Which page of the Florida Holocaust Museum Web site unifies all of the parts of the site?

_____

4. Scan the Florida Holocaust Museum site. What tabs and links do you find on the navigation bar? Explain how each of these works with the others to produce a coherent web browsing experience.

_____

WRITE ABOUT IT **Timed Writing: Evaluation (15 minutes)**

Think about the museum Web site from this lesson. Then, answer the following questions.

• Does the home page unify the site?

_____

• Is the information included on the Web site coherent?

_____

• Does the site meet its goal?

_____

_____

Water Names

The **oral tradition** is stories that were once told out loud. These stories were passed down from older people to younger people. Stories in the oral tradition have these elements:

- **Theme:** a central message about life. Some themes are **universal**. Universal themes appear in many cultures and many time periods.

- **Heroes** and **heroines:** men and women who do great and often impossible things.

Storytellers tell their stories aloud. They need to hold their listeners' attention. Look at the chart for some ways that storytellers make stories more interesting and entertaining for their audiences.

Technique	Definition	Example
Hyperbole	exaggeration or overstatement, often to make people laugh	That basketball player was as tall as the Empire State Building.
Personification	human qualities or characteristics given to animals or things	The clouds shed tears.
Idioms	expressions in a language or culture that do not mean exactly what they say	"a chip off the old block" "as easy as pie"

American folk literature is a living tradition. This means that it is always changing. Many of the subjects and heroes from American folk literature can be found in the movies, sports heroes, or even politics of today.

There are different types of stories in the oral tradition.

- **Myths:** stories about the actions of gods, goddesses, and heroes. Some myths tell how things came to be. Every culture has its own **mythology**. A mythology is a collection of myths.

- **Fables:** short stories that usually have a moral. A moral is a lesson. The characters in fables are often animals that act like humans.

- **Tall tales:** stories that use exaggeration to make them funny. This kind of exaggeration is called **hyperbole**. Heroes of tall tales often do impossible things. Tale tales are one kind of **legend**. A legend is a story that is based on fact but that becomes less true with each telling.

- **Epics:** long poems about great heroes. These heroes go on dangerous journeys called **quests**. The quests are an important part of the history of a culture or nation.

Word List A

Study these words from "Water Names." Then, complete the activities.

abruptness [uh BRUPT nuhs] *n.* a way of ending things suddenly
When Dad shouted, I ended my telephone call with abruptness.

bulk [BUHLK] *n.* the large size of something
The bulk of a ship that carries people across the ocean is amazing.

forbidden [fuhr BID in] *adj.* not allowed
Forbidden to drive the car, I took the train into the city.

glittered [GLIT uhrd] *v.* shone with a sparkling light
Her eyes glittered from the tears she held back.

gorges [GAWRJ ez] *n.* deep, narrow valleys cut through rock
Gorges are cut through rocks by water moving through them over thousands of years.

reflection [ri FLEK shuhn] *n.* image you see when you look in a mirror or shiny surface
The small boy was surprised to see his reflection in the shiny bumper of the new car.

remote [ri MOHT] *adj.* far away
The wealthy, unhappy man chose to live alone on a remote island.

rippling [RIP uh ling] *adj.* having small waves on the surface
The rippling water relaxed me as I sat by the stream.

Exercise A

Fill in each blank in the paragraph below with an appropriate word from Word List A. Use each word only once.

As we turned the corner, the [1] _____ of the mountain rose up suddenly before us. Below it, a lake [2] _____ brightly in the sunlight. The water was as smooth as a mirror. As I looked, I could see the mountain's [3] _____ in it. I had heard that small fingers of the lake pushed into deep [4] _____ along the sides of the mountain. Because many of these areas were private, visitors were [5] _____ there. We rolled down the car windows to feel the fresh breeze and listen to the [6] _____ water. Since we were miles from any town, we noticed the quiet of this [7] _____ area right away. With [8] _____, we forgot the stress of our busy city life and relaxed at last.

1. Underline the words that give a clue about the meaning of <u>remote</u>. Then, write your own definition of *remote*.

2. Circle the words describing how the river has *glittered*. Then, explain what *glittered* means.

3. Underline the words naming the source of the *abruptness* that is described. Then, tell about another natural disaster that comes with *abruptness*.

4. Circle two words naming one feature of <u>gorges</u>. Then, explain what *gorges* are.

5. Underline all the words in the paragraph describing the <u>bulk</u> of the Three Gorges Dam. Then, describe the *bulk* of something huge you have seen.

6. Circle the words naming what the Chinese people are <u>forbidden</u> to do. Then, explain what *forbidden* means.

7. Circle the word that gives a clue to the meaning of <u>reflection</u>. Describe two different types of *reflections* that you might see in the Yangtze River.

Read the following passage. Pay special attention to the underlined words. Then, read it again, and complete the activities. Use a separate sheet of paper for your written answers.

The Yangtze River in China is the third longest river in the world. It flows more than 3,700 miles, through cities, towns, and <u>remote</u> areas that few people ever see. The scenery along the river is some of the most beautiful on Earth. The river has <u>glittered</u> like a jewel in the hearts and minds of Chinese people for centuries. Today, more than 350 million people live along its shores.

Although the Yangtze gives people important gifts, it also can kill them. With the <u>abruptness</u> that comes from sudden flooding, whole villages can be wiped out. At these times, the <u>rippling</u> waters become a raging enemy. Animals, people, and all other living things are at risk. As waters rise, the high walls of deep <u>gorges</u> can suddenly seem low. Terror strikes all along the banks of the swollen river.

To control the floods, the Chinese government has built dams along the Yangtze. The biggest of these projects is the Three Gorges Dam. Begun in 1994, the dam should be finished in 2009. The planned <u>bulk</u> of it is amazing. It will be one and a half miles wide and 610 feet tall. The lake it creates will hold five trillion gallons of water. Electricity produced by the dam will meet one-ninth of China's needs.

Not everyone is happy about the project. However, Chinese people, <u>forbidden</u> to speak out against the government, keep their opinions to themselves. Nearly two million people, however, will have to find new homes as the dam waters rise. Some types of wildlife could be wiped out forever.

Most agree that the Three Gorges Dam will have both advantages and disadvantages. No matter what happens, the mighty Yangtze will continue to be important to China. Whether looking at a <u>reflection</u> in a peaceful spot, fishing, or taking water from the river for farming, Chinese people will continue to be thankful for this grand gift of nature.

Water Names
Lan Samantha Chang

Summary Three girls sit on a back porch on the prairie. Their grandmother Waipuo reminds them of how important China's longest river was in the lives of their ancestors. She tells them a story in Chinese about a girl who falls in love with a water ghost.

Note-taking Guide

Use this chart to record details about the story within the story.

In the present

Who:

three girls and their grandmother

Where:

What happens:

1,200 years ago

Who:

Wen Zhiqing and his daughter

Where:

What happens:

Activate Prior Knowledge

Think of a family that moved to America from another country. How would the grandparents of that family be different from the grandchildren?

_____

_____

_____

_____

Themes in American Stories

A **legend** is a story that is based on a true story from long ago but that becomes less true each time it is told. How many years ago does the grandmother's story take place? Underline the answer in the text. Is it possible that the grandmother is retelling a legend? Explain.

_____

_____

_____

Stop to Reflect

How is the river important in the lives of the girls' ancestors? Explain.

_____

_____

_____

Water Names

Lan Samantha Chang

During summer evenings, the sisters would sit on the back porch. They would fight and argue with one another. Their grandmother scolded the girls for fighting. The sisters would stop their arguing immediately. Some nights their grandmother sat quietly in her chair. Other times, she would tell stories about China.

◆ ◆ ◆

"In these prairie crickets I often hear the sound of rippling waters, of the Yangtze River," she said. "Granddaughters, you are descended on both sides from people of the water country, near the mouth of the great Chang Jiang, as it is called, where the river is so grand and broad that even on clear days you can scarcely see the other side."

◆ ◆ ◆

The grandmother tells the girls that they are related to great men and women. The family has lived through floods and bad times. It runs together like rain. It has the spirit of the river. But even people of the river must be careful of water.

When the grandmother was young, her own grandmother told her a story. Twelve hundred years ago, Wen Zhiqing lived near the Yangtze River. He trained birds to catch fish for him. The birds would sit on the side of the boat. Then they would dive into the water.

Wen Zhiqing had a beautiful daughter. She loved the river. She also loved to go out in the boat to fish. She did not worry about the dangers of the river.

◆ ◆ ◆

"One clear spring evening, as she watched the last bird dive off into the blackening waters, she said, 'If only this catch would bring back something more than another fish!'

"She leaned over the side of the boat and looked at the water. The stars and moon reflected back at her. And it is said that the spirits living underneath the water looked up at her as well. And the spirit of a young man who had drowned in the river many years before saw her lovely face."

◆　◆　◆

The bird was gone for a long time. It came back with a very large fish. Inside the fish Wen found a pearl ring.

Wen's daughter was happy that her wish came true. In the evenings she stared at the water. Sometimes she thought she saw a young man looking back. She longed for the young man. She became sad and afraid. She knew that she would leave her family soon.

Her father told her that she was seeing only the moon's reflection in the water. The daughter told him that there was a kingdom in the river. The prince wanted to marry her. The ring was a gift to her father. Wen did not believe his daughter. He told her to stay away from the water.

For a year, nothing happened. Then a terrible flood came in the spring. The flood destroyed almost everything.

◆　◆　◆

"In the middle of the torrential rain, the family noticed that the daughter was missing. She had taken advantage of the confusion to hurry to the

© Pearson Education

Read Fluently

A preposition describes *where* or *how* a noun does something. Some prepositions are *at, over, in, under, off,* and *on*. Circle the prepositions in the bracketed passage.

Themes in American Stories

Many stories from the oral tradition have **heroes or heroines** who are larger-than-life or perform impossible tasks. Is Wen's daughter a heroine? Explain.

_____

_____

_____

_____

_____

Reading Check ✏

Wen caught a fish. What did Wen find in the fish's stomach? Underline the answer.

Vocabulary Development

torrential (tuh REN shuhl) *adj.* describing large amounts of water moving very quickly in a particular direction

Themes in American Stories

Theme is a central message about life. One theme in this story is about the desire for a treasure, or something better. How is this theme shown by Wen's daughter?

_____

_____

_____

_____

Stop to Reflect

How do the girls feel when the story is over? Underline the words that tell what they think and do. Summarize what they feel on the lines below.

_____

_____

Reading Check ✏️

What did the people think happened to Wen's daughter? Circle the answer in the text.

river to visit her beloved. The family searched for days but they never found her."

♦ ♦ ♦

The grandmother stopped talking. One of the sisters asked what happened to the girl.

♦ ♦ ♦

"Who knows?" Waipuo said. "They say she was seduced by a water ghost. Or perhaps she lost her mind to desiring."

♦ ♦ ♦

The grandmother answered no more questions. She rose from her chair. Soon the light went on in her bedroom.

The sisters stayed on the porch. They did not talk. They were thinking about Wen Zhiqing's daughter. They wondered what she looked like. They wondered how old she was. They wondered why no one remembered her name.

♦ ♦ ♦

While we weren't watching, the stars had emerged. Their brilliant pinpoints mapped the heavens. They glittered over us, over Waipuo in her room, the house, and the small city we lived in, the great waves of grass that ran for miles around us, the ground beneath as dry and hard as bone.

Vocabulary Development

seduced (si DOOST) _v._ persuaded someone to do something by making it seem very attractive or interesting

emerged (i MERJD) _v._ appeared after being hidden

Themes in American Stories

1. **Infer:** The girls learn how important the great river was in their family's past. How do they and their grandmother feel about the river?

_____

_____

_____

2. **Interpret:** Two unusual events from the story are listed in the first column of the chart. List different ways to explain these events in the second column. Then, use the third column to explain why you agree or disagree with each explanation.

Event	Explanation	Why You Agree or Disagree
Face in the water	The reflection of the moon	
Ring in the fish		

3. **Themes in American Stories:** A **theme** is a central idea or message that is revealed in a story. What do you think is the theme of this story?

_____

_____

_____

4. **Themes in American Stories:** Think about the way the story is told. Identify one example of a storytelling technique or detail that is part of the **oral tradition**.

_____

_____

_____

Storytelling Hour

Plan a **storytelling hour** during which you will retell a variety of Chinese folk tales. Follow these steps to gather information for your storytelling hour.

- Go to the library and search the online catalog for collections of Chinese folklore. Record the titles and short summaries of stories that you think will interest the class.

What I found: _____

_____

_____

- Search the Internet. Search for "Chinese folklore" or "Chinese folk tales." Record short summaries of the stories that you find.

What I found: _____

_____

_____

- Watch the video interview with Lan Samantha Chang. Review your source material. Use this information to record additional information for your storytelling hour.

Additional information: _____

_____

_____

_____

_____

_____

_____

_____

Use your notes to prepare your storytelling hour.

Coyote Steals the Sun and Moon • Why the Waves Have Whitecaps

Reading Skill

A **summary** presents the main ideas of a text. It is much shorter than the original work. To write a summary, you must focus on the most important information. This helps you remember the main point of the story. Use these steps to summarize:

- **Reread to identify main events or ideas** in the story.

- Put the main ideas in order.

- Use your notes to write a summary that has the main ideas.

- Use as few words as possible.

Remember that summaries do not have details. Reading a summary cannot replace the experience of reading the whole work.

Literary Analysis

A **myth** is an ancient story. It tells the beliefs or customs of a culture. A culture is a group of people. Every culture has its own **mythology**. A mythology is a group of myths. Myths explain events in nature or in a people's history. They often describe the actions of gods. Some have animals that act like people. Myths often have natural forces, such as wind and rain, that act like people.

It is helpful to know about a culture to understand its myths. Use this chart to find cultural connections that help explain the myths in this section.

Detail from Mythology	Cultural Connections
Prometheus steals fire from Zeus, king of the gods, and gives it to humans.	To ancient Greeks, fire was essential for cooking, forging weapons, and providing warmth.

Word List A

Study these words from "Coyote Steals the Sun and Moon." Then, complete the activity.

chattering [CHAT uhr ing] *v.* knocking together
  My teeth started chattering as the cold wind blew harder and harder.

coyote [kye OH tee] *n.* a small, wild dog that lives in the West.
  The man was alarmed when he heard the coyote howling.

curiosity [kyoor ee AHS uh tee] *n.* the desire to know something
  Steve's curiosity about how hockey began led him to the library.

eagle [EE guhl] *n.* a large bird that feeds on small animals
  An eagle has a hooked beak and long, powerful wings.

lend [LEND] *v.* to give something for just a short time
  Carly hoped her brother would lend her his CD player.

nudged [NUJD] *v.* pushed or poked gently
  My partner nudged me in the ribs with his elbow to get my attention.

panting [PANT ing] *v.* breathing quickly and loudly
  After rushing up the stairs, I was panting and starting to sweat.

produce [pruh DOOS] *v.* to make something happen
  Does Ms. Conklin actually think her jokes will produce laughter?

Exercise A

Fill in each blank in the paragraph below with an appropriate word from Word List A. Use each word only once.

The woman's teeth were [1] _____, not from cold but from fear. She was lost in the desert. Every time a [2] _____ howled, she became more scared. She was sorry for her [3] _____, which had led her to explore something away from the group. She was [4] _____ from the heat, wishing she had taken the hat a friend offered to [5] _____ her for the trip. Anything that would [6] _____ shade would be welcome. Then, a shadow fell on her. Looking up, she saw a huge [7] _____. Its wings gave her shade. Suddenly she felt as if someone had [8] _____ her and made her turn east. Within minutes, she spotted her group. The eagle left her as she reached them.

Read the following passage. Pay special attention to the underlined words. Then, read it again, and complete the activities. Use a separate sheet of paper for your written answers.

When I was small, my mother used to make up stories to tell me. Because I had such a huge curiosity about all things, she found that books often would not hold my attention. At the least, I would interrupt nearly every sentence to ask questions. Sometimes, I even nudged her to get her attention.

So, each night Mom would request that I give her a list of three characters. Then, she would produce a story that featured them. Always, the stories were great, and by the time a story ended, I was usually panting with excitement and asking for more. However, Mom's limit was one story per night.

My requested characters were always animals. A favorite was the magnificent eagle. I think Mom liked the eagle as a character, too. She usually talked about its keen eyes, but really meant that the graceful bird had great wisdom. I also often chose the sly coyote. I think Mom usually made this tricky animal the bad guy, but in a humorous way.

I only wish someone had written down Mom's stories because I would love to have been able to lend them to my own children to read today. I've never been a very good oral storyteller. It feels too much like public speaking, a scary situation that usually leaves my teeth chattering. So, I could never tell the stories to others.

Still, I think Mom's art with words probably led me toward my career. As a writer of stories based on myths, I can craft them with carefully selected words. I work alone, with just my imagination and research beside me. The reader I keep in mind is myself as a curious, questioning young boy.

I'm sorry that my readers cannot listen to my mom, inventing clever plots that twist and turn all along the way. How in the world was she so wonderfully creative on the spot?

1. Underline the sentence that describes the boy's curiosity. Then, describe something that brings out your *curiosity*.

2. Underline the words that help to understand nudged. Write a sentence using *nudged*.

3. Circle the word naming what Mom would produce. Then, explain what *produce* means.

4. Underline the words telling when the boy was panting. Explain why *panting* may happen when someone is excited.

5. Circle one word that describes the eagle and one that describes the coyote. Then, write a sentence using a different descriptive word for each animal.

6. Underline the words naming what the writer would like to lend. Then, explain what *lend* means.

7. Circle the two words that name what leaves the writer's teeth chattering. Then, list three times when your teeth have been *chattering*.

Coyote Steals the Sun and Moon
Zuñi Myth, Retold by Richard Erdoes and Alfonso Ortiz

Summary This myth tells about how the sun and the moon got into the sky. Coyote and Eagle team up to steal the sun and moon to light up their dark world. Coyote's curious nature causes them to lose both. The sun and moon escape into the sky.

 Writing About the Big Question

Are yesterday's heroes important today? "Coyote Steals the Sun and Moon" explains a specific event in nature and features Coyote, a popular character in mythology. Complete this sentence:

Myths and their heroes have **endured** through the ages because they

_____:

Note-taking Guide
Use this chart to write the explanations this myth gives for questions about nature.

Questions About Nature	Explanations
• How did the sun and the moon get into the sky? • Why do we have the seasons of fall and winter?	

Coyote Steals the Sun and Moon

Zuñi Myth, Retold by Richard Erdoes and Alfonso Ortiz

The main characters of this story are two animals: Coyote, an eager but bad hunter, and Eagle, a very good hunter. Eagle catches many rabbits, but Coyote only catches little bugs because he has trouble seeing in the dark. So Coyote decides to team up with Eagle to get more food. Eagle agrees.

So the two hunters begin to look for the light. They set out to find the sun and the moon.

◆ ◆ ◆

At last they came to a pueblo,[1] where the Kachinas[2] happened to be dancing. The people invited Eagle and Coyote to sit down and have something to eat while they watch the sacred dances. Seeing the power of the Kachinas, Eagle said, "I believe these are the people who have light."

◆ ◆ ◆

Coyote sees two boxes, one large and one small. The Kachinas open these boxes whenever they want light. The big box gives off more light than the small box.

◆ ◆ ◆

Coyote nudged Eagle. "Friend, did you see that? They have all the light we need in the big box. Let's steal it."

Activate Prior Knowledge

Describe an animal in a folk tale or fairy tale you read when you were younger. What human qualities did the animal have?

_____

_____

_____

Literary Analysis

Myths often explain something in nature. What do you think this tale will explain? Underline a sentence in the bracketed passage that helps you figure out the answer. Then, write the answer below.

_____

_____

Stop to Reflect

Why do you think Coyote wants to steal the sun and the moon?

_____

What do you think he will do with them?

_____

_____

Vocabulary Development

sacred (SAY krid) *adj.* holy; worthy of worship

---

1. **pueblo** (PWEB loh) *n.* Native American village in the southwestern United States.

2. **Kachinas** (kuh CHEE nuhz) *n.* masked dancers who imitate gods or the spirits of their ancestors.

© Pearson Education

Read Fluently

A dialogue is a conversation between characters. Quotation marks often point out a dialogue. Circle any sentences spoken by Eagle in the first bracketed passage. Underline any sentences spoken by Coyote.

Reading Skill

A **summary** is a short statement that presents the key ideas and main points of a text. Read the second bracketed paragraph. Write the numbers *1*, *2* and *3* next to the three sentences that tell the main points of this paragraph. Then, summarize the paragraph.

_____

_____

_____

Reading Check

What were the Kachinas doing when Coyote and Eagle stole their light? Bracket the sentence that tells you.

"You always want to steal and rob. I say we should just borrow it."

"They won't lend it to us."

"You may be right," said Eagle. "Let's wait till they finish dancing and then steal it."

◆ ◆ ◆

After the Kachinas go to sleep, Eagle scoops up the large box and flies off. Coyote runs along as fast as he can, but he can't keep up. Coyote begs Eagle to let him carry the box a little way. But Eagle refuses.

◆ ◆ ◆

"No, no," said Eagle, "you never do anything right."

He flew on, and Coyote ran after him. After a while Coyote shouted again: "Friend, you're my chief, and it's not right for you to carry the box; people will call me lazy. Let me have it."

"No, no, you always mess everything up." And Eagle flew on and Coyote ran along.

◆ ◆ ◆

Coyote keeps begging to carry the box. Finally, Eagle agrees to let him carry the box for a while. But first he makes Coyote promise not to open it. Coyote gives his promise not to open the box. But as Eagle flies ahead, Coyote gets more and more curious. He hides behind a hill and sneaks a look inside the box. Coyote finds that Eagle has put both the sun and the moon in a single box.

When Coyote opens the box, the moon flies high into the sky. All the plants shrivel up and turn brown. The leaves fall off the trees. Winter comes. Then the sun flies out into the sky. All the fruits of the earth shrivel up and turn cold.

◆ ◆ ◆

Eagle turned and flew back to see what had delayed Coyote. "You fool! Look what you've done!" he said. "You let the sun and moon escape, and now it's cold." Indeed, it began to snow, and Coyote shivered. "Now your teeth are chattering," Eagle said, "and it's your fault that cold has come into the world."

It's true. If it weren't for Coyote's curiosity and mischief making, we wouldn't have winter; we could enjoy summer all the time.

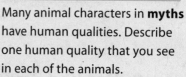

TAKE NOTES

Reading Skill

When you **summarize** a story, you explain its main points in your own words. Summarize how the world changes in this myth after Coyote opens the box.

_____

_____

_____

_____

Literary Analysis

Many animal characters in **myths** have human qualities. Describe one human quality that you see in each of the animals.

_____

_____

_____

Reading Check

Whose fault is it that we have winter every year? Circle the name in the story.

Coyote Steals the Sun and Moon

1. **Compare and Contrast:** Explain one way that Coyote and Eagle are the same. Explain one way that they are different.

   _____

   _____

   _____

2. **Infer:** What does the way Coyote acts in this story tell you about him?

   _____

   _____

3. **Reading Skill:** The graphic organizer below splits this story up into four parts. In the blank next to each part, list the most important events in that part. This will help you **summarize** the story. **The Hunt** has been summarized for you.

Detail	Cultural Connections
The Hunt	Eagle catches many rabbits. Coyote catches only bugs.
At the Kachinas' Dance	
Running Away	
Coyote's Mistake	

4. **Literary Analysis:** Most **myths** explain something in nature. What event in nature does this myth explain?

   _____

   _____

Writing: Myth

A **myth** is a story that often explains something in nature. Write your own myth that answers a question about the natural world.

- What is something in nature that interests you? _____

- What is a possible explanation for your choice? _____

  _____

- Write a brief description of the characters you will use. Tell whether they are humans or animals. List the qualities they have. _____

  _____

  _____

- What is a good title for this myth? _____

Listening and Speaking: Oral Presentation

Prepare an **oral presentation** about Zuñi culture. Use the Internet and library references to gather information.

Make a list of questions you will need to answer for your report. Use this list to help focus your research.

1. _____

   _____

2. _____

   _____

3. _____

   _____

4. _____

   _____

5. _____

   _____

Word List A

Study these words in dialect from "Why the Waves Have Whitecaps." Then, complete the activity.

Ah *pron.* **I**
> Ah don't want to have to tell you again!

ast *v.* asked
> Your mother has ast you three times to clean your room.

'bout *prep.* about
> Dan told me 'bout your plans to go hiking tomorrow.

de *art.* **the**
> After de bad day you had, you must have gone home and cried.

dem or 'em *pron.* them
> Did you see dem shopping last night?
> Can you take 'em out to eat with you?

git *v.* get
> Did you git lots of presents for your birthday?

mo' *adj.* more
> Jenny has mo' clothes than any other girl we know.

tole *v.* told
> Dad tole you to call home if you were going to be late.

Exercise A

Fill in each blank in the paragraph below with the correct word to replace the dialect word from Word List A.

Every winter my Aunt Sylvia calls to tell us [1] _____

the wonderful Florida weather. "We went walking barefoot on

[2] _____ beach yesterday," she might say. My brothers visited

her last year, but they did not take my sisters or me with [3] _____.

We [4] _____ to go [5] _____ than a hundred times. Mama

[6] _____ us we were too young. Anyway, [7] _____ am just

waiting for that phone call this year. In Atlanta, people say we will not

[8] _____ any cold weather for two more weeks. When Aunt Sylvia

calls, we are ready to talk about wearing shorts and T-shirts!

Read the following passage. Pay special attention to the underlined words. Then, read it again, and complete the activities. Use a separate sheet of paper for your written answers.

Dialect is spoken language that is special to a certain part of the country. For example, some people in the southern United States have unique ways of talking.

For a dialect to develop, two things must be true. First, people have to live together in a small area. Second, this group must be separate from other groups.

Sometimes the way of talking relates to how words are pronounced. For example, *th* at the beginning of words can be replaced by *d*. Instead of *the*, people might say <u>de</u>. A sentence with a bunch of *th-* words might sound like this:

> On de dird Dursday of de month, we always eat dinner together, so we can see <u>dem</u>.

Ending sounds also change—for example, *asked* is said <u>ast</u> in some parts of the South.

Other ways of talking in dialect involve dropping sounds from words. Instead of saying *more*, some people say <u>mo'</u>. Speakers also drop the first sounds of words, saying <u>'bout</u> instead of *about*, for example. To describe people who are needy, some might say:

> Those po' people need mo' money, and I'm talkin' 'bout givin' it to all of 'em right now!

Sometimes, vowel sounds are stretched out or changed in dialects. Someone with a drawl, in which sounds are stretched out and changed, says <u>Ah</u> instead of *I*, for example. On the other hand, the short *i* sound is very popular in some places. Instead of *get*, people say <u>git</u>. So, you might hear a woman call her pet like this:

> Binji, Ah have ast you dree times to git in de house. Come on now!

If all of this seems confusing, just remember that lots of older people cannot understand your Internet chat dialect. That's right, no one ever <u>tole</u> them that *lol* means "laugh out loud" and not "lots of love."

1. Look at the dialect sentence with *dem* in it. Underline the other words using *d* for *th*. Then, list them with the standard English words beside them.

2. Find and circle <u>ast</u>. What does it mean in standard English? Now, change the word *risked* to dialect. Write a sentence using it.

3. Underline the words with dropped sounds in the sentence with <u>mo'</u> and <u>'bout</u>. Then, list the words with the standard English words beside them.

4. Find and circle <u>Ah</u>. Notice how *I* changes to *Ah* in dialect. Write a sentence in dialect using as many long *i* words as you can. Read it aloud to a friend.

5. In an area where <u>get</u> is said *git*, how would you pronounce *pen*? Explain.

6. Rewrite the dialect sentence in which the woman calls her pet, using standard English.

7. Underline the dialect word in the last paragraph. What word does it represent in standard English?

Why the Waves Have Whitecaps

Zora Neale Hurston

Summary The story is an African American folk tale. Mrs. Wind brags about her children. Mrs. Water grows tired of it and drowns the children. Mrs. Wind looks for her children but sees only white feathers on the water. That is why there are whitecaps. Storms at sea are the wind and water fighting over children.

Writing About the Big Question

Are yesterday's heroes important today? "Why the Waves Have Whitecaps" is a story in which characters act in ways that are humorous, but unheroic. Complete this sentence:

I think that story characters who (do/do not) behave admirably

have more relevance today because _____

_____.

Note-taking Guide

Record the sequence of events of "Why the Waves Have Whitecaps" in this chart.

Mrs. Wind and Mrs. Water sit and talk. →	→	

↓ →	Whitecaps are feathers coming up when Mrs. Wind calls for her children. →	The storms at sea are the wind and water fighting over the children.

Why the Waves Have Whitecaps

1. **Infer:** Mrs. Wind and Mrs. Water were friends at the beginning of the story. Why did they start fighting?

   _____

   _____

2. **Cause and Effect:** What happens because of their fight?

   _____

   _____

3. **Reading Strategy:** The chart shows the three parts of the story. Use this chart to **summarize** each part of the story. Use your own words.

Section	Summary
Mrs. Water and Mrs. Wind Compete	
Mrs. Water's Revenge	
Whitecaps and Storms	

4. **Reading Strategy:** A **summary** includes the most important facts of a text. Use your chart to summarize this myth. Use only a few sentences. Do not include small details.

   _____

   _____

5. **Literary Analysis: Myths** explain things in life. What does this myth explain?

   _____

Writing: Myth

Create your own **myth**. In it, explain something that takes place in nature. For example, you could explain a rainbow, the seasons, or an animal behavior. Begin by thinking of a list of possible ideas. Use the graphic organizer below to help you choose your subject.

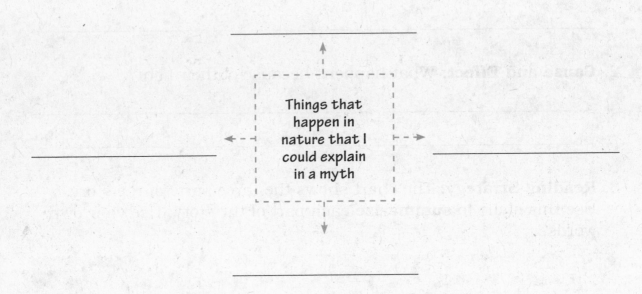

Things that happen in nature that I could explain in a myth

Choose one of your ideas to explain in your myth.

Listening and Speaking: Oral Presentation

Prepare an **oral presentation** about African myths and folk tales that were brought to the Americas. Do your research in the library or on the Internet. Look for ways in which history and traditional stories have affected African Americans. Make a list of topics you could use to search for information.

_____

_____

_____

Use your list to help you find information for your oral presentation.

Chicoria • from The People, Yes • Brer Possum's Dilemma • John Henry

Reading Skill

A **summary** is a short statement. It gives the main points of a piece of writing. Summaries do not include the minor details. They are a quick way to preview or review a work. Follow these steps to create a summary:

- Decide which events are important enough to be included.

- **Use graphics** to help you put the information in order. You could use a timeline to put the events of a story in order.

Literary Analysis

Storytellers pass on legends, songs, folk tales, tall tales, and stories in the **oral tradition**. This means that they are passed from generation to generation by word of mouth. These stories are written down later. They are written in a **dialect**. A dialect is the language and grammar of a certain region. Reading these tales can help you learn about the values of a culture. As you read, use this chart to note characteristics of the oral tradition.

Oral Tradition	Story Detail
Repetition and exaggeration	
Heroes who are brave, clever, or strong	
Animal characters that act like human beings	
Dialect and informal speech	
Traditions of a culture	

© Pearson Education

Word List A

Study these words from the selections. Then, complete the activities.

accord [uh KAWRD] *n.* doing something without being asked
  Brett surprised us by taking out the garbage of his own accord.

cyclone [SY klohn] *n.* tornado; a storm with strong winds
  The cyclone roared through town, damaging many houses.

poets [POH uhts] *n.* people who write poems
  Some poets write their poems in rhyme, while others don't.

recited [ri SYT id] *v.* said aloud from memory
  On July 4, an actor recited the Declaration of Independence.

shame [SHAYM] *n.* embarrassment or loss of honor
  Will blurted the answer without thinking and felt shame afterward.

spinning [SPIN ing] *n.* the telling of stories that you have made up
  While spinning tales of the Wild West, the storyteller showed slides.

straddling [STRAD ling] *adj.* with legs on either side of something
  Betty rode the donkey with her legs loosely straddling the animal.

yarns [yahrnz] *n.* long tales that are not completely true
  Late nights around the campfire, we told yarns of pirates and sailors.

Exercise A

Fill in each blank in the paragraph below with an appropriate word from Word List A. Use each word only once.

In our little town, there were no published [1] _____ or novelists.

Yet, just about everyone loved to stay up nights telling and listening to

[2] _____ of pioneer days. Sometimes, friends took turns and

[3] _____ parts of a well-known tale. Other times, they made up

new ones. No one had to be coaxed to speak, but did it of his or her own

[4] _____. In [5] _____ tales of olden times, our townsfolk

could cause any professional storyteller great [6] _____. My favorite

tale was of the [7] _____ of '79. That twister was so mighty, it was

supposedly lifted our first mayor and his horse hundreds of feet into the

air. When they came down, there was the trusty horse, [8] _____

the mayor!

Read the following passage. Pay special attention to the underlined words. Then, read it again, and complete the activities. Use a separate sheet of paper for your written answers.

Where do those <u>yarns</u> we call tall tales come from? Why are they still popular today?

Gathering to hear stories and poems is a very old form of entertainment. Before radio, television, and movies, people amused one another by <u>spinning</u> stories. <u>Poets</u> spoke their verses for others to hear and pass on.

Settlers on the frontier were the first to tell tall tales. These stories, full of daring deeds and folksy humor, captured people's imaginations. Some tales told about fictional heroes. Others revealed larger-than-life stories about real people, such as Davy Crockett, Daniel Boone, and Johnny Appleseed.

Pecos Bill, another heroic character, was a cowboy. He made friends with wild animals and even rode a mountain lion instead of a horse. He was seen <u>straddling</u> a <u>cyclone</u> to bring that twister under control.

John Henry was the hero of railroad workers. He could hammer spikes into railroad tracks faster than anyone else. When a machine is invented to do the job, John Henry decides—of his own <u>accord</u>—to try to beat the machine. He does, but dies wearing himself out. Of course, there is no <u>shame</u> in that!

Daniel Boone and Davy Crockett, real-life characters, lived colorful lives on the frontier. Stories about them made their lives more amazing. Crockett himself <u>recited</u> many of the stories about his feats.

Johnny Appleseed was the nickname of John Chapman. In real life, he traveled the wilderness planting apple trees. Many stories grew up around this gentle man who believed that beautiful fruit orchards would improve settlers' lives.

We still enjoy tall tales today because they are so entertaining. In a way, comic-book superheroes of today are like tall-tale heroes. Both are larger-than-life characters give people hope in a difficult world.

1. Circle two words that tell what <u>yarns</u> are. Name one of your favorite *yarns*.

2. Circle the word in paragraph three that means about the same as <u>spinning</u>? Explain what *spinning* means.

3. Underline what <u>poets</u> spoke aloud. Name one of your favorite *poets*.

4. Circle the word in the previous sentence that gives a clue to the meaning of <u>straddling</u>. Describe what *straddling* a *cyclone* might look like.

5. Underline the word that gives a clue to the meaning of <u>accord</u>. Describe something that you did of your own *accord*.

6. Underline the words in the previous sentence that tell what there is no <u>shame</u> in. Rewrite the sentence with *shame*, substituting a word or phrase with the same meaning.

7. Circle the words that tell what Crocket <u>recited</u>. Name something that you have *recited* lately.

Chicoria • from The People, Yes

Summaries In "Chicoria," a rancher invites a poet to dinner. The poet is asked to share poetry, but not to eat. The poet uses a folk tale to point out the rancher's rude behavior. In the selection from *The People, Yes*, the speaker talks about his love for America. He describes the adventures of famous characters from American folklore, such as Paul Bunyan and John Henry.

Writing About the Big Question

Are yesterday's heroes important today?
In both "Chicoria" and the excerpt from *The People, Yes*, the values and beliefs of a culture are passed on by showing what qualities and abilities that culture finds **admirable** in its heroes. Complete these sentences:

In today's stories, qualities such as _____ and _____

may be considered **outdated** for a heroic character. On the other hand,

qualities such as **bravery,** honesty, and _____ are still relevant.

Note-taking Guide

Use this graphic organizer to record how "Chicoria" and the selection from *The People, Yes* have some of the same folk story traits. Put one example in each box.

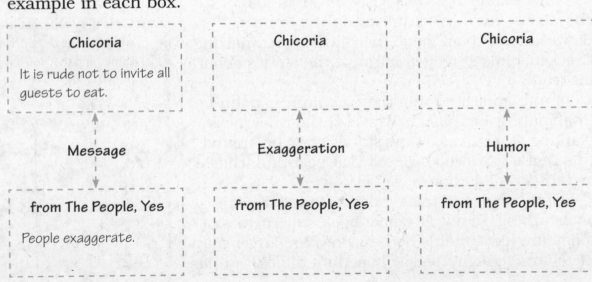

Chicoria • from The People, Yes

1. **Analyze:** Why is Chicoria so sure that he will eat at the rancher's table?

   _____

   _____

2. **Evaluate:** Identify two characters in the selection from *The People, Yes*. Tell how their abilities help them survive in a wild, new country.

   _____

   _____

3. **Reading Skill:** Fill in the cluster diagram below. **Summarize** images in the selection from *The People, Yes*. State the main idea behind the images.

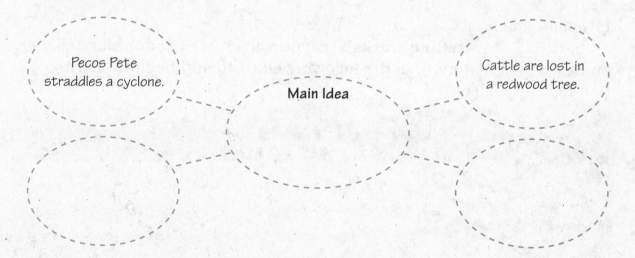

4. **Literary Analysis:** Why might people from New Mexico like the story of Chicoria enough to pass it on through the **oral tradition**?

   _____

   _____

Writing: Critical Analysis

Write a **critical analysis** to explain how language and idioms affect the tone and mood in folk stories. Be sure to give examples from "Chicoria" and the selection from *The People, Yes*. Use the chart below to write notes for your critical analysis.

Example of Language or Idiom Used	How it Affects Mood of Work

Listening and Speaking: Storytelling Workshop

As part of a **storytelling workshop**, you will create tips for storytellers as well as tell a story. Use the following chart to add helpful information for storytellers.

Storytelling Tips	
How to Choose a Story	
Making Eye Contact	
How to Use Gestures to Dramatize	
How to Add Humor	

Word List A

Study these words from "Brer Possum's Dilemma." They are all dialect words from the Old South, where this tale originated. Regional dialect is the language of everyday speech in an area. Some writers use dialect to capture the speech of their characters. If you find this language hard to understand, try reading the words aloud. Then, complete the activity.

a-doin' [uh-DOO-in] *v.* doing
He was always busy a-doin' something for others.

Brer [BRER] *n.* brother; used before a name
Brer Rabbit walked down the road and met Brer Fox.

critters [KRIT erz] *n.* creatures; animals
He didn't like to see critters, large or small; in trouble.

offa [AWF uh] *prep.* off of
Won't you help get that tree limb offa me?

outa [OWT uh] *prep.* out of
I need a ladder to get the cat outa the tree.

you's [YOOZ] *contraction* you is; standard English, you are
You's too kindhearted to say a bad word to anyone.

Exercise A

Fill in each blank in the paragraph below with an appropriate dialect word from Word List A. Use each word only once.

[1] _____ in for a real treat when you read about [2] _____ Rabbit and his friends. Of all the [3] _____ of the fields and woods, he was the trickiest. He was always [4] _____ something to get himself into the worst trouble. Then, he had to be clever to get himself [5] _____ the trouble. There was one time when he got stuck on a tar baby. The fox had made this figure out of tar to catch the troublesome rabbit. The rabbit, however, was so clever that he got the fox to pull him [6] _____ the tar baby. How did he do that? Read the tale to find out.

1. Circle the word that is standard English for brer. Write a sentence in which you use *Brer* with another animal name.

2. Write the standard English word for critters. List some of the *critters* that appeared in African American folk tales.

3. Circle the words in standard English that mean the same as *you's*. Following that example, write this sentence in dialect: *We are going now.*

4. Write the standard English for *a-doin'*. Following the example of *a-doin'*, write a sentence using the dialect form of *hoping*.

5. Circle the words in standard English that mean the same as *outa* and *offa*. Following these examples, write the words *full of* in dialect and then use the new word in a sentence.

Read the following passage. Pay special attention to the underlined words. Then, read it again, and complete the activities. Use a separate sheet of paper for your written answers.

Brer, or "Brother" Rabbit and the other beloved critters of the Old South did not spring from the mind of writer Joel Chandler Harris, as some people used to think. Harris is the author known for introducing whites in America to African American tales that use dialect, or local speech.

Harris was a teenager in Georgia. After the Civil War, he remembered stories that slaves had told him and recorded them. He then invented a character he called Uncle Remus to be the storyteller. Many versions of the stories, including ones about Brer Rabbit, exist today.

Actually, the character of Brer Rabbit had its origins before the pre-Civil War South. There was a long tradition of trickster tales in African folk tales. African storytellers later brought their tales to America. In the new land, they created tales in which animals took on the traits of people among whom they lived.

The stories of Brer Rabbit and his world are all the livelier for the southern dialect that is used in them. Here are some examples. Brer Fox would not say, "I see what you are doing." Instead, he would say, "I see what you's a-doin'. Brer Rabbit wouldn't think, "I can get myself out of this trouble." Instead, he would think, "I kin git myself outa dis trouble." Nor would he announce, "I just have to get off of this log and run as fast as I can." Instead, he would think, "I jist gotta git offa dis log and run lickety split."

The rhythm of this speech is natural and musical. Just listen as the storytellers of long ago spin their delicious tales. It's no wonder these tales have lasted and become favorites today.

Brer Possum's Dilemma • John Henry

Summary In "Brer Possum's Dilemma," Brer Snake asks Brer Possum for help. "John Henry" is a ballad, or song, that tells the story of an African American hero who races a steam drill.

 Writing About the Big Question

Are yesterday's heroes important today? The human-like animal characters in "Brer Possum's Dilemma" and the larger-than-life folk hero in "John Henry" are typical one-dimensional folk tale characters. Complete this sentence:

Although the **accomplishments** of folk heroes are exaggerated,

these stories have value because _____

_____.

Note-taking Guide

Folk tales often pass along important life lessons. Use this chart to record the lessons in each folk tale.

Folk Tale	What Lesson It Taught
Brer Possum's Dilemma	
John Henry	Nothing is impossible when you set your mind to it.

Activate Prior Knowledge

Describe a time when you were fooled by someone. What did you learn from the experience?

_____

_____

_____

_____

Reading Skill

A **summary** presents the main points of a story. It does not include minor details. What events from this page of the story would you include in a summary?

_____

_____

_____

Reading Check

What are Brer Possum and Brer Snake like? Circle the paragraph that describes Brer Possum. Put a box around the paragraph that describes Brer Snake.

Brer Possum's Dilemma
Jackie Torrence

Back in the days when the animals could talk, there lived ol' Brer[1] Possum. He was a fine feller. Why, he never liked to see no critters[2] in trouble. He was always helpin' out, a-doin' somethin' for others.

♦ ♦ ♦

While walking one day, Brer Possum saw a big hole in the road. He looked in. He saw Brer Snake in the bottom of the hole. Brer Snake had a brick on his back. Brer Possum decided to leave. He knew that Brer Snake might bite him. He began to walk away.

Brer Snake called out for help. Brer Possum went back. Brer Snake asked Brer Possum to help get the brick off his back.

♦ ♦ ♦

Brer Possum thought.

"Now listen here, Brer Snake. I knows you. You's mean and evil and lowdown, and if'n I was to git down in that hole and git to liftin' that brick offa your back, you wouldn't do nothin' but bite me."

Ol' Brer Snake just hissed.

"Maybe not. Maybe not. Maaaaaaaybe not."

♦ ♦ ♦

Brer Possum saw a dead branch hanging from a tree. He climbed up the tree and broke off the branch. He poked the brick off Brer Snake's back. Then he ran away.

Brer Snake called for help again. Brer Possum went back to the hole. Brer Snake said that he could not get out of the hole. He asked Brer Possum to help. Brer Possum again said that he was afraid that Brer Snake

1. **Brer** (brĕr) dialect for "brother," used before a name.
2. **critters** dialect for "creatures"; animals.

would bite him. Brer Snake said that he might not bite him. Brer Possum pushed the dead branch under Brer Snake. He lifted Brer Snake out of the hole and tossed him into the tall grass. Then Brer Possum ran away.

Brer Snake called for help once more. Good-hearted Brer Possum once again went back to the hole. Brer Snake said that he was cold. He asked Brer Possum to put him in Brer Possum's pocket.

Brer Possum refused. If he put Brer Snake in his pocket, Brer Snake would bite him. Brer Snake said that he might not bite him. Brer Possum began to feel sorry for him.

♦ ♦ ♦

"All right," said Brer Possum. "You must be cold. So jist this once I'm a-goin' to put you in my pocket."

♦ ♦ ♦

Brer Snake was quiet and still. Brer Possum forgot about him. Suddenly, Brer Snake crawled out of the pocket. He hissed at Brer Possum.

♦ ♦ ♦

"I'm a-goin' to bite you."

But Brer Possum said, "Now wait a minute. Why are you a-goin' to bite me? I done took that brick offa your back, I got you outa that hole, and I put you in my pocket to git you warm. Why are you a-goin' to bite me?"

Brer Snake hissed.

"You knowed I was a snake before you put me in you pocket."

And when you're mindin' your own business and you spot trouble, don't never trouble trouble 'til trouble troubles you.

Reading Skill

Write a **summary** of the two ways Brer Possum helps Brer Snake in this story.

_____

_____

_____

Literary Analysis

What features of the **oral tradition** are contained in "Brer Possum's Dilemma?"

_____

_____

_____

Read Fluently

A **dialect** is the language used by people in a certain region. Reading a story written in a dialect that is not your own can be difficult. It can help to rewrite passages written in dialect in your own words. Rewrite the bracketed passage in your own words below.

_____

_____

_____

_____

_____

John Henry
Henry

John Henry was a lil baby,
Sittin' on his mama's knee,
Said: 'The Big Bend Tunnel on the
    C. & O. road[1]
Gonna cause the death of me,
5 Lawd, Lawd, gonna cause the death of me.'

Cap'n says to John Henry,
'Gonna bring me a steam drill 'round,
Gonna take that steam drill out on the job,
Gonna whop that steel on down,
10 Lawd, Lawd, gonna whop that steel
    on down.'

John Henry tol' his cap'n,
Lightnin' was in his eye:
'Cap'n, bet yo' las, red cent on me,
Fo' I'll beat it to the bottom or I'll die,
15 Lawd, Lawd, I'll beat it to the bottom or
    I'll die.'

Sun shine hot an' burnin',
Wer'n't no breeze a-tall,
Sweat ran down like water down a hill,
That day John Henry let his hammer fall,
20 Lawd, Lawd, that day John Henry let his
    hammer fall.

John Henry went to the tunnel,
An' they put him in the lead to drive,
The rock so tall an' John Henry so small,
That he lied down his hammer an' he cried,
25 Lawd, Lawd, that he lied down his hammer
    an' he cried.

Literary Analysis

Poems in the **oral tradition** often have words or phrases that are repeated. Underline the words that are repeated in the poem. Why do you think these words are repeated?

_____

_____

_____

Reading Skill

What is the first important event in this story that you would include in a **summary** of this poem?

_____

Why is this event important?

_____

_____

Stop to Reflect

What qualities do you think a hero should have?

_____

_____

_____

---

1. **C. & O. road** Chesapeake and Ohio Railroad. The C&O's Big Bend railroad tunnel was built in the 1870s through a mountain in West Virginia.

John Henry started on the right hand,
The steam drill started on the lef—
'Before I'd let this steam drill beat
    me down,
I'd hammer my fool self to death,
30 Lawd, Lawd, I'd hammer my fool self
    to death.'

John Henry had a lil woman,
Her name were Polly Ann,
John Henry took sick an' had to go to bed,
Polly Ann drove steel like a man,
35 Lawd, Lawd, Polly Ann drove steel like
    a man.

John Henry said to his shaker,
Shaker, why don' you sing?
I'm throwin' twelve poun's from my hips
    on down,
Jes' listen to the col' steel ring,
40 Lawd, Lawd, jes' listen to the col' steel ring.'

Oh, the captain said to John Henry,
'I b'lieve this mountain's sinkin' in.'
John Henry said to his captain, oh my!
'Ain' nothin' but my hammer suckin' win',
45 Lawd, Lawd, ain' nothin' but my hammer
    suckin' win'.'

John Henry tol' his shaker,
'Shaker, you better pray,
For, if I miss this six-foot steel,
Tomorrow'll be yo' buryin' day,
50 Lawd, Lawd, tomorrow'll be yo' buryin' day.'

TAKE NOTES

Reading Skill

Reread the bracketed stanza. Write a brief **summary** of the information you learn about John Henry and his wife in this stanza.

_____

_____

_____

_____

_____

Stop to Reflect

How might writing a summary of this poem help you understand it more clearly?

_____

_____

_____

Reading Check

What does John Henry tell his shaker to listen to? Circle the line that tells you.

Vocabulary Development

shaker (SHAY kuhr) n. person who sets the spikes and places the drills for a steel-driver to hammer

Literary Analysis

Poems in the **oral tradition** often use dialect to show the ways that different people speak. Reread the underlined text in the first stanza. Write the meaning of the lines below.

_____

_____

_____

_____

Read Fluently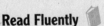

Read the bracketed stanza. Then, rewrite the stanza in your own words below. Write in complete sentences.

_____

_____

_____

_____

_____

_____

Read Fluently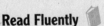

How does John Henry die? Circle the lines that tell you.

John Henry tol' his captain,
'Look yonder what I see—
Yo' drill's done broke an' yo' hole's
    done choke,
An' you cain' drive steel like me,
55 Lawd, Lawd, an' you cain' drive steel
    like me.'

The man that invented the steam drill,
Thought he was mighty fine.
John Henry drove his fifteen feet,
An' the steam drill only made nine,
60 Lawd, Lawd, an' the steam drill only
    made nine.

The hammer that John Henry swung,
It weighed over nine pound;
He broke a rib in his lef'-han' side,
An' his intrels² fell on the groun',
65 Lawd, Lawd, an' his intrels fell on
    the groun'.

All the womens in the Wes',
When they heared of John Henry's death,
Stood in the rain, flagged the eas'-boun
    'train,
Goin' where John Henry fell dead,
70 Lawd, Lawd, goin' where John Henry
    fell dead.

John Henry's lil mother,
She was all dressed in red,
She jumped in bed, covered up her head,
Said she didn' know her son was dead,
75 Lawd, Lawd, didn' know her son was dead.

2. **intrels** (IN trelz) *n.* dialect for entrails—internal organs.

Dey took John Henry to the graveyard,
An' they buried him in the san',
An' every locomotive come roarin' by,
Says, 'There lays a steel-drivin' man,
80 Lawd, Lawd, there lays a steel-drivin' man.'

TAKE NOTES

Literary Analysis

Which features of stories in the **oral tradition** are present in this poem?

_____

_____

_____

Reading Skill

Summarize the ending of this poem.

_____

_____

_____

Reading Check

What comes by the graveyard that John Henry was buried in? Circle the word in the text.

© Pearson Education

Brer Possum's Dilemma • John Henry

1. **Infer:** Brer Possum helps Brer Snake even though he does not trust the snake. Is Brer Possum meant to look foolish or very kind in the story? Explain.

_____

_____

_____

2. **Deduce:** Brer Possum does not help Brer Snake right away. Why might Brer Possum think it is safe to trust Brer Snake?

_____

_____

3. **Reading Skill:** A **summary** tells the main points of a story. Knowing the important events in a story can help you summarize it. Complete this timeline to help you summarize "John Henry."

Baby John Henry foresees his death.					John Henry is buried.

4. **Literary Analysis:** Think about how John Henry is described in this ballad. Why do you think "John Henry" has been passed down from generation to generation in the **oral tradition**?

_____

_____

Writing: Writing a Critical Analysis

Write a **critical analysis** to explain how language and idioms affect mood and tone in folk literature. Use this chart to help you list certain dialect or idioms from the stories. Note their meanings. Use your notes to help you write your critical analysis.

Dialect and Folk Idioms	Meaning

Listening and Speaking: Storytelling Workshop

Prepare for a **storytelling workshop**. Select a tale to perform. The following prompts will help prepare you to perform your tale.

- How will you use your voice and body to dramatize the action? Give specific examples of what you will do at different points in the tale.

_____

_____

- What informal language or dialect can you add to your performance?

_____

_____

- In which parts of the story will you make eye contact? _____

_____

Reviews

About Reviews

A **book review** gives a feeling or opinion about a book. You can find book reviews in different places, such as newspapers, magazines, television, or online.

Some book review writers know a great deal about a book's topic or author. Most book reviews have these parts:

- basic information such as author, price, and publisher
- a summary of the book
- opinions about the book's good and bad points
- an opinion about whether the book is worth reading

Reading Skill

Text features organize and highlight information in a written work. When you read, you can **use text features to analyze information,** which will help you understand the text. For example, looking at headings and subheadings will help you identify main ideas. Study the graphic organizer below to learn more about using text features to analyze information.

Structural Features of Book Reviews

- **heading:** large, bold text that identifies the book being reviewed
- **byline:** a line that shows who wrote the review
- **introduction:** an opening section that briefly describes the book being reviewed or provides information that is useful for context
- **conclusion:** a closing section that sums up the book's contents and the reviewer's opinion of it

A Life in Letters

Book Review
by Zakia Carter

Zora Neale Hurston: A Life in Letters.

Edited by Carla Kaplan
Doubleday; October 2002;
896 pages

Within days of having *Zora Neale Hurston: A Life in Letters* in my possession, I was inspired to devote the total of my lunch hour to selecting beautiful blank cards and stationery, a fine ink pen and a book of stamps. By the end of the day, I had penned six letters, the old-fashioned way, to friends and relatives—something I haven't done since summer camp. In our haste to save time, we check our inboxes with an eagerness that was once reserved for that moment before pushing a tiny silver key into a mailbox door. E-mail has replaced paper and pen, so much so that the U.S. Postal Service is losing business. But the truth of the matter is, folks will neither salvage nor cherish e-mail as they might a handwritten letter.

And so *A Life in Letters* is a gift. It includes more than 500 letters and postcards written by Zora Neale Hurston over four decades. The 800-plus-page collection reveals more about this brilliant and complex woman than perhaps the entire body of her published works combined, including her notoriously unrevealing autobiography, *Dust Tracks on the Road*. Amazingly, the urgency and immediacy (typos and all) we associate with e-mail can also be found in Zora's letters. She writes to a veritable who's who in American history and society, including Langston Hughes, Carl Van Vechten, Charlotte Osgood Mason, Franz Boas, Dorothy West and W.E.B. Du Bois

---

Text Structure

A book review includes basic information about a book. You can use this information to find the book. Circle the title, editor, publisher, and publication date for *A Life in Letters*. Why would these pieces of information be useful to a reader?

_____

_____

Vocabulary Builder

Multiple-Meaning Words The verb *penned* has more than one meaning. *Penned* can mean "wrote a note or a letter with a pen." It can also mean "prevented a person or an animal from leaving an enclosed area." What does *penned* mean in the first paragraph?

_____

_____

Cultural Understanding

The United States Postal Service began in 1775 when Benjamin Franklin was appointed the first Postmaster General. Postage stamps were introduced in 1847. Packages began traveling through the mail in 1913.

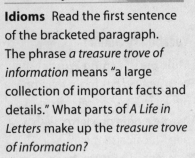

Vocabulary Builder

Uncommon Terms Find the word *pundit* in the first full paragraph on this page. *Pundit* means "someone who knows a lot about a particular subject." About what subject does the author believe Zora knows a lot?

_____

Vocabulary Builder

Idioms Read the first sentence of the bracketed paragraph. The phrase *a treasure trove of information* means "a large collection of important facts and details." What parts of *A Life in Letters* make up the *treasure trove of information?*

_____

_____

_____

Comprehension Builder

Summarize the main points of this book review.

_____

_____

_____

_____

_____

among others, sometimes more than once or twice a day. In these, her most intimate writings, Zora comes to life.

While we are familiar with Zora the novelist, essayist, playwright and anthropologist, *A Life in Letters* introduces us to Zora the filmmaker; Zora the Barnard College undergrad and Columbia University student; Zora the two-time Guggenheim fellow; Zora the chicken specialist; Zora the thrice-married wife; and Zora the political pundit. Zora's letters are at times flip, ironic, heartbreaking and humorous. They are insightful, biting and candid as journal entries. One can only wish for responses to Zora's words, but the work is not incomplete without them.

A treasure trove of information, in addition to the annotated letters, a chronology of Zora's life, a glossary of the people, events, and institutions to which she refers in her letters, and a thorough bibliographical listing are generously included by editor Carla Kaplan. Each decade of writing is introduced by an essay on the social, political, and personal points of significance in Zora's life. Kaplan's is a fine, well edited and utterly revealing work of scholarship into the life of one of the greatest and often most misunderstood American writers. In many ways, *A Life in Letters* is, in fact, a long love letter for Zora. It is a reminder to salvage and cherish what should not be forgotten and an admonishment to write what you love on paper.

—Zakia Carter is an editor at Africana.com.

Thinking About the Book Review

1. The reviewer says that there is some information in *A Life in Letters* that is not in Hurston's other books. What kind of information would not be found in other books?

   _____

   _____

2. A **book review** gives an opinion about a book. Some readers know Hurston only as a novelist and storywriter. What is in the review that might surprise these readers?

   _____

   _____

 **Reading Skill**

3. What information does the heading of this review provide?

   _____

4. How does the author organize the first complete paragraph on page 362?

   _____

WRITE ABOUT IT **Timed Writing: Summary (20 minutes)**

Summarize the **review**. Include the author's main points and opinions. Use this chart to get started.

What does Carter think about *A Life in Letters*?	
What does Carter think readers will gain from reading *A Life in Letters*?	

Ellis Island • from Out of the Dust

Reading Skill

Setting a purpose for reading helps you pay attention when you read. Think about when you read about people from a different time and place. Your purpose might be to learn about the way they see the world and the problems they face.

One way to set a purpose for reading is to **ask questions**. The "K-W-L" chart can help you organize your thoughts. Fill in the first two boxes before you begin to read "Ellis Island." Fill in the last box after you are done reading.

K	W	L
What I already know about the topic	Questions that explore what I want to know	Answers that show what I learned

Literary Analysis

Each work of literature has a **cultural context**. The cultural context is the society and point in history in which the characters live. Cultural contexts are shaped by many things, such as war and money issues.

Knowing about the cultural context helps you understand the characters better. As you read, look for things that characters say or do that are based on a cultural issue.

Word List A

Study these words from Out of the Dust. Then, complete the activity.

brewing [BROO ing] *v.* getting ready to happen soon
Looking at all of those dark clouds, I think a storm is brewing.

dampen [DAM puhn] *v.* to make something slightly wet
Before you iron, you can use a spray bottle to dampen the clothes.

fleeing [FLEE ing] *v.* leaving quickly, usually to escape danger
A shark was spotted, so people were all fleeing from the ocean.

harvest [HAHR vist] *n.* the act of gathering ripe crops
In many farming towns, the harvest means hard work and celebration.

relief [ri LEEF] *n.* the happy feeling you have when something bad has ended or not happened
I sighed with relief when there was no pop math quiz today.

stumbled [STUHM buhld] *v.* almost fell while walking
Too many people have stumbled over that crack in the sidewalk.

Exercise A

Fill in each blank in the paragraph below with an appropriate word from Word List A. Use each word only once.

It was a clear morning in late fall, just after the [1] _____. A few cars sat in the huge parking lot of the state fair. Still, a feeling of excitement dangled in the air, the knowledge that something big was [2] _____. Within two hours, things had gotten very busy in the lot—and very hot. I was constantly using a wet towel to [3] _____ my forehead and neck. Suddenly, I noticed a crowd spilling out of the gates of the fair. They seemed to be frightened and were [4] _____ from something. Several people [5] _____, and I was afraid someone would get hurt in the rush. With [6] _____, I watched a dozen security guards arrive and start to bring order to the somewhat wild crowd. "Had a bull gotten loose?" I wondered.

1. Underline the words naming the group for whom problems were <u>brewing</u>. Then, explain what *brewing* means.

2. Circle the words explaining why farmers were <u>fleeing</u> to cities. Then, describe another time when people were seen *fleeing* from a bad situation.

3. Underline the words telling what modern machines do during a <u>harvest</u>. Then, explain what happens during *harvest*.

4. Circle the words naming the group that has felt <u>relief</u>. Then, tell about a recent time†when you felt *relief*.

5. Underline the words naming where some people have <u>stumbled</u>. Then, explain why the visitors might have *stumbled* in these areas.

6. Underline the words identifying what <u>dampens</u> the farmers' clothes. Then, write a sentence using *dampen*.

Read the following passage. Pay special attention to the underlined words. Then, read it again, and complete the activities. Use a separate sheet of paper for your written answers.

In the 1930s, major problems were <u>brewing</u> for small farmers in the United States. They were finding it harder and harder to make money. The government did step in with aid. The troubles did not stop, however. By the 1970s, millions of American farmers had given up. Families that had farmed for generations were <u>fleeing</u> to cities to find jobs.

As a result, much farming today looks more like a big business. Farming companies use huge new tractors and other machines that are very expensive. Such equipment allows the work to be done on very large areas of land. During <u>harvest</u>, for example, these machines churn out the crops at high speeds and with little waste. How can a small farmer without modern equipment compete?

Many Americans have noticed the loss of small farms. They want to reverse the process. As the United States Department of Agriculture (USDA) has said: "[Small farms] are a unique part of our heritage, a tradition older than the nation itself, and a national treasure that must be preserved. . . . Bigger is not necessarily better."

Farmers in the twenty-first century have welcomed with <u>relief</u> the new help offered by the USDA. Since 1998, the USDA has been working to reach 146 goals. These have been set to help America's small farmers and ranchers succeed.

Many Americans shop in ways that support the small farmer. They stop at roadside stands to buy fruits and vegetables. They ask their stores to offer locally grown foods. Some shoppers have even <u>stumbled</u> through the fields at small "pick your own" farms. Americans seem to be willing to pay a bit more for food grown by small farmers.

Perhaps you have seen pictures of proud American farmers hard at work. The sweat of their labors may <u>dampen</u> their clothes but not their spirits.

from Out of the Dust
Karen Hesse

Summary "Out of the Dust" includes three poems. The speaker in "Debts" describes the faith her father has that it will rain again. "Fields of Flashing Light" describes a dust storm on the prairie. In "Migrants," people leave their dried-up farms behind.

 Writing About the Big Question

Are yesterday's heroes important today? In *Out of the Dust,* Hesse explores the responses of ordinary people to the destructive effects of a long drought and an economic depression. Complete these sentences:

Courage can come from unexpected places. One person that others

might not consider heroic, but I do, is _____

because _____.

Note-taking Guide
Use this chart to list the ways that dust and drought affect the people in each of the three poems.

Effects of Dust and Drought		
Debts	Fields of Flashing Light	Migrants

Debts

Activate Prior Knowledge

Describe a time when bad weather affected your life.

_____

_____

_____

_____

Reading Skill

Setting a purpose for reading helps you focus your attention as you read a literary work. Read the title and the first three lines of this poem. What will your purpose be in reading this poem?

_____

_____

_____

Literary Analysis

The **cultural context** of a literary work is the social and historical environment in which the characters live. Underline three words and/or phrases that tell you about what life is like for the people in this poem. Explain one choice below.

_____

_____

_____

_____

Daddy is thinking
of taking a loan from Mr. Roosevelt and his men,[1] . . .

◆　◆　◆

Daddy will use the money to plant new wheat. His winter crop has dried up and died. He will not have to repay the money until he harvests the crop. He is sure that it will soon rain and the wheat will grow.

Ma worries that it might not rain. Daddy disagrees. Ma tells Daddy that there has not been enough rain in the last three years.

Daddy is angry. He goes to the barn. He does not want to argue with Ma. The speaker asks Ma why Daddy is sure that it will rain. Ma says that it rains just enough to give people hope.

◆　◆　◆

But even if it didn't
your daddy would have to believe.
It's coming on spring,
and he's a farmer."

March 1934

---

1. **. . . . a loan from Mr. Roosevelt and his men.** In 1933, President Franklin D. Roosevelt began a series of government programs, called the New Deal, to help Americans suffering from the effects of the Great Depression. Among these programs were government loans to help Dust Bowl farmers.

Fields of Flashing Light

The wind woke the speaker from sleep. The speaker went outside to watch the lightning. Then the speaker heard the dust coming. It destroyed the fields of winter wheat.

♦   ♦   ♦

I watched the plants,
surviving after so much <u>drought</u> and so much wind,
I watched them fry, . . .

♦   ♦   ♦

The dust began to blow at the house. The speaker ran back inside the house. When the dust blew against the windows, Daddy woke up. He quickly went out into the storm.

♦   ♦   ♦

his overalls half-hooked over his union suit.
"Daddy!" I called. "You can't stop dust."

♦   ♦   ♦

Ma asked the speaker to cover the beds. The speaker pushed rugs against the doors and wet the rags around the windows. Ma made coffee and biscuits. She waited for Daddy to return.

After four in the morning, Ma sat down. She covered her face. Daddy was gone for many hours. It started to snow. At first, they were glad to see the snow. But the wind blew the snow away. All that was left was dust. Daddy returned. He sat down and blew his nose.

♦   ♦   ♦

Mud streamed out.
He coughed and spit out
mud.
If he had cried,
his tears would have been mud too,
but he didn't cry.
And neither did Ma.

March 1934

Read Fluently

A preposition relates a noun or pronoun following it to another word in the sentence. Some prepositions are *at, over, in, under, into,* and *on.* Circle the prepositions in the first bracketed passage.

Reading Skill

Sometimes your **purpose** for reading a poem or story may be to get new or unusual information about an event. Read the second bracketed passage. What information about the Dust Bowl do you find here that you could not get from a history textbook?

_____
_____
_____
_____

Reading Check

What does the speaker do to keep the dust out of the house? Underline the lines that tell you.

Literary Analysis

Economic forces, or money issues, are part of a **cultural context**. Read the beginning of "Migrants." What economic force is driving the people away?

_____

_____

_____

_____

Stop to Reflect

How would a drought such as the one experienced in the 1930s affect you and your neighborhood?

_____

_____

_____

_____

Reading Check 🖊

Where are the neighbors going? Circle the answers in the text.

Migrants

The neighbors say that they will return when it rains again. They fill their cars with everything they own. The springs on their cars sag with heavy loads. They ask the speaker's family to remember them.

◆　◆　◆

And so they go,
Fleeing the blowing dust, . . .

◆　◆　◆

The neighbors say that they will come back. Some of them will travel to Texas or to Arkansas. They hope to rent a farm and start over. Still, they promise to come back when it rains. They take everything they own. Some of them are going to California. They might stay there if life is better.

◆　◆　◆

Don't forget us, they say.
But there are so many leaving,
how can I remember them all?

April 1935

from Out of the Dust

1. **Cause and Effect:** The storm in "Fields of Flashing Light" destroys the wheat that the family planted. How will this affect the family's income?

_____

_____

2. **Speculate:** The family's neighbors move away in "Migrants." What might happen to the people who are left behind?

_____

_____

3. **Reading Skill: Setting a purpose for reading** helps you focus your attention on what you are reading. What purpose did you set for reading the three poems?

_____

_____

4. **Literary Analysis:** Complete this chart by explaining what each detail from the poems from "Out of the Dust" tells you about the poems' **cultural context**, or the ways of life and attitudes of farmers during the Dust Bowl.

Detail	Ways of Life and Attitudes
Dust blew away crops, covering items and people.	
Ma and Pa do not cry when their wheat crop is destroyed.	Farmers had to be tough and not show emotion.
Pa decides to plant again, but other families decide to move away.	

Writing: Writing a Research Proposal

Write a short **research proposal** for a report on how the Dust Bowl affected farmers in the 1930s. A research proposal is an outline or description of information you plan to research. Complete these steps to help you organize your proposal.

Title of the report: _____

List at least two sources for your report: _____

_____

_____

Explain what you will describe first in your report: _____

_____

Explain what you will describe last in your report: _____

_____

Research and Technology: Letter

Use the following chart to list ideas for your **letter**. Imagine what you might experience on a long trip from Oklahoma to California.

Experiences	How I Felt
What Did I See?	
What Did I Do?	

Word List A

Study these words from the poetry of Joseph Bruchac. Then, complete the activity.

knowledge [NAHL ij] *n.* understanding; learning
Everyone in our family has knowledge of camping.

memory [MEM uh ree] *n.* something remembered from the past
My father has no memory of the first house he lived in.

native [NAY tiv] *adj.* referring to the place one is born
Is Spanish or English your native language?

sickness [SIK nuhs] *n.* disease; illness; bad condition
They suffered from the sickness for only two days

slips [SLIPS] *v.* moves smoothly and quietly
After the boat slips up to the dock, we tie it to a post.

veins [VAYNZ] *n.* tubes in the body through which blood flows
Blood for testing is taken from veins near the surface of the arm.

Exercise A

Fill in each blank in the paragraph below with an appropriate word from Word List A. Use each word only once.

The rowboat [1] _____ quietly through the water, nearing the shore. Looking back, one of the sailors sees the ship getting smaller and smaller. The pulse of excitement runs through the sailor's arteries and [2] _____. None of his shipmates has any better [3] _____ than he has of the land they are about to explore. Will they meet any [4] _____ peoples in the new land? Will they be friendly or hostile? The sailor's [5] _____ of his last landfall remains strong. The crew was unprepared for the rough greeting they received. A small military force drove them back to their ship. "Is it a [6] _____ to want to explore new territory?" he wonders. "If it is, then it is an illness of the most wonderful kind."

Read the following passage. Pay special attention to the underlined words. Then, read it again, and complete the activities. Use a separate sheet of paper for your written answers.

1. Circle the words that suggest the meaning of memory. Write about a *memory* you have.

2. Underline the knowledge that the author cannot shake. Tell about some *knowledge* you would rather not have.

3. Circle the word in the paragraph that contrasts with the author's native country. Tell about the place to which you are *native*.

4. Circle the word that is the opposite of sickness. Write about a time you had to stay home because of *sickness*.

5. Underline the two things that the author imagines flowing through his children's veins. Describe your *veins* based on what you can see.

6. Underline the words in the next sentence that identify what the author compares with a memory that slips through his mind. Explain how a memory *slips* through one's mind.

When I came to this country, I felt reborn. Still, I feel it is important to preserve every memory I can of the old country to pass something along to my children—and their children. Why do I feel that I need to hold on to things from my past? I will try to explain it to you.

I move among American-born residents of this city, knowing that my story is very different from theirs. I will never take this country for granted. I can't shake the knowledge of the horrible things my native country's government did to its people in the name of security.

In America, I no longer fear arrest or torture. I no longer fear for my life. In sickness or in health, I will be able to live peacefully here, and I will not be thrown into the gutter if I become too ill to work or even stand up. I will pass along to my children the gift of freedom that will rush through their veins along with their blood.

Now and again, in a moment of quiet, a memory of the old country slips through my mind. It is noiseless, like muffled paddles rowing smoothly across the water of a calm lake. A picture of the old life sometimes comes into my mind's eye, but it never seems to have any words. If it did what words would it have—those of my native language or those of English?

"Get on with your life," people tell me, and I do. I don't live in the past, nor do I want to. Still, I do not want to stop remembering the past. The moment I do, the reasons that brought me here would lose their grip. I might become like some Americans who, born in the U.S.A., take the country for granted.

Ellis Island
Joseph Bruchac

Summary The poet imagines his Slovak grandparents as they arrive in the United States. Their first stop in the land of their dreams was Ellis Island in New York. He then writes of his Native American grandparents. He points out that they had always lived in America. Their way of life was destroyed when the Europeans came.

Writing About the Big Question

Are yesterday's heroes important today? In "Ellis Island," Joseph Bruchac writes of the conflicting feelings the famous immigrant processing station awakens in him. Complete this sentence:

Many people view the accomplishments of their immigrant ancestors

with pride because _____

_____.

Note-taking Guide

Some of the phrases in the poem are hard to understand. They use words that paint pictures and stand for other things. Use this graphic organizer to record some of the hidden messages.

the red brick of Ellis Island	the island of the tall woman	green as dreams of forests and meadows	nine decades the answerer of dreams
↓	↓	↓	↓
The building at Ellis Island is made of red bricks.			

Ellis Island

1. **Interpret:** The word "native" means to be a member of or belong to the first group of people. The speaker uses the phrase "native lands within this nation." What does the phrase mean?

_____

2. **Analyze:** The speaker had one set of grandparents who came from Europe. He had another set who were Native American. How do his grandparents affect his feelings about Ellis Island?

_____

_____

3. **Reading Skill:** Your **purpose** for reading is the reason you read a text. What was your purpose for reading "Ellis Island"?

_____

_____

_____

4. **Literary Analysis:** The **cultural context** shows the setting in which the characters lived. What did you learn about the cultural context in the late 1800s? To answer, fill in the rest of the chart.

Detail	Cultural Conditions and Attitudes
Immigrants were kept in quarantine before entering the United States.	Immigrants were considered to be a possible source of disease.
Immigrants dreamed of owning their own land.	
Native American lands were invaded "when the earth became owned."	
Native Americans had "knowledge of the seasons in their veins."	

Writing: Research Proposal

Write a short **research proposal** for a report on immigrants' experiences as they passed through Ellis Island in the 1890s and early 1900s. A research proposal is an outline or description of information you plan to research. Complete these steps to help you organize your proposal.

Title of the report: _____

List at least two sources for your report: _____

_____

_____

Explain what you will describe first in your report: _____

_____

Explain what you will describe last in your report: _____

_____

Use your observations to help you get ideas for a research proposal.

Research and Technology: Letter

Write a **letter** to a friend back home as if you are an immigrant at Ellis Island. Use the list below to help you choose what information to include in your letter.

• Where I am coming from: _____

• Reasons for leaving the "old country": _____

_____

• What the journey to America was like: _____

_____

• What I felt when I first saw land: _____

_____

• How I was treated when I arrived: _____

_____

Choice: A Tribute to Martin Luther King, Jr. • An Episode of War

Reading Skill

Before you start to read, it is a good idea to **set a purpose for reading**. Deciding on a purpose gives you a focus. Then, you can **adjust your reading rate** to go with the goal. When you adjust your reading rate, you choose a reading speed.

- When you read to learn new information, read *slowly* and carefully. Take time to think about what you read. Reread if you do not understand.

- When you read for fun, read as *quickly* as you like. Reread if something is extra interesting to you.

The chart below shows examples of reading rates. Fill in the blanks in the empty chart to show your reading plan for the selections.

Source	Magazine article on rock star	Source	Biography of John F. Kennedy	Source	
Purpose	Entertainment	Purpose	Research report	Purpose	
Reading Rate	Read quickly to find interesting details.	Reading Rate	Read slowly, selecting facts for your report.	Reading Rate	

Literary Analysis

An **author's influences** are the things that affect his or her writing. History and culture play an important role in what an author writes.

You can better understand what you read if you know about an author's influences. Read about the author's life. Then, follow these steps when reading the text:

- Note details that show values or attitudes.
- Note historical figures or happenings that are included.

Word List A

Study these words from "Choice: A Tribute to Dr. Martin Luther King, Jr." Then, complete the activity.

capable [KAY puh buhl] *adj.* having the skill needed to do something
  It surprised us that Jane was capable of doing cartwheels.

cemetery [SEM uh ter ee] *n.* a place where dead people are buried
  After the funeral service, Grandpa was buried in the cemetery.

fearless [FEER lis] *adj.* not afraid of anything
  When it comes to trying new sports, John is surprisingly fearless.

heritage [HER uh tij] *n.* the beliefs, values, and traditions of a group
  On national holidays, people celebrate their rich heritage.

importance [im PORT uhns] *n.* the quality of being meaningful
  The outcome of the Civil War had great importance to our country.

inherited [in HER it id] *v.* received something after someone has died
  My mother inherited a diamond necklace from her grandmother.

resistance [ri ZIS tuhns] *n.* standing firm against others' actions
  The citizens showed resistance to cooperating with the invaders.

rotted [RAHT id] *v.* crumbled away from natural decay
  After many years of neglect, the wooden house rotted away.

Exercise A

Fill in each blank in the paragraph below with an appropriate word from Word List A. Use each word only once.

Antonio's family was from the "old school." Long after they arrived in America, they kept alive their [1] _____, which connected them with their family's roots. On every holiday, older family members told about the [2] _____ of keeping traditions alive. They believed that each generation [3] _____ much more than material goods. Traditions such as holiday gatherings and visiting the [4] _____ where relatives were buried provided the glue [5] _____ of keeping he family together. Younger family members, who seemed [6] _____, were urged to overcome their [7] _____ to "old-fashioned" customs. Too much "modern" life, they were told, [8] _____ away the fabric that held families together.

1. Circle two words in the paragraph that help explain Keisha and Miles's <u>heritage</u>. Tell about two parts of your *heritage*.

2. Underline the two words that help to understand the meaning of <u>importance</u>. What is of great *importance* to you?

3. Underline the phrase that suggests the meaning of <u>inherited</u>. Describe something someone you know has *inherited*.

4. Circle the words that suggest the opposite of <u>resistance</u>. Write about something to which you have *resistance*.

5. Underline the words that define <u>cemetery</u>. Use two synonyms for *cemetery* in a sentence.

6. Circle the smaller word in <u>capable</u> that tells its meaning. What two things are you *capable* of?

7. Underline the antonym of <u>fearless</u>. Describe something about which you are *fearless*.

8. Rewrite the sentence with <u>rotted</u>, using a different word.

Read the following passage. Pay special attention to the underlined words. Then, read it again, and complete the activities. Use a separate sheet of paper for your written answers.

"Why can't we go to Orlando?" Keisha asked her parents. "That's my idea of a real vacation."

"Because, Keisha, dear," her mother answered, "we think it's time we introduced you to your <u>heritage</u>. We want you to spend some time in Georgia. Our people lived there for two hundred years. I cannot overstate the <u>importance</u> of experiencing that land and culture."

"But we've seen the family Bible that Daddy <u>inherited</u> from his father," Miles said. He had his own <u>resistance</u> to going along with his parents' plan. "What's the difference if we actually go to the <u>cemetery</u> where all those folks are buried? We can't see them anyhow."

"Your father and I think you're both <u>capable</u> of getting a lot out of visiting the old homestead, and Cousin Maggie is sure looking forward to our visit."

"If it's so great down there," Keisha said, "why did you ever leave?"

"In those days, there wasn't much opportunity for black people in that part of Georgia. Your grandparents thought my brothers and I would have a better chance of getting an education up north. People like your granddaddy were <u>fearless</u> in trying to change things, but my mamma was afraid it would take too long for us to be able to benefit from any changes. She said she wanted us to move before our brains <u>rotted</u> away."

Keisha smiled. "Oh, I guess it will be all right. Are you sure Cousin Maggie still has that old tire swing and that the pond hasn't dried up?"

Her mother laughed. Then, she said quietly, "You know, your daddy and I were thinking that if we all like it enough, maybe we'll move down there. I understand there's a brand-new community college that's looking for a few good teachers. It would be a great way to build a future—by reconnecting with the past."

Choice: A Tribute to Martin Luther King, Jr.
Alice Walker

Summary The author describes Dr. King's successes with the civil rights movement. She explains how Dr. King inspired African Americans to appreciate their heritage.

Writing About the Big Question

Are yesterday's heroes important today? In "Choice," Alice Walker recalls the tremendous influence of Martin Luther King, Jr. on herself and her community. Complete this sentence:

A figure from the past, besides King, who continues to influence

people today is _____ because

_____.

Note-taking Guide

Use this diagram to recall the reasons that Alice Walker looks up to Martin Luther King, Jr.

He was not afraid to be arrested for his beliefs.

Why Alice Walker looks up to Martin Luther King, Jr.

Activate Prior Knowledge

Describe a person you admire who leads, or has led, a fight for an important cause. What qualities do you admire in this person?

_____

_____

_____

Reading Skill

When you **set a purpose for reading**, you decide what to focus on as you read. Scan this page of text, and look closely at the first paragraph. What do you think your purpose will be in reading this text?

_____

_____

Read Fluently

Commas, semicolons, and periods show relationships between groups of words. Read the bracketed passage. Circle the commas, periods, and semicolons. Then rewrite this sentence as two separate sentences.

_____

_____

_____

_____

Choice: A Tribute to Martin Luther King, Jr.

Alice Walker

This address was made in 1973 at a Jackson, Mississippi, restaurant that had refused to serve people of color until forced to do so by the civil rights movement a few years before.

◆ ◆ ◆

Walker begins by telling the story of her great-great-great-grandmother, a slave who walked with two babies from Virginia to Eatonton, Georgia, and describing the family cemetery in which generations of ancestors are buried.

◆ ◆ ◆

Yet the history of my family, like that of all black Southerners, is a history of <u>dispossession</u>. We loved the land and worked the land, but we never owned it; . . .

◆ ◆ ◆

Walker and others of the 1960s generation were compelled to leave the South to avoid having happy memories replaced by bitter recollections of brutal treatment.

◆ ◆ ◆

It is a part of the black Southern <u>sensibility</u> that we treasure memories; for such a long time, that is all of our homeland those of us who at one time or another were forced away from it have been allowed to have.

◆ ◆ ◆

In 1960, Walker first saw Dr. Martin Luther King, Jr. on television being arrested for

---

Vocabulary Development

dispossession (dis puh ZESH uhn) *n.* state of having had one's property or land taken

sensibility (sen suh BIL uh tee) *n.* moral, artistic, or intellectual outlook

demonstrating in support of Hamilton Holmes and Charlayne Hunter,[1] who were attempting to enter the University of Georgia. Dr. King's calmness and bravery impressed her; his example changed her life.

◆ ◆ ◆

At the moment I saw his resistance I knew I would never be able to live in this country without resisting everything that sought to <u>disinherit</u> me, and I would never be forced away from the land of my birth without a fight.

He was The One, The Hero, The One Fearless Person for whom we had waited.

◆ ◆ ◆

Walker reminds listeners of the public acts of Dr. King: his speeches, his philosophy, his books, his preaching, his honors, and his deep concern for all displaced people. She also notes that people of color would not be permitted to eat in the restaurant in which she is speaking but for Dr. King's struggles. Walker also thanks Dr. King for an equally important, yet perhaps less obvious, gift.

◆ ◆ ◆

He gave us back our heritage. He gave us back our homeland; the bones and dust of our ancestors, who may now sleep within our caring *and* our hearing. . . .

He gave us <u>continuity</u> of place, without which community is ephemeral.[2] He gave us home.

Vocabulary Development

disinherit (dis in HER it) *v.* to take away someone's property or rights as a citizen

continuity (kahn tuh NOO uh tee) *n.* state of continuing, without problems, interruptions, or changes

---

1. **Hamilton Holmes and Charlayne Hunter** students who made history in January 1961 by becoming the first two African Americans to attend the University of Georgia.

2. **ephemeral** (i FEM uhr uhl) *adj.* short-lived; fleeting.

TAKE NOTES

Literary Analysis 🔍

An **author's influence** are the factors that affect his or her writing. List three things that influenced Walker in this essay.

_____

_____

_____

Reading Check ✏

What does Walker say Dr. King gave her people? Circle three things.

Stop to Reflect 📖

How do you think Walker's message affects or applies to modern readers?

_____

_____

_____

_____

Choice: A Tribute to Martin Luther King, Jr.

1. **Connect:** Walker made this speech in a restaurant that had refused to serve African Americans. What is important about this place?

   _____

   _____

2. **Interpret:** Walker saw Martin Luther King, Jr. arrested on television. What did she notice about the way he acted?

   _____

   _____

3. **Reading Skill:** Suppose that you are writing a report on Dr. King's accomplishments as a civil rights leader. You would need to find information about what he did to help African Americans. Would this speech be a good source of information for that **purpose**? Explain.

   _____

   _____

   _____

4. **Literary Analysis:** Complete this chart to show how the **author's influences** affected her writing.

	Influences	Effect on Her Portrayal of Dr. King
Time and place of Walker's birth	Walker was born in pre-Civil Rights Era Georgia.	Walker could document the personal impact of Dr. King's actions.
Walker's cultural background		
Major news events		

Writing: Speech

A **speech** is meant to be read aloud to a group. Prepare a speech for the dedication of a local monument to Martin Luther King, Jr. Your speech should celebrate Dr. King's accomplishments and leadership in the civil rights movement. Use your notes from the prompts to write your speech.

- List three of Dr. King's values: _____

_____

- Explain three reasons why Dr. King should be remembered: _____

_____

_____

_____

- Explain why Dr. King's ideas are still important today: _____

_____

_____

Research and Technology: Newspaper Article

Use the following chart to record information for your **newspaper article**. Remember that a newspaper article answers the questions *who, what, where, when,* and *how.*

Information about King	
Quotes from King, Walker, and Others	

Word List A

Study these words from the "An Episode of War." Then, complete the activity.

ambulances [AM byuh luhns uhz] *n.* hospital vehicles
  Ambulances took the injured workers to the hospital.

assault [uh SAWLT] *n.* an attack, often by an army
  During the assault on our fort, we were pelted with snowballs.

assistance [uh SIS tuhns] *n.* help
  I would welcome your assistance to move the dresser.

corps [KAWR] *n.* military group trained for special duties
  The hospital corps was close to the battlefield.

encouragement [en KER ij muhnt] *n.* support that helps someone
  My parents give me a lot of encouragement to succeed in school.

engaged [en GAYJD] *v.* took part in
  I engaged in a tug-of-war with my brother for the remote control.

menace [MEN is] *n.* someone or something that is dangerous
  The club on the corner is a menace to our peace and quiet.

representatives [rep ri ZEN tuh tivz] *n.* people acting for others
  Representatives of the committee met to discuss school issues.

Exercise A

Fill in each blank in the paragraph below with an appropriate word from Word List A. Use each word only once.

In the [1] _____ on our stronghold, many of our soldiers received bullet holes in their skin or other flesh wounds. Emergency teams, arriving in [2] _____, managed to get the worst hit soldiers off the hill and on toward the hospital in town. With the able [3] _____ of caring medical staff, we hoped they would all recover. As the wounded were lifted or walked into the vans, we gave them as much [4] _____ as we could. I even managed a smile. Then, [5] _____ of our military [6] _____ gathered the rest of us together. They [7] _____ us in some quick strategy planning, for we knew the [8] _____, or present danger, was far from over. With skill and luck, we would have the strength to hold off another attack.

Read the following passage. Pay special attention to the underlined words. Then, read it again, and complete the activities. Use a separate sheet of paper for your written answers.

In the mid-1800s, how did the leaders of the divided northern and southern states put together armies to fight the Civil War?

The Civil War was the first war for which the American government tried to draft men into the army. Actually, the threat of being forced to join was enough to make many men enlist, or sign up. Fewer than 50,000 men had to be forced to give <u>assistance</u> to their country. To get Americans to sign up, some had to be given <u>encouragement</u> in the form of cash awards.

The northern and southern armies were each made up of <u>representatives</u> of all states and all walks of life. There were many ways to support the war effort besides taking part in an <u>assault</u> on the enemy. Workers were needed to load and unload supplies. Strong men were needed to operate the <u>ambulances</u>, wagons used to remove the sick and injured from the battlefield. In field hospitals, doctors and nurses tended these soldiers.

At first, soldiers' spirits ran high. The North was fighting to protect the country from the <u>menace</u> of southern states seceding, or withdrawing, from the Union. Meanwhile, the South was fighting for that very right.

The war dragged on. As thousands of soldiers died, morale dropped. Younger and younger men—boys, actually—were needed. Some <u>engaged</u> in draft dodging, or avoiding being taken into the army. Rich families could do so legally. A man with money could simply pay someone to take his place. A business even grew up to find substitute soldiers for those who could not find them on their own.

Sometimes, a soldier found the war too painful. Then, he deserted, or illegally left, his <u>corps</u>. In some cases, soldiers got out of service legally because of personal or physical problems. Thousands of soldiers, however, plodded through the war, despite everything. They were probably the true heroes. Fortunately, some lived to tell their horrible wartime experiences.

1. Circle the words that tell what some men were forced to give <u>assistance</u> to. Describe a time when you gave *assistance*.

2. Circle the words that tell what was used for <u>encouragement</u>. What kind of *encouragement* helps you do something?

3. Circle the words that describe the army's <u>representatives</u>. Describe something you know that has *representatives*.

4. Underline the word that helps you understand <u>assault</u>. Describe an *assault* in war today.

5. Underline what <u>ambulances</u> were during the Civil War. Describe modern *ambulances*.

6. Circle the words that identify the <u>menace</u>. Name a *menace* today.

7. Circle what some soldiers <u>engaged</u> in. Rewrite the sentence, replacing *engaged* with a word or phrase.

8. Circle the word in the following sentence that helps to understand <u>corps</u>. Explain what *corps* means.

© Pearson Education

An Episode of War
Stephen Crane

Summary A Civil War lieutenant is shot by a stray bullet. The other soldiers are worried for him. The doctors and medical staff act as if he is a bother. The lieutenant is ashamed that he was not shot in battle. His arm is removed. The lieutenant tells his family that missing an arm does not really matter.

 Writing About the Big Question

Are yesterday's heroes important today? "An Episode of War" explores various reactions to the wounding of a soldier, including those of the soldier himself. Complete this sentence:

The concept of heroism (is/is not) outdated in our times because

_____.

Note-taking Guide

Use this chart to record the attitudes of the different characters in "An Episode of War."

Characters	Attitudes	Reasons for Attitudes
Lieutenant		
Other soldiers	awed and sympathetic	
Surgeon		
Lieutenant's family		

An Episode of War

1. **Analyze:** The lieutenant was not shot in battle. He was dividing coffee when he was shot. How does this fact make you feel bad for him?

   _____

   _____

2. **Interpret:** The lieutenant's family cries when he returns with his arm amputated. He tells them, "I don't suppose it matters so much as all that." Why do you think he says this?

   _____

   _____

3. **Reading Skill:** Think about writing a research report about leadership in the Civil War. Would this text be helpful for that **purpose**?

   _____

   _____

4. **Literary Analysis:** Read the information about the author on page 1016 of the textbook. Fill in the chart to show the **author's influences** on his writing.

	Influences	Effect on "An Episode of War"
Crane's Interests	He was interested in the Civil War.	
Crane's Research		

Writing: Speech

Prepare a **speech** for the dedication of a local Civil War memorial. The memorial will honor those who died or were injured in the war. Begin by answering these questions:

- When did the Civil War take place? _____

- Did any Civil War battles take place near your community? _____
  If so, where and when? _____

- Did people in your community fight for the Union or the Confederacy?

  _____

- Why do you think those who fight in the Civil War, on either side, deserve to be honored?

  _____

  _____

  Use your notes to help you write your speech.

Research and Technology: Newspaper Article

Write a **newspaper article** about the experience and cost of fighting in the Civil War. Make up statements that might have been made by the lieutenant in "An Episode of War."

What do you think the lieutenant would say about the kind of men with whom he served?	
What do you think the lieutenant would say about military hospitals?	
How do you think the lieutenant felt about having to live the rest of his life without an arm?	

Use the quotations from your chart in your newspaper article.

Transcripts

About Transcripts

Transcripts are written records of speech. They use the exact words of the speakers. Transcripts provide a complete record of what was said at an event. They do not include opinions or rewording. People use transcripts to record:

- radio or television shows
- trials or government hearings
- interviews or oral histories
- debates or speeches

Reading Skill

Analyze the treatment, scope, and organization of ideas to help you understand information in a transcript. The treatment reveals the purpose of the piece of writing. The purpose of a transcript is to record what was said during an event. The scope of the transcript includes the entire record of what was said by all participants at an event. The scope can be broad and cover lots of topics. It can also be narrow and cover a specific subject. The organization of a transcript follows the questions and comments of the participants in the order in which they were spoken.

Checklist for Evaluating Treatment, Scope, and Organization

❑ Has the author addressed the topic in a way that is neutral or biased?

❑ Does the author cover different sides of an issue or only one?

❑ Does the author present ideas in a logical sequence?

❑ Are details organized in a way that enhances the author's points?

Build Understanding

Knowing these words will help you read this transcript.

paralyzed veterans (PAR uh lyzd VET uhr uhnz) *n.* people who have been in the military and now have arms and/or legs that cannot move

paraplegics (par uh PLEE jiks) *n.* people who have both legs paralyzed

spinal cord injuries (SPY nuhl KORD IN juh reez) *n.* damage to the nerves that run from the brain down the back

You can use the text structure to understand transcripts. Look at the heading on this transcript. Circle the date the program aired and the name of the program. What was the program about on this day?

_____

_____

Comprehension Builder

Reading transcripts can be confusing. Different people are involved, but you cannot see any of them. So, you have to keep them straight by looking at their names. You also have to remember how each person is involved in the discussion. Explain how each person below is involved in this radio show.

Bob Edwards: _____

Joe Shapiro: _____

Ken Seaquist: _____

MORNING EDITION,

NATIONAL PUBLIC RADIO

November 11, 2003

PROFILE: **World War II veterans who founded the Paralyzed Veterans of America.**

BOB EDWARDS, host: This is MORNING EDITION from NPR News. I'm Bob Edwards.

In February of 1947, a small group of World War II veterans gathered at Hines VA Hospital near Chicago. The fact that they were there at all was considered extraordinary. The men were paralyzed, living at a time when paraplegia was still an unfamiliar word and most people with spinal cord injuries were told they would die within a few years. But these wounded veterans had other ideas, so they came from hospital wards across the country to start a national organization to represent veterans with spinal cord injuries. Today on Veterans Day, NPR's Joseph Shapiro tells their story.

JOSEPH SHAPIRO reporting: The logo of the Paralyzed Veterans of America looks a bit like the American flag, except that it's got 16 stars, one for each of the men who started the PVA when they gathered at that first convention nearly 57 years ago. Today only one of those 16 paralyzed veterans is still alive. His name is Ken Seaquist. He lives in a gated community in Florida. . . . It's there that Seaquist sits in his wheelchair and flips through some yellowed newspaper clippings . . .

MR. KEN SEAQUIST: Oh, here it is. OK.

SHAPIRO: . . . until he finds a photo. . . . The picture shows that convention. It was held in a veterans hospital just outside Chicago. A large room is filled with scores of young men in wheelchairs. Others are in their pajamas and hospital beds, propped up on white pillows.

MR. SEAQUIST: There's Bill Dake. He came with us and then Mark Orr. Three of us came in the car from Memphis. Mark had one good leg, his right leg, and he was the driver of the car.

SHAPIRO: Ken Seaquist was a tall, lanky 20-year-old in an Army mountain ski division when he was wounded in Italy. He was flown back to the United States to a veterans hospital in Memphis. He came back to a society that was not ready for paraplegics.

MR. SEAQUIST: Before the war, people in our condition were in the closet. They never went out hardly. They didn't take them out.

SHAPIRO: Few people had ever survived for more than a few years with a spinal cord injury. Infections were common and deadly. But that was about to change. David Gerber is a historian at the University at Buffalo. He's written about disabled veterans.

MR. DAVID GERBER (UNIVERSITY AT BUFFALO): With the development of antibiotics, which came into general use in World War II, there were many healthy spinal cord-injured veterans who were able to survive and begin to aspire to have a normalized life.

SHAPIRO: Gerber says neither the wounded veterans, nor the world around them at that time knew what to make of men who were seen as having gone from manly warriors to dependent invalids.

MR. GERBER: The society is emphatically not ready for them, and nor is the medical profession. To this extent, it was often the paralyzed veterans themselves who were pioneers in the development of a new way of life for themselves.

SHAPIRO: Seaquist and the others set out to overcome the fear and pity of others. After Seaquist was injured, he never heard from his girlfriend. His mother's hair turned white in a matter of months. People stared when he went out in public. It was a time when a president with polio felt he had to hide the fact that he

© Pearson Education

TAKE NOTES

Text Structure ✏️

The names of the speakers stand out in the formatting of the text. Circle the names of the three people who are talking on this page.

Note that a person's full name is given the first time the person talks. After the first time, names are written in shorter ways. Underline the names of a person who is talking for the first time on this page.

Vocabulary Builder

Prefixes Recall that a prefix is a word part added to the beginning of a base word. Find the word *antibiotics* in this transcript. The prefix *anti-* means "against." The base word *biotic* relates to bacteria, or very small living things that can cause diseases. What do you think the word *antibiotics* means?

_____

_____

Cultural Understanding

The president that Shapiro refers to is President Franklin D. Roosevelt. He was president of the United States from 1933–1945. He is the only president to serve four terms in office.

Fluency Builder

When people speak, they may not use grammatically correct language. Read the sentence spoken by Mr. Seaquist that begins "The ramping and." Rewrite the entire sentence using grammatically correct language. You may need to incorporate ideas from other sentences in the paragraph.

_____

_____

_____

Now, read the entire paragraph aloud.

Vocabulary Builder

Proper Nouns A proper noun names a specific person, place, or thing. Proper nouns begin with capital letters. Read the paragraph beginning "shapiro: There were about." Circle the proper nouns in this paragraph.

Comprehension Builder

How did injured soldiers' lives change due to the influence of Dr. Ernst Bors? Summarize the changes on the lines below.

_____

_____

_____

_____

used a wheelchair. Beyond attitudes, there was a physical world that had to change. When Seaquist arrived at the Memphis hospital, he could not get off the ward. There were steps in the way.

MR. SEAQUIST: They had no idea of what they had to do for wheelchairs. So when we got there, they had to put in all these long ramps and this is what we were talking about. The ramping and just to get around the hospital and get out ourselves, you know; not having somebody help us all the time. We were an independent bunch.

SHAPIRO: There were about 2,500 soldiers with spinal cord injuries, most of them living in military hospitals around the country. Pat Grissom lived at Birmingham Hospital in California. He would become one of the first presidents of the PVA, but he was unable to travel from California to Chicago for that first convention. Grissom, too, had come back from war with little hope for his future.

MR. PAT GRISSOM: I just suppose that we were going to live the rest of our lives either in the hospital or go to an old soldiers home. We were just going to be there taking medicine and if you got sick, they would try to take care of you and you'd have your meals provided and your future was the hospital or the old soldiers home.

SHAPIRO: At Birmingham Hospital, Grissom met a doctor who was about to become a pioneer in the new field of spinal cord medicine. Dr. Ernst Bors did a lot to improve the physical care of paraplegics. He also pushed the men at Birmingham to set goals for their lives, to go back to school, get jobs and marry. Bors and the veterans at Birmingham Hospital were the subject of a Hollywood film, _The Men._ The realistic and sympathetic portrayal helped the American public better understand paralyzed veterans. In the film, the kindly doctor in a lab coat is based on Bors. He urges on a wounded soldier in a white T-shirt, played by a young Marlon Brando.

(Soundbite of The Men)

MR. MARLON BRANDO: Well, what am I going to do? Where am I going to go?

Unidentified Actor: Into the world.

MR. MARLON BRANDO: I can't go out there anymore.

Unidentified Actor: You still can't accept it, can you?

MR. MARLON BRANDO: No. What did I do? Why'd it have to be me?

Unidentified Actor: Is there an answer? I haven't got it. Somebody always gets hurt in the war.

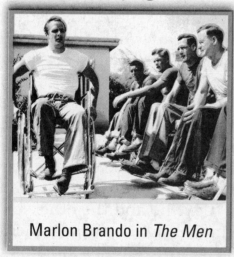

Marlon Brando in *The Men*

SHAPIRO: For Grissom and the other paralyzed veterans, there was something else that helped them go out into the world, a new technology. The introduction of automatic transmission meant that a car could be modified with hand controls for the gas and brakes. Pat Grissom.

MR. GRISSOM: Oldsmobile came up with the hydromatic drive and they put on hand controls and they sent people out to start giving driving lessons to us and we started having visions of saving up enough money to get a car and then things were looking better all the time.

SHAPIRO: Ken Seaquist says driving opened up all kinds of possibilities, from going out to a restaurant with a bunch of friends to romance.

MR. SEAQUIST: In Memphis, we had—our favorite place was called the Silver Slipper and they welcomed us with open arms and we had maybe 10, 12 wheelchairs going with our dates. Generally it

Text Structure

Read the bracketed passage. How is this passage different from the rest of the **transcript?**

_____

_____

_____

_____

Cultural Understanding

Long ago, all cars had manual transmissions. The driver had to change gears frequently while driving, in the same way that you might change gears on a bicycle while riding uphill. The automatic transmission changed gears when necessary without any action by the driver. *Oldsmobile* is a manufacturer of cars.

TAKE NOTES

Fluency Builder

With a partner, take turns reading aloud the first speech by Shapiro on this page. Read his words as though you were a radio announcer.

Comprehension Builder

Why did Mr. Seaquist and others found the PVA? Underline the sentences that tell the answer.

Vocabulary Builder

Multiple-Meaning Words The verb *push* can mean "move a person or thing by pressing with your hands." It can also mean "try to persuade someone to accept or do something." What meaning does the verb have in the bracketed passage?

_____

_____

Car modified with hand controls

was our nurses that we dated, 'cause, you know, we couldn't get out anywhere. We took the girls with us, you know. Eventually I married one of them.

SHAPIRO: Seaquist and his wife quickly had two daughters. And with a young family, he had to find work. He went to school and became a landscape architect. Ken Seaquist stopped seeing himself as an invalid and became a man with a future. So in 1947, he and the other founders of the PVA met in Chicago to put together a collective voice to express their dreams and what they needed to accomplish them. They came up with a slogan to get others to join, 'Awaken, gentlemen, lest we decay.' Ken Seaquist explains what it meant.

MR. SEAQUIST: If they forget us, we're going to decay. We're going to be left in the closet. We've got to get out there and speak out, getting things done so we can roll around this country and have access to the whole country.

SHAPIRO: The PVA quickly won some important legislative victories in Washington: money for paralyzed veterans to modify automobiles and houses, money for medical care. Later they would help push for laws that would make buildings and streets accessible to wheelchair users. The PVA has continued to advocate for veterans with spinal cord injuries through every war since World War II.

Joseph Shapiro, NPR News.

Thinking About the Transcript

1. Why were veterans of World War II more likely to survive their injuries?

_____

2. Why did the veterans form the Paralyzed Veterans of America?

_____

_____

TALK ABOUT IT **Reading Skill**

3. How does the organization of the transcript help you identify the comments by the veterans?

_____

_____

4. Describe the scope of the information presented in this transcript. Is the scope broad or narrow? Explain.

_____

_____

WRITE ABOUT IT **Timed Writing: Explanation (20 minutes)**

Paralyzed veterans face many stereotypes. Write a paragraph explaining why stereotyping can be hurtful.

- Identify examples of stereotypes from the transcript.

_____

_____

- Use these examples to explain why stereotyping can hurt people.

_____

_____

The exercises and tools presented here are designed to help you increase your vocabulary. Review the instruction and complete the exercises to build your vocabulary knowledge. Throughout the year, you can apply these skills and strategies to improve your reading, writing, speaking, and listening vocabulary.

The following list contains common word roots with meanings and examples. On the blank lines, write other words you know that have the same roots. Write the meanings of the new words.

Root	Meaning	Example and Meaning	Your Words	Meanings
-brev-	brief; short	*brevity:* the quality of lasting for a short time		
-cede-	go	*recede:* move or go away or move or go back		
-dict-	say or tell	*predict:* tell what might happen next		
-fac-	make	*factory:* place where things are made		
-fer-	bring; carry	*reference:* something you say or write that mentions another person or thing, something that brings or carries more information		
-ject-	throw	*eject:* push or throw out with force		
-manu-	hand	*manual:* operated or done by hand		

Root	Meaning	Example and Meaning	Your Words	Meanings
-phon-	hearing; sound	*telephone*: a device that brings sound over long distances		
-port-	carry	*support*: carry or hold something up		
-scrib-	write	*scribble*: write something quickly in a messy way		
-sequ-	follow	*consequence*: effect that follows a cause		
-similis-	same	*similar*: alike in some way		
-spec-	look; see	*inspect*: look carefully at something		
-sum-	take; use	*assumption*: something that you think is true or take as true		
-tele-	far; distant	*telescope*: instrument that makes distant objects look larger		
-vali-	strong; worth	*valid*: true, based on strong reasons or facts		
-ver-	truth	*verify*: make sure something is true		

PREFIXES

The following list contains common prefixes with meanings and examples. On the blank lines, write other words you know that begin with the same prefixes. Write the meanings of the new words.

Prefix	Meaning	Example and Meaning	Your Words	Meanings
anti-	against	*antisocial*: not liking to meet and talk to people; against friendliness		
aud-	hearing; sound	*auditorium*: a room for hearing concerts or speeches		
con-	with; together	*concur*: agree with		
de-	down; from	*decrease*: become less		
dis-	not	*disorganized*: not organized		
in-	without; not	*incapable*: not able		
inter-	between	*intermission*: short period of time between the parts of a play or concert		
ir-	without; not	*irregular*: not regular		

Prefix	Meaning	Example and Meaning	Your Words	Meanings
mis-	wrong; bad	*misspell:* spell wrong; spell incorrectly		
multi-	many	*multicolored:* having many colors		
non-	without; not	*nonfat:* without fat		
ob-	against	*obstacle:* something that works against another, something that makes it difficult for you to succeed		
post-	after	*post-test:* a test given after instruction		
pre-	before	*preview:* look before		
re-	again	*remake:* make again		
sub-	below, under	*submarine:* a ship that moves under the ocean		
super-	above; over	*superior:* better than another		
un-/an-/a-	not	*unbelievable:* not believable		

Prefixes V5

SUFFIXES

The following list contains common suffixes with meanings and examples. On the blank lines, write other words you know that have the same suffixes. Write the meanings of the new words.

Suffix	Meaning	Example and Meaning	Your Words	Meanings
-able/-ible	able to be	*movable*: able to be moved		
-al	relating to	*financial*: relating to money		
-ance/-ence	act of; state of; quality of	*assistance*: act of giving help		
-ate	make	*motivate*: make someone feel eager to do something		
-en	make	*weaken*: make something less strong		
-er/-or	one who	*actor*: person who acts		
-ful	filled with	*joyful*: filled with happiness		
-hood	state or quality of	*manhood*: the state of being an adult male		

Suffix	Meaning	Example and Meaning	Your Words	Meanings
-ic	like; pertaining to	*heroic:* like a hero; brave		
-ish	resembling	*foolish:* not sensible		
-ist	one who	*violinist:* person who plays the violin		
-ize/-yze	make	*publicize:* make public; tell people about		
-less	without	*powerless:* without power		
-ly	in a way	*quickly:* done in a short amount of time		
-ment	act or quality of	*excitement:* feeling of being excited		
-ness	state or quality of	*kindness:* friendly and caring behavior		
-ous	having; full of	*famous:* having fame; known and recognized by many people		
-sion/-tion	act or process of	*persuasion:* act of convincing someone		

Use a **dictionary** to find the correct spelling, the meaning, the pronunciation, and the part of speech of a word. The dictionary will show you how the plural is formed if it is irregular. You can also find the word's history, or *etymology,* in a dictionary. Etymology explains how words change, how they are borrowed from other languages, and how new words are invented, or "coined."

Here is a sample entry from a dictionary. Notice what it tells about the word. Then, follow the instructions.

> **lemon** (lem´ ən) *n.* [ME *lymon* < MFr *limon* < Ar *laimūn* < Pers *līmūn*]
> **1** a small, egg-shaped, edible citrus fruit with a yellow rind and a juicy, sour pulp, rich in ascorbic acid **2** the small, spiny, semitropical evergreen citrus tree (*Citrus limon*) bearing this fruit **3** pale yellow **4** [slang] something, esp. a manufactured article, that is defective or imperfect

1. Circle the *n.* in the dictionary entry. It stands for *noun.* Write what these other parts of speech abbreviations mean: *v.* _____, *adv.* _____, *adj.* _____, *prep.* _____.

2. Underline the origins of the word *lemon.* ME stands for Middle English, Ar stands for Arabic, and Pers. stands for Persian. What do you think MFr stands for? _____

3. Put a box around the pronunciation.

4. How many noun definitions does the entry have? _____

5. Which definition is slang? _____

6. Which definition of *lemon* is used in the following sentence? _____
   The car that my dad bought turned out to be a lemon.

Activity: Use a dictionary to learn about the origins of these words.

Activity: Use a dictionary to learn about the origins of these words.

1. literature _____ / _____ / _____
      pronunciation   main part of speech original language(s)

_____ / _____
   1st meaning   other meanings

_____

_____

_____

_____

2. language _____ / _____ / _____
      pronunciation   main part of speech original language(s)

_____ / _____
   1st meaning   other meanings

_____

_____

_____

Activity: Look up each of the following words in a dictionary. Then, write a definition of the word and a sentence using the word.

moment _____

_____

popular _____

_____

remedy _____

_____

blur _____

_____

lazy _____

_____

Use these word study cards to break big words into their parts. Write the word at the top of the card. Then, divide the word into its prefix, root, and suffix. Note that not all words have prefixes and suffixes. List the meaning of each part of the word. Next, find three words with the same root and write them on the card. Finally, write the word's part of speech and its definition. Use a dictionary to help you. One example has been done for you.

Word:	invisible	
Prefix	**Root**	**Suffix**
in: not	**vis:** see	**ible**-able to be

Root-related Words
1. vision
2. revise
3. visibility

Definition: invisible *adj.* not able to be seen

Word:		
Prefix	**Root**	**Suffix**

Root-related Words
1.
2.
3.

Definition:

Word:

Prefix	Root	Suffix

Root-related Words
1.
2.
3.

Definition:

Word:

Prefix	Root	Suffix

Root-related Words
1.
2.
3.

Definition:

Word:

Prefix	Root	Suffix

Root-related Words
1.
2.
3.

Definition:

achieve (uh CHEEV) *v.* succeed; accomplish

analyze (AN uh lyz) *v.* study the parts of something

anticipate (an TIS uh payt) *v.* look forward to, expect

determine (dee TER muhn) *v.* figure out

establish (uh STAB lish) *v.* show or prove

formulate (FOHR myoo layt) *v.* make a statement, form an idea

intention (in TEN shuhn) *n.* purpose; goal

modify (MAHD uh fy) *v.* change

predict (pree DIKT) *v.* make a logical assumption about future events

revise (ri VYZ) *v.* correct, improve, or change

A. True/False For each of the following, mark T or F to indicate whether the italicized vocabulary word has been used correctly in the sentence. If you have marked F, correct the sentence by using the word properly.

1. _____ If you *modify* your answer, you leave it exactly the same as it is.

2. _____ You can *predict* how a story will end by paying attention to the author's clues.

3. _____ Based on reliable evidence, the scientist will *formulate* a new theory.

4. _____ Rita *anticipates* the trip that she went on last week.

5. _____ Most students *achieve* their goals in school by failing tests.

6. _____ When you *analyze* a story, you look at the plot details.

7. _____ Roger uses the blinker on his car to *determine* where he is going to turn.

8. _____ When you *revise* an essay, you usually try to make it incorrect.

9. _____ The author's *intention* is to bore readers.

10. _____ Use facts to *establish* what is true.

B. Use each word pair in an original sentence that illustrates the meaning of the academic vocabulary word.

achieve/goal _____

_____

analyze/situation _____

_____

anticipate/party _____

_____

determine/truth _____

_____

establish/rules _____

_____

formulate/idea _____

_____

intention/persuade _____

_____

modify/answer _____

_____

predict/conclusion _____

_____

revise/errors _____

_____

aspect (AS pekt) *n.* the specific part that you are observing or studying

conclude (kuhn KLOOD) *v.* decide by reasoning

differentiate (dif uhr EN shee ayt) *v.* show how things are different

evidence (EV uh duhns) *n.* facts that serve as clues or proof

examine (eg ZAM uhn) *v.* study carefully

indicate (IN di kayt) *v.* show; hint at

infer (in FER) *v.* draw conclusions based on facts

logical (LAHJ i kuhl) *adj.* reasonable; sensible

similar (SIM uh luhr) *adj.* alike

unique (yoo NEEK) *adj.* having nothing that is similar or equal

A. True/False For each of the following, mark T or F to indicate whether the italicized vocabulary word has been used correctly in the sentence. If you have marked F, correct the sentence by using the word properly.

1. _____ It is *logical* to think that monkeys can fly.

2. _____ What can you *infer* about the main character from the way he dresses?

3. _____ Ben can *differentiate* between books by describing how they are the same.

4. _____ Two pens that look exactly alike are *unique*.

5. _____ The left blinker in the car is used to *indicate* a left turn.

6. _____ Jason found *evidence* to support his theory.

7. _____ Facts *examine* the author's purpose.

8. _____ What can you *conclude* from the details in the story?

9. _____ *Examine* the tent carefully for leaks.

10. _____ How *similar* was the movie version to the book?

B. Use each word pair in an original sentence that illustrates the meaning of the academic vocabulary word.

aspect/character _____

_____

conclude/detail _____

_____

differentiate/novels _____

_____

evidence/prove _____

_____

examine/details _____

_____

indicate/correct _____

_____

infer/details _____

_____

logical/answer _____

_____

similar/traits _____

_____

unique/characteristic _____

_____

accurate (AK yuh ruht) *adj.* free from error; correct; exact

bias (BY uhs) *n.* unfair preference or dislike for someone or something

cite (SYT) *v.* refer to an example or fact as proof

credible (KRED uh buhl) *adj.* believable; reliable

focus (FOH kuhs) *n.* the central point of a work

focus (FOH kuhs) *v.* concentrate on one thing

imply (im PLY) *v.* hint at; suggest

implied (im PLYD) *adj.* suggested

pertinent (PERT uhn uhnt) *adj.* relevant; having a connection

suggest (suhg JEST) *v.* show indirectly; imply

support (suh PORT) *v.* provide evidence to prove or back up an idea

topic (TAHP ik) *n.* the subject

A. Code Name Use the code to figure out each vocabulary word. Each letter is represented by a number or symbol. This exercise will help you learn how to spell and recognize the vocabulary words.

%	5	•	*	2	#	!	7	^	&	9	¶	£	$	3	¥	+	=	?	÷	4	¢	6	§	«	ç
a	b	c	d	e	f	g	h	i	j	k	l	m	n	o	p	q	r	s	t	u	v	w	x	y	z

1. # 3 • 4 ? _____

2. ¥ 2 = ÷ ^ $ 2 $ ÷ _____

3. ^ £ ¥ ¶ ^ 2 * _____

4. % • • 4 = % ÷ 2 _____

5. • = 2 * ^ 5 ¶ 2 _____

6. ? 4 ¥ ¥ 3 = ÷ _____

7. ÷ 3 ¥ ^ • _____

8. 5 ^ % ? _____

9. • ^ ÷ 2 _____

10. ? 4 ! ! 2 ? ÷ _____

B. Answer each question. Then, explain your answer.

1. Would drama be a good *topic* for a science paper? _____

_____

2. If an answer is *accurate*, are there mistakes in it? _____

_____

3. When you are trying to *focus* on homework, is it a good idea to watch

television? _____

_____

4. If a suggestion is *implied*, is it generally stated aloud? _____

5. Would a *pertinent* comment have anything to do with the topic being

discussed? _____

_____

6. Would you expect someone with a *bias* to always be fair? _____

_____

7. Is it a good idea to *support* your ideas with facts and examples? _____

_____

8. If someone you knew told a lot of lies, would she be *credible*? _____

_____

9. If an article *suggests* that there is life on Mars, would it be directly stated? ____

_____

10. If the author *cites* the work of someone else, does she mention the work? ____

_____

adapt (uh DAPT) *v.* change something to make it more suitable

clarify (KLAR uh fy) *v.* explain; make clearer

confirm (kun FERM) *v.* make certain; prove to be correct

context (KAHN tekst) *n.* text surrounding an unfamiliar word

convey (kuhn VAY) *v.* carry meaning; communicate

emphasize (EM fuh syz) *v.* stress

reflect (ri FLEKT) *v.* mirror an image; express or show

restate (ree STAYT) *v.* express the same idea in a different way

restatement (ree STAYT muhnt) *n.* expressing the same idea in different words

synonymous (si NAHN uh muhs) *adj.* having the same, or nearly the same, meaning

A. Completion Complete each sentence that has been started for you. Your sentence completion should be logical and illustrate the meaning of the vocabulary word in italics.

1. Some words that are *synonymous* with happy are _____

_____

2. The teacher tried to *clarify* _____

_____

3. A smile can *convey* _____

_____

4. A writer might *adapt* a story to _____

_____

5. It is a good idea to *restate* a poem so that _____

_____

6. You can *confirm* a fact by _____

_____

7. If you look at the *context* surrounding an unfamiliar word, you may be able to

_____

_____

8. One way to *emphasize* an important idea in writing is to _____

_____

9. A good reason for a *restatement* of an idea is _____

_____

10. A restatement should *reflect* _____

_____

B. Using the word pair, write an original sentence that illustrates the meaning of the academic vocabulary word.

reflect/image _____

_____

convey/meaning _____

_____

emphasize/main point _____

_____

restate/words _____

_____

adapt/story _____

_____

synonymous/words _____

_____

restatement/idea _____

_____

confirm/report _____

_____

context/unfamiliar _____

_____

clarify/difficult _____

_____

assumption (uh SUMP shuhn) *n.* something one supposed to be true, without proof

connect (kuh NEKT) *v.* show how things are related

consequence (KAHN si kwens) *n.* result; outcome

evaluate (ee VAL yoo ayt) *v.* judge; determine the worth or strength of something

factor (FAK tuhr) *n.* something that helps bring about a result

impact (IM pakt) *n.* the power to produce changes or effects

influence (IN floo uhns) *n.* ability to affect results

rational (RASH uhn uhl) *adj.* based on reason; logical

reaction (ree AK shuhn) *n.* response to an influence or force

valid (VAL id) *adj.* based on facts and strong evidence; convincing

A. Completion Complete each sentence that has been started for you. Your sentence completion should be logical and illustrate the meaning of the vocabulary word in italics.

1. One *consequence* of a heavy rain might be _____

   _____

2. Do not make *assumptions* if _____

   _____

3. A *valid* conclusion would _____

   _____

4. A strange *reaction* to a scary movie would be _____

   _____

5. One *factor* in success in school is _____

   _____

6. A *rational* reason to go to bed early is _____

   _____

7. If you *connect* all the facts, you will _____

   _____

8. One way that teachers *evaluate* students is _____

   _____

9. The event that has had the biggest influence on my life so far is _____

_____

10. Books can have an impact on _____

_____

B. Using the academic word pair, write an original sentence that illustrates the meaning of the words.

factor/influence _____

_____

consequence/impact _____

_____

reaction/rational _____

_____

assumption/valid _____

_____

evaluate/connect _____

_____

critique (kri TEEK) *v.* write a critical essay or review

disorganized (dis OHR guh nyzd) *adj.* not arranged in a logical order

essential (uh SEN shuhl) *adj.* necessary

extract (ek STRAKT) *v.* deduce; obtain

focus (FOH kuhs) *v.* direct one's attention to a specific part of something

identify (y DEN tuh fy) *v.* recognize; find and name

organized (OHR guh nyzd) *v.* arranged in a logical order

revise (ri VYZ) *v.* change; adjust

sequence (SEE kwuhns) *n.* order

skim (SKIM) *v.* read quickly, skipping parts of the text

A. True/False For each of the following, mark T or F to indicate whether the italicized vocabulary word has been used correctly in the sentence. If you have marked F, correct the sentence by using the word properly.

1. _____ A telephone book should be *organized* in alphabetic order.

2. _____ If you *skim* a book, you read every single word.

3. _____ When you *revise* an essay, you should not change anything.

4. _____ We will *identify* the dishes after dinner.

5. _____ Please, *critique* my essay for me before I turn it in.

6. _____ A dictionary is an *essential* tool for an English student.

7. _____ If something is out of *sequence*, it is in the correct order.

8. _____ A *disorganized* desk would be very neat and orderly.

9. _____ If you are supposed to *focus* on a reading, you should sit in a quiet place.

10. _____ To *extract* important information from a text, only read every other word.

B. Answer each question. Then, explain your answer.

1. Is a television *essential* for life in the United States? _____
   _____

2. How would you *extract* information from an encyclopedia? _____
   _____

3. Will a *disorganized* summary help you remember key ideas? _____
   _____

4. Should words in a dictionary be *organized* in order of importance? _____
   _____

5. What would be a logical *sequence* for events in a story? _____
   _____

6. Why might you *revise* your essay? _____
   _____

7. If you were asked to *skim* a magazine article, would you read it slowly and
   carefully? _____
   _____

8. Could you *critique* a novel without reading it? _____
   _____

9. If you are asked to *focus* on a sentence, should you flip through the whole
   book? _____
   _____

10. If you were asked to *identify* the main character in a story, what would you do?
    _____

Use this page to write down academic words you come across in other subjects, such as social studies or science. When you are reading your textbooks, you may find words that you need to learn. Following the example, write down the word, the part of speech, and an explanation of the word. You may want to write an example sentence to help you remember the word.

dissolve *verb* to make something solid become part of a liquid by putting it in a liquid and mixing it

The sugar *dissolved* in the hot tea.

_____

_____

_____

_____

_____

_____

_____

_____

_____

_____

_____

_____

_____

Use these flash cards to study words you want to remember. The words on this page come from Unit 1. Cut along the dotted lines on pages V25 through V32 to create your own flash cards or use index cards. Write the word on the front of the card. On the back, write the word's part of speech and definition. Then, write a sentence that shows the meaning of the word.

lurking	burdened	finery
innumerable	preliminary	descendants
virtuous	retribution	unobtrusively

---

verb

ready to spring out, attack;
existing undiscovered

The man was lurking in the
shadows so we did not
see him.

---

adjective

too numerable to be counted

There are innumerable stars
in the desert sky.

---

adjective

moral; upright

A virtuous man respects
the rights of others.

---

adjective

weighted down by work,
duty, or sorrow

The old man seemed to
be burdened with worry.

---

adjective

introductory; preparatory

The dinner began with a
preliminary appetizer.

---

noun

punishment for wrongdoing

The victim wanted retribution
from the man who robbed him.

---

noun

fancy clothing and accessories

The girls felt glamorous in their
borrowed finery.

---

noun

children, grandchildren, and
continuing generations

The old man willed all
of his possessions to
his many descendants.

---

adverb

without calling attention
to oneself

She slipped out of the
room unobtrusively.

Use these flash cards to study words you want to remember. Cut along the dotted lines on pages V25 through V32 to create your own flash cards or use index cards. Write the word on the front of the card. On the back, write the word's part of speech and definition. Then, write a sentence that shows the meaning of the word.

Use a fold-a-list to study the definitions of words. The words on this page come from Unit 1. Write the definition for each word on the lines. Fold the paper along the dotted line to check your definition. Create your own fold-a-lists on pages V35 through V38.

sinister _____

_____

compliance _____

_____

tangible _____

_____

impaired _____

_____

rigorous _____

_____

inexplicable _____

_____

celestial _____

_____

exertion _____

_____

maneuver _____

_____

ascent _____

_____

Fold In ←

Write the word that matches the definition on each line.
Fold the paper along the dotted line to check your work.

threatening harm or evil   _____

agreement to a request   _____

able to be perceived by
the senses   _____

made weaker or less useful   _____

very harsh or strict   _____

not possible to explain   _____

heavenly   _____

energetic activity; effort   _____

series of planned steps   _____

the act of climbing or rising   _____

Fold In ←

Write the words you want to study on this side of the page. Write the definitions on the back. Then, test yourself. Fold the paper along the dotted line to check your definition.

Word: _____

_____

Word: _____

_____

Word: _____

_____

Word: _____

_____

Word: _____

_____

Word: _____

_____

Word: _____

_____

Word: _____

_____

Word: _____

_____

Word: _____

_____

Fold In ←

Write the word that matches the definition on each line.
Fold the paper along the dotted line to check your work.

Definition: _____

Definition: _____

Definition: _____

Definition: _____

Definition: _____

Definition: _____

Definition: _____

Definition: _____

Definition: _____

Definition: _____

Fold In ←

The list on these pages presents words that cause problems for many people. Some of these words are spelled according to set rules, but others follow no specific rules. As you review this list, check to see how many of the words give you trouble in your own writing. Then, add your own commonly misspelled words on the lines that follow.

abbreviate	auxiliary	census	deficient
absence	awkward	certain	definitely
absolutely	bandage	changeable	delinquent
abundance	banquet	characteristic	dependent
accelerate	bargain	chauffeur	descendant
accidentally	barrel	chief	description
accumulate	battery	clothes	desert
accurate	beautiful	coincidence	desirable
ache	beggar	colonel	dessert
achievement	beginning	column	deteriorate
acquaintance	behavior	commercial	dining
adequate	believe	commission	disappointed
admittance	benefit	commitment	disastrous
advertisement	bicycle	committee	discipline
aerial	biscuit	competitor	dissatisfied
affect	bookkeeper	concede	distinguish
aggravate	bought	condemn	effect
aggressive	boulevard	congratulate	eighth
agreeable	brief	connoisseur	eligible
aisle	brilliant	conscience	embarrass
all right	bruise	conscientious	enthusiastic
allowance	bulletin	conscious	entrepreneur
aluminum	buoyant	contemporary	envelope
amateur	bureau	continuous	environment
analysis	bury	controversy	equipped
analyze	buses	convenience	equivalent
ancient	business	coolly	especially
anecdote	cafeteria	cooperate	exaggerate
anniversary	calendar	cordially	exceed
anonymous	campaign	correspondence	excellent
answer	canceled	counterfeit	exercise
anticipate	candidate	courageous	exhibition
anxiety	capacity	courteous	existence
apologize	capital	courtesy	experience
appall	capitol	criticism	explanation
appearance	captain	criticize	extension
appreciate	career	curiosity	extraordinary
appropriate	carriage	curious	familiar
architecture	cashier	cylinder	fascinating
argument	catastrophe	deceive	February
associate	category	decision	fiery
athletic	ceiling	deductible	financial
attendance	cemetery	defendant	fluorescent

foreign	minuscule	proceed	_____
fourth	miscellaneous	prominent	
fragile	mischievous	pronunciation	_____
gauge	misspell	psychology	
generally	mortgage	publicly	_____
genius	naturally	pursue	
genuine	necessary	questionnaire	_____
government	neighbor	realize	
grammar	neutral	really	_____
grievance	nickel	recede	
guarantee	niece	receipt	_____
guard	ninety	receive	
guidance	noticeable	recognize	_____
handkerchief	nuisance	recommend	
harass	obstacle	reference	_____
height	occasion	referred	
humorous	occasionally	rehearse	_____
hygiene	occur	relevant	
ignorant	occurred	reminiscence	_____
immediately	occurrence	renowned	
immigrant	omitted	repetition	_____
independence	opinion	restaurant	
independent	opportunity	rhythm	_____
indispensable	optimistic	ridiculous	
individual	outrageous	sandwich	_____
inflammable	pamphlet	satellite	
intelligence	parallel	schedule	_____
interfere	paralyze	scissors	
irrelevant	parentheses	secretary	_____
irritable	particularly	siege	
jewelry	patience	solely	_____
judgment	permanent	sponsor	
knowledge	permissible	subtle	_____
lawyer	perseverance	subtlety	
legible	persistent	superintendent	_____
legislature	personally	supersede	
leisure	perspiration	surveillance	_____
liable	persuade	susceptible	
library	phenomenal	tariff	_____
license	phenomenon	temperamental	
lieutenant	physician	theater	_____
lightning	pleasant	threshold	
likable	pneumonia	truly	_____
liquefy	possess	unmanageable	
literature	possession	unwieldy	_____
loneliness	possibility	usage	
magnificent	prairie	usually	_____
maintenance	precede	valuable	
marriage	preferable	various	_____
mathematics	prejudice	vegetable	
maximum	preparation	voluntary	_____
meanness	previous	weight	
mediocre	primitive	weird	_____
mileage	privilege	whale	
millionaire	probably	wield	_____
minimum	procedure	yield	

When you are reading, you will find many unfamiliar words. Here are some tools that you can use to help you read unfamiliar words.

Phonics

Phonics is the science or study of sound. When you learn to read, you learn to associate certain sounds with certain letters or letter combinations. You know most of the sounds that letters can represent in English. When letters are combined, however, it is not always so easy to know what sound is represented. In English, there are some rules and patterns that will help you determine how to pronounce a word. This chart shows you some of the vowel digraphs, which are combinations like *ea* and *oa*. Two vowels together are called vowel digraphs. Usually, vowel digraphs represent the long sound of the first vowel.

Vowel Diagraphs	Examples of Usual Sounds	Exceptions
ee and *ea*	steep, each, treat, sea	head, sweat, dread
ai and *ay*	plain, paid, may, betray	plaid
oa, ow, and *oe*	soak, slow, doe	now, shoe
ie and *igh*	lie, night, delight	friend, eight

As you read, sometimes the only way to know how to pronounce a word with an ea spelling is to see if the word makes sense in the sentence. Look at this example:

The water pipes were made of *lead*.

First, try out the long sound "ee." Ask yourself if it sounds right. It does not. Then, try the short sound "e." You will find that the short sound is correct in that sentence.

Now try this example.

Where you *lead*, I will follow.

Word Patterns

Recognizing different vowel-consonant patterns will help you read longer words. In the following sections, the V stands for "vowel" and the C stands for "consonant."

Single-syllable Words

CV – go: In two letter words with a consonant followed by a vowel, the vowel is usually long. For example, the word *go* is pronounced with a long *o* sound.

In a single syllable word, a vowel followed only by a single consonant is usually short.

CVC – got: If you add a consonant to the word *go*, such as the *t* in *got*, the vowel sound is a short *o*. Say the words *go* and *got* aloud and notice the difference in pronunciation.

Multi-syllable words

In words of more than one syllable, notice the letters that follow a vowel.

VCCV – robber: A single vowel followed by two consonants is usually short.

VCV — begin: A single vowel followed by a single consonant is usually long.

VCe — beside: An extension of the VCV pattern is vowel-consonant-silent *e*. In these words, the vowel is long and the *e* is not pronounced.

When you see a word with the VCV pattern, try the long vowel sound first. If the word does not make sense, try the short sound. Pronounce the words *model, camel,* and *closet*. First, try the long vowel sound. That does not sound correct, so try the short vowel sound. The short vowel sound is correct in those words.

Remember that patterns help you get started on figuring out a word. You will sometimes need to try a different sound or find the word in a dictionary.

As you read and find unfamiliar words, look the pronunciations up in a dictionary. Write the words in this chart in the correct column to help you notice patterns and remember pronunciations.

Syllables	Example	New words	Vowel
CV	go		long
CVC	got		short
VCC	robber		short
V/CV	begin open		long long
VC/V	closet		short

Mnemonics are devices, or methods, that help you remember things. The basic strategy is to link something you do not know with something that you *do* know. Here are some common mnemonic devices:

Visualizing Create a picture in your head that will help you remember the meaning of a vocabulary word. For example, the first four letters of the word *significance* spell *sign*. Picture a sign with the word *meaning* written on it to remember that significance means "meaning" or "importance."

Spelling The way a word is spelled can help you remember its meaning. For example, you might remember that *clarify* means to "make clear" if you notice that both *clarify* and *clear* start with the letters *cl*.

To help you remember how to spell certain words, look for a familiar word within the difficult word. For example:

Believe has a *lie* in it.

Separate is *a rat* of a word to spell.

Your *principal* is your *pal*.

Rhyming Here is a popular rhyme that helps people figure out how to spell *ei* and *ie* words.

i before *e* — except after *c* or *when sounding like* **a** *as in neighbor and weigh.*

List words here that you need help remembering. Work with a group to create mnemonic devices to help you remember each word.

_____   _____

_____   _____

_____   _____

_____   _____

List words here that you need help remembering. Work with a group to create mnemonic devices to help you remember each word.

_____   _____

_____   _____

_____   _____

_____   _____

_____   _____

_____   _____

_____   _____

_____   _____

_____   _____

_____   _____

_____   _____

_____   _____

_____   _____

_____   _____

Use these sentence starters to help you express yourself clearly in different classroom situations.

Expressing an Opinion

I think that _____

I believe that _____

In my opinion, _____

Agreeing

I agree with _____ that _____

I see what you mean.

That's an interesting idea.

My idea is similar to _____'s idea.

My idea builds upon _____'s idea.

Disagreeing

I don't completely agree with you because _____

My opinion is different than yours.

I got a different answer than you.

I see it a different way.

Reporting a Group's Ideas

We agreed that _____

We decided that _____

We had a different approach.

We had a similar idea.

Predicting

I predict that _____

I imagine that _____

Based on _____ I predict that _____

Paraphrasing

So you are saying that _____

In other words, you think _____

What I hear you saying is _____

Offering a Suggestion

Maybe we could _____

What if we _____

Here's something we might try.

Asking for Clarification

I have a question about that.

Could you explain that another way?

Can you give me another example of that?

Asking for a Response

What do you think?

Do you agree?

What answer did you get?

VOCABULARY BOOKMARKS

Cut out each bookmark to use as -a handy word list when you are reading. On the lines, jot down words you want to learn and remember. You can also use the bookmark as a placeholder in your book.

TITLE		TITLE		TITLE	
Word	**Page #**	**Word**	**Page #**	**Word**	**Page #**
_____	___	_____	___	_____	___
_____	___	_____	___	_____	___
_____	___	_____	___	_____	___
_____	___	_____	___	_____	___
_____	___	_____	___	_____	___
_____	___	_____	___	_____	___
_____	___	_____	___	_____	___
_____	___	_____	___	_____	___
_____	___	_____	___	_____	___
_____	___	_____	___	_____	___
_____	___	_____	___	_____	___
_____	___	_____	___	_____	___
_____	___	_____	___	_____	___
_____	___	_____	___	_____	___

Cut out each bookmark to use as -a handy word list when you are reading. On the lines, jot down words you want to learn and remember. You can also use the bookmark as a placeholder in your book.

TITLE		TITLE		TITLE	
Word	**Page #**	**Word**	**Page #**	**Word**	**Page #**
_____		_____		_____	
_____		_____		_____	
_____		_____		_____	
_____		_____		_____	
_____		_____		_____	
_____		_____		_____	
_____		_____		_____	
_____		_____		_____	
_____		_____		_____	
_____		_____		_____	
_____		_____		_____	
_____		_____		_____	
_____		_____		_____	
_____		_____		_____	

VOCABULARY BUILDER CARDS

Use these cards to record words you want to remember. Write the word, the title of the story or article in which it appears, its part of speech, and its definition. Then, use the word in an original sentence that shows its meaning

Word: _____ Page _____

Selection: _____

Part of Speech: _____

Definition: _____

_____

My Sentence _____

_____

Word: _____ Page _____

Selection: _____

Part of Speech: _____

Definition: _____

_____

My Sentence _____

_____

Word: _____ Page _____

Selection: _____

Part of Speech: _____

Definition: _____

_____

My Sentence _____

_____

Use these cards to record words you want to remember. Write the word, the title of the story or article in which it appears, its part of speech, and its definition. Then, use the word in an original sentence that shows its meaning

Word: _____ Page _____

Selection: _____

Part of Speech: _____

Definition: _____

_____

My Sentence _____

_____

Word: _____ Page _____

Selection: _____

Part of Speech: _____

Definition: _____

_____

My Sentence _____

_____

Word: _____ Page _____

Selection: _____

Part of Speech: _____

Definition: _____

_____

My Sentence _____

_____

Using the Personal Thesaurus

The Personal Thesaurus provides students with the opportunity to make connections between words academic words, familiar words, and even slang words. Students can use the Personal Thesaurus to help them understand the importance of using words in the proper context and also avoid overusing words in their writing.

Use the following routine to foster frequent use of the Personal Thesaurus.

1. After students have read a selection or done some writing, have them turn to the Personal Thesaurus.

2. Encourage students to add new entries. Help them to understand the connection between their personal language, which might include familiar words and even slang, and the academic language of their reading and writing.

3. Call on volunteers to read a few entries aloud. Point out that writers have many choices of words when they write. Help students see that audience often determines word choice.

N

nice

admirable

friendly

agreeable

pleasant

cool

phat

A

B

C

D

E

F

G

H

I

J

K

L

M

N

O

P

Q

R

S

T

U

V

W

X

Y

Z

(Acknowledgments continued from page ii)

Dramatic Publishing
From *Anne Frank & Me* by Cherie Bennett with Jeff Gottesfeld. Copyright © 1997 by Cherie Bennett. Printed in the United States of America. CAUTION: Professionals and amateurs are hereby warned that *Anne Frank & Me,* being fully protected under the copyright Laws of the United States of America, the British Empire, including the Dominion of Canada, and all other countries of the Universal Copyright and Berne Conventions, are subject to royalty. All rights, including professional, amateur, motion picture, recitation, lecturing, public reading, radio and television broadcasting, and the rights of translation into foreign languages, are strictly reserved. All inquiries regarding performance rights should be addressed to Dramatic Publishing, 311 Washington St., Woodstock, IL 60098. Phone: (815) 338-7170.

Farrar, Straus & Giroux, LLC
"Charles" by Shirley Jackson from *The Lottery.* Copyright © 1948, 1949 by Shirley Jackson and copyright renewed © 1976, 1977 by Laurence Hyman, Barry Hyman, Mrs. Sarah Webster and Mrs. Joanne Schnurer.

Florida Holocaust Museum
Florida Holocaust Museum Press Release from *www.flholocaustmuseum.org.* Copyright © Florida Holocaust Museum, 2001, 2005.

Richard Garcia
"The City is So Big" by Richard Garcia from *The City Is So Big.*

Harcourt, Inc.
"Choice: A Tribute to Martin Luther King, Jr." by Alice Walker from *In Search Of Our Mothers' Gardens: Womanist Prose.* Copyright © 1983 by Alice Walker. "For My Sister Molly Who in the Fifties" from *Revolutionary Petunias & Other Poems,* copyright © 1972 and renewed 2000 by Alice Walker.

HarperCollins Publishers, Inc.
From *An American Childhood* by Annie Dillard. Copyright © 1987 by Annie Dillard.

Hill and Wang, a division of Farrar, Straus & Giroux
"Thank You, M'am" from *Short Stories* by Langston Hughes. Copyright © 1996 by Ramona Bass and Arnold Rampersad.

Holiday House
"January" from *A Child's Calendar* by John Updike. Text copyright © 1965, 1999 by John Updike. All rights reserved.

Georgia Douglas Johnson
"Your World" by Georgia Douglas Johnson from *American Negro Poetry.*

The Estate of Dr. Martin Luther King, Jr. c/o Writer's House LLC
"The American Dream" by Dr. Martin Luther King, Jr. from *A Testament Of Hope: The Essential Writings Of Martin Luther King, Jr.* Copyright © 1961 Martin Luther King Jr.; Copyright © renewed 1989 Coretta Scott King.

Alfred A. Knopf, Inc.
"Harlem Night Song" from *The Collected Poems of Langston Hughes* by Langston Hughes, edited by Arnold Rampersad with David Roessel, Associate Editor, copyright © 1994 by The Estate of Langston Hughes. "The 11:59" by Patricia C. McKissack from *The Dark Thirty* by Patricia McKissack illustrated by Brian Pinkney, copyright © 1992 by Patricia C. McKissack. Illustrations copyright © 1992 by Brian Pinkney.

Liveright Publishing Corporation
"Runagate Runagate" Copyright © 1966 by Robert Hayden, from *Collected Poems of Robert Hayden,* edited by Frederick Glaysher.

Robert MacNeil
"The Trouble with Television" by Robert MacNeil condensed from a speech, *November 1984 at President Leadership Forum, SUNY.* Copyright © 1985 by Reader's Digest and Robert MacNeil.

Eve Merriam c/o Marian Reiner
"Thumbprint" from *A Sky Full of Poems* by Eve Merriam. Copyright © 1964, 1970, 1973, 1986 by Eve Merriam.

N. Scott Momaday
"New World" by N. Scott Momaday from *The Gourd Dancers.*

National Public Radio
"Profile: World War II veterans who founded the Paralyzed Veterans of America" from *National Public Radio, November 11, 2003.* Copyright © 2005 National Public Radio.

Naomi Shihab Nye
"Words to Sit in, Like Chairs" by Naomi Shihab Nye from *911: The Book of Help.* "Hamadi" by Naomi Shihab Nye from *America Street.*

Harold Ober Associates, Inc.
"Cat!" by Eleanor Farjeon from *Poems For Children.* Copyright © 1938 by Eleanor Farjeon, renewed 1966 by Gervase Farjeon.

Oxford University Press, Inc.
"Summary of The Tell-Tale Heart" by James D. Hart from *The Oxford Companion To American Literature.* Copyright © 1983.

Pantheon Books, a division of Random House Inc.
"Coyote Steals the Sun and Moon" by Richard Erdoes and Alfonso Ortiz from *American Indian Myths and Legends,* copyright © 1984 by Richard Erdoes and Alfonso Ortiz.

PHOTO AND ART CREDITS

Cover: *False Start*, 1959, oil on canvas, Johns, Jasper (b.1930)/Private Collection, Lauros/Giraudon;/www.bridgeman.co.uk/Cover art © Jasper Johns/Licensed by VAGA, New York, NY; **6:** Hulton Archive/Getty Images Inc.; **9:** Courtesy of Diane Alimena; **19:** Jeff Greenberg/PhotoEdit; **29:** New York State Historical Association, Cooperstown, New York; **35:** Paul Fusco/Magnum Photos, Inc.; **43:** Pearson Education/PH School Division; **47:** © Charles E. Rotkin/CORBIS; **48:** © Charles E. Rotkin/CORBIS; **49:** © Charles E. Rotkin/CORBIS; **54:** Pearson Education; **62:** Getty Images; **68:** Corel Professional Photos CD-ROM™; **68:** © Daryl Benson/Masterfile; **71:** The Granger Collection, New York; **73:** Corel Professional Photos CD-ROM™; **79:** Charles Krebs/CORBIS; **80:** © Daryl Benson/Masterfile; **81:** The Granger Collection, New York; **82:** Prentice Hall; **88:** Courtesy National Archives, photo no. (542390); **97:** © Peter Frischmuth/argus/Peter Arnold, Inc.; **107:** California Department of Parks & Recreation; **112:** Courtesy of the Library of Congress; **113:** © Ulf Sjostedt/FPG International Corp.; **123:** Courtesy of the Library of Congress; **127:** Courtesy of the Library of Congress; **134:** SuperStock; **143:** Dianna Sarto/CORBIS; **149:** Sid Grossman (1913–1955), Photographer, Reprinted by permission of the Museum of the City of New York, Gift of the Federal Art Project, Work Projects Administration; **157:** Pure Pleasure, Pat Scott/The Bridgeman Art Library, London/New York; **161:** Image courtesy of the Advertising Archives; **168:** NASA; **177:** Getty Images; **180:** Bettmann/CORBIS; **185:** Harriet Tubman Quilt made by the Negro History Club of Marin City and Sausalito, CA, 1951, 120 x 96 inches, cotton appliqued. Designed by Ben Irvin. Gift of the Howard Thurman Educational Trust to the permanent collection of the Robert W. Woodruff Library, Atlanta University Center, Atlanta, GA; **191:** Paul Conklin/PhotoEdit; **200:** Courtesy National Archives, photo no. (NWDNS-200-HN-PO-5); **204:** Bettmann/CORBIS; **211:** Jon Feingersh/CORBIS; **219:** Courtesy of the Library of Congress; **225:** Hulton Archive/Getty Images Inc.; **233:** NASA; **237:** Norman Chan/istockphoto.com; **246:** Playground, P.J. Crook/The Bridgeman Art Library, London/New York; **246:** *t.* StockFood; **246:** *b.l.* Eising Food Photography/StockFood America—All rights reserved.; **246:** *b.r.* Snowflake Studios Inc./StockFood America—All rights reserved.; **246:** background Getty Images; **247:** background Getty Images; **256:** Getty Images; **264:** Anne-Marie Weber/CORBIS; **270:** Bruce Forster/Getty Images; **278:** Corel Professional Photos CD-ROM™; **287:** USDA Photo; **297:** Pearson Education; **300:** Lon C. Diehl/PhotoEdit; **303:** *The Magpie*, 1869, Claude Monet, Reunion des Musées Nationaux/Art Resource, NY; **315:** *Crawling Turtle II*, Barry Wilson/SuperStock; **326:** Courtesy of Pensacola Little Theatre; **334:** Photofest; **341:** Lon C. Diehl/PhotoEdit; **346:** Copyright ANNE FRANK-Fonds, Basle/Switzerland; **362:** The Granger Collection, New York; **362:** Random House Inc.; **366:** Courtesy of the Florida Holocaust Museum; **373:** Kevin Schafer/CORBIS; **382:** Corel Professional Photos CD-ROM™; **390:** Warren Bolster/Getty Images; **390:** Bettmann/CORBIS; **391:** Richard Oliver/CORBIS; **396:** Paul & Lindamarie Ambrose/Getty Images; **401:** Illustration from "Count Your Way Through Mexico" by Jim Haskins; illustrations by Helen Byers. Illustrations copyright ©1989 by Carolrhoda Books, Inc.; **411:** Random House Inc.; **417:** AP/Wide World Photos; **425:** Felix Zaska/CORBIS; **431:** AP/Wide World Photos; **438:** Art Resource, NY; **444:** Bettmann/CORBIS; **446:** Richard Oliver/CORBIS